About Island Press

Since 1984, the nonprofit Island Press has been stimulating, shaping, and communicating the ideas that are essential for solving environmental problems worldwide. With more than 800 titles in print and some 40 new releases each year, we are the nation's leading publisher on environmental issues. We identify innovative thinkers and emerging trends in the environmental field. We work with world-renowned experts and authors to develop cross-disciplinary solutions to environmental challenges.

Island Press designs and implements coordinated book publication campaigns in order to communicate our critical messages in print, in person, and online using the latest technologies, programs, and the media. Our goal: to reach targeted audiences—scientists, policymakers, environmental advocates, the media, and concerned citizens—who can and will take action to protect the plants and animals that enrich our world, the ecosystems we need to survive, the water we drink, and the air we breathe.

Island Press gratefully acknowledges the support of its work by the Agua Fund, Inc., Annenberg Foundation, The Christensen Fund, The Nathan Cummings Foundation, The Geraldine R. Dodge Foundation, Doris Duke Charitable Foundation, The Educational Foundation of America, Betsy and Jesse Fink Foundation, The William and Flora Hewlett Foundation, The Kendeda Fund, The Forrest and Frances Lattner Foundation, The Andrew W. Mellon Foundation, The Curtis and Edith Munson Foundation, Oak Foundation, The Overbrook Foundation, the David and Lucile Packard Foundation, The Summit Fund of Washington, Trust for Architectural Easements, Wallace Global Fund, The Winslow Foundation, and other generous donors.

The opinions expressed in this book are those of the author(s) and do not necessarily reflect the views of our donors.

URBAN
TRANSFORMATION

- -

URBAN TRANSFORMATION

Understanding City Design and Form

by Peter Bosselmann

ISLANDPRESS

WASHINGTON · COVELO · LONDON

Library of Congress Cataloging-in-Publication Data

Bosselmann, Peter.
    Urban transformation : understanding city design and form / Peter Bosselmann.
        p. cm.
    Includes bibliographical references and index.
    ISBN-13: 978-1-59726-480-8 (cloth : alk. paper)
    ISBN-10: 1-59726-480-6 (cloth : alk. paper)
    ISBN-13: 978-1-59726-481-5 (pbk. : alk. paper)
    ISBN-10: 1-59726-481-4 (pbk. : alk. paper)
    1. Cities and towns—Study and teaching. 2. Sociology, Urban—Study and teaching.
    3. Social structure—Study and teaching. 4. City planning—Study and teaching. I. Title.
    HT110.B67 2008
    307.76071—dc22   2008013301

Printed on recycled, acid-free paper

Design by Lyle Rosbotham

Manufactured in the United States of America
10 9 8 7 6 5 4 3 2 1

Contents

List of Illustrations

Acknowledgments

The ideas discussed in this book emerged in the context of a humanistic urban design tradition at the University of California, Berkeley. Over the last four decades, a group of urban designers developed methods to gain knowledge about cities and their changing form. The members have roots in design practice and therefore share an interest in gathering information that led to a normative stance, emphasizing more the prescriptive, "what should be," and less the descriptive, reflective mode, emphasizing the "what is."

It was possible for such a humanistic tradition to emerge because those who practiced held a commitment to an integrated view of education and with a relatively high tolerance for each other's approaches. Like all humanistic traditions, the Berkeley urban design school arose in response to aspirations for a better state of human affairs. The design of buildings, neighborhoods, cities, and regions should not be dictated by doctrine of any persuasion but should be genuinely concerned with the conditions of all human beings, or as many as possible.

The group of colleagues that I am referring to include Christopher Alexander, Donald Appleyard, Clare Cooper Marcus, and Dan Solomon. Those four colleagues taught at Berkeley when I joined in 1976. I worked with all of them during my first few years. Allan Jacobs, whom I worked with for many years, came to Berkeley at roughly the same time. He is highly skilled in keeping the group focused on urban design research and its relevance to the profession. Donlyn Lyndon and Randolf Hester came to Berkeley when Richard Bender became dean at the College of Environmental Design. In the mid-1980s Michael Southworth joined to fill Appleyard's position (he had died in a car accident in September 1983). Nezar Allsayyad joined after he completed his doctorate with Spiro Kostof. Later Rene Davids, Walter Hood, and Louise Mozingo joined (the last two both Berkeley graduates). They were followed by Rene Chow, who came from MIT. Until recently Elizabeth MacDonald, also a contributor to this book, was the most recent member of the group. In 2006 Nicolas De Montchaux took on that role. That core group was and is complemented by a larger community. Until his death in 1992, the historian Spiro Kostof could be counted on as an initiator of ideas. Edward Arens, Joe McBride, John Radke, Robert Cervero and Matt Kondolf continue to inform us as scientists. Tony Dubrovsky teaches our students to see the city through the eyes of an artist. Urban design students are continually drawn to Paul Growth, who as a geographer and historian introduces them to reading the cultural landscape.

Academic groups need jolters. Mel Webber jolted the early members of the group with his thesis that local place was growing less important as society was becoming more and more placeless.[1] The polemics of the discussion made students in the simulation laboratory work on a film "Webberville versus Applelandia." In one the curtains are drawn to keep out the glare as residents communicate with their peers in faraway places; the other has the residents in the streets erecting barricades to protest against traffic and environmental degradation and for greater social justice. Peter Hall told us that increasingly the form of urban regions would need to be studied. He was right, we started that line of work with some delay. He suggested that the Randstad in Holland could serve as a model for a conurbation where residents live at relatively high density and a relatively low dependency on the automobile. Manuel Castells pointed us to a major shift in how society uses space. The information age had changed how people interacted socially at all levels. Daniel Solomon jolted us when he became a founding member of the new urbanism movement. He was also the first to point out that the thrust of the movement was not new, nor had the products at that time been necessarily very urban. T. J. Kent, Fran Violich, and Vernon DeMars jolted us in a manner typical for an older generation who, earlier in their career had pursued similar aspirations. It was their privilege to be impatient and to remind us that mindless urban development had started during the post–World War decades; it had only grown more acute.

This is the milieu that produced a large number of urban designers, practitioners, and academics.

Five, now former, students as research assistants made direct contributions to this book. Neil Hrushowy reviewed three decades of research that had accumulated in a research methods class and wrote a summary of the work. Neil's work provided structure and some of the content described in chapter 3. Elizabeth Macdonald was coauthor of a research project on the Olmsted boulevards in New York City. We published the results together with Thomas Kronenmeier in the *Journal of the American Planning Association*. I have summarized the research in chapter 3. Stefan Pellegrini collaborated with me on an essay about the transformation of downtown Oakland. In modified form this essay with its illustrations became chapter 3. Cheryl Parker collaborated with me on urban simulation projects in San Francisco, no longer as a student, but as a professional; examples of her Urban Explorer's GIS work are found in chapter 6. Finally, Katie Standke produced paintings of the San Francisco Bay. They are reproduced with her kind permission in chapter 7.

As students at Berkeley, their work was supported by grants from the Graham Foundation, the Beatrix Farrand Fund, and the Geraldine Knight Scott Landscape Architecture History Fund. The same funds also supported students from the Masters of Urban Design Program, Vijo Cherian, Simone LeGrande, and Anne Forsberg in the preparations of drawings for chapter 5. The Oakland project discussed in chapter 4 began in late 1999 as commissioned work by the City of Oakland. Shunji Suzuki helped in the modeling of various density scenarios and area-specific clusters. Hiro Sasaki helped with a focus on neighborhood improvement strategies.

The maps compiled in chapter 1 were also created with the help of urban design students at the University of California, Berkeley. Shunji Suzuki was the first to manually trace satellite images and to help clarify the graphic conventions of the production. Geeti Silval and Maria Vasileva digitized the process. Briesh Bhatha completed the collection and georeferenced all maps with help from Anders Flodmark at the Geographic Information Science Center. Ashish Karode and Stefan Pellegrini produced graphic representations of the Bay Area region, and the entire Spring 2002 class helped with the collection of satellite images. This group included Sunai Beri, Jennifer Henry, Abha Kapadia, Jun Kato, Derrin Nordahl, Kartika Rachmawati, Champaka Rajagopal, Mathew Robinson, Geeti Silval, Ana Sverco, Stephanie Tencer, and Tetsuya Yaguchi. Swapneel Patil worked on the graphic layout and Cao Yu together with Corinne Hartnet completed the project in the fall of 2005.

Illustrations for the final book were compiled in the fall of 2007 by Nadine Soubotin, Rachel Edmonds, and Trudy Garber. Thanks go to Noah Freedman who created an image of streets that treat water and special thanks go to John Sugrue who created the image on suburban transformations and helped me during the final six months with the management of all digital image files.

I am very grateful to all the Berkeley students and to the faculty committees that provided funding for their work; to Rasmus Bolvig Hanson, student at the Royal Danish Academy who took the pictures for me in Copenhagen; and David Moffat, who helped with editing the material on the metropolitan landscape. I enjoy my collaboration with John Kriken, who is a colleague in the urban design program and who, together with Ellen Lou, directed the work on the Transbay Terminal Area Plan in San Francisco.

Material for the book was gathered over a period of seven years, including a six-month stay in Copenhagen and a year-long stay in Milan. Both places have left major traces in the book. I owe Jan Gehl much gratitude for our long friendship and for being my host in Copenhagen together with Lars Gemzoe and Michael Varming, whom I dearly miss. In Milan, I owe much thanks to Fausto Curti for giving me the opportunity to set up a simulation laboratory at the Politecnico di Milano. The simulated images of Milan's skyline were produced there with the help of Barbara Piga, Anna Galli, Ali Ustum, and Valerio Signorelli.

The book was written in the Città Alta of Bergamo, at a place of great prospect and refuge. Reflecting on knowledge about city design and transformation in a place where the urban structure has been continuously adapted must have influenced the writing.

The narrative of the chapters has gained in clarity through the insistent probing by Heather Boyer from Island Press.

Our daughters Thea and Sophia have supported my efforts in ways that are clear only to me. I am grateful to Dorit for putting up with the author during the many phases of the project, helping me to rework the material numerous times and giving inspiration to my writing.

The book is dedicated to the memory of Kirk Bosselmann, 03/25/1983–11/27/2004.

Introduction

What is known to us about cities and landscapes is partly a matter of our own experiences and partly what has reached us in one form or another from other sources. This book combines the experiential knowledge that was committed to memory with the knowledge of concepts that were read—or listened to and that, at times, have lit up whole landscapes around us.

This book focuses on the transformation of cities, the knowledge of the changing form of cities, and how cities compare with each other. We are curious about the underlying structure of the built landscape, the social and the natural world, one shaping the other. The book is intended to give an introduction to the field of city design, an overview of the issues that city designers address, the knowledge base needed, and how such knowledge is acquired.

Stephen Jay Gould[1] wrote that knowledge falls into three domains: the knowledge of science, the knowledge of values, and the knowledge of art, each a distinct domain with established methods of inquiry and resulting theories. City design draws from all three domains. The need for knowledge of the natural sciences has increased, because it is widely recognized that the form of cities and the activities inside remain subject to the forces of nature. This is not a new observation, but one that has been glossed over too frequently and not only during the modernist area. Knowledge of values is important, because city design is concerned with human experience, and the ideals, customs, perceptions and cognitions, memory, attachment, and dependencies of a society. Drawing upon values emphasizes the humanistic tradition in design.

The domain of art brings a spiritual dimension to the discipline because art seeks meaning in everyday life. I am thinking primarily about the mutual reinforcement between detailed observation and the knowledge of causes that influence art as a form of seeing, expressing, and interpreting.

Cities are not a form of art, but the process of city design involves the art of creating cities that heighten daily experiences, preferably good experiences, but the bad cannot be ignored.

This book is intended to make a contribution to a field of knowledge that is expanding because of the growing need for professionals equipped to deal with the challenges of the rapidly urbanizing world, depletion of natural resources, and mounting social problems in cities. In the transformation of cities much attention is given to economic forces. Rightfully so, but designing the qualities of the physical settings, and the process of shaping environments requires knowledge that goes beyond an understanding of market forces. Those interested in becoming city designers learn to balance monetary gains with social and ecological gains. City design remains a political, social, and environmental affair.

Urban history cannot be explained without reflecting on the inertia that exists in city transformations. The demographic trends, environmental crisis, and problems with social health and wealth have been identified for many decades. Collectively we know the coming decade will need to be decisive because of the significant increases in urban populations and the need to live with the associated diminishing resources. Of course, the same could have been said in more or less regular intervals throughout urban history, but that is the point. Urban history is again in such a decisive period. To direct, or at least influence, the current urban transformations we need to evaluate what has influenced our selection of knowledge and how knowledge can be used to direct urban transformation in the future.

Peter Hall and Ulrich Pfeiffer address the rapidly urbanizing world and refer to the millennial challenge with an appeal for greater social coherence and solidarity, including greater citizen involvement and a return to more forceful local planning.[2] Thomas Sieverts,[3] in his book *Cities without Cities,* calls upon the city design professions to reassess their position on traditional urban form and to identify a new urban form capable of enabling cities to survive. His is a call for creative solutions that address the wasted land in the fragmented, dissolving city. From Italy, comes a third voice. Bernardo Secchi[4] reflects upon continuity and discontinuity in urban history. He points to previous urban reforms when societies have selectively taken from urban structures, abandoning some structures and adopting what can be used in the transformation to new urban structures. I have selected these three recent references because they all highlight the value of the sensory form of cities and city regions.

One category largely missing from the literature[5] is about professional knowledge, the knowledge designers acquire through their professional work. While this book makes use of secondary sources, the focus is on knowledge that is gained directly by employing seven activities typical to design practice: to compare, to observe, to measure, to transform, to define, to model, and to interpret. Each chapter illustrates one such activity.

The first chapter, entitled To Compare, examines a collection of forty-one maps produced from satellite data. They include twenty of the world's largest urban agglomerations, which have populations above ten million inhabitants. All forty-one maps share a water city typology. Most maps show cities in a river landscape, some near natural harbors, such as bays or estuaries. Others show delta cities and cities located on ocean straits. The collection of maps allows for a comparison of city form and water. It is easy to understand that cities originated near water, and how transportation routes and cities were established in response to water— the ease of reaching water at the seashore, or crossing it and following it along valleys that were created by water. While the natural historical role of water might be taken for granted, the importance of water to sustain life cannot. Water remains an essential part of city structure. One could argue that all cities owe their existence to water. Knowledge about the importance of water influences the transformation of cities.

Patterns of urbanization in parts of the world follow dramatically different forces. In the developing world ever greater numbers of people concentrate, while in other parts of the world more and more people disperse. Comparisons of relative information become meaningful if we introduce a common denominator. A square of fifty by fifty kilometers is superimposed on the maps; the surface area of the forty-one cities is computed as a percentage of such a square. This simple computation makes possible the comparisons between the maps and makes concrete the stunning differences in densities that exist among urban populations and the human tolerance for such differences.

As consequential, but less recognized, in the map comparisons are the differences in the scale dimensions of the cities. A city designer's chief contribution to city transformation is setting the dimensions of streets and lanes, blocks and parcels, building setbacks, entrances and driveways, building heights, separation between buildings, and the size of building footprints. These decisions determine the scale of a city and the human experience of space—the length of a walk, the likelihood of encountering others, the amount of light that is received, protection from wind, exposure to noise, what meets our eyes, when we feel intimacy, when we are participants on a civic stage. In short, city scale determines all aspects of human experience, including the energy needed to transport us and the energy needed to heat or cool dwellings and commercial places.

The second chapter, To Observe, uses an approach similar to the way observation is used in anthropology. The observer strives toward an unprejudiced interpretation of phenomena that can be independently verified, and if a potential conflict is identified, a designer will order the information into a system related toward design intervention. Like hypotheses, the phenomena observed generate ideas that can be tested through design. The current transformations of Copenhagen's city center are used as an example.

The third chapter, To Measure, reminds us of the need to measure those qualities in cities that cannot be measured according to agreed upon conventions, but can nevertheless be measured in relative terms. Such qualities include livability, vitality, and sense of place, which need to be measured empirically on a scale that resembles a continuum. When such qualities are measured repeatedly under different conditions, the knowledge gained is meaningful in demonstrating conditions of general validity. The chapter reports on research that measures mixed use, density, and public life as attributes of *vitality* in cities. Traffic calming, ease of walking, centrality in neighborhoods, and inclusion of nature are attributes contributing to *livability,* and sense of place and sense of time can be attributes of the sense of belonging.

The fourth chapter, To Transform, uses a method that explores the morphology of a city in order to find its essential structures. All cities have such a structure; in some cities it is stronger than in others. The goal is to discover a process of transformation of precedent, extending the structure without destroying its essential components. The urban morphology of Oakland, California, serves as an example.

Chapter five, To Define, explains design principles that shape the form of cities. Defining principles means setting rules that are based upon a generalizable rationale. More than any other structure, streets define the character of cities. This chapter discusses the discovery of principles that generate good streets. Although the examples address the streets of San Francisco, the principles can be applied to many other cities. The chapter examines the various grids of the city and the activities these grids support. It also demonstrates how streets can be designed to improve urban ecology, specifically streets as places that have a comfortable microclimate, serve as meaningful collectors of water, and function well as connectors between open-space systems.

Chapter six, To Model, emphasizes the need to communicate the abstract concepts of the design profession in a manner that makes them understandable to the public. Much knowledge can be gained through modeling, not only for the benefit of those who otherwise would not understand the implications of decision making, but importantly for the designer and his or her colleagues. Through the process of modeling, city design enters into the realm of political discourse. Modeling possible futures unleashes public discussions about who gains and who loses. Such discussions are necessary in a society that embraces local democracy.

The final chapter, To Interpret, focuses on art as a distinct domain of human knowledge. Art tries to capture essential aspects of life. Knowledge cumulates when it finds expression through art. In addition to the domains of science, and the values helping to explain phenomena in cities, civilizations have produced *art* as a form of expression. Throughout time, artists have frequently addressed city form and city milieu in a manner that goes beyond the earlier two domains. The chapter presents abstractions of the shoreline of the San Francisco Bay that can be understood as a *commons,* shared by the adjoining communities. Paintings and photos allude to the character of these commons—its shape and condition, light, texture, and mood.

Thus the book is about methods. The methods used in understanding and transforming through design the elements of the city: streets and promenades, blocks with buildings, edges, waterfronts, and centers—the essential structure of cities.

CHAPTER ONE

To Compare

Cities, Size, Scale, and Form

Coastlines, lakeshores, rivers, and mountain ridges are chiefly responsible for the shape of cities. Views from space suggest that even the largest of the world's great cities were shaped by their natural location. The ground plain for the city of Los Angeles originated through crustal upheaval, and the rivers that emerged on its slopes have almost disappeared, but on a satellite image the shape of the large drainage basin that the city occupies is impressive and understandably its most important form-giving element.

Only recently have new parts of Cairo started to climb away from the Nile River valley onto the rim of the Sahara desert, where they have begun to encroach on the pyramids. Likewise, Shanghai has only recently crossed the Huangpu River, even if future satellite images will almost certainly show it stretched out onto the large fertile plain of the Yangtze River Delta.

As urban population grows, it will be highly relevant to watch the cities

of this world from space—and not only the expanding cities of the developing world but also the dispersing cities[1] in the developed world. If one were to

Figure 1.1 Venice Biennale on the Future of Cities held at the Venice Arsenal in 2006. Three-dimensional models show population density in relation to surface area for the world's largest cities.

Figure 1.2 Los Angeles from space. The ground plain for the city of Los Angeles originated through an upheaval of the earth's crust, and the rivers that emerged on its slopes have almost disappeared, but on a satellite image the shape of the large drainage basin that the city occupies is impressive and is understandably the city's most important form-giving element. (Courtesy NPA Satellite Mapping)

Figure 1.3 Cairo from space. Only recently have new parts of Cairo started to climb away from the Nile River plain onto the rim of the Sahara desert, where they have begun to encroach on the pyramids. (Courtesy NPA Satellite Mapping)

imagine for a moment that it would be possible to direct the growth of cities in the developing world—that is, not to stop the influx of rural migration but to direct the renewal and expansion at their outskirts—future satellite images would show a web of linear gaps in settlement patterns, where now continuous urbanization occurs. These gaps would coincide with the existing water drainage patterns. For reasons that we well understand, new urbanization would stay at a distance from water: from creeks, rivers, bays, and estuaries. Of all physical measures, the preservation of land near water would provide the greatest benefits for human health, health of vegetation and animal life, quality of the air, and a more comfortable climate.

The same understanding of natural systems would direct the dispersed cities in the developed world. In both worlds, the result would lead to a better integration of cities with the forces of nature. This concern for the integration of natural processes into city design will surface again in other chapters of this book.

The second major theme of the book relates city form to human experience. The comparison of city maps in this chapter helps us reflect on the quality of life in cities. The primary urban resource, the amount of space available to each individual, is stunningly variant. The comparison between the maps should not lead us to the conclusion that more space equals a higher or better quality of life; rather, we should conclude that land is a precious resource, to be used deliberately and not to be wasted.

At first disbelief sets in when the maps of the San Francisco Bay Area are shown next to Hong Kong, and next to a map of the Randstad, the urban concentration in The Netherlands that forms a ring and includes Amsterdam, Utrecht, The Hague, and Rotterdam. The comparison suggests that all inhabitants of the San Francisco Bay Area could live together in Sausalito and the urbanized areas of a small county to the north of San Francisco under conditions Bay Area residents would find extremely uncongenial, that is, if they were to live on the same

land area and at the same density as the seven million people of Hong Kong. The rest of the Bay Area would be unpopulated. When shown to Bay Area residents the comparison produces a sense of shock and disbelief. All three maps were reproduced at the same graphic scale; all three show urbanized regions that accommodate nearly the same number of inhabitants, seven million people. The comparison is made possible by computing the surface of each of the three urbanized areas and expressing it as a percentage of a fifty by fifty kilometer square.

In the year 2000 when this collection of maps was started, the population of the San Francisco Bay Area was approaching seven million people and covered 83.75 percent of such a square; Hong Kong has since exceeded seven million inhabitants, but it still covers only 6 percent of a fifty by fifty kilometer square, whereas the Randstad in The Netherlands with its 6.6 million covers 42.7 percent of the same size square. Cities in different cultures with relatively equal numbers of inhabitants accommodate people at strikingly different densities. The conditions associated with the high density of Hong Kong are quickly explained. They are chiefly related to history, the influx of refugees from mainland China, and the political status of the former British colony. But the reasons for the high density are also explained by reflecting on Hong Kong's topography. Most of the available and buildable land area is urbanized. The same is true for the San Francisco Bay Area; topography defines the extent of urbanization. Since the Bay Area has so much more buildable land, it is used at a dramatically different density. The Randstad on the other hand makes for a different comparison; the Rhine–Meuse–Scheldt Delta has much open land available, but by comparison the cities of this urbanized region have only modestly expanded into the agricultural land. The collective political will has limited the extent of the urbanization. Historically, all land above water was precious and had to be protected from flooding. As a result, residents here have lived at relatively high densities because

Figure 1.4 San Francisco Bay Area from satellite data recorded in April 2007. A solid loop has formed around the San Francisco Bay that includes—in addition to San Francisco—the major cities of San Jose in the south and Oakland to the east. (Courtesy NPA Satellite Mapping)

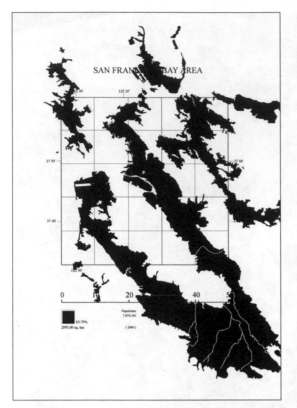

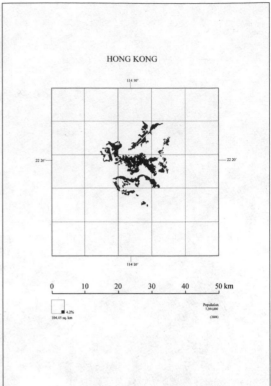

Figure 1.5 San Francisco Bay Area (top) compared to Hong Kong (top right) and the Randstad (right). The three maps were reproduced at the same graphic scale; all three show urbanized regions that accommodate nearly the same number of inhabitants, seven million people. The comparison is made possible by computing the surface of each of the three urbanized areas and expressing it as a percentage of a fifty by fifty kilometer square.

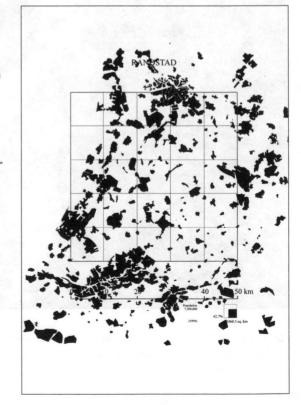

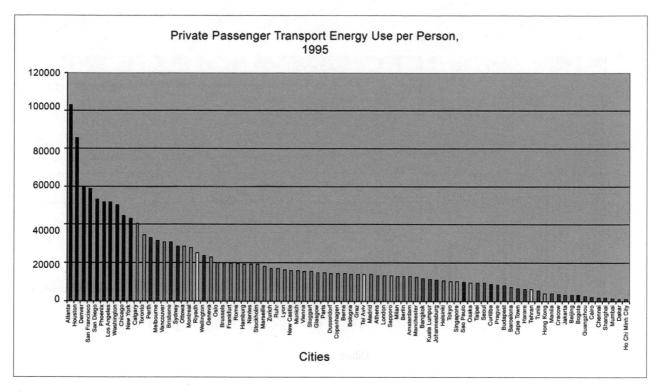

Figure 1.6 Per capita energy consumption for private vehicles in the world's largest cities, 1995. (Courtesy Jeff Kenworthy and Peter Newman, Global City Data Base, CUSP Institute, Curtin University, Perth, Australia)

they have also lived in settlement patterns barely at sealevel, frequently below.

It is fair to conclude from the comparison of the three urban regions that human tolerance for density varies significantly, but the metrics of density as they relate to human ecology are not very well understood. Thus the comparisons between available space in cities and numbers of people using it allow us to interpret human population as part of the earth's ecosystem.

It is possible to apply other metrics, in addition to geographic size, to a comparison between these three urban settlements; for example, car ownership, average length of journeys to work, number of trips made by public transit, air quality, per capita energy consumption, human health statistics, distance to open space—in short, all measures that attempt to quantify sustainable life in cities. Some of this work had its beginning in a metropolitan

world atlas.[2] For example, the atlas compares trips by public or private transportation. Hong Kong residents use transit for 61 percent of their work-related trips, Randstad residents for 49 percent, and Bay Area residents for only 4.7 percent. According to the atlas, the carbon monoxide (CO) emissions for the Bay Area amount to 313.3 tonne per square kilometer, double the CO emissions of Randstad's 167 tonne. But Hong Kong's emissions are 757.9 tonne. In making these comparisons we might not always find direct causality in relation to density and spatial distribution of people because of the many and complex variables that also influence such metrics, but hidden in these comparisons lies a sustainability index that is waiting for discovery. A research group in Australia has correlated automobile use to density. The group at Curtin University[3] has collected data on energy consumption for private automobile use for the

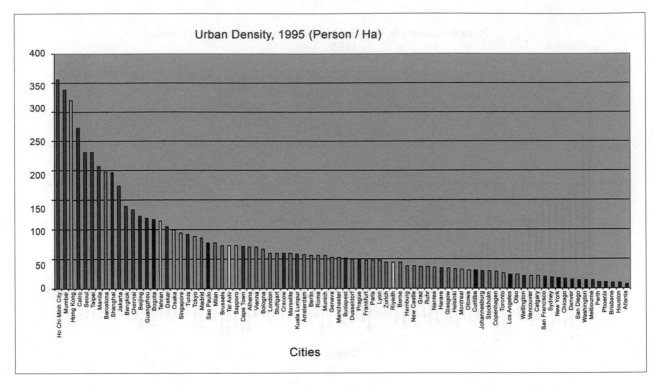

Figure 1.7 Population density in the world's largest cities, 1995. (Courtesy Jeff Kenworthy and Peter Newman)

world's one hundred largest cities and compared it to population density. This global Cities Database was a challenge to compile because of the variable methods used in compiling population statistics worldwide. The work has been criticized for this reason, but the conclusions are correct. The graphs show an inverse correlation between density and private energy use for cars. The densest cities in the world also use the lowest amount of energy for private transportation. The reverse is equally true: the cities of lowest density use by far the highest amount of fuel for private cars. This conclusion might be obvious. However, the magnitude of the difference explains many social, geo-political, and environmental conditions of our time.

The urban region of Atlanta, for example, with its four million inhabitants, consumes 103,000 megajoules (MJ) of energy per person per year for private transportation. Houston ranks close behind with 95,000 MJ followed by Denver, the San Francisco Bay Area, San Diego, Phoenix, Los Angeles, Washington, Chicago, and New York in descending order. These U.S. cities are followed by Australian and Canadian cities. The European cities

Figure 1.8 A map of the San Francisco Bay Area produced from Landsat 7 data 2000. The satellite orbits Earth on a sixteen-day cycle. Through multispectral analysis using data bands 7, 4, 5 of the eight bands sent by Landsat 7 back to Earth the continuously urbanized areas can be delineated. The data analysis process is not entirely unsupervised. Test sites are selected that contain urbanized areas that could be mistaken for nonurbanized areas, or vice versa. Since May 2003 Landsat 7 imagery is only partially readable due to a technical failure of the scan line corrector.

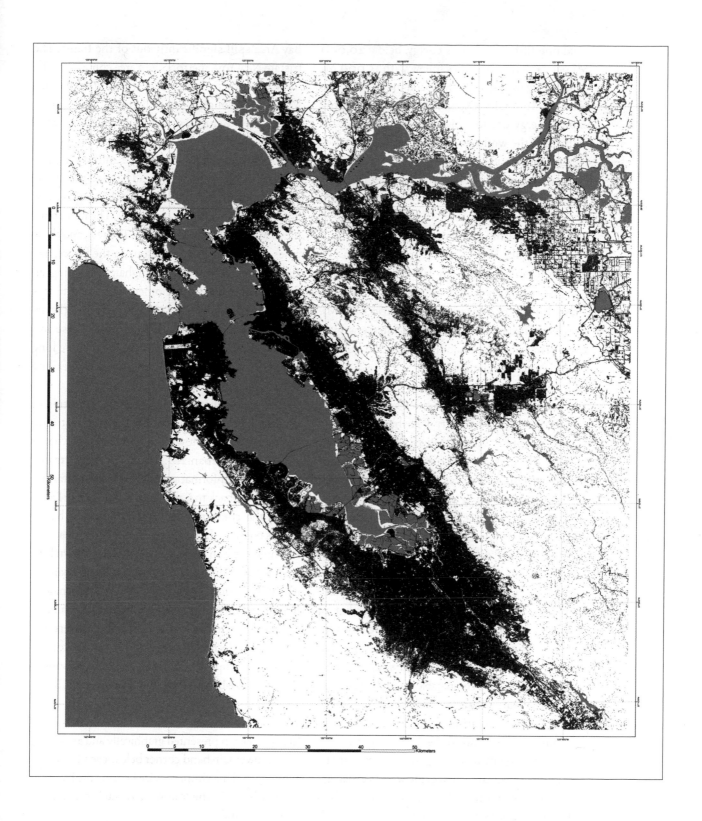

used one fifth of Atlanta's energy, below 20,000 MJ per capita. Asian cities follow with 15,000 MJ descending to just a few thousand megajoules like Ho Chi Minh City. One needs to add up the per capita energy use for private automobile use for thirteen of the world's very dense and largest cities from the collection of maps in this book to come close to the per capita energy consumption for private vehicles in Atlanta. In fact such a list would include, in ascending order starting with the lowest users, Mumbai, Shanghai, Cairo, Beijing, Jakarta, Manila, Hong Kong, Tehran, Seoul, Taipei, São Paulo, and Tokyo. Cumulatively the per capita energy consumption for private transportation in these thirteen cities is equivalent to 100,000 MJ. In these thirteen cities transport-related energy is used primarily for public transportation but at a much lower per capita rate.

These are 1995 statistics; they will not stay the same. Residents in Chinese cities are motorizing rapidly. For example, the city of Foshan, a city of six million people in the Pearl River Delta, was registering 5,665 cars every month in 2007. The neighboring city Guangzhou has ten million inhabitants. In 2006, it was adding 274 cars to its streets every day, a total of 8,228 a month. These are averages. There was a month in 2007 when 16,268 cars were added in Guangzhou, which equates to 542 per day.[4] But even if the private per capita energy consumption of Chinese cities would increase one hundred-fold, it would still be well below that of Atlanta. Even if all the growing Chinese cities increase the consumption of energy for private transport, which is happening, they would still be significantly below a comparable number of cities in the United States, Canada, and Australia. However, globally these comparisons raise much concern.

Comparisons between the world's largest cities are made possible by placing them into a fifty by fifty kilometer square. Most of the world's urban agglomerations fit into such a square. Some, such as Tokyo, Los Angeles, Chicago, and the San Francisco Bay Area spill significantly out of the frame. The tristate New York metropolitan area comes surprisingly close to fitting inside; it barely spills out. Moscow fits snugly; so does Paris, if it were not for its five satellite cities. London spills out a little. Sydney almost fits into the square, but it contains only four million inhabitants. The 3.4 million inhabitants of Melbourne have spread beyond this frame in the southeast. São Paulo, one of the world's most populous cities still, but barely, fits. The more populous Mexico City no longer fits. The rest, and these cities will be the most populous in the future, like Cairo, Mumbai, Calcutta, Shanghai, and Beijing, all fit amply into the fifty-kilometer square. And it is here, of course, where the transformation of the urbanized area will be most noticeable. These five cities—relatively small in surface area—have long bypassed the ten million mark; some are heading for twenty million inhabitants by 2015.

The maps follow a morphological definition of metropolitan areas. Independent of administrative boundaries, they show the boundaries of what is continuously urbanized. The maps were created from satellite information. Eight bands of information are sent back to Earth from satellites like Landsat 7; the combination of three spectral bands makes possible the mapping of urbanized areas. For example, the San Francisco Bay Area is shown here mapped according to such a multispectral analysis. The information is checked against aerial imagery and placed into a fifty by fifty kilometer square.

To select a frame of fifty by fifty kilometers was an arbitrary decision, but when the frame is consistently superimposed onto all maps, comparisons of scale and size become possible. For example, Rome can be compared to cities of similar population size or to cities with similar surface areas. The surface areas are also represented graphically and are shown in the lower left-hand corner below each black and white map. This simple device became the basis for comparisons in the following discussions on city size, scale, and form.

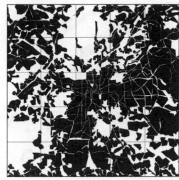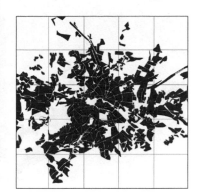

Collection of City Maps

Making of the Maps

In a global comparison involving many cities, it was not possible to verify on the ground the urban boundary delineation. Therefore, we checked the boundaries against visual information. In the case of the San Francisco Bay Area we compared the map with the 2007 image created from satellite data shown in figure 1.4, which we purchased from the NPA Group, Edenbridge, UK. In addition to the San Francisco Bay Area, we used Landsat 7 information to map Rome, Calcutta, Cairo, and Mexico City. These maps resulted from multispectral analysis, a method that uses data bands 7, 4, and 5 of the eight bands sent by Landsat 7 back to Earth. The information contained in these three spectral bands permits the delineation of the continuously urbanized areas. For the rest of the cities in the collection we used feature extraction analysis. From the European Space Agency 2001 publication, "Mega Cities," Geospace, Salzburg, Austria, we read information from their satellite imagery. This helped to create the black and white maps of Bangkok, Beijing, Berlin, Buenos Aires, Mexico City, Cairo, Calcutta, Chicago, Delhi, Hong Kong, Istanbul, Jakarta, Lagos, Lima, London, Los Angeles Manila, Moscow, Mumbai, New York, Paris, Rio de Janeiro, Rome, São Paulo, Seoul, Shanghai, Sydney, Teheran, Tian-

jin, and Tokyo. We also used imagery from the NPA Group in Edenbridge, U.K., which we found in the 2003 *Oxford Atlas of the World*. They include Los Angeles, New York, Santiago de Chile, Cairo, Teheran, Tokyo, and Sydney. In general, we preferred to make maps from data that we could compare to multiple sources; we found images in books and on the Internet. We georeferenced the images, compared the planar projection against a consistent source, the city map portion of the 2003 *Oxford Atlas of the World* and used a feature extraction method in a conventional graphic application program to check the boundaries. The majority of the maps in this collection were produced in this manner. The feature extraction method involved composite viewing or layering of two, sometimes up to four, satellite images for interpretation of visible features along the urban edge. We then traced the extent of settlements in a consistent manner. The comparisons between satellite imagery from different years made us aware of the pace of change in the rapidly expanding cities in this collection. These cities include Beijing, Shanghai, and Tianjin, but also the three cities in India, Calcutta, Mumbai, and Delhi, as well as Lagos in Nigeria. For example, satellite imagery from the year 2000 shows a highly compact Shanghai still neatly framed by agricultural land use; five years later urbanization punctured

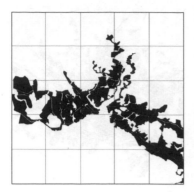 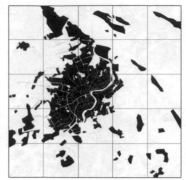 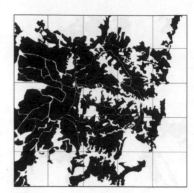

that line in many places. In many Chinese cities the process of urban expansion has continued at an accelerated pace.

Frequently, we had to remind ourselves that geographic information system application software had been designed to conduct analysis at a far greater precision than necessary for a comparison where the size, shape, and form of cities would be compared within a five-inch square. For example, to produce the "footprint of a city" in a black-and-white graphic convention, we needed to establish a relatively precise line defining the edge of urban development. However, in reality this line rarely exists unless it is coincident with the edge of a water body, or the toe line of mountains. On the ground, instead of a line, the edge of a city is frequently a zone, and therefore any line is an approximation. But given the large graphic scale of the representation the decisions where to draw the lines were obvious ones. More difficult to make out were the distinctions between constructed patterns and those found in nature. An established suburb under a dense tree canopy can be difficult to discern; likewise, hillside squatter settlements, with their fine resolution of built elements and irregular shapes, can easily be misinterpreted for patterns found in nature. In general, squatter settlements rarely show on political maps of cities; a high resolution is also

needed to detect them on satellite images. When in doubt, Google Earth became a much used tool to "fly" along the edges of urbanized areas to view in detail the transition zone between urban and nonurbanized areas. But it is important to remember that Google Earth imagery shows conditions with a significant delay and not simultaneously with conditions that exist on the ground when the request to visit the Google site is made.

Mapping the Natural Systems and Historic Core Areas

The black-and-white footprint maps that emerged from this process were highly abstract. They looked like inkblots. Early on in the project there was a desire to create a second type of map that depicted some of the natural context within which these cities are located. We were also interested to show unattached neighboring cities. Therefore, on the left-hand side of each double page, rivers, shorelines, mountain ridges, or other large open-space systems are shown in order to understand the context of each urban agglomeration. For this second set of maps the urbanized areas were depicted in gray, and the extent of the historic core was rendered in black. For a global comparison of cities no single source exists that reliably shows the extent of all cities at a given time in history. Again, we used

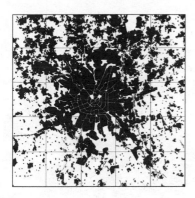 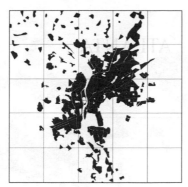 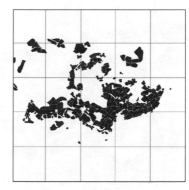

multiple sources. Generally, the black area on the left-hand maps depicts the city between the 1850s and 1900. We used Melville C. Branch, 1978, *Atlas of Rare City Maps*, (Princeton Architectural Press) to delineate the maps of Amsterdam, Berlin, Calcutta, Constantinople, Copenhagen, London, Milan, Moscow, New York, Paris, Stockholm, and Rome. Large urban agglomerations joined over time with adjacent cities. Rarely did we have access to historical maps that show the historic core area of all surrounding cities now connected by urban fabric into one continuous metropolis. As a result only the main city's historical boundaries are shown. We were fortunate to have historical data for the cities surrounding Berlin from W. Ribbe and J. Schmadeke, 1988; the cities comprising the Randstad from Polynet.org.uk/Randstad; the San Francisco Bay Area from various historic maps in the University of California–Berkeley's map library; and Tokyo from *Tokyo, A Bilingual Atlas*, 1991, published by Kodansha.

Population Statistics

For the purpose of density calculations, population numbers are difficult to evaluate because the methods used to create population statistics vary widely. Few sources reveal the exact geographic areas for which the numbers are gathered. For all cities such numbers also depend on the quality and age of the census data. For that reason, it was not possible to compute a consistent comparison of inhabitants to surface area. The population numbers used in the map collection came from the United Nations Population Division (UN), which maintains a Web site with population statistics for all the world's cities with more than 100,000 inhabitants. In many instances the population statistics were supplemented by data from the "World Gazetteer" (WG) at www.world-gazetteer.com, the 1999 *Oxford Essential Geographical Dictionary* (Ox); and Thomas Brinkhoff, "City Populations" (BCP) at www.citypopulation.de. In all instances, we found the population statistics for metropolitan areas to be inconsistent: due to the incomparability of the term "urban agglomeration," different sources appear to base their population counts upon different geographic areas and/or different census information.

ATLANTA

84 20'

33 50'

84 20'

33 40'

3 40'

84 30'

84 20'

0   10   30   40   50 km

1. Atlanta, Georgia
The city is located atop a ridge south of the Chattahooches River, in Fulton and
DeKalb counties. Named in 1847. Population 4,247,981 (2004 U.S. Census).
Source: www.geology.com; Google Earth 2005.

ATLANTA

33 50'

33 40'

84 20'

84 30'

8 40'

0   10   40   50 km

96.0%

2400.5 sq. km

Population
4,247, 981

(2003)

AUCKLAND

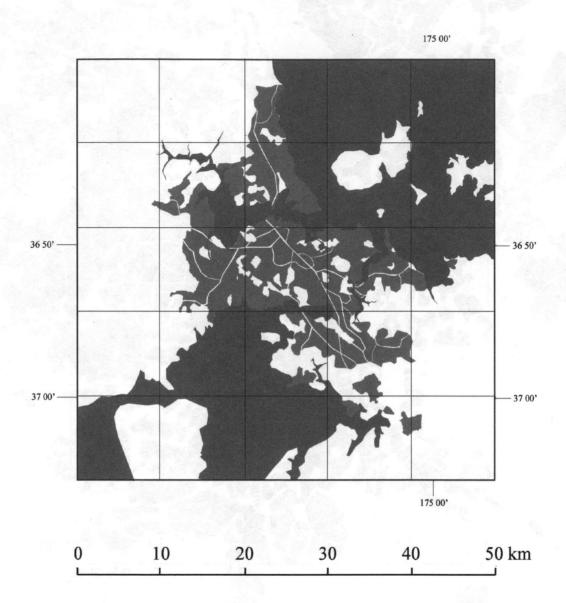

175 00'

36 50'

37 00'

0   10   20   30   40   50 km

2. Auckland, New Zealand
New Zealand's largest city and capital from 1854 to 1865. The city is located on
an isthmus that has its origin as a volcanic field between the Tasman Sea and
the Hauraki Gulf. Population 1.6 million (UN 2005).
Source: Google Earth 2005.

AUCKLAND

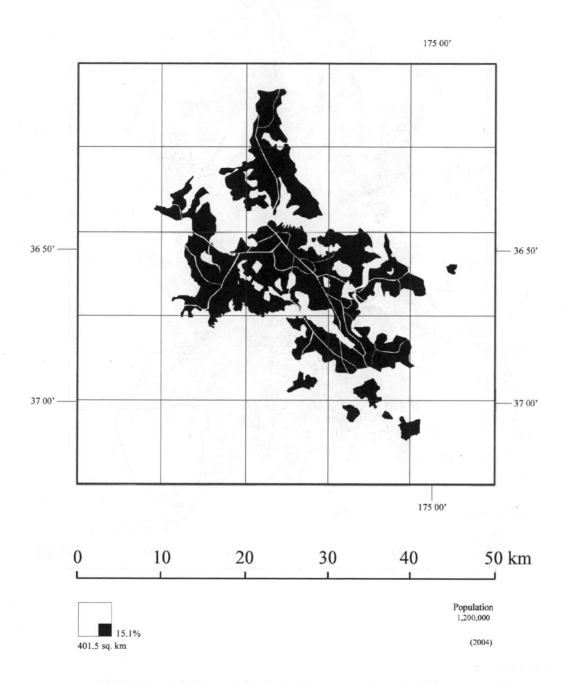

175 00'

36 50' — — 36 50'

37 00' — — 37 00'

175 00'

0   10   20   30   40   50 km

15.1%
401.5 sq. km

Population
1,200,000

(2004)

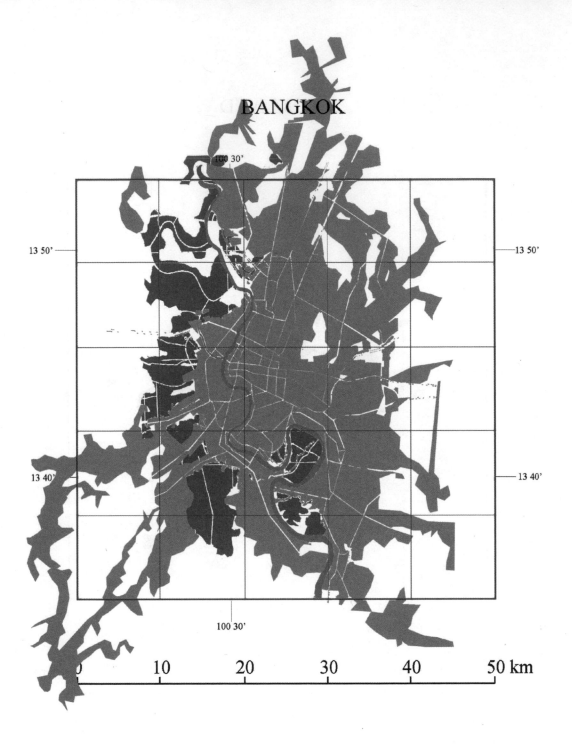

BANGKOK

100 30'

13 50'   13 50'

13 40'   13 40'

100 30'

0 10 20 30 40 50 km

3. Bangkok, Thailand

Bangkok, like a great number of cities in Southeast Asia is located in the coastal flood plain of a major river. The Chao Phraya River meanders toward the Gulf of Thailand. Population 5,876,000 (Ox 1999); 6,593,700 (UN 2005) greater metropolitan area 7.8 million (Ox 1999). According to UN estimates Bangkok will reach 10.4 million in 2015 and rank twenty-fourth among the world's largest cities.
Source: European Space Agency 2001; Google Earth 2005.

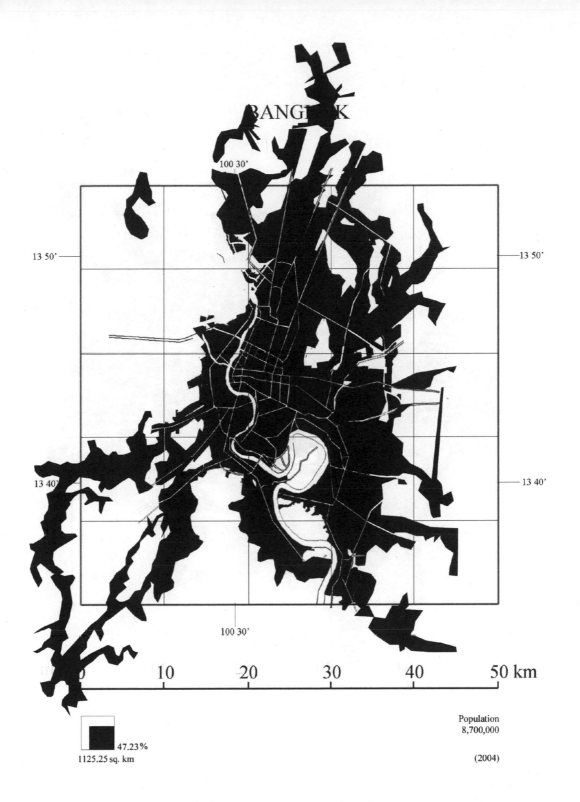

BANGKOK

100 30'

13 50'   13 50'

13 40'   13 40'

100 30'

10   20   30   40   50 km

47.23%
1125.25 sq. km

Population
8,700,000

(2004)

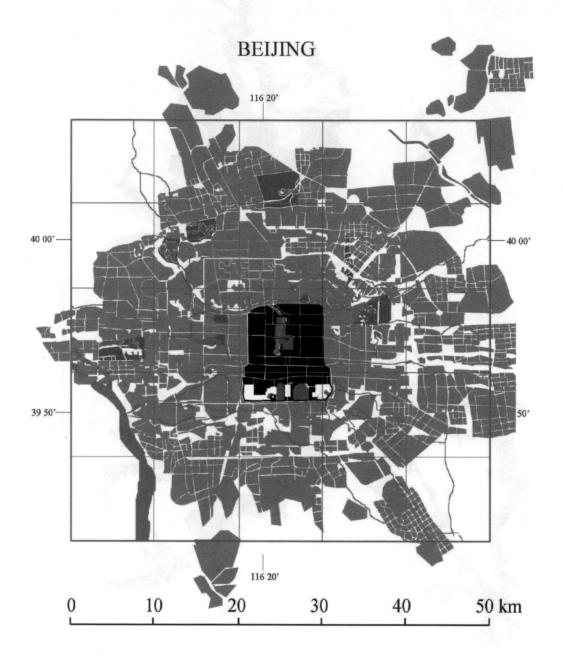

BEIJING

116 20'

40 00'   40 00'

39 50'   50'

116 20'

0   10   20   30   40   50 km

4. Beijing, China

Located 43.5 m above sea level. Founded in 1057 BC. Capital of China since 1421 during the Ming dynasty. Historically known as Ji, Zhongdu, and Dadu. The city is located between two tributaries of the Hai River system. Population 7,209,900 (WG 2004); greater metropolitan area 10,717,000 (UN 2005); 13,569,194 (WG 2004). According to UN estimates the urban agglomeration of Beijing will reach 19.6 million in 2015 and rank sixth among the world's largest cities.
Source: European Space Agency 2001; Google Earth 2005.

BEIJING

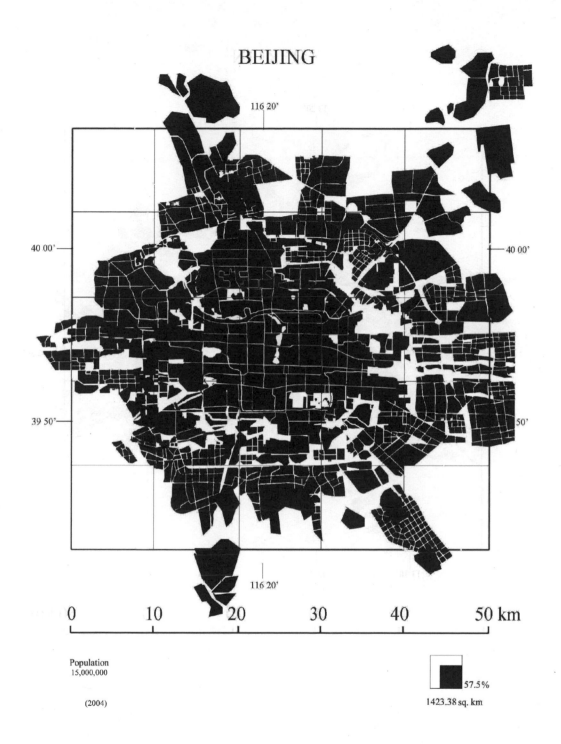

116 20'

40 00'   40 00'

39 50'   50'

116 20'

0   10   20   30   40   50 km

Population
15,000,000

(2004)

57.5%

1423.38 sq. km

BERLIN

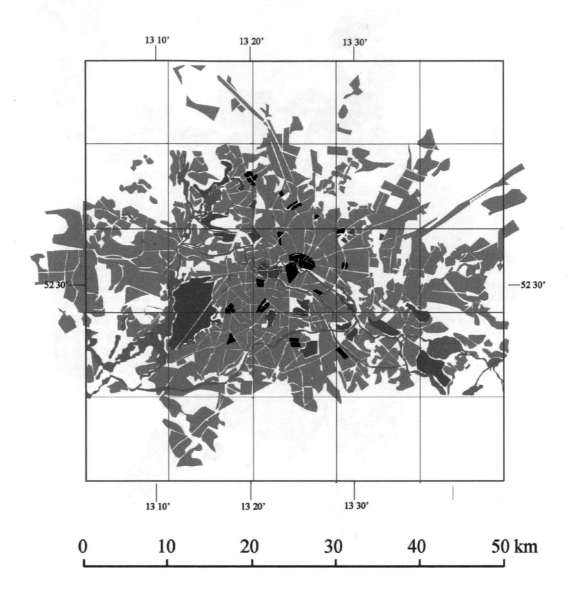

5. Berlin, Germany

Capital of Germany 1871–1949 and since 1990. The city is located in the Spree–Havel River valley. Population 3,102,500 (Ox 1999), 3,385 667 (UN 2005), 4,100,000 (BCP 2004).
Source: European Space Agency 2001; Google Earth 2005.

BERLIN

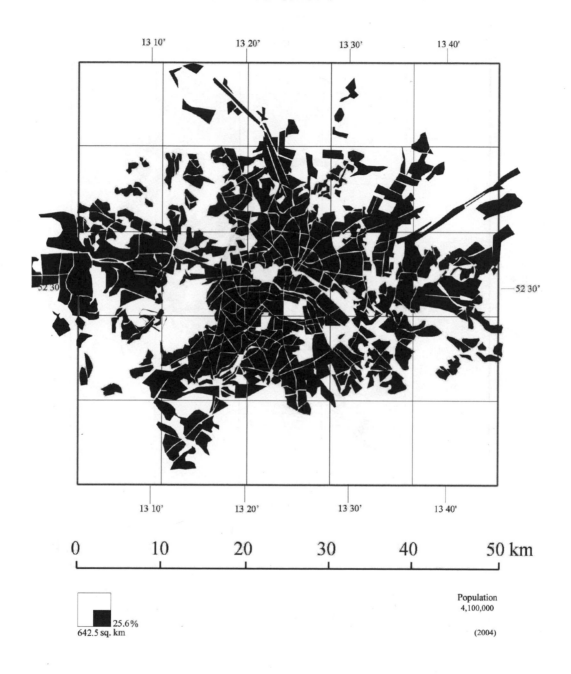

0   10   20   30   40   50 km

25.6%
642.5 sq. km

Population
4,100,000

(2004)

BRASILIA

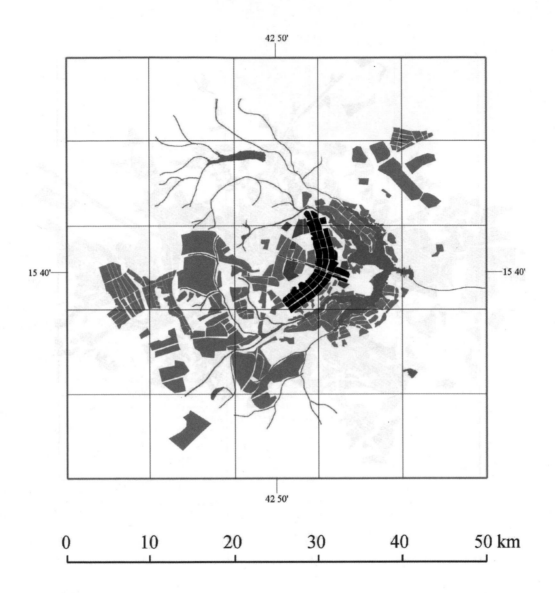

42 50'

15 40'   15 40'

42 50'

0   10   20   30   40   50 km

6. Brasilia, Brazil
Capital of Brazil since 1960. The city is located between the Preto and
Descoberto rivers. Population 1,601,100 (Ox 1999); 3,341,000 (UN 2005).
Source: Google Earth 2005.

BRASILIA

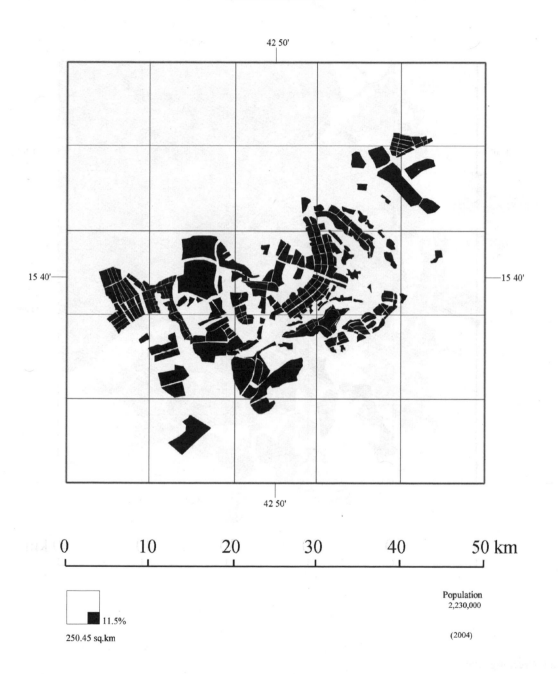

42 50'

15 40' — — 15 40'

42 50'

0   10   20   30   40   50 km

250.45 sq.km   11.5%

Population
2,230,000

(2004)

BUENOS AIRES

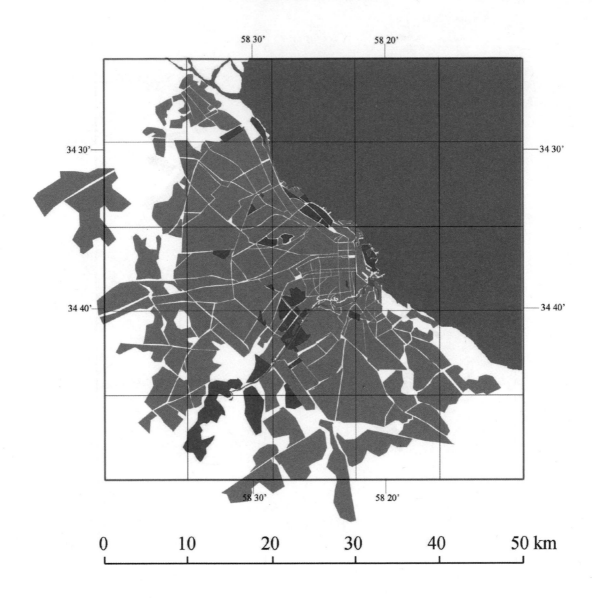

7. Buenos Aires, Argentina
Founded in 1536 and located at the mouth of the Rio de la Plata. Population of
the city 3,961,608 (UN 2000); greater metropolitan area 12,550,000 (UN 2005).
According to UN estimates the greater metropolitan area of Buenos Aires will
remain at 12.5 million in 2015, or rank nineteenth among the world's largest cities.
Source: European Space Agency 2001; Google Earth 2005.

BUENOS AIRES

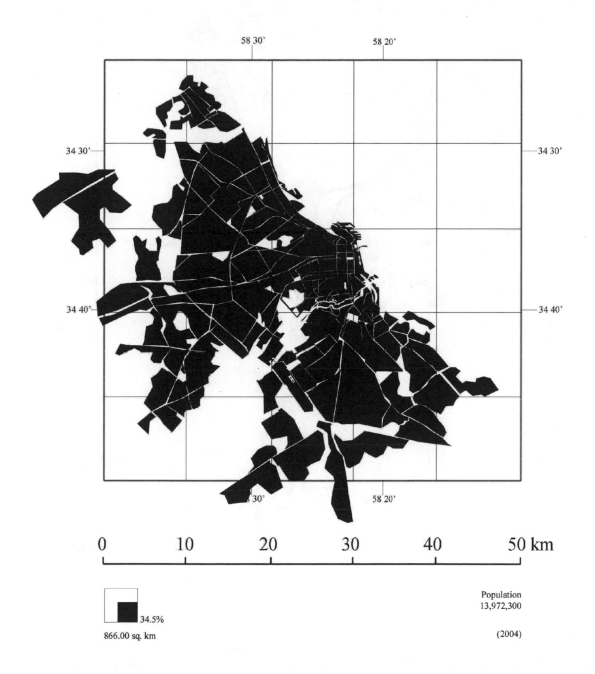

58 30'   58 20'

34 30'   34 30'

34 40'   34 40'

58 30'   58 20'

0   10   20   30   40   50 km

34.5%

866.00 sq. km

Population
13,972,300

(2004)

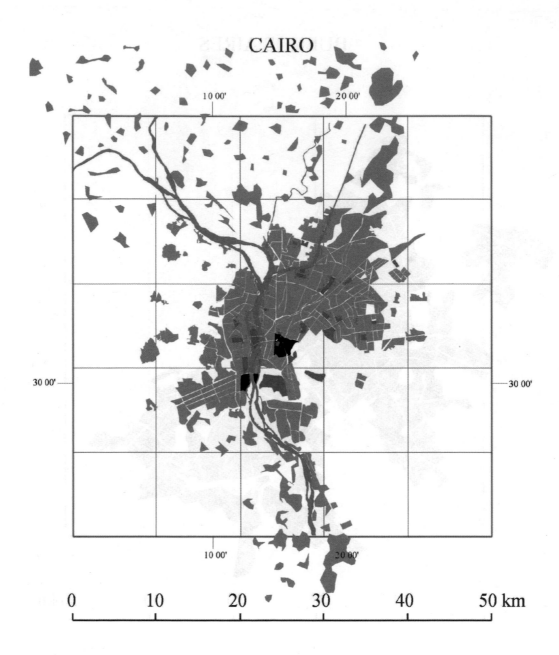

CAIRO

0   10   20   30   40   50 km

8. Cairo, Egypt

Founded by Rome as Babylon-in-Egypt at the site of a Pharaonic river crossing of the Nile River. In the eighth century conquering Muslims started a tent city and mosque to the north of the Roman walls and called the city Fustal. In 750 a permanent city was built further to the north and named Al-Quatai. In 969, a fortified city, Al-Quahira, was built just to the north of the former. Capital of Egypt since the tenth century. Population 7,609,700 (WG 2004); greater urban area 11,128,000 (UN 2005). According to UN estimates Cairo will reach 14.7 million inhabitants in 2015, or rank sixteenth among the world's largest cities. According to other estimates the urban agglomeration has already grown to 15,863,300 (BCP 2004).

Source: Landsat 7; European Space Agency 2001; Oxford World Atlas 2003; NPA Group, Edenbridge, UK 1999; Google Earth 2005.

CAIRO

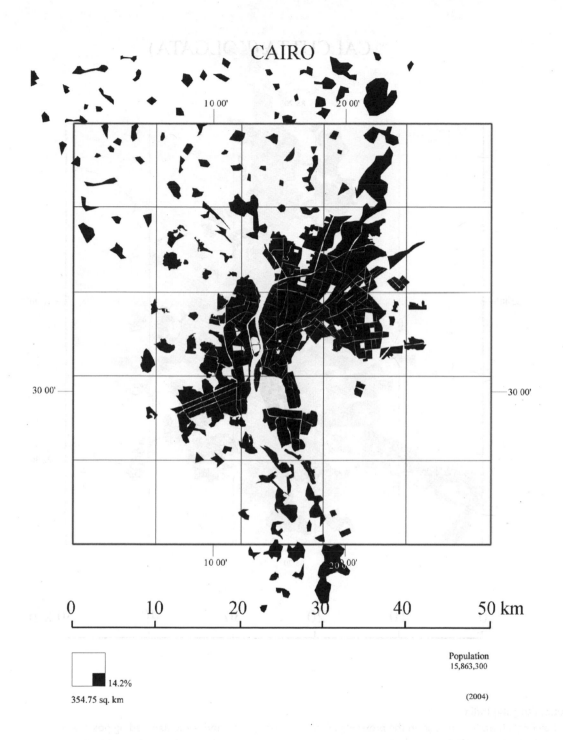

10 00' 20 00'

30 00' 30 00'

10 00' 20 00'

0 10 20 30 40 50 km

14.2%

354.75 sq. km

Population
15,863,300

(2004)

CALCUTTA (KOLGATA)

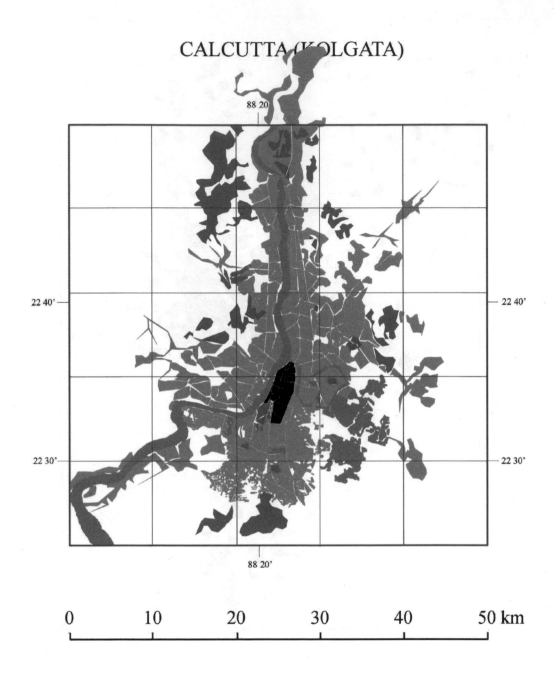

9. Calcutta, (Kolgata) India
Founded by English traders in 1690 in the proximity of Danish, Portuguese, and Armenian trading posts on the Hugli River in the Ganges Delta at 1.5 to 9.0 meters above sea level. Capital of India during the rule of the East India Company until 1912, then capital of West Bengal, it is the largest city in India. Population 10,916,000 (Ox 1999), 14,277,000 (UN 2005). The greater metropolitan area includes nineteen cities adjacent and attached to Calcutta. According to UN estimates Calcutta will reach 17.6 million in 2015 or rank eleventh among the world's largest cities.
Source: Landsat 7; European Space Agency 2001; Google Earth 2005.

CALCUTTA (KOLGATA)

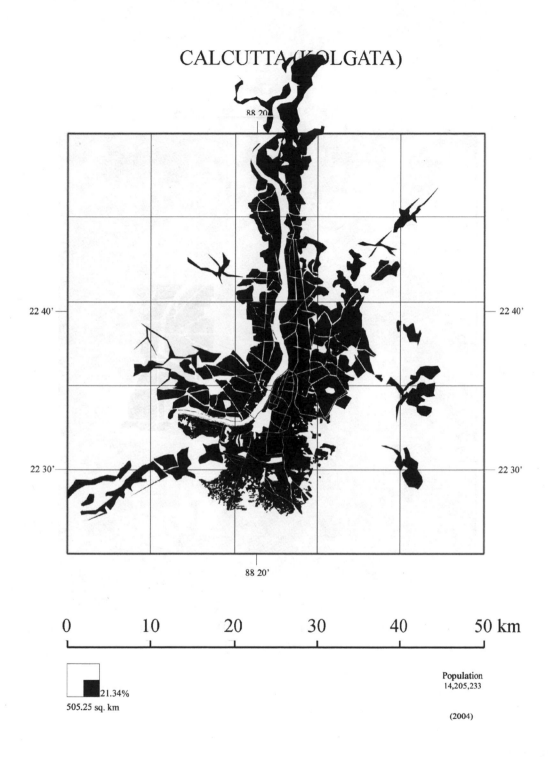

0   10   20   30   40   50 km

21.34%

505.25 sq. km

Population
14,205,233

(2004)

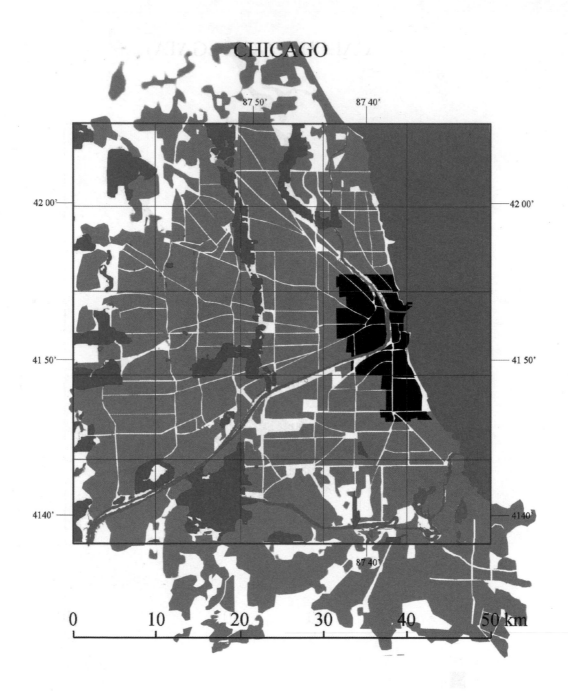

10. Chicago, USA
Founded in 1833 in a location on a continental divide at Lake Michigan between the
Great Lakes and Mississippi watersheds, 176 m above sea level. Population 2,783,730 (OX
1999) for the city; 9,443,000 (UN 2005) for the Consolidated Metropolitan Area.
Source: European Space Agency 2001, America From Space 1998, Google Earth 2005.

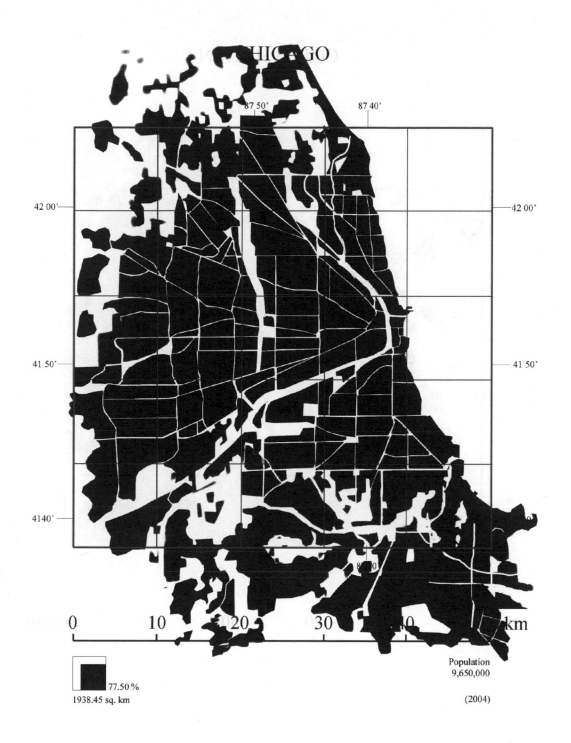

CHICAGO

87 50'   87 40'

42 00'   42 00'

41 50'   41 50'

4140'

87 10'

8 10'

0   10   20   30   40   km

◼ 77.50 %
1938.45 sq. km

Population
9,650,000

(2004)

COPENHAGEN

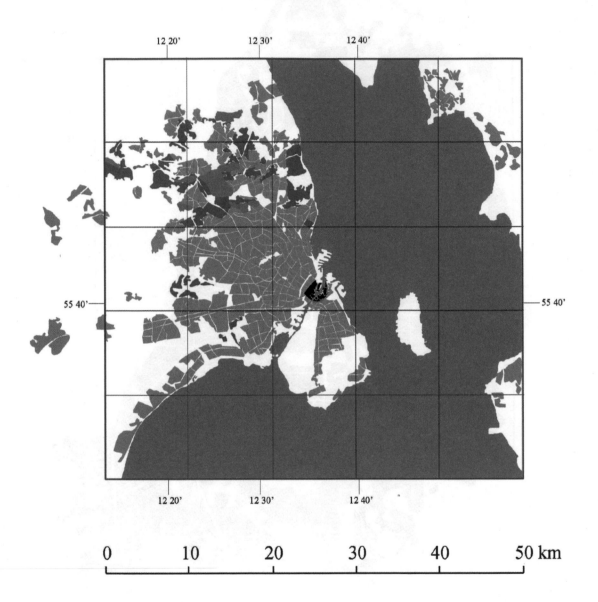

11. Copenhagen, Denmark
First mentioned in 1043, located on the Øresund, a strait that connects the
Baltic with the Kattegat, to the Skagerrak and to the North Sea. Population
466,700 (Ox 1999); greater metropolitan area, one million (UN 2005).
Source: Royal Danish Geographic Service 2000, Google Earth 2005.

COPENHAGEN

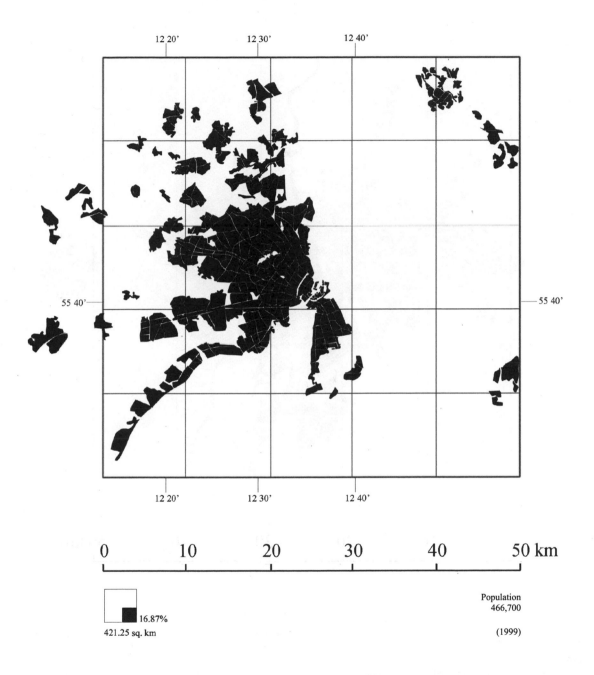

0   10   20   30   40   50 km

16.87%

421.25 sq. km

Population
466,700

(1999)

DELHI

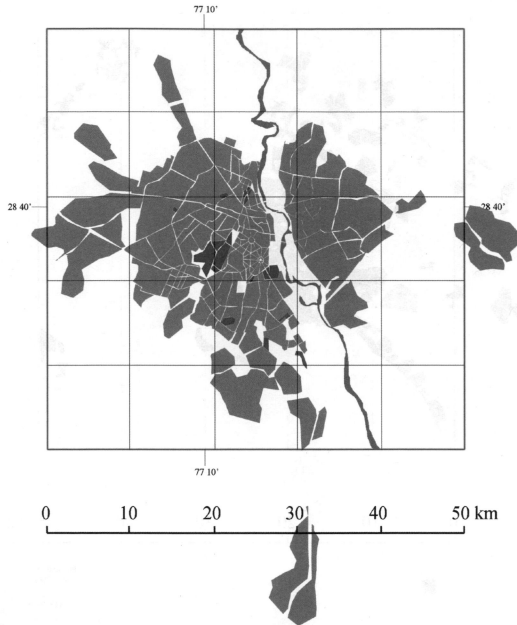

77 10'

28 40'

28 40'

77 10'

0   10   20   30   40   50 km

12. Delhi, India

Capital of the Mogul Empire in 1638. New Delhi, capital of India since 1912. The city is located on the Yamuna River. Population 7,175,000 (Ox 1999), 8,419,084 (UN) 1999, urban agglomeration in 2004 estimated 17,367,300 (WG 2004). According to UN estimates Delhi will reach 17.5 million, or rank twelfth among the world's largest cities. Already estimated at 18,700,000 (BCP 2004).
Source: European Space Agency 2001; Google Earth 2005.

DELHI

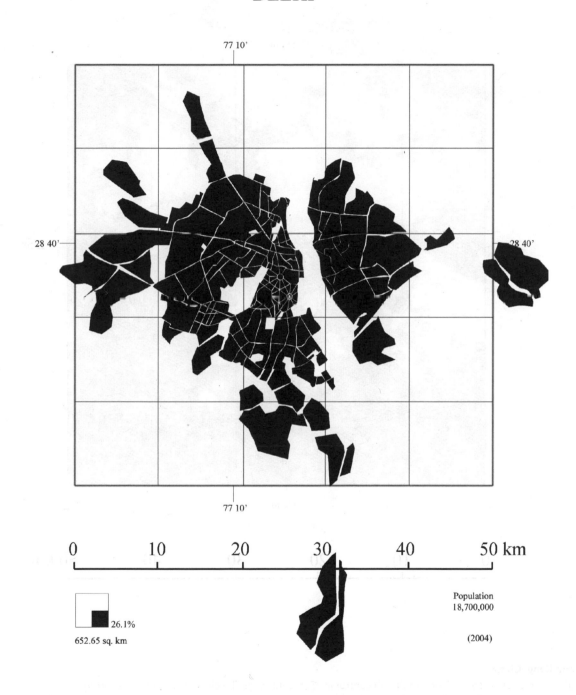

77 10'

28 40'   28 40'

77 10'

0   10   20   30   40   50 km

26.1%

652.65 sq. km

Population
18,700,000

(2004)

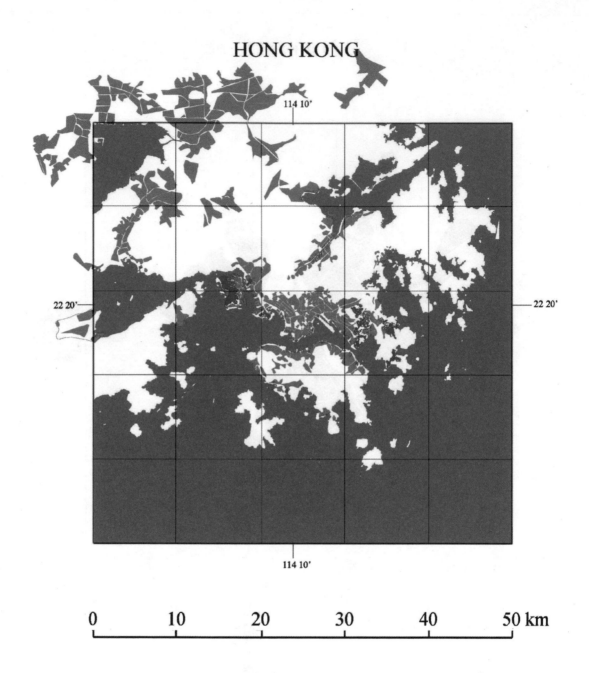

HONG KONG

114 10'

22 20' — — 22 20'

114 10'

```
0        10        20        30        40      50 km
├────────┼────────┼────────┼────────┼────────┤
```

13. Hong Kong, China

Special Administrative Zone. Ceded to British control in 1842 until 1997. The city consists of three territories in the South China Sea at the mouth of the Pearl River estuary: Hong Kong Island, Kowloon Peninsula, and New Territories. The narrow strait between the island and the peninsula is known as Victoria Harbour.
Population 5,900,000 (Ox 1999); 6,843,000 (UN) 1999; 7,394,000 (BCP 2004).
Source: European Space Agency 2001; Google Earth 2005.

HONG KONG

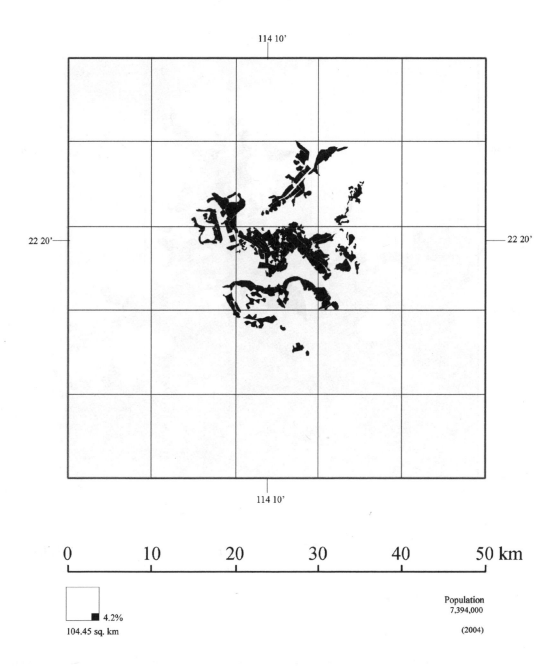

114 10'

22 20'   22 20'

114 10'

0   10   20   30   40   50 km

4.2%

104.45 sq. km

Population
7,394,000

(2004)

ISTANBUL

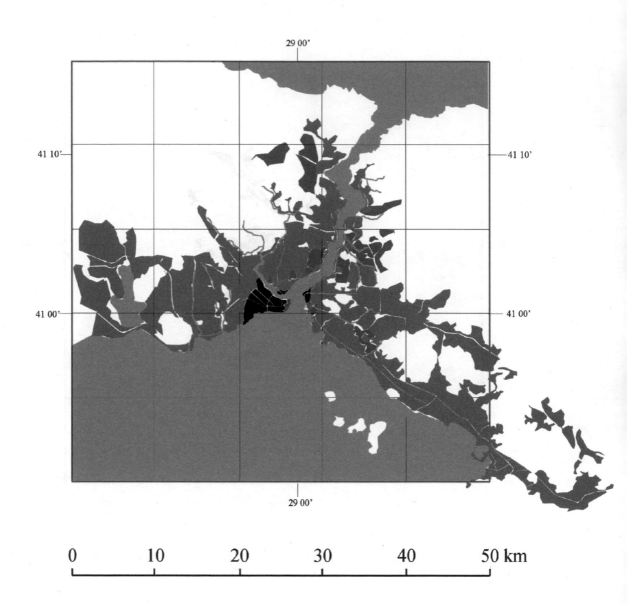

14. Istanbul, Turkey

Founded as Bythantium in the seventh century BC. Capital of East Rome, named Constantinople from 330 until 1453 when it was captured by Ottoman Turks and became the capital of the Ottoman Empire; capital of Turkey until 1923. The metropolitan region is located on the European side of the Bosporus but incorporates historic settlements on the Asian shore and spreads noticeably along the Aegean Sea. Population 7,309,000 (Ox 1999); 8,506,026 (UN 1999); 14,879,000 (BCP 2004). According to UN estimates Istanbul will reach 12.1 million in 2015 and will rank twentieth among the world's largest cities.
Source: European Space Agency 2001; Google Earth 2005.

ISTANBUL

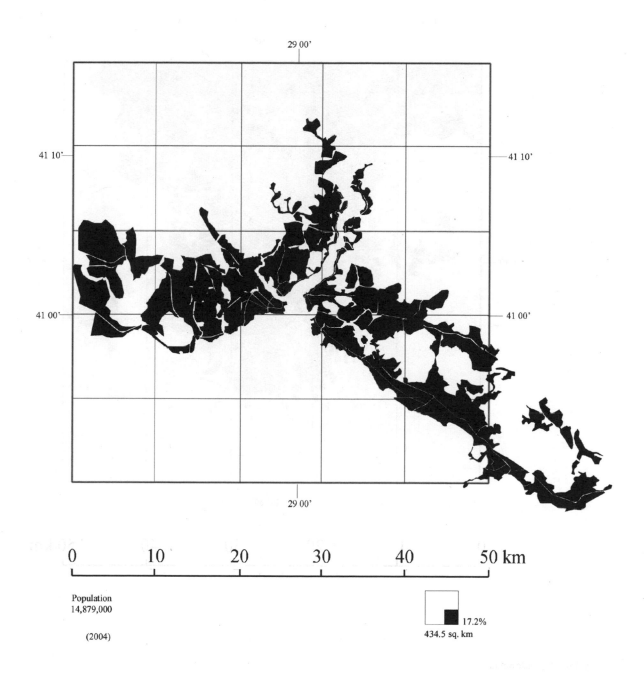

29 00'

41 10'   41 10'

41 00'   41 00'

29 00'

| 0 | 10 | 20 | 30 | 40 | 50 km |

Population
14,879,000

(2004)

17.2%

434.5 sq. km

JAKARTA

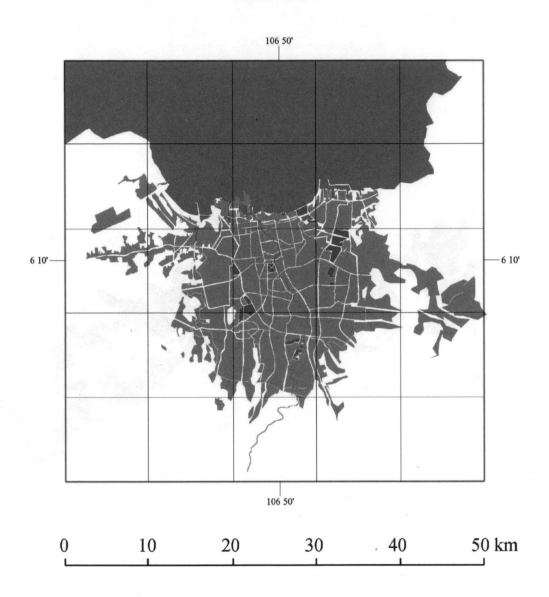

106 50'

6 10' — — 6 10'

106 50'

0   10   20   30   40   50 km

15. Jakarta, Indonesia
Capital of Indonesia since 1949. Named Batavia under Dutch rule. Population
8,222,500 (Ox 1999), 8,987,800 (WG 2004), urban agglomeration 18,206,700
(WG 2004). According to UN estimates Jakarta will reach 21.5 million in 2015,
or rank fifth among the world's largest cities.
Source: European Space Agency 2001; Google Earth 2005.

JAKARTA

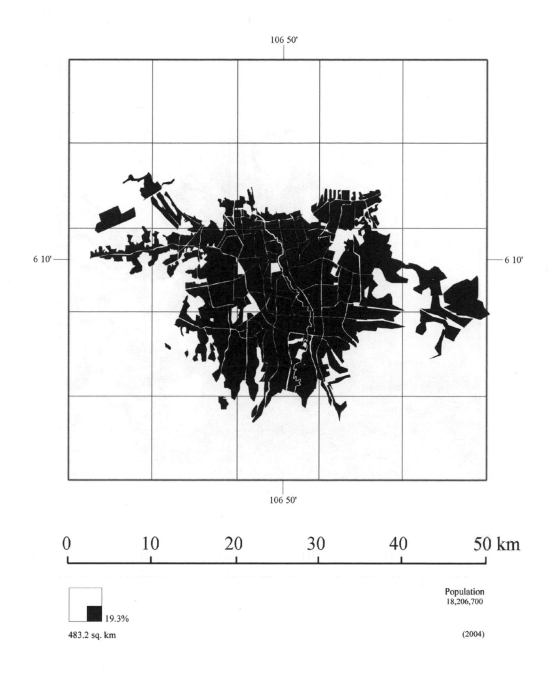

106 50'

6 10'   6 10'

106 50'

0   10   20   30   40   50 km

19.3%

483.2 sq. km

Population
18,206,700

(2004)

KARACHI

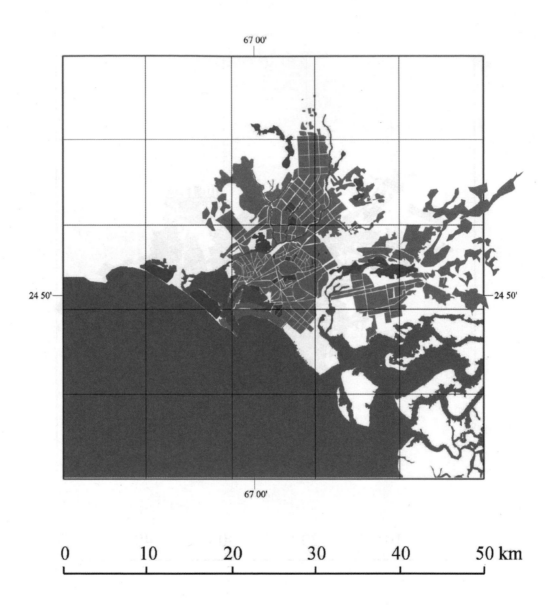

16. Karachi, Pakistan

Capital of Pakistan from 1947 to 1959. The city is located on the Arabian Sea, at the mouth of the Malir and Lyari rivers at the edge of the Indus River Delta. Population 6,700,000 (Ox 1999); 14,870,000 (UN 2004). According to UN projections Karachi will reach 20.8 million inhabitants, or rank seventh among the world's largest cities. *Source:* Oxford World Atlas 2003; European Space Agency 2001; Google Earth 2005.

KARACHI

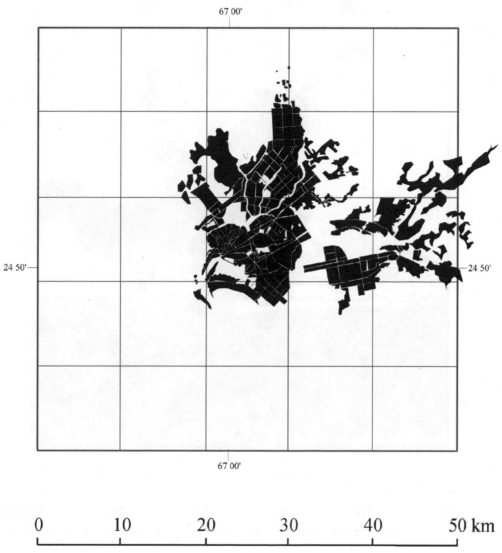

67 00'

24 50'   24 50'

67 00'

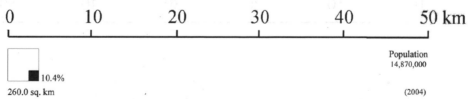

0   10   20   30   40   50 km

10.4%

260.0 sq. km

Population
14,870,000

(2004)

LAGOS

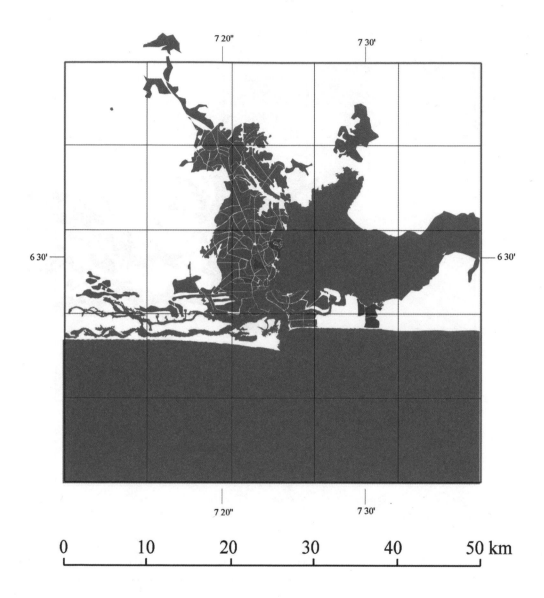

0   10   20   30   40   50 km

17. Lagos, Nigeria

Population in 1975, the year for which UN figures are available 1,060,848 (UN 1975); 5,195,200
(Webster 1991). Most current estimate puts Lagos at 10,650,000 (BCP 2004). The city is located
on islands in a lagoon at the Nigerian coast of Africa. According to UN estimates Lagos will
reach 24 million inhabitants by 2015, or rank third among the world's largest cities.
Source: European Space Agency 2001; Google Earth 2005.

LAGOS

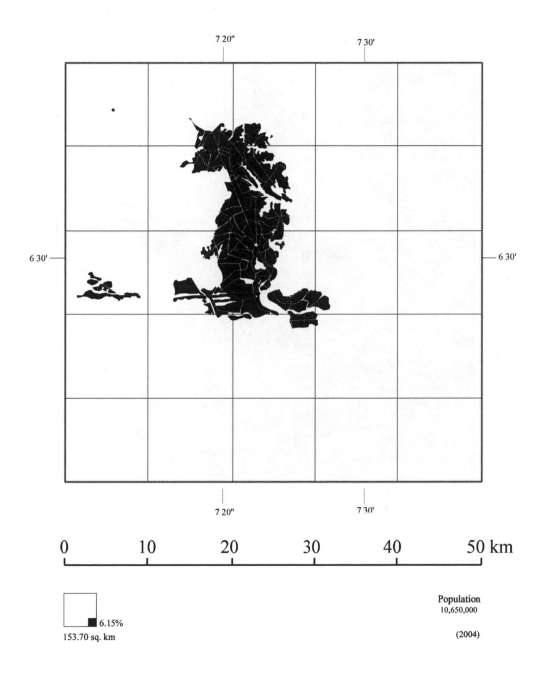

7 20"   7 30'

6 30'   6 30'

7 20"   7 30'

0   10   20   30   40   50 km

6.15%

153.70 sq. km

Population
10,650,000

(2004)

LIMA

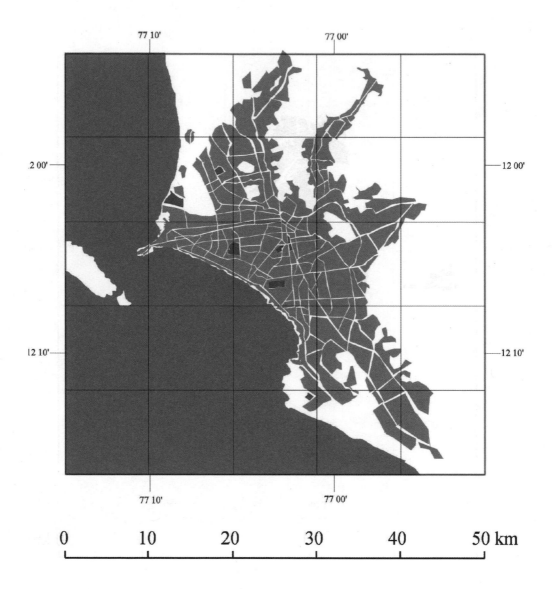

18. Lima, Peru

Founded in 1553, capital of the Spanish colonies in South America until liberation from Spain in the nineteenth century. The city is located on a coastal plain between the Chillon, Rimac, and Lurin rivers. Population 5,700,000 (Ox 1999); 6,321,173 (UN 1993); 8,300,000 (BCP 2004). According to UN estimates Lima will reach 10.1 million inhabitants, or rank twenty-sixth among the world's largest cities. *Source:* European Space Agency 2001; Google Earth 2005.

LIMA

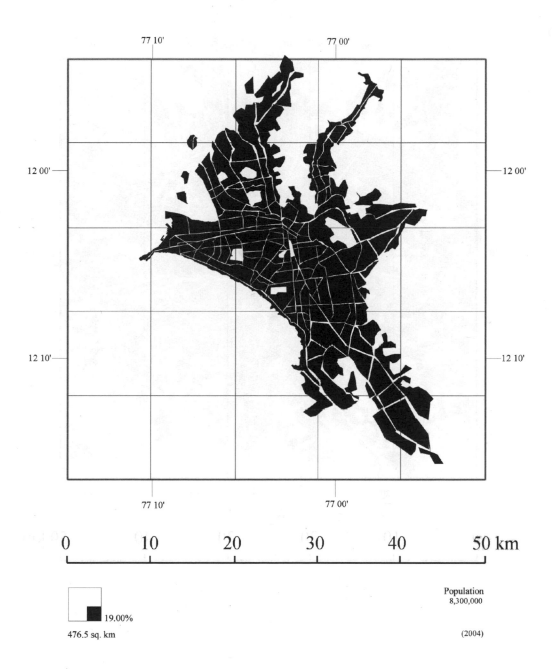

0   10   20   30   40   50 km

19.00%

476.5 sq. km

Population
8,300,000

(2004)

LONDON

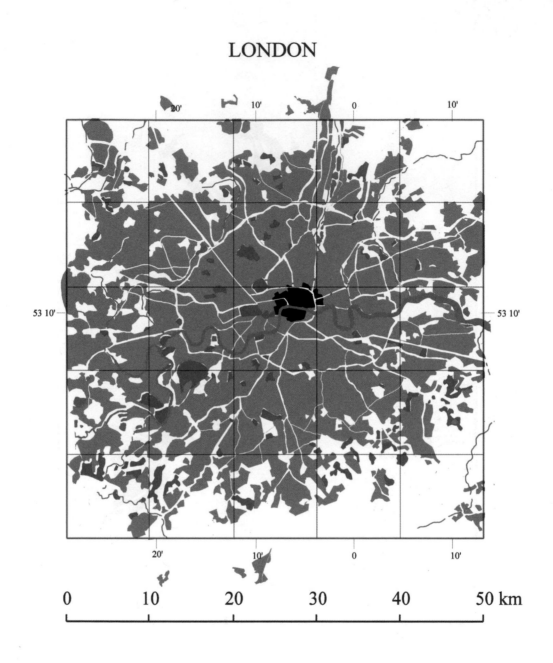

19. London, United Kingdom
Settled in AD 43; capital of the United Kingdom. The city is located in the tidal reach of the North Sea on the River Thames and numerous smaller rivers. Population 7,593,300 (WG 2000); 8,278,251 (BCP 2004). City of London plus thirty-two surrounding boroughs of Greater London; urban agglomeration 11,950,000 (BCP 2004).
Source: Oxford World Atlas 2003; European Space Agency 2001; Google Earth 2005.

LONDON

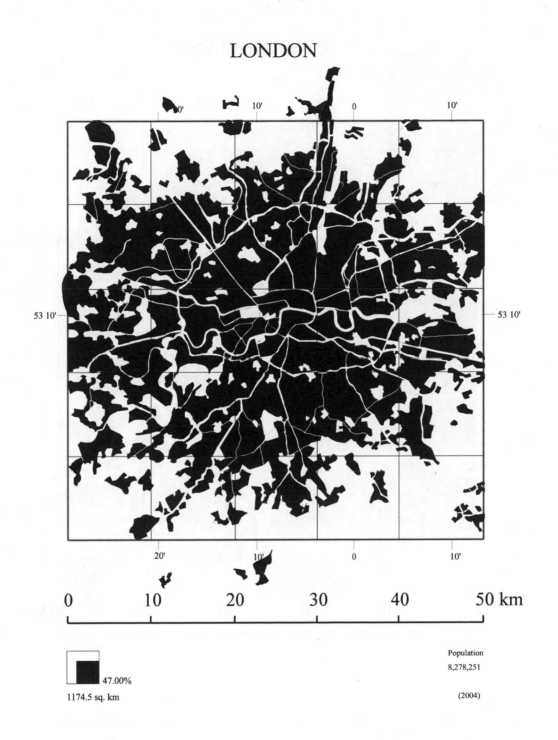

0'   10'   0   10'

53 10'   53 10'

20'   10'   0   10'

0   10   20   30   40   50 km

47.00%

1174.5 sq. km

Population
8,278,251

(2004)

LOS ANGELES

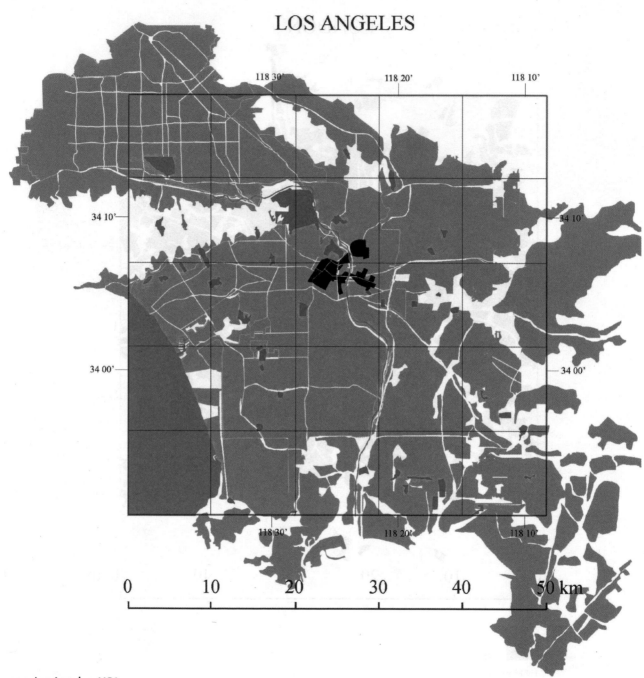

20. Los Angeles, USA

Founded by Spain in 1781, the city had its origin near the Los Angeles River, a large seasonal stream. Population of the City of Los Angeles 3,485,398 (Ox 1999); Greater Los Angeles area, 16,373,645 (UN 2000); 16,710,400 (WG 2004) includes the consolidated metropolitan area, urbanized areas of Los Angeles County, Riverside, Orange County, Long Beach County, San Bernardino County, and Ventura County. According to UN estimates Los Angeles will have 14.5 million inhabitants in 2015 and rank seventeenth among the world's largest cities. (Note: the United Nations must be using different area boundaries for its 2015 estimates.)
Source: Oxford World Atlas 2003; NPA Group Edenbridge UK 1999; European Space Agency 2001; Google Earth 2005.

LOS ANGELES

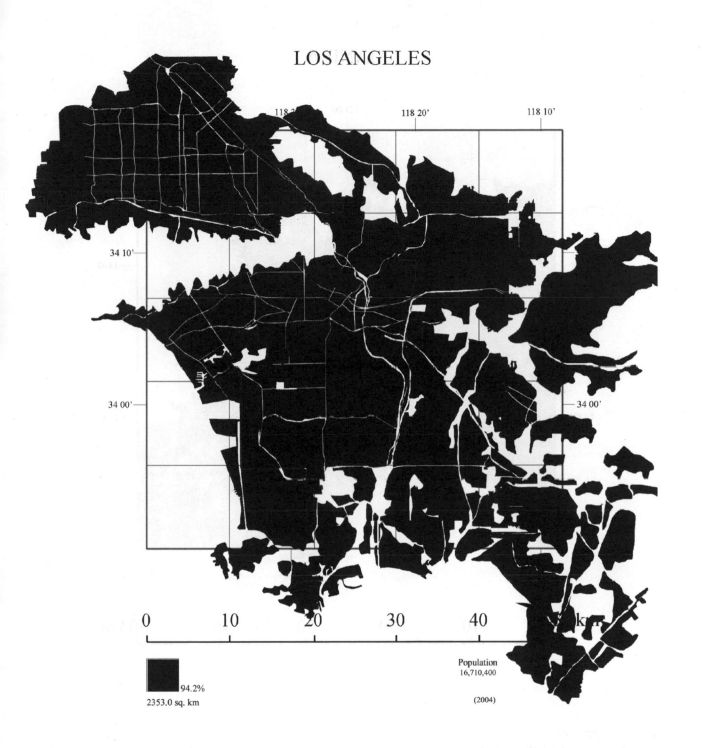

118 30'   118 20'   118 10'

34 10'

34 00'   34 00'

0   10   20   30   40   km

94.2%

2353.0 sq. km

Population
16,710,400

(2004)

MANILA

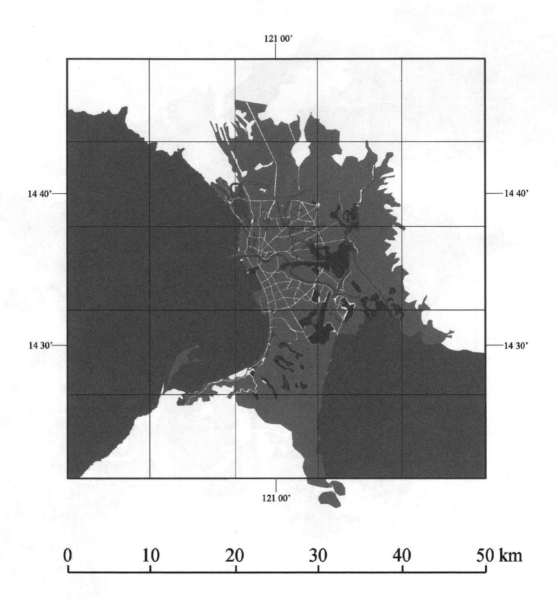

121 00'

14 40'   14 40'

14 30'   14 30'

121 00'

0   10   20   30   40   50 km

21. Manila, Philippines
Founded in 1571, capital of the Philippines. Under Spanish rule until 1898, taken by the United States, since 1945 independent. The city is located at the mouth of the Pasing River at Manila Bay. Population 1,654,761 (UN 1995); greater metropolitan area 8,590,000 (UN 1999); 10,330,100 (WG 2004). According to UN estimates Manila will reach 15.5 million inhabitants in 2015 and rank fifteenth among the world's largest cities.
Source: European Space Agency 2001; Google Earth 2005.

MANILA

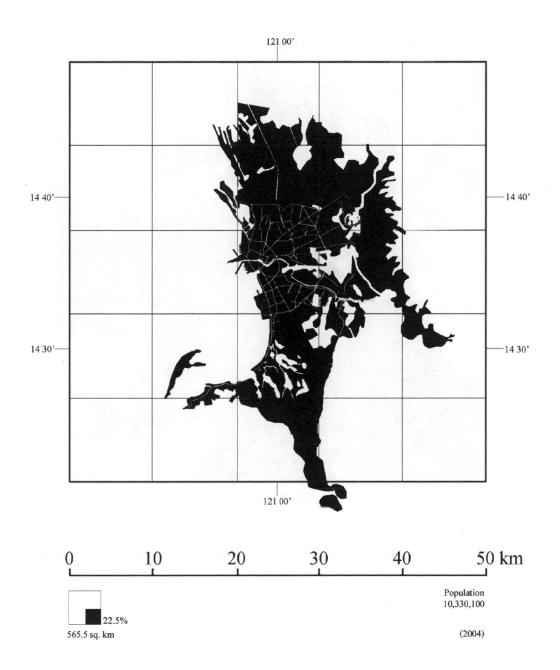

121 00'

14 40'   14 40'

14 30'   14 30'

121 00'

0   10   20   30   40   50 km

22.5%

565.5 sq. km

Population
10,330,100

(2004)

MELBOURNE

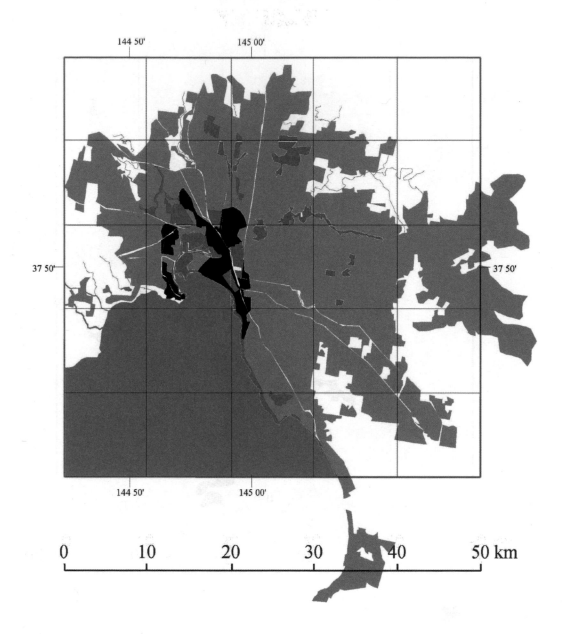

22. Melbourne, Australia
Capital of Australia from 1901 until 1927. The city was settled in 1835 and incorporated in 1847 on the banks of the Yarra River near Port Phillip, a natural bay of the Tasman Sea. Population 2,762,000 (Ox 1999); 3,413,894 (UN 1999).
Source: www.Geology.com; Google Earth 2005.

MELBOURNE

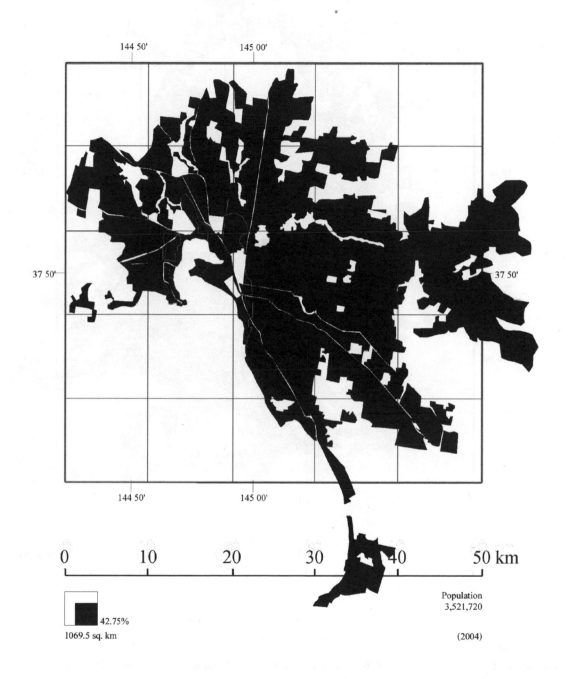

144 50'   145 00'

37 50'   37 50'

144 50'   145 00'

0   10   20   30   40   50 km

42.75%

1069.5 sq. km

Population
3,521,720

(2004)

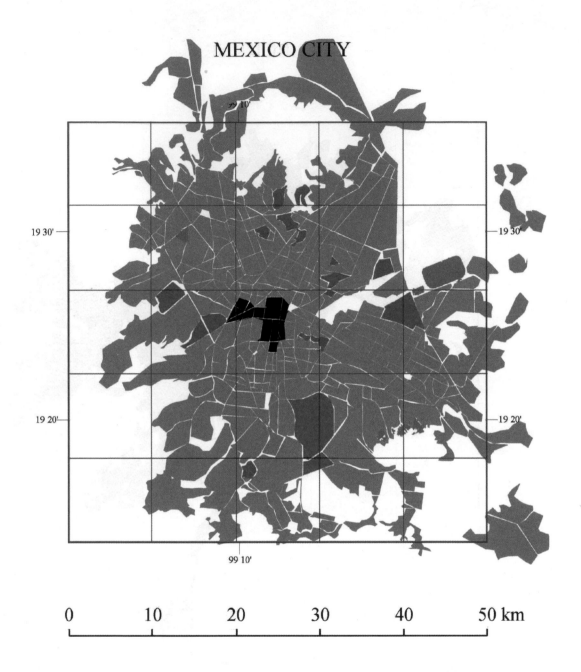

MEXICO CITY

19 30' — — 19 30'

19 20' — — 19 20'

99 10'

0   10   20   30   40   50 km

23. Mexico City, Mexico

Capital of Mexico; founded in 1325 as the Aztec capital of Tenochtitlan; 1521 conquered by Spain; 1821 independence and capital of the Republic of Mexico. The city originated in the Anáhuac basin on an island in Lake Texcoco. Population 8,703,100 (WG 2004); urban agglomeration 13,636,000 (Ox 1999); 15,047,685 (UN 1999). According to UN estimates Mexico City will reach 19.1 million in 2015 and rank tenth among the world's largest cities. Estimates for current population already exceed this projection, 21,503,700 (WG 2004).
Source: Landsat 7; European Space Agency 2001; Google Earth 2005.

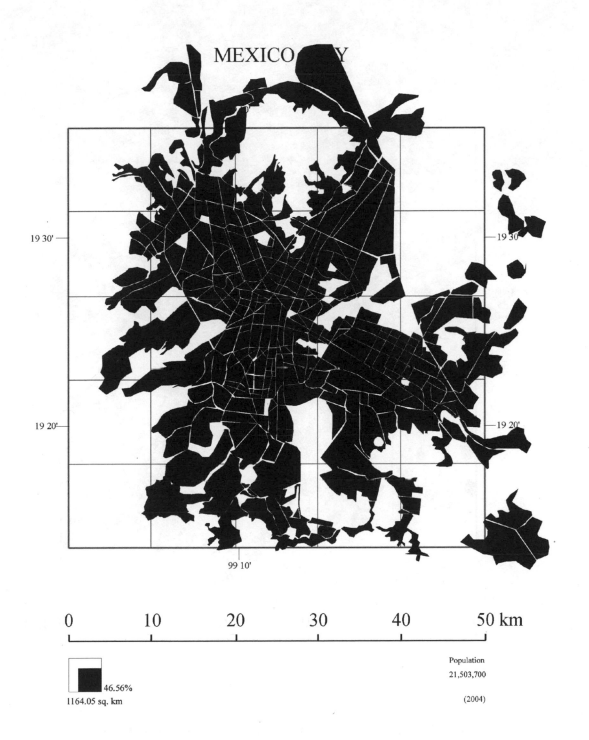

MEXICO CITY

19 30'

19 20'

99 10'

0   10   20   30   40   50 km

46.56%

1164.05 sq. km

Population
21,503,700

(2004)

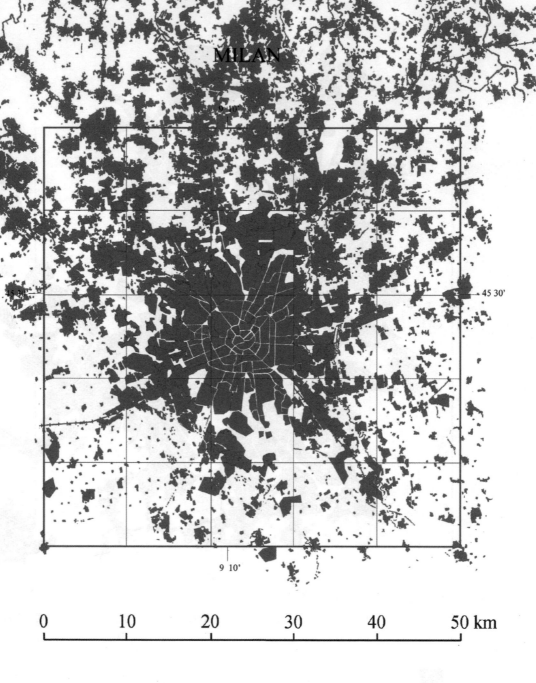

MILAN

24. Milan, Italy
Italy's largest city. Of Celtic origin, subdued by Rome 222 BC. Seat of Roman emperors from AD 305 to 402.
Capital of Lombardy. The name is a corruption of *medio lemorum,* between two rivers, the Olona and Sevestro.
The greater metropolitan area is located in a river landscape of several small rivers and two major rivers, the Ti-
cino and the Adda, both originating in the Alps and joining the Po River south of Milan. Population 1,980,000
(UN 2004). Greater metropolitan area totals seven million including Varese, Como, Lecco and Bergamo.
Source: Casabella 2005; La Città di Città 2006.

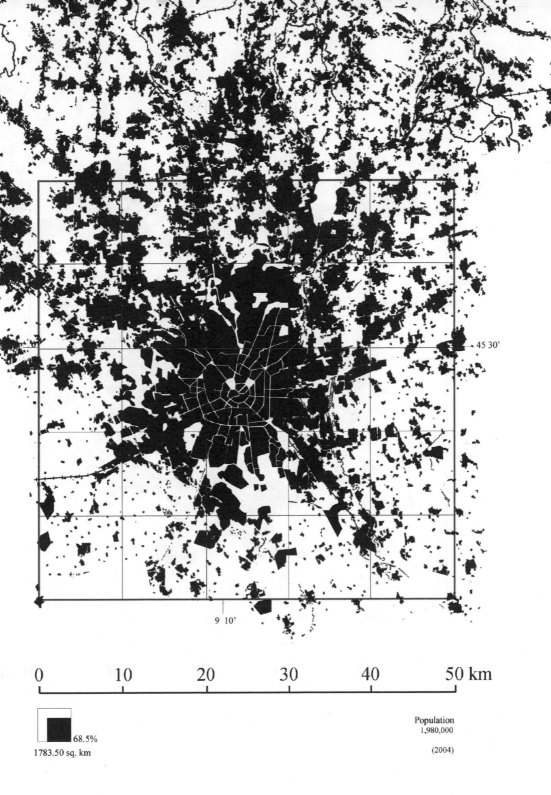

45 30'

9 10'

0   10   20   30   40   50 km

68.5%

1783.50 sq. km

Population
1,980,000

(2004)

MOSCOW

0   10   20   30   40   50 km

25. Moscow, Russian Federation
First mentioned in 1147. Capital of Russia in the 16th century and after 1917.
Capital of the Russian Federation, named after the Moskva River. Population
9,000,000 (Ox 1999); 11,273,400 (UN 2004), 10,126,424 (BCP 2004).
Source: European Space Space Agency 2001; Google Earth 2005.

MOSCOW

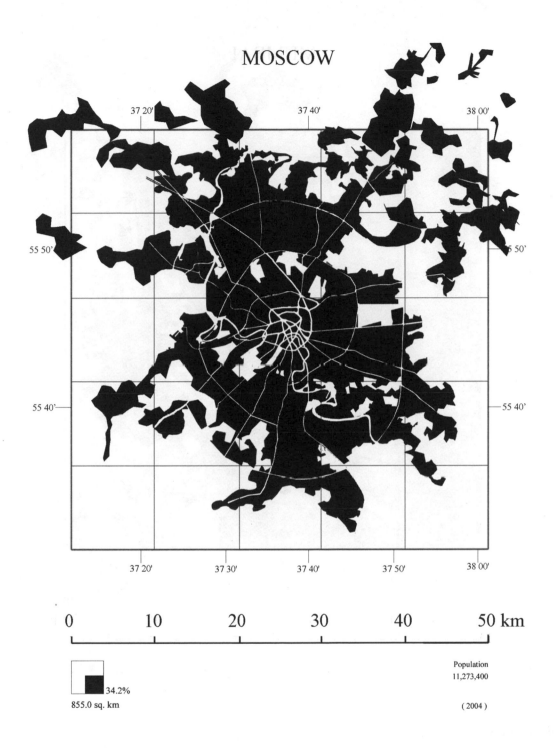

0   10   20   30   40   50 km

34.2%

855.0 sq. km

Population
11,273,400

(2004)

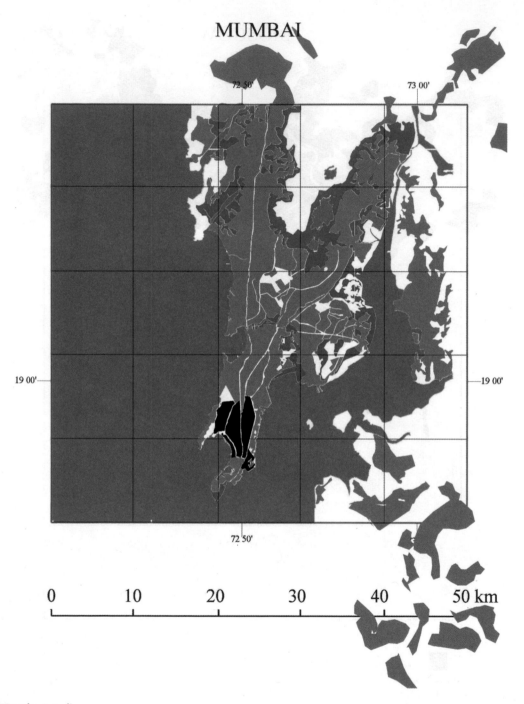

MUMBAI

26. Mumbai (Bombay), India
Capital of the State of Maharashtra; traces of a settlement date back to 250 BC. Colonized by Portugal in 1534, ceded to England in 1661. Under British rule until 1947. Located on Salsette Island at the mouth of the Ulhas River. Population 9,990,000 (Ox 1999); 17,564,430 (UN 2004); 12,622,500 (WG 2004); urban agglomeration 17,340,400 (WG 2004); 18,200,000 (BCP 2004). According to UN estimates Mumbai will reach 27.4 million by 2015 and will rank second among the largest cities of the world. *Source:* European Space Agency 2001; Google Earth 2005.

MUMBAI

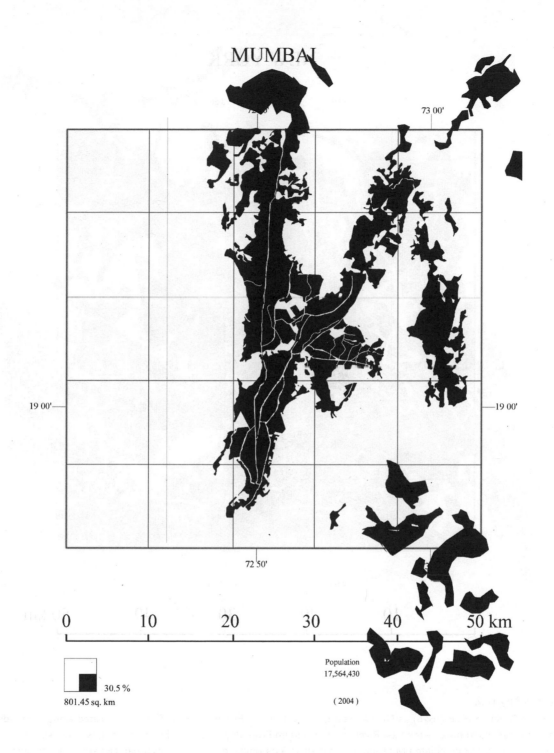

73 00'

19 00'

19 00'

72 50'

0   10   20   30   40   50 km

30.5 %

801.45 sq. km

Population
17,564,430

(2004)

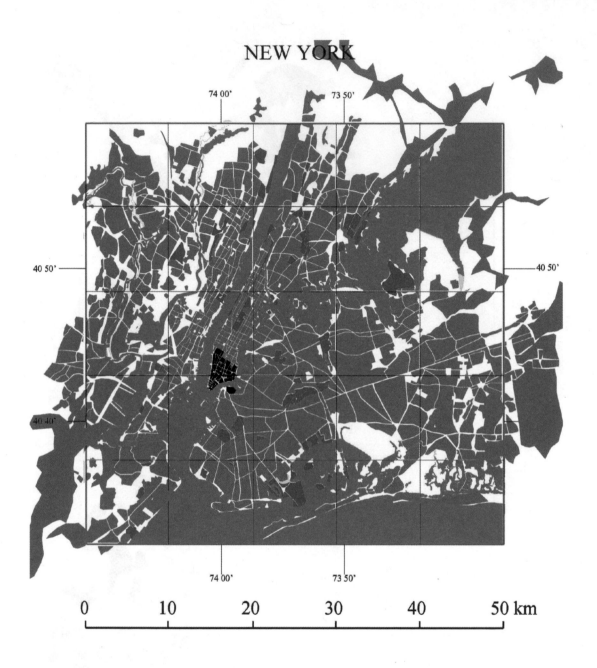

NEW YORK

27. New York City, USA

Settled by the Dutch in 1606 (1626) as New Amsterdam. Captured by Britain in 1664. The city is located along the Hudson River and tidal estuaries, most notably the East River and the Harlem River. Population in the five boroughs: 7,322,564 (Ox 1999); 8,008,278 (UN 2000); Consolidated Metropolitan Statistical Area (includes the adjacent urbanized areas of New Jersey, Connecticut, and Long Island) 21,199,865 (UN 2000). According to UN estimates the Greater New York Area will have 17.4 million inhabitants by 2015 and rank thirteenth among the world's biggest cities. (Note: Other UN projections exist within different boundaries for the 2015 projection.)
Source: Oxford World Atlas 2003; European Space Agency 2001; Google Earth, 2005.

NEW YORK

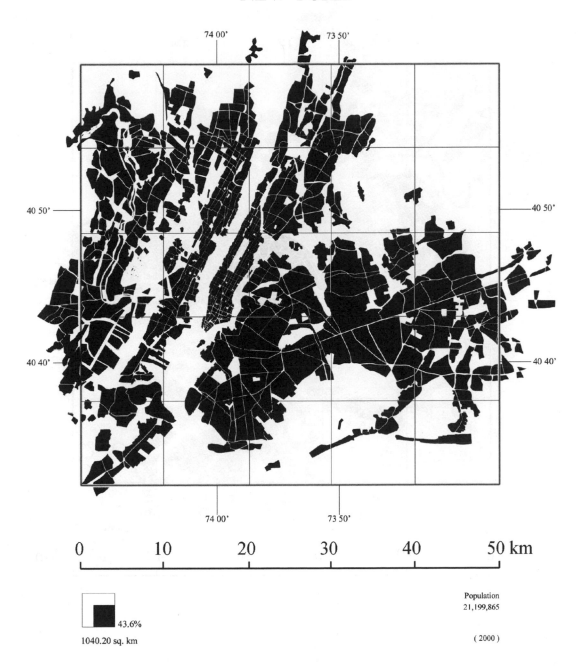

74 00'   73 50'

40 50'   40 50'

40 40'   40 40'

74 00'   73 50'

0   10   20   30   40   50 km

43.6%

1040.20 sq. km

Population
21,199,865

(2000)

PARIS

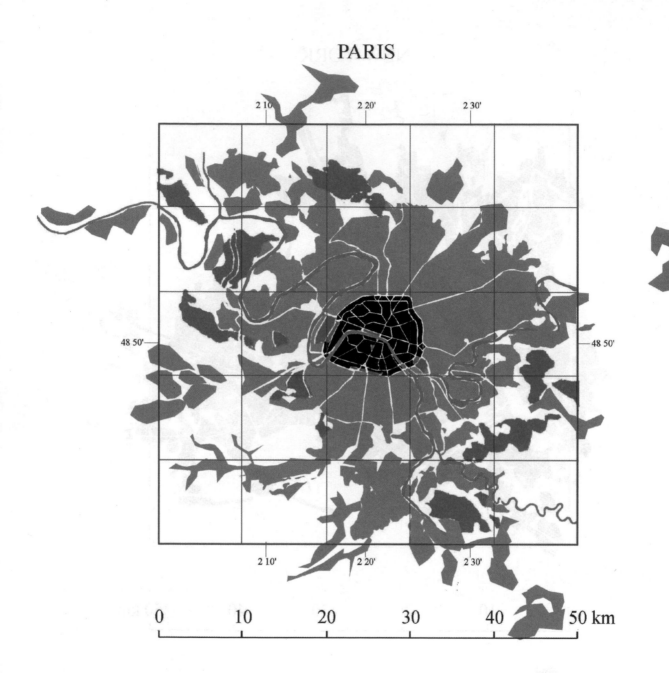

28. Paris, France

Capital of France since 987; known as Lutetia in Roman times. The city is located in the Ile de France, the Seine River valley between the Marne and Oise River tributaries. Population 2,175,000 in the twentieth Arrondissement (Ox 1999); in the greater metropolitan area 9,319,367 (UN, 1999); 11,419,400 (WG 2004) include 162 communes in four departments adjacent to Paris.
Source: European Space Agency 2001; Google Earth 2005.

PARIS

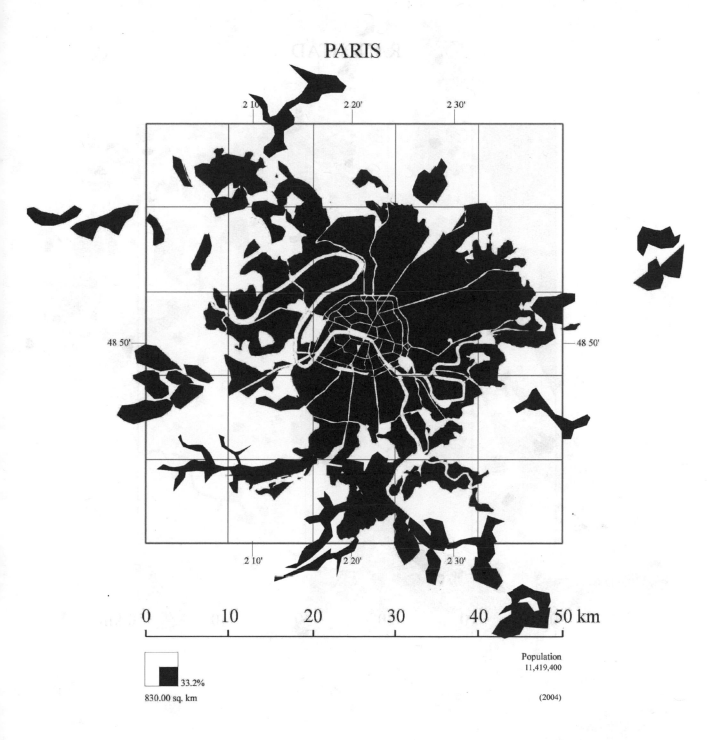

2 10'   2 20'   2 30'

48 50'   48 50'

2 10'   2 20'   2 30'

0   10   20   30   40   50 km

33.2%

830.00 sq. km

Population
11,419,400

(2004)

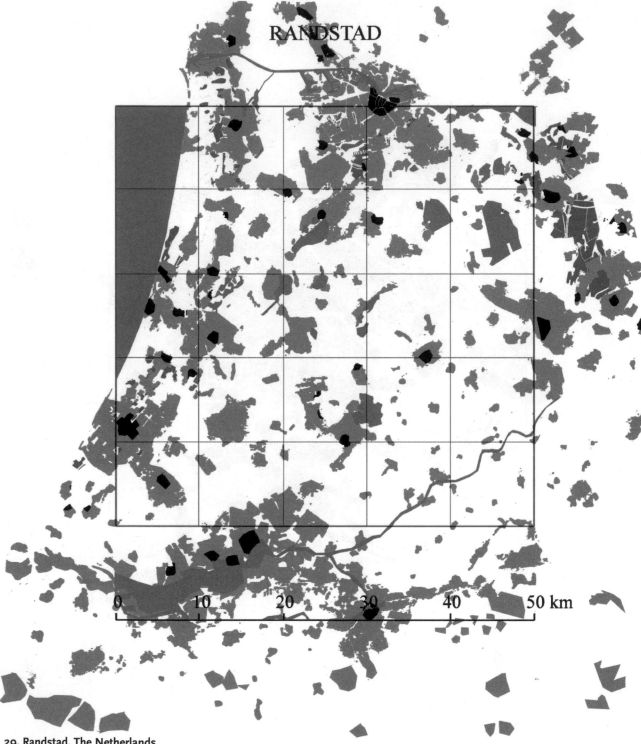

RANDSTAD

29. Randstad, The Netherlands

Located in the delta of the Rhine, Mense, and Scheldt rivers on largely reclaimed land containing twelve cities and fourteen smaller towns. Population 7,200,000 (UN 1999), a conurbation that includes Amsterdam (735,080 inhabitants in 2003), The Hague and Delft (89,400), Rotterdam (987,615), and other smaller towns.

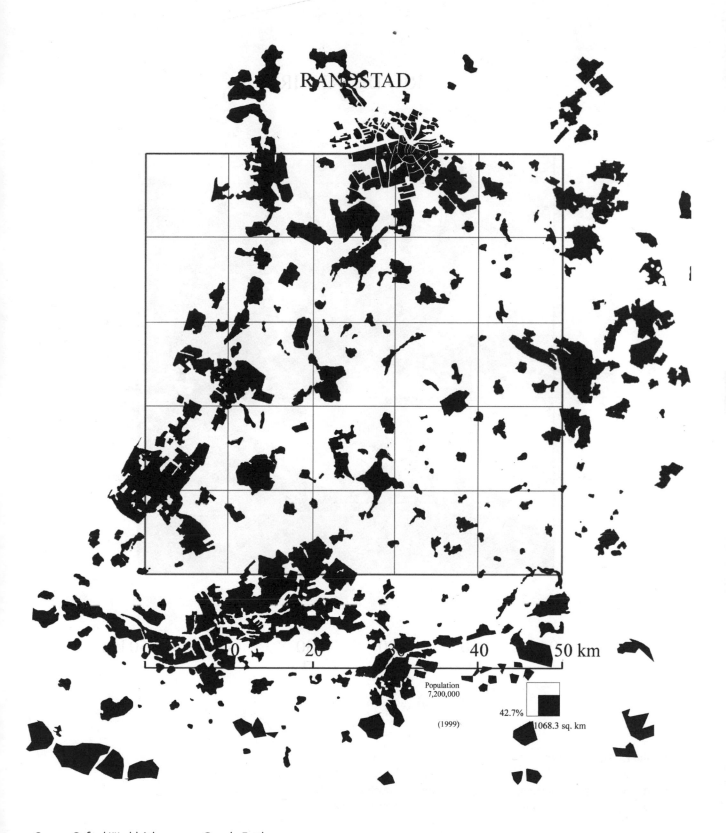

RANDSTAD

50 km

Population
7,200,000

(1999)

42.7%

1068.3 sq. km

Source: Oxford World Atlas, 2003; Google Earth 2005.

RIO DE JANEIRO

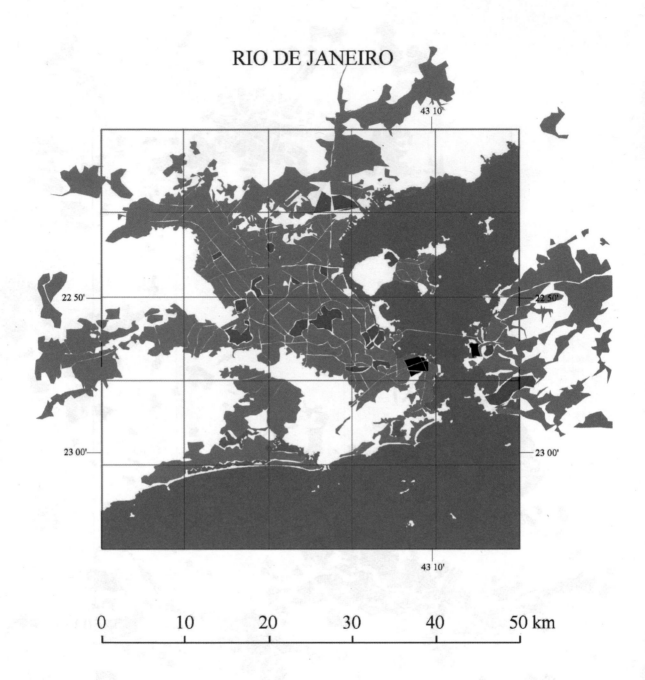

30. Rio De Janeiro, Brazil
Founded in 1565. Capital of Brazil from 1763 to 1960. Located on Guanabara Bay. Population
5,481,000 (Ox 1999); 5,613,897 (UN 1999), greater metropolitan area 11,566,770 (WG 2004).
According to UN estimates Rio de Janeiro will have 11.3 million inhabitants in 2015 and rank
twenty-first among the world's largest cities. Current population already exceeds this estimate.
Source: European Space Agency 2001; Google Earth 2005.

RIO DE JANEIRO

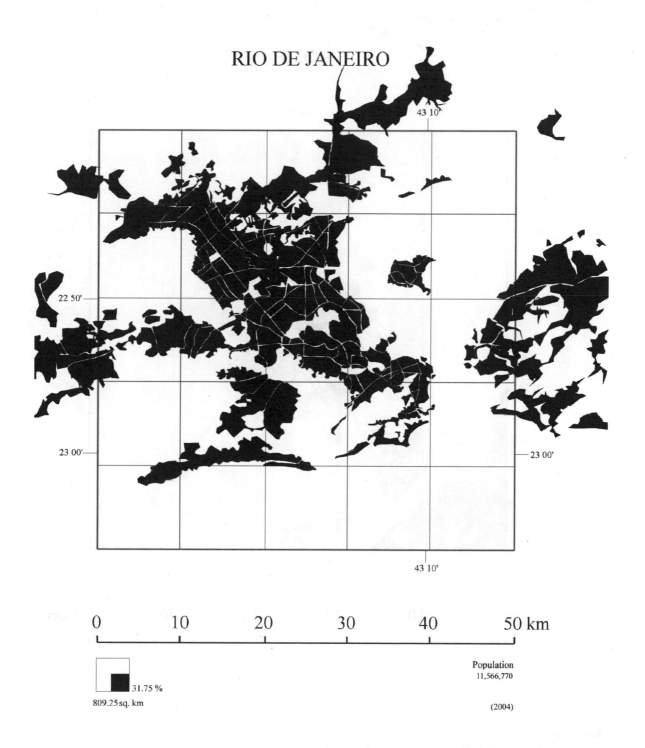

43 10'

22 50'

23 00'   23 00'

43 10'

0   10   20   30   40   50 km

31.75 %

809.25 sq. km

Population
11,566,770

(2004)

ROME

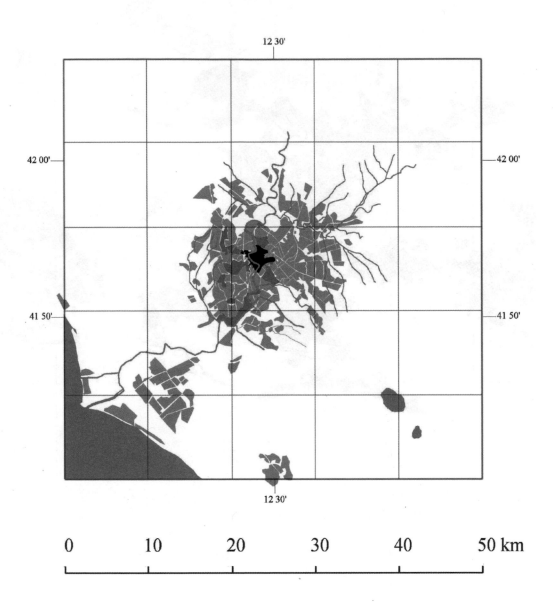

12 30'

42 00'

41 50'

12 30'

| 0 | 10 | 20 | 30 | 40 | 50 km |

31. Rome, Italy
Founded in 753 BC, since 510 BC the capital of the Roman Republic, later
Roman Empire, and Papal State. In 1871 Rome became the capital of a unified
Italy. The city is located at the confluence of the Aniene and Tiber rivers.
Population 2,791,000 (Ox 1999); 2,648,843 (UN 1999).
Source: Landsat 7; European Space Agency 2001; Google Earth 2005.

ROME

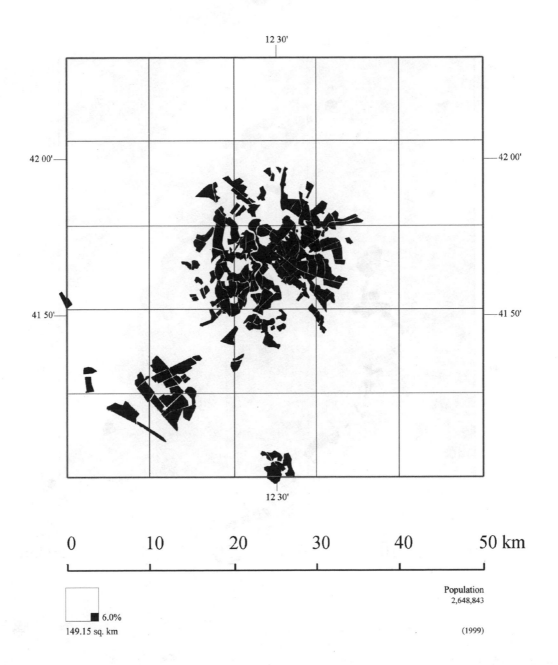

12 30'

42 00'

42 00'

41 50'

41 50'

12 30'

| 0 | 10 | 20 | 30 | 40 | 50 km |

6.0%

149.15 sq. km

Population
2,648,843

(1999)

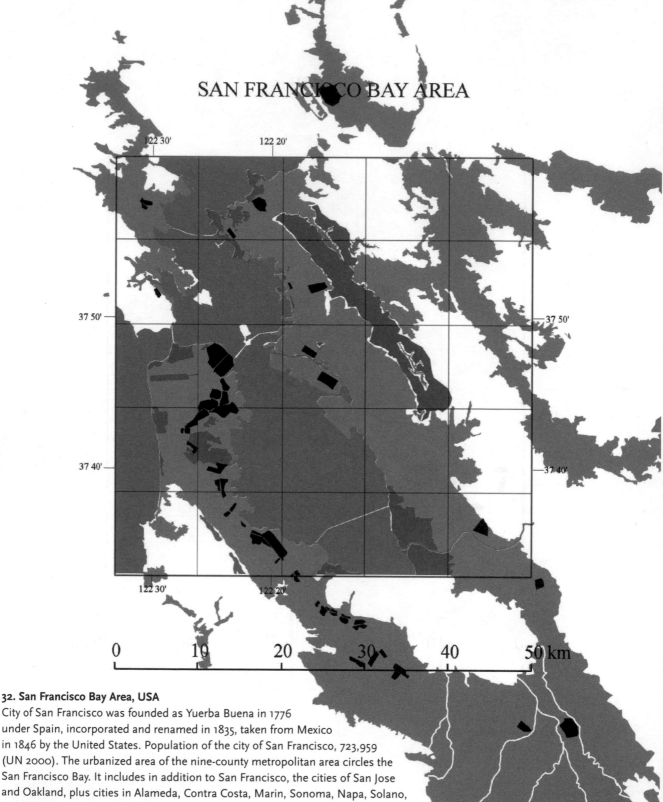

SAN FRANCISCO BAY AREA

32. San Francisco Bay Area, USA

City of San Francisco was founded as Yuerba Buena in 1776
under Spain, incorporated and renamed in 1835, taken from Mexico
in 1846 by the United States. Population of the city of San Francisco, 723,959
(UN 2000). The urbanized area of the nine-county metropolitan area circles the
San Francisco Bay. It includes in addition to San Francisco, the cities of San Jose
and Oakland, plus cities in Alameda, Contra Costa, Marin, Sonoma, Napa, Solano,
San Mateo, and Santa Clara counties, 7,039,362 (UN 2000).
Source: Landsat 7; NPA Group, Edenbridge, UK 2007; European Space Agency 2001;
Google Earth 2005.

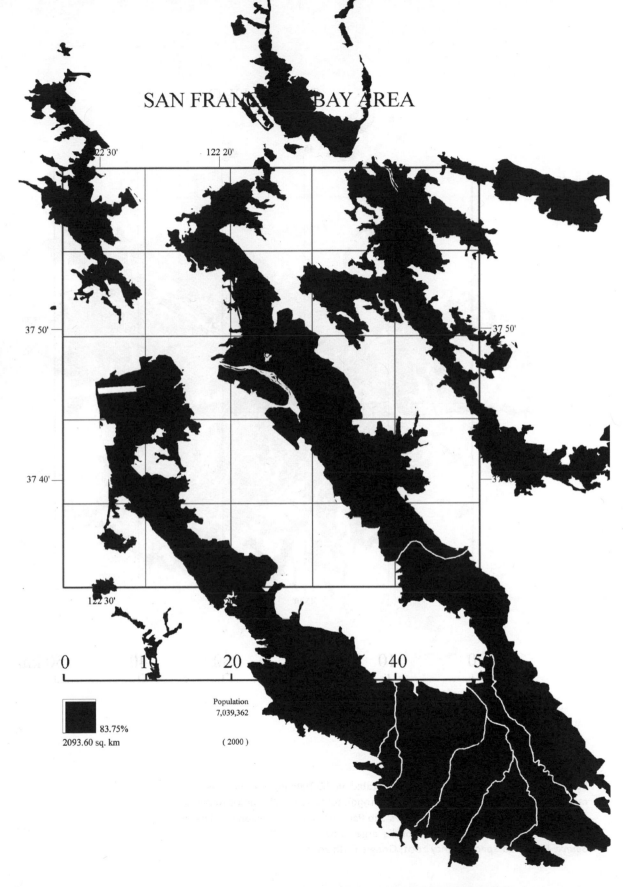

SAN FRANCISCO BAY AREA

122 30' 122 20'

37 50' 37 50'

37 40' 37 40'

122 30'

0   10   20   40   5

Population
7,039,362

83.75%
2093.60 sq. km

(2000)

SÃO PAULO

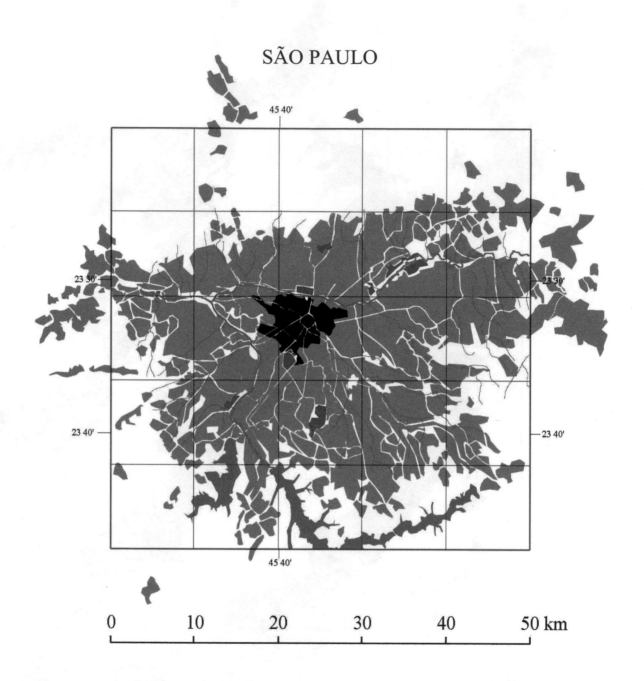

33. São Paolo, Brazil
Founded in 1552 by Jesuit missionaries. Located on the Tietê River in the coastal
range of Brazil. Population 9,700,000 (Ox 1999); 10,009,231 (UN 1999); 19,090,200
(WG 2004). According to UN estimates São Paolo will reach 21 million inhabitants
in 2015 and rank sixth among the world's largest cities.
Source: European Space Agency 2001; Google Earth 2005.

SÃO PAULO

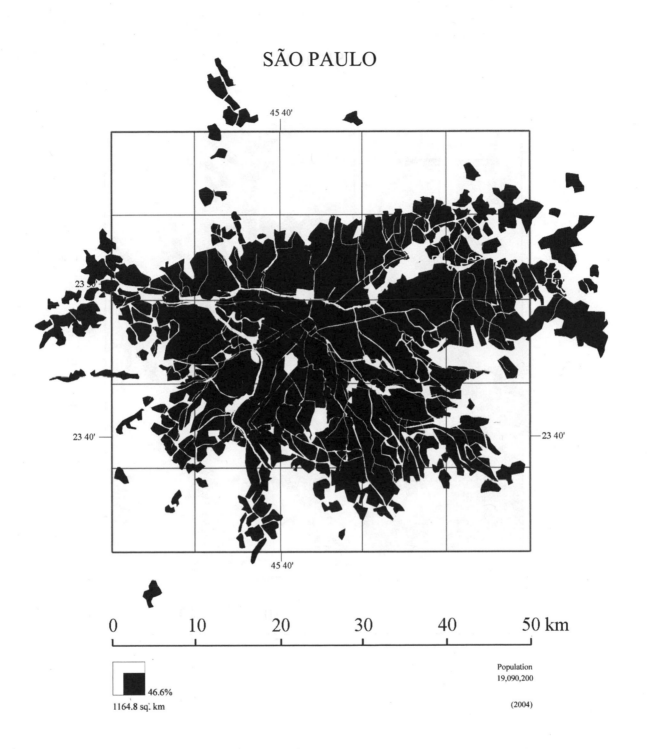

45 40'

23 30'

23 40'   23 40'

45 40'

| 0 | 10 | 20 | 30 | 40 | 50 km |

46.6%

1164.8 sq. km

Population
19,090,200

(2004)

SEOUL

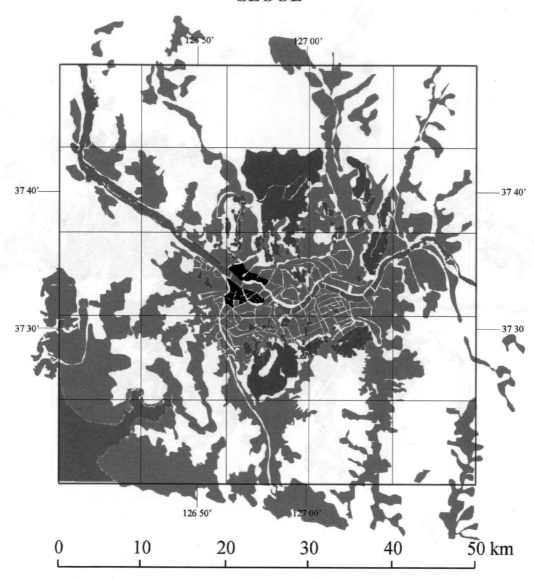

34. Seoul, South Korea

Capital of the Yi dynasty from the fourth century until 1910 when Korea was annexed by the Japanese until 1945. Located on the Han River. Population 10,628,000 (Ox 1999); 10,231,217 (UN 1995); greater metropolitan area 10,165,100 (WG 2004). According to UN estimates Seoul will reach 13.1 million inhabitants in 2015 and will rank eighteenth among the world's largest cities. *Source:* European Space Agency 2001; Google Earth 2005.

SEOUL

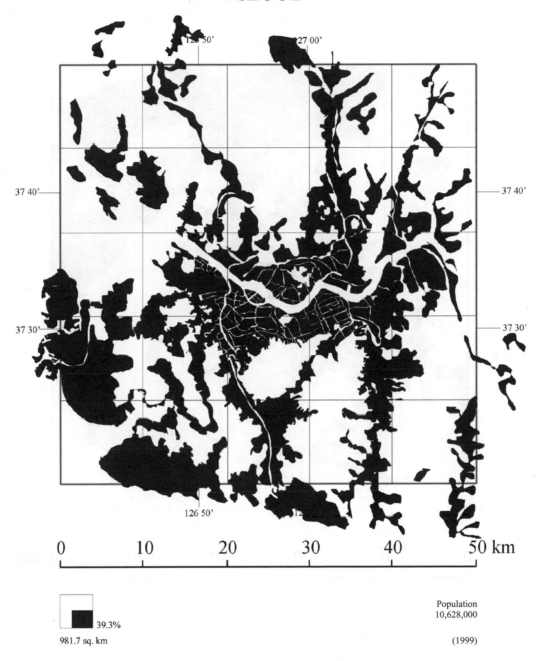

127 00'

126 50'

37 40'

37 30'

126 50'

0   10   20   30   40   50 km

39.3%

981.7 sq. km

Population
10,628,000

(1999)

SHANGHAI

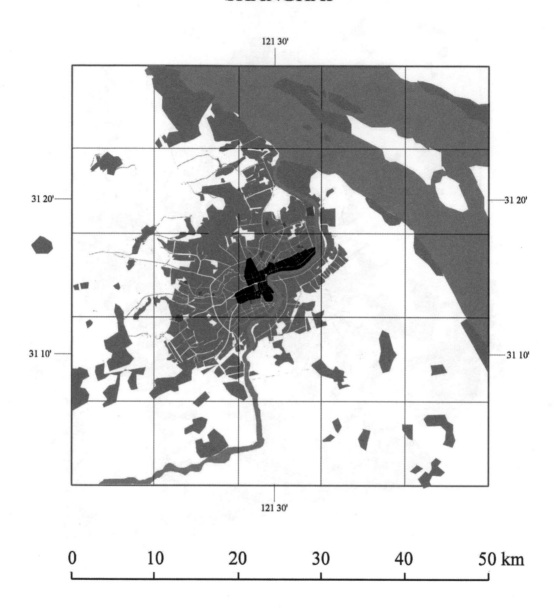

121 30'

31 20'   31 20'

31 10'   31 10'

121 30'

0   10   20   30   40   50 km

35. Shanghai, China

Original settlement since the seventh century AD. British trading post in 1842, French in 1847. International settlement until 1949. Located on both sides of the Huangpu River. Population 7,780,000 (Ox 1999); 8,214,384 (UN 1999); 13,278,700 (WG 2004); greater metropolitan area 16,407,734 (BCP 2004). According to UN estimates Shanghai will reach 23.2 million inhabitants by 2015 and rank fourth among the world's largest cities.
Source: European Space Agency 2001; Google Earth 2005.

SHANGHAI

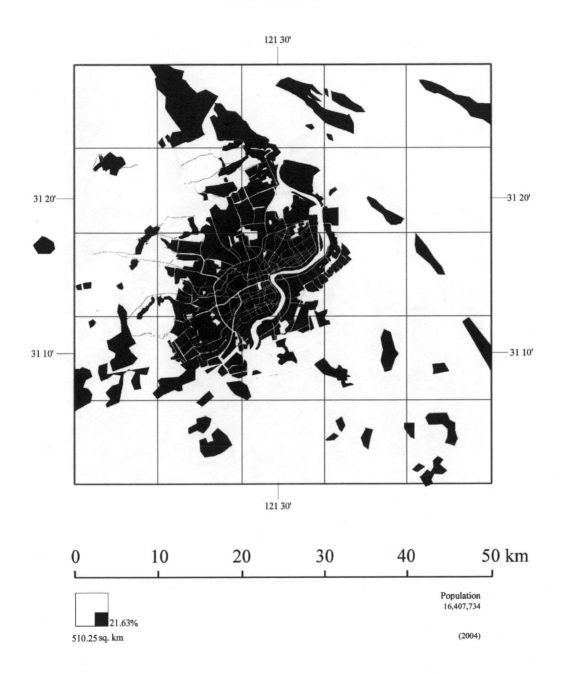

121 30'

31 20'   31 20'

31 10'   31 10'

121 30'

0   10   20   30   40   50 km

21.63%

510.25 sq. km

Population
16,407,734

(2004)

SINGAPORE

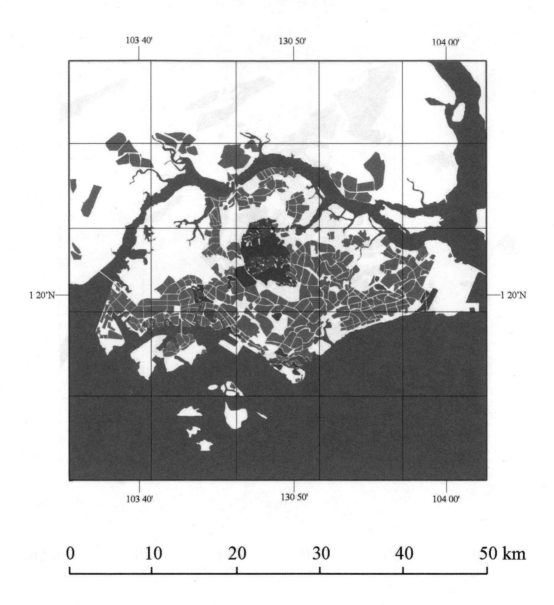

36. Singapore City, Singapore

A city-state, named by a Malay prince in the fourteenth century. Located at the Singapore
River on Jonor Island. British colony from 1819 until 1963, capital of Singapore since
1965. Population 3,045,000 (Ox 1999); 3,894,000 (UN 1999); 4,637,500 (WG 2004).
Source: www.satimagingcorp.com; Google Earth 2005.

SINGAPORE

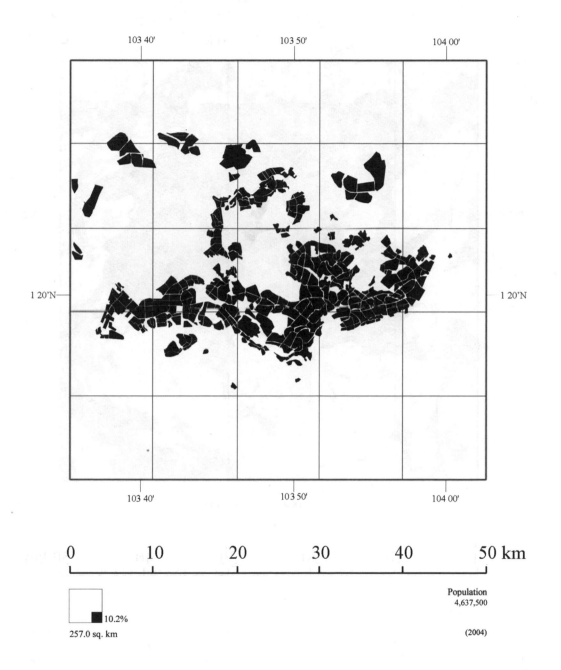

0   10   20   30   40   50 km

10.2%

257.0 sq. km

Population
4,637,500

(2004)

STOCKHOLM

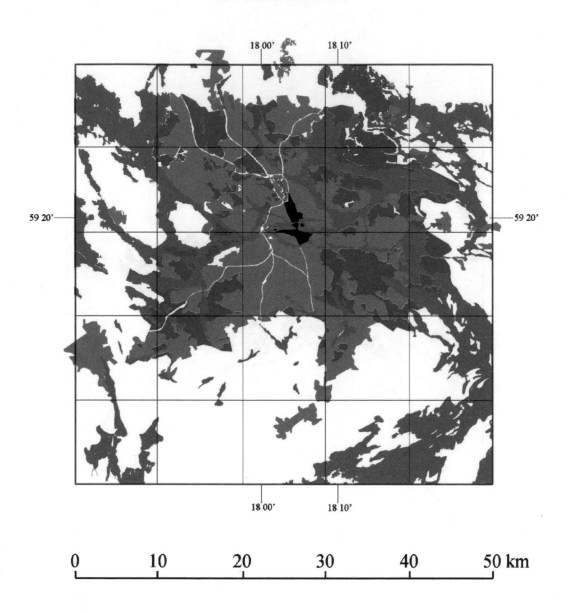

37. Stockholm, Sweden
Founded in AD 1252. Capital of Sweden since 1493. Located on
fifteen islands in an archipelago where the Mälaren Lake joins
the Baltic Sea. Population 1,643,366 (UN 1999).
Source: Geology.com; Google Earth 2005.

STOCKHOLM

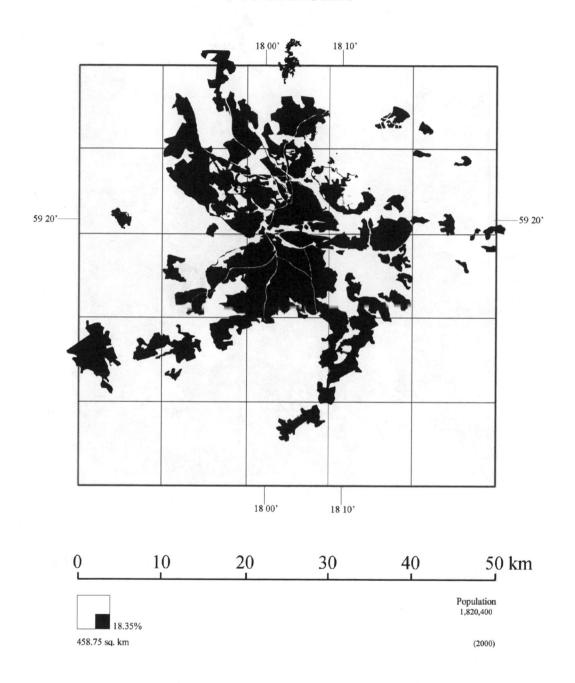

18 00' 18 10'

59 20'   59 20'

18 00' 18 10'

0   10   20   30   40   50 km

18.35%

458.75 sq. km

Population
1,820,400

(2000)

SYDNEY

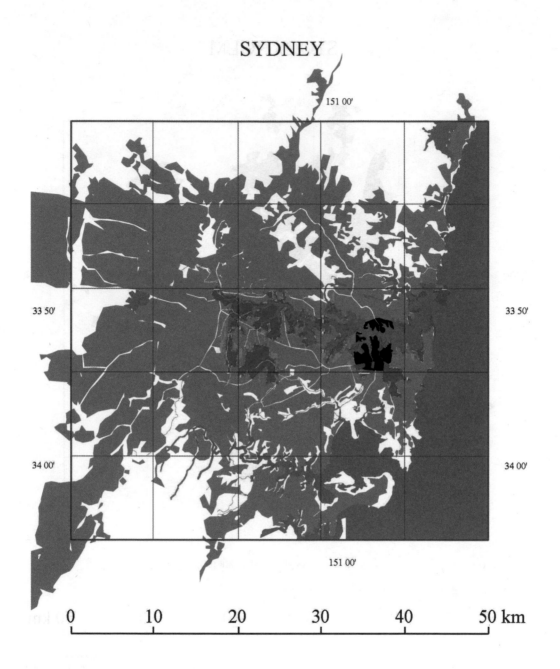

151 00'

33 50'   33 50'

34 00'   34 00'

151 00'

0   10   20   30   40   50 km

38. Sydney, Australia
Founded in 1788 at the mouth of the Hawesbury River and a large bay known as
Sydney Harbour. Population 3,098,000 (Ox 1999); 4,238,420 (UN 2004).
Source: Oxford World Atlas 2003; European Space Agency 2001; Google Earth 2005.

SYDNEY

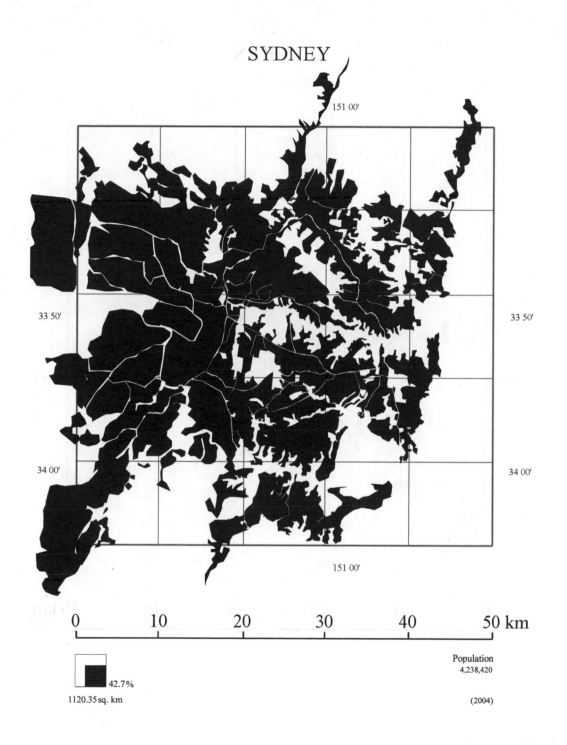

151 00'

33 50'   33 50'

34 00'   34 00'

151 00'

| 0 | 10 | 20 | 30 | 40 | 50 km |

42.7%

1120.35 sq. km

Population
4,238,420

(2004)

TEHERAN

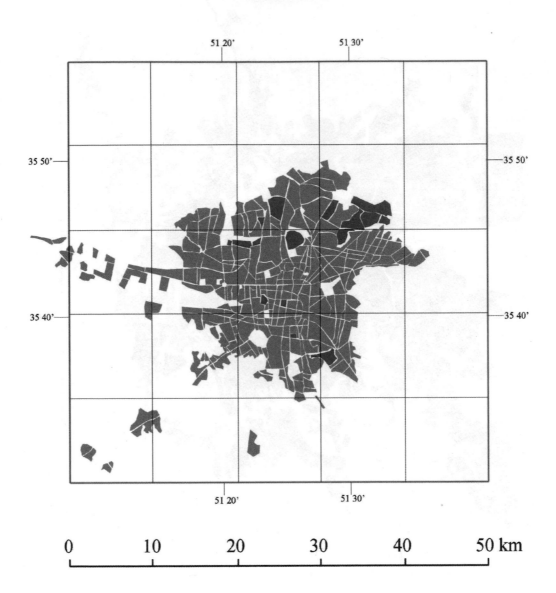

39. Teheran, Iran
Origins date back to the 6000 BC. Population 6,750,000 (Ox 1999); 6,758,845 (UN 1996); 11,474,200 (WG 2004). According to UN estimates Teheran will reach ten million inhabitants in 2015 and rank twenty-seventh among the world's largest cities.
Source: Oxford World Atlas 2003; European Space Agency 2001; Google Earth 2005.

TEHERAN

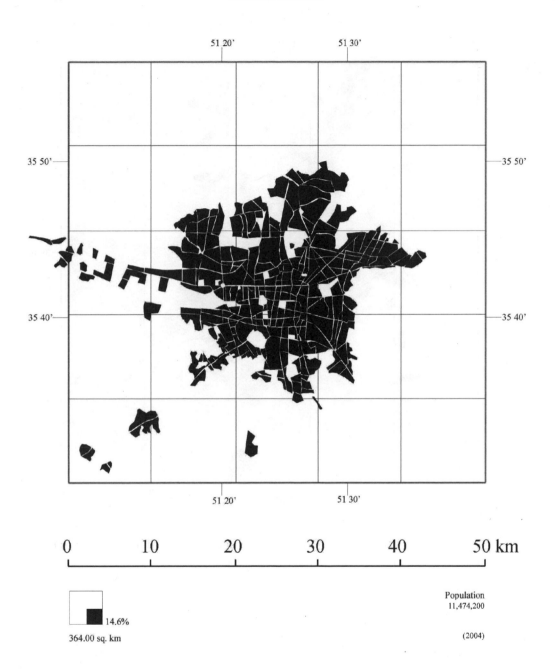

51 20'   51 30'

35 50' — — 35 50'

35 40' — — 35 40'

51 20'   51 30'

0   10   20   30   40   50 km

14.6%

364.00 sq. km

Population
11,474,200

(2004)

TIANJIN

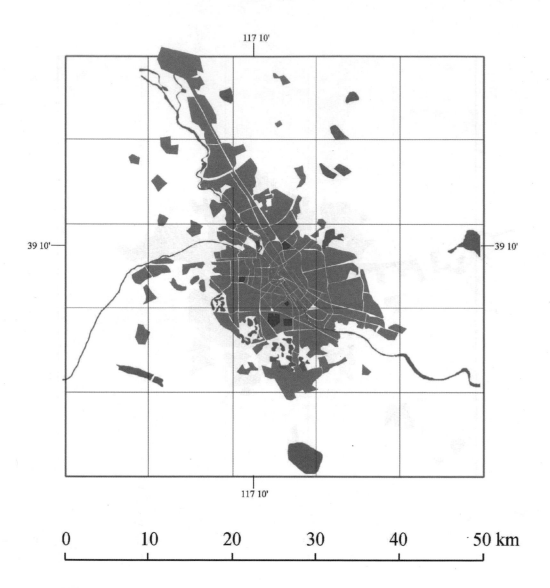

117 10'

39 10'   39 10'

117 10'

```
0        10        20        30        40      · 50 km
```

40. Tianjin, China
At the mouth of the Hai He River into the Gulf of Bohai. The city is also near the confluence with the Ziya, Daqing, and Yongding rivers as well as the northern terminus of the Grand Canal of China. Population 5,700,000 (Ox 1999); 5,855,044 (UN 1999); 6,321,100 (WG 2004). According to UN estimates Tianjin will reach 17.1 million inhabitants in 2015 and rank seventeenth among the world's largest cities.
Source: European Space Agency 2001; Google Earth 2005.

TIANJIN

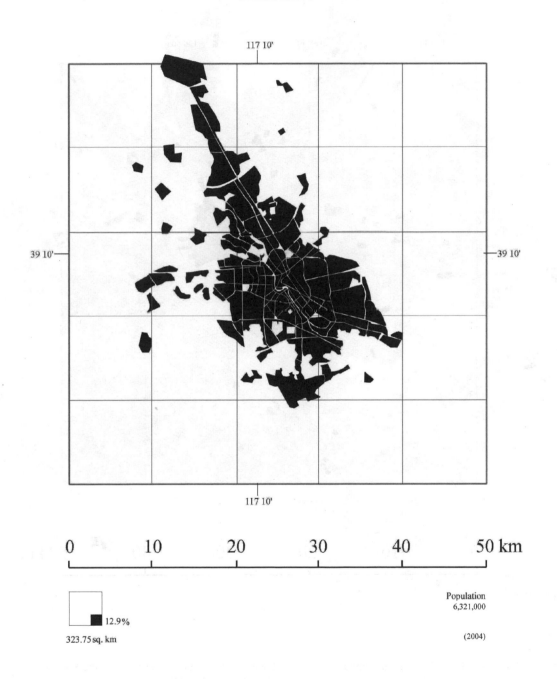

117 10'

39 10'   39 10'

117 10'

0   10   20   30   40   50 km

12.9%

323.75 sq. km

Population
6,321,000

(2004)

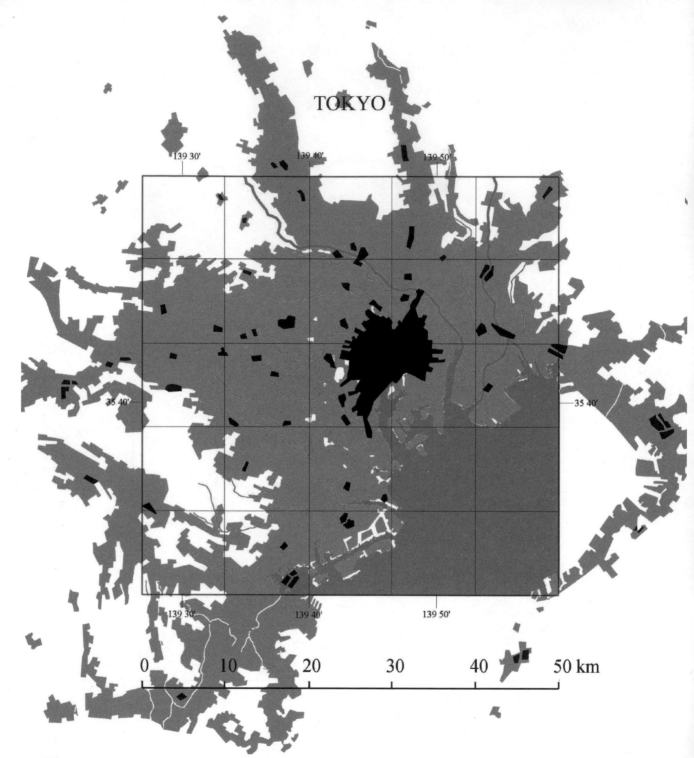

41. Tokyo, Japan

Western capital of Japan since 1868; earlier named Edo or Yedo. Located on the Sumida River and Tama River. Population 8,163,000 (Ox 1999); 12,059,237 (UN 2000) includes the twenty-three ku (wards) of Tokyo prefecture plus fourteen urban counties, eighteen towns, and eight villages. The urban agglomeration with cities in five surrounding prefectures has 31,224,700 (WG 2004) inhabitants. According to UN estimates the Tokyo metropolitan area will continue to rank as the largest conurbation in the world in 2015.

Source: Oxford World Atlas 2003; European Space Agency 2001; Google Earth 2005.

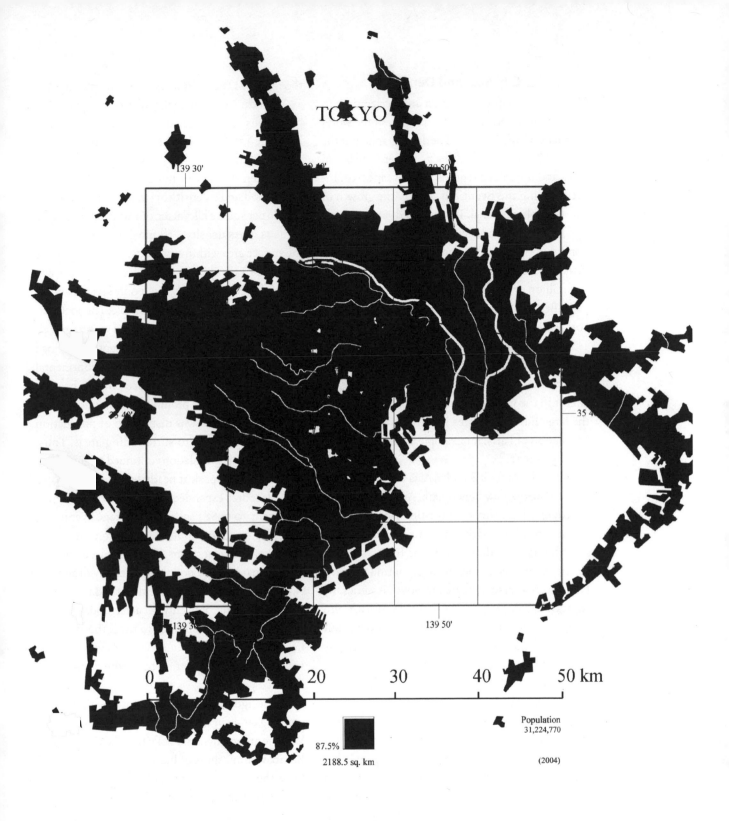

TOKYO

139 30'   139 40'   139 50'

35 40'   35 4

139 3   139 50'

0   20   30   40   50 km

87.5%
2188.5 sq. km

Population
31,224,770

(2004)

City Size and Density

The dynamics of urbanization are accelerating. In the early twentieth century 10 percent of the world population lived in cities. The demographers at the United Nations[5] predict that 75 percent will live in cities and urbanized regions by the year 2050. Indeed, during the twentieth century the growth of cities was phenomenal. Two hundred years ago only London approached the one million mark. By 1850 London's population had grown to two million, and Paris had reached one million. In 1900 cities with one million or more inhabitants included London, Paris, Berlin, Vienna, Moscow, St. Petersburg, New York, Chicago, Philadelphia, Tokyo, and Calcutta. This group of eleven cities grew to 100 cities by 1960. But already by midcentury, European and North American cities were no longer among the largest in the world. Indeed, population growth in the large European cities had stagnated; thus the population of Paris, for example, started to decline as early as 1932.[6]

But in the Americas and in Asia ten million people became the new benchmark. And by the end of the twentieth century twenty cities had grown past the ten million mark. Such urban population growth was most dramatic on the Indian subcontinent and in East Asia, but large, continuously urbanized areas also appeared in South America. By contrast urban growth was slower in Africa. Cairo remained the largest city on that continent, but even Cairo has now begun to expand noticeably beyond its former compact core as a new perimeter road has invited settlements in the desert above the Nile River valley. Meanwhile, Lagos, Nigeria, is currently the fastest-urbanizing city in the world. It is expected to grow to 24.1 million by 2015. But this projection remains somewhat of a puzzle because the latest numbers available from the United Nations put the population of Lagos at 10,886,000 people in 2005. In the past, demographers frequently had to revise their estimates. Yet, even if at times they have vastly overestimated the populations of cities in developing countries,

the reality of their numbers is still staggering.

We included Berlin in the collection of maps, but not because of its large population. In 2000 Berlin had only 3,386,667 inhabitants, significantly less than in 1940, when it had close to five million. But, more interestingly, one hundred years ago the city accommodated a density of twenty-nine thousand people per square kilometer, or 120 people per acre. (This is gross density—all inhabitants divided by the surface area within city limits, minus large lakes and parks.) Until 1900 the surface area of the city was highly constricted to about only seventy square kilometers for its two million people. The social dimensions of such density impressed writers and visual artists of the early 1900s, who aptly described the Berlin milieu. After 1919, like other continental European cities, Berlin "exploded" in size because further crowding had prohibited economic growth.

The only option was dispersion of production and worker housing to surrounding areas. Thus, even though its population continued to grow from two million to a peak at nearly five million in 1939, its surface area expanded thirteen times its original size, from 70 to 883 square kilometers. Eventually, Berlin came to incorporate seven large cities and sixty-eight smaller towns. That magnitude of spatial expansion made population density drop from twenty-nine thousand to five thousand people per square kilometer, or twenty per acre.[7] Today, Berlin's density has further dropped to three thousand inhabitants per square kilometer or only twelve persons per acre, roughly one-tenth the density of a hundred years ago.

These figures pose an important question for the growing cities in the rest of the developing world. Will the growth dynamics of cities like Calcutta and Bombay mimic those of European cities like Berlin? Or is the magnitude of population growth in Asia so different that additional cities will need to absorb it? The latter seems to be true in the case of Calcutta. The chief planners at a meeting in Calcutta were clearly relieved to learn that earlier demographic projections for the city had been far too high.[8] Instead, recent findings by UN demographers showed that the nineteen cities on both sides of the Hugli River that together with Calcutta hold an estimated 17.6 million people were not growing as fast as smaller cities throughout West Bengal. Other cities offer opportunities to those who decide to leave rural areas of India and have absorbed more population than Calcutta. But even if this trend holds true, Calcutta will still need more space. The gradual and mostly unauthorized additions to living and work space that are in evidence everywhere—something that all city executives at the Calcutta meeting viewed as a major problem—are creating significant momentum for the consumption of yet more space.

Space in the rapidly urbanizing cities has

Figure 1.9 *Cliff Dwellers,1913*, by George Bellows, 1882–1925, courtesy Los Angeles County Museum of Art, Los Angeles County Fund, #16.4. Photograph © 2007 Museum Associates/LACMA. Bellows's urban New York reminds us that conditions of high population density now common in cities like Calcutta or Lagos were common in cities like New York one hundred years ago.

become a significant resource. It taxes our common sense to imagine how Calcutta with its almost eighteen million people fits into the surface area of the city of San Francisco plus the county to the south, San Mateo, where altogether one million people live. Imagine that a space occupied by one person on a San Francisco sidewalk, in a park, inside a lobby, or in an apartment building would need to be shared with eighteen additional others. People in many Asian cities have lived at such densities, and many additional millions will live under such conditions in the future.

City size is relative and can only be fully grasped when compared to conditions one knows well. The people of the San Francisco Bay Area look down at the sprawl and resulting car culture of Los Angeles. The Los Angeles metropolitan area with its sixteen million people covers a 94 percent surface area of a fifty by fifty kilometer square. For Bay Area residents it is important to remember that LA's surface area is only 11 percent larger than the San Francisco Bay Area. But Los Angeles accommodates more than twice as many people. The fact that the Los Angeles region is far more densely populated compared to other West Coast cities is not very well known.

Tokyo covers 87 percent of a fifty by fifty kilometer square. That makes Tokyo with its thirty-one million people only twice as dense as Los Angeles. Atlanta is the only metropolitan area in this collection that exceeds 100 percent of the surface area available in a fifty by fifty kilometer square. It houses only four million people. That makes Los Angeles four times as dense as Atlanta, and Tokyo eight times as dense.

City Scale

In comparing the scale of cities we reflect on the dimensions of the elements in the urban fabric and how these elements relate to human experience. Everyone with a recently built computer can connect to a well-known global map server and slowly fly across cities. In Beijing a ten-kilometer long virtual flight above Chang An Street, starting to the

east of the center, at Yuyuantan Park—not long ago at the city's edge, now well within it—will take us clear across the center, to Tian'anmen Square and on to the Guomao area near Beijing's new rail station. It seems as if a gigantic rake has plowed through the fabric eradicating narrow lanes and small-scale housing, leaving equally spaced high slabs of buildings in its path that are placed according to simple sun access rules. No streets in the traditional sense are left inside these large super-blocks, until we reach Beijing's second ring. From that point on, the pattern changes; some of the old fabric is still visible. In Beijing, the authorities created large units of land to accommodate the influx of a new urban population and to replace residents from areas where a finely scaled building pattern was common.

As Beijing transforms its scale, the city consciously loses its link to its past. It is easy to understand how the small lanes, or *hutongs*, lined with courtyard houses are despised because of overcrowding, poverty, and, for some, a political history that evokes disdain.[9]

Beijing, founded in 1057 BC, predates Rome by three hundred years. A ten kilometer flight above Rome from the Castello Sant'Angelo near the Vatican along the Corso Vittorio Emmanuelle, the Piazza de Venezia, past the Imperial Forum, and the Coliseum would take us through the Aurelian Wall out on Via Appia Nuova to Cine Città, at Rome's southeastern edge. Rome has its share of monumental buildings, even a good number of monumental streets. We would pass many of them on the ten kilometer flight. But the larger-scaled elements of the urban fabric are embedded in a small-scaled texture of a very fine grain. Importantly, the buildings fronting streets form continuous facades. It is not the age of buildings in Rome that determines the scale. The buildings surrounding the historic monuments of Rome are not old; most date from the nineteenth and twentieth centuries. However, the property configurations and parcel dimensions are much older. The ownership pattern of relatively small parcels has been resilient and continues to define the scale of Rome's urban fabric to the present day. In Beijing the transformation in scale is possible because all land is continuously owned by the state; private landownership is only now emerging as a concept.

This collection of maps is not the first comparative study on the subject of city scale. Many authors have used this method. Sten Eiler Rassmussen might have been the first to use it when he compared London and Paris to demonstrate the difference between dispersed and compact city scale, and when he showed the size of Paris and London over time at the same graphic scale.[10] Influential for compiling the present collection was Richard Saul Wurman's small book, which he produced in 1963 with his students at North Carolina State University.[11] He asked his students to prepare fifty city maps at a scale of 600 feet to the inch (1:7200). They were carved into white plasticene and mounted on sixteen by sixteen inch Masonite panels. The photographs of these panels are stunningly beautiful. His book emphasizes planned cities in cultures as diverse as Tikal and Pompeii. Incidentally, both cities covered very much the same surface area, but the scale of Tikal's physical fabric is much larger than Pompeii's. Miletus, the Greek colonial town laid out by Hippodamus ca. 1000 BC at the mouth of the Meander River in Asia Minor was bigger than colonial Savannah laid out seventeen miles up the Savannah River by James Oglethorpe in 1733. But both cities are noted for their similarly scaled street grid. There is also Paris next to Rome, and Rome appears to be so much smaller in scale. Manhattan at Forty-second Street is just as wide as Philadelphia along Market Street between the Delaware and Schuykill rivers, and just as wide as the diameter of Venice, between the train station and the exposition area for the Biennale near the Arsenal. Once discovered, these scale comparisons are not easily forgotten because they reveal unexpected information. At first disbelief sets in; but after the graphic scale is checked and rechecked, the reader is forced to think about the true scale of cities relative to the information stored in one's mind.

An earlier book compared the relative nature of distance and time in a collection of maps.[12] The maps were the product of a collaboration between Allan Jacobs and the author. Whenever one of us worked on a project over the years, we produced a figure ground map of the area at 200 feet to the inch drawn into a frame of eight by eight inches. A large collection emerged by the mid-1990s. A red line drawn on each map delineated a walk of four minutes or one thousand feet in length. It is quite clear from comparing these maps that one walk appears not as long—or as short—as the other. A person stepping out of the National Archives on 700 Pennsylvania Avenue and walking across Ninth and Tenth avenues will reach the entrance of the Old Post Office in four short minutes and encounter six buildings. On a walk of identical length a person walking at the same pace along Copenhagen's pedestrian street will encounter in four seemingly much longer minutes forty-two buildings.

Distance and time are perceived quantities, and their duration differs according to the amount of information available to the human senses. More information, more to be experienced, equals slower passage of time. The map comparisons led to experiments with groups of people who were taken on walks of identical length. It became clear that those who walked judged the elapsed time according to the spatial complexity of their experience.[13] A summary of these experiments is reported in the third chapter: smaller spatial dimensions, more variation, more changes in direction, and shorter block dimensions influence people to estimate longer duration, close to 50 percent longer than the actual time it took to walk the distance. The experiment confirms what William James wrote in 1892: "A time filled with varied and interesting experiences seems short in passing, but long as we look back. On the other hand a tract of time empty of experiences seems long in passing, but in retrospect short."[14]

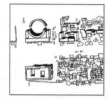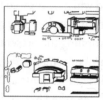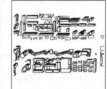

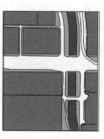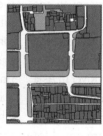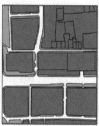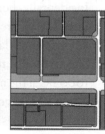

Figure 1.10
Beijing transect, ten kilometers along Chang An Street from Yuyuantan Park across Tian'anmen Square to the Guamao area to Beijing's new train station. Tree coverage and building shapes were traced from Google Earth, 2007.

Ten Kilometers on Beijing's Chang An Street

0   400   800   1200   1400 feet

0   100   200   300   400   500 meters

km 0
Military Museum

km 1.3
Yongdin River

km 2.5
Nao Shiko

km 3.4
Commercial Street

km 3.9
Nan Linshi

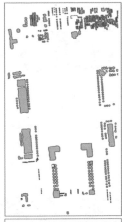

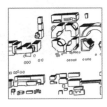

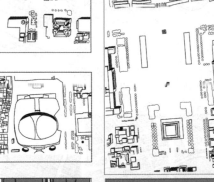
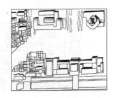

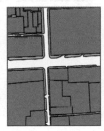
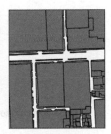

Km 4.7
Sidan Street
km 6.5
Opera House

km 6.75
Tiananmen Square

km 7.5
Nan Heyan Street

km 7.9
Wangfuijing Street

km 9.2 Beijing
International Hotel
km 10 Chaoyommen
South Street

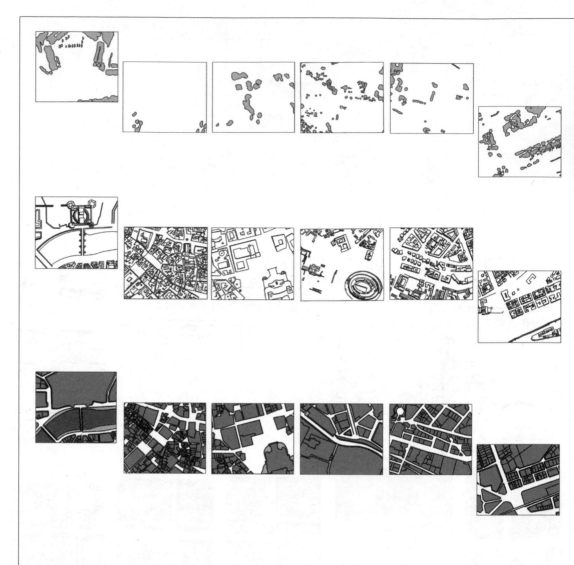

Figure 1.11
Rome transect, from Castello de San Angelo, past the Imperial Forum and the Coliseum, leaving historic Rome at Porta San Giovanni and traveling on Via Appia Nuova to Cine Città.
Source: Atlante di Roma, 1995, Marsilio, Google Earth, 2007.

Rome, from Castello de San Angelo

| 0 | 400 | 800 | 1200 | 1400 | feet |
| 0 | 100 | 200 | 300 | 400 | 500 | meters |

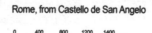

| km 0 | km 1 | km 1.8 | km 2.8 | km 3.6 | km 4.2 |
| Ponte San Angelo | Campo die Fiori | Piazza Venezia | Piazza dei Colosseo | Piazza San Giovanni | Porta San Giovanni; Piazza de Appio |

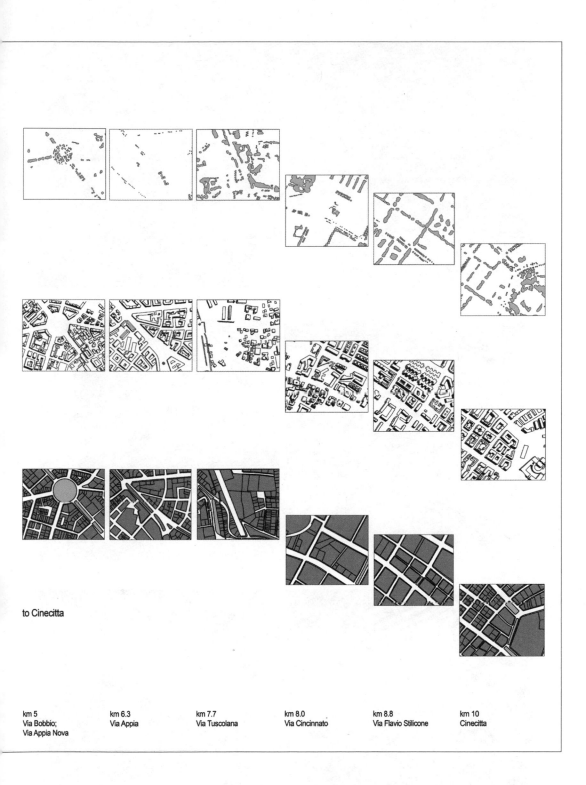

to Cinecitta

km 5
Via Bobbio;
Via Appia Nova

km 6.3
Via Appia

km 7.7
Via Tuscolana

km 8.0
Via Cincinnato

km 8.8
Via Flavio Stilicone

km 10
Cinecitta

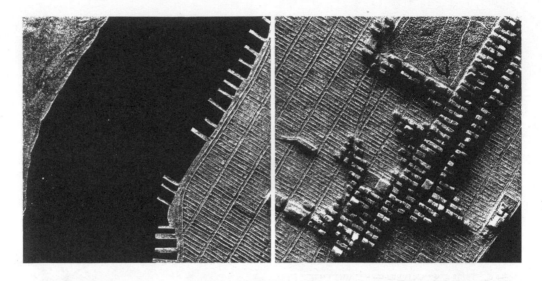

Figure 1.12 New York City (top), Philadelphia (middle), and Venice (bottom) at the same scale. Fifty city maps were prepared at a scale of 600 feet to the inch (1:7200), then carved into white plasticene and mounted on sixteen by sixteen inch Masonite panels. These allow us to see that Manhattan at Forty-second Street is just as wide as Philadelphia along Market Street between the Delaware and Schuykill rivers, and just as wide as the diameter of Venice between the train station and the exposition area for the Biennale near the Arsenal. (Courtesy Richard Saul Wurman)

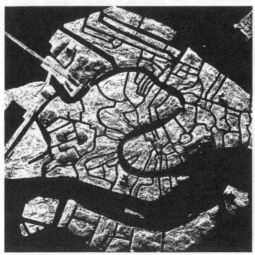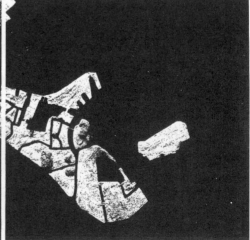

Cities have their own sense of time: time passes more slowly in Rome and faster in Milan, more slowly in Manhattan and faster in Los Angeles, because a mile is simply not the same in any of these cities.

Comparing the scale of cities and relating it to human psychology reflects on how residents spend their time in the daily life of a city; the comparisons also explain the far-reaching consequences of city scale on sustainability. The dimensions of streets and blocks, the distances between concentrations within a city, and the distribution of activities determine travel time and modes of travel, whether a person can walk, take transit, or is forced to drive. Thus city scale influences energy consumption, the use of other nonrenewable resources, as well as human health.

This discussion about the scale of cities is not likely to leave a lasting impression on staff members working for the large state-run planning and design firms in China, or in a different context for the International Monetary Fund or the World Bank, but it should. As funding is made available to support urbanization in the developing world, modern planning and engineering standards are applied to road construction and the layout of new subdivisions. The scale of the new infrastructure and the dimensions of land set aside to settle the growing urban population is in marked contrast to the existing fabric. This is intended, because what is being financed should result in progress. But the investors should know that building amply spaced slabs and towers that are set in green spaces is not a product of the latest thinking. Over time this building typology has been rejected in Berlin as well as in U.S. cities, Paris suburbs, and many other places. Granted, at first, families eagerly moved away from narrow lanes and crowded apartments into modern, well-lit accommodations. But soon the empty spaces between buildings were no longer seen as an amenity—residents ultimately felt segregated and ghettoized. The green spaces turned out to be cold, windswept, and deserted, and there was no community with eyes on the street. There are no streets, in the conventional

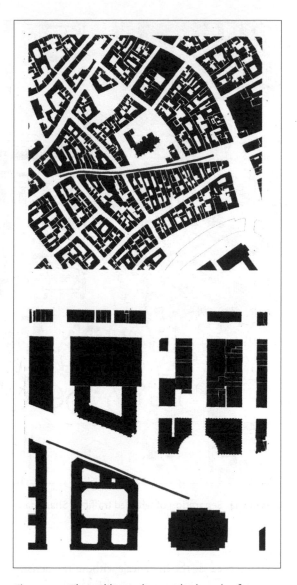

Figure 1.13 The red line indicates the length of two four-minute walks, one in Copenhagen (top) and one in Washington, DC (bottom). Shown here on maps reproduced at the same scale. (Maps courtesy Allan Jacobs, in Bosselmann, 1998, *Representation of Places*, UC Press)

sense. What is being financed is resentment that will manifest in a few decades. Paradoxically, once those residents who now crowd the narrow *hutongs* have left, the wealthier will be attracted to repair what is left of the traditional row housing or courtyard

Figure 1.14 Separation of wheeled traffic in Shanghai.

housing because the finer scale without the density is highly conducive to inner-city life.[15]

Like Beijing, Shanghai is rapidly transforming; a new center has emerged across the Hung Po River. The city is renewing its housing stock and the roads that serve the new neighborhoods. The dynamics are fiercely modern. What is troublesome is the use of Western road standards. Traffic lanes on major streets do not have to be four or four and one-half meters wide. Such design is intended to speed up traffic, but it makes bicycling a dangerous mode of transportation. Exactly for that reason, in Shanghai, bicycles are now banned from major new streets and directed to a separate the web of roadways. The

widening of traffic lanes on major streets has already led to much congestion and will grow worse as automobile use increases. If the lane width, for example, on all newly planned streets were reduced by only 0.60 meters per lane, for every kilometer of six-lane road a land area of thirty-six hundred square meters could be saved. That equates to the ground-level space needed for one eight-story apartment building with six hundred units of housing.

City Form

No two city maps in this collection have the same form. There might be a growing similarity between cities on the ground, but when seen from space all cities have a distinct shape. What gives each city such fundamental authenticity may often be found in the natural history of its locations. In simple terms, the topography of the earth's surface and the location and flow of water have shaped the construction of roads, buildings, and city blocks. Thus Melbourne, located on relatively undifferentiated terrain with its three million inhabitants, occupies the same amount of space as Sydney with four million inhabitants. Again, there may be historic reasons for these differences in density between the two cities. But the map comparisons suggest that the far more differentiated landforms of eastern Sydney are responsible for its unique settlement pattern, its higher overall density, and the greater identity of its districts.

City Form Typologies

Over a period of one hundred years the form of cities in this collection has changed in a manner that cannot simply be labeled as a continuation of their historic shape and form. Cities have grown out of the old *core city* typology and mutated toward *radial*, *concentric*, or *dispersed* city models.[16] In 1949 Patrick Geddes coined the term "conurbation" to describe a region of cities that forms one large urban agglomeration.[17] The twenty-six towns and cities of the Randstad provide the clearest image of a conurbation that is composed of multiple, but separate centers. Other conurbations, like the one hundred cities that make up the San Francisco Bay Area, or the fifty-eight municipalities that define Mexico City, have grown together into a single continuous urbanized area. Thus most conurbations in this collection of maps are continuous, and only traces of the old typologies can still be seen. There are exceptions; Beijing still follows the concentric ring pattern. The freeway grid still defines the form of Los Angeles. Chicago with its radial pattern remains highly concentrated in the loop at its core. The map comparisons suggest a new typology, one that makes reference to natural systems.

A Typology of Urban Form Based upon Natural Systems

All cities in this collection are water cities; they were shaped by water systems. Most cities in this collection had their origins in a river landscape like Paris, London, or Beijing. In a related category are those cities situated on river branches that form a large delta like Calcutta or the Randstad in Holland. Equally numerous are cities that originated as harbors, located at the mouth of a river and along the shores of an open sea like Jakarta or Chicago. Cities around a large bay like Tokyo or Sydney belong in a fourth category. There are only two cities in the collection, Auckland and Atlanta, that are located along a ridgeline where two water systems join; in the case of Atlanta, one that drains toward the Atlantic Ocean and one that drains toward the Gulf of Mexico. Finally, there is a small group of cities that stretch out along the shores of a narrow or strait like Victoria Harbour at Hong Kong, the Bosporus at Istanbul, or the Øresund between Copenhagen and Malmø. All cities in the collection are water cities, and in all categories the water system has been severely challenged by the growing settlement patterns. Among the river cities (or sometimes an inland body of water Lake Texcoco in Mexico City) only remnants of the river system or inland water body have remained (e.g., Los Angeles and Milan). But in river cities, including Los Angeles, Paris, London, and Milan, there is a renewed interest in reclaiming riverfront land, made available by industrial closures, to re-create river landscapes. It will never be possible to repair the original water systems to their natural conditions, but on such recently vacated land the new uses can be laid out in a manner that repairs the natural forces of the river, sometimes to make room for periodic flooding, such as along the Waal River just outside the Randstad, sometimes through increased access and vegetation to shade the riverbanks. The same type of repair takes place in harbor cities and bay cities. Tokyo has large tracts

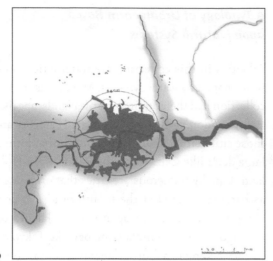

1840

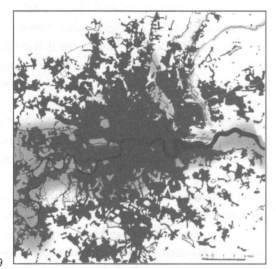

1929

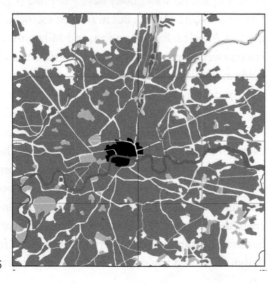

2005

of former harbor land under regeneration around Tokyo Bay.[18]

The observation that all urban agglomerations in this collection were shaped by water systems instills optimism because a better understanding of natural systems that existed and that were altered can inform the design of new cultural landscapes, landscapes that can be designated as *commons* for a large metropolitan area. Such commons would improve the urban ecology of city regions and their social conditions. At the same time the correlation between water system and urban form can also be deadly serious. For example, six urban concentrations in this collection—and they are among the world's most populated cities—are situated barely above sea level. They are located in the floodplains or deltas of large rivers and depend, like New Orleans, on levees for protection from flooding. The design and management of such metropolitan commons therefore require knowledge of systems that recognize the forces of nature and natural processes as well as the potential for social gain.

It was not foresight but rather a remnant of the feudal system that preserved the Thames River landscape deep into the heart of London. Today we understand the open spaces from Kensington Garden to Green Park and Pall Mall, all the way to St. Martin in the Fields on Trafalgar Square as a sequence of parks.

But in the development of London's spatial morphology, these park areas were first part of the river landscape; they became hunting grounds for the aristocracy prior to being opened to the public. Today such green spaces provide a significant

Figure 1.15 Thames River landscape in London. The two maps on the left, 1840 and 1929, were redrawn from maps by Steen Eiler Rasmussen for his 1939 book *London, the Unique City* (Cambridge, MA: MIT Press,1967). The 2005 map shows today's traces of the Thames River landscape. Note the site of the 2012 Olympics in the Lower Lee Valley in the former industrial East London.

Figure 1.16 Milan's web of green streets connecting the city to the river landscape of the Po River tributaries, the most notable being the Ticino on the west and the Lambro to the east, redrawn from *La Citt di Citt* (A City of Cities), Milan: Provincia di Milano, 2006.

resource, but ecologists would also argue that such connected green spaces are essential to the biological health of a city. Plant and animal life need sufficient room, and parks need to be connected to encourage migration of species. The human population benefits from such constructed landscapes. The health and diversity of vegetation contribute to a more moderate climate, improved air, and water quality.

Again, it was not foresight but the same remnants of feudal rights that make Parisians enjoy the Seine River landscape, right in the heart of the city in the Bois de Vincennes, originally enclosed in 1183 by King Phillip Auguste to keep wild animals, or in the Bois de Boulonge. Louis Napoleon opened up both large forests as parks for the people of Paris. It is said that the emperor directed much of the landscaping himself, cutting new drives and creating artificial cascades.[19] Leading to the Bois de Boulonge was the most resplendent and most expensive of all the new thoroughfares that he laid out together with his chief designer Haussmann. This linear green, the Avenue Foch, as it is named today, ran through rural scenes; today, lined with large trees, the boulevard makes an ecological link between the large park and Paris' web of tree-lined streets. By comparison, Paris' tree lined streets are well known, the boulevards of central Milan are less well-documented. Their pattern is shown in Figure 1.16 with their important connection to the tributaries of the Po River.

In the center of Calcutta, the Maidan has more complicated origins. After a 1756 uprising the East India Company built Fort William at the location of the old village Govindapur. The Company cleared the surrounding jungle and created a large glacis to defend the Europeans from potential future attacks. Over time trees have grown back selectively and the former glacis, the Maidan, is the Central Park of Calcutta. Literally millions of people enjoy the Maidan as a place to breathe fresh air and to approach the Hugli River, which, as part of the Ganges, has sacred importance for the nation of Bengal.

The opportunity to connect large open-space systems made us look at the satellite images of cities in developing countries to see what opportunities might be claimed now to satisfy ecological concerns in the future. For example, Santiago de Chile has a curious-looking mountain spur that extends from the Andes deep into the center of the city and directs the Mapocho River along its course. These two elements, the river and the mountain spur, with their connection to the Andes, can be fur-

Figure 1.17 Calcutta with the Maidan in 1842. (Melville Branch, *Atlas of Rare City Maps: Comparative Urban Design, 1830–1842*, courtesy Princeton Architectural Press)

ther developed into a continuous landscape that will contribute to the health of five million people.

Large open spaces can be spotted on satellite images. Possible connections between them can be found and designed as linear greenways. It is possible to create such green connectors within the right of way of a typical arterial street. An ecologically healthy greenway has trees and vegetation planted close together. The movement of cars and people takes place underneath the canopy of such trees. Striking examples are the streets of Ho Chi Min City with its tall rain-forest-type trees that were planted by the French colonial rulers.

It is important to connect as many open spaces as possible into a system and to connect such a system to the area outside of the city, to mountains, shorelines, and lakes. If this were done consistently, future satellite images would show a thin green web weaving together a fabric of natural elements that improves the quality of air, water, and climate.

Comparing the maps in this collection led to the conclusion that each city has an authentic shape, and that this shape makes reference to a city's original landform. Thus the only permanent authenticity visible on the maps in this collection refers to how a city is placed and has grown inside the landform of its region. One day, out of necessity for water conservation, this authenticity might be tied to a new program of urban ecology. Such a program will be a key to decoding how the widely used term "sustainability" might apply to

Figure 1.18 Santiago de Chile from satellite. Note the narrow mountain spur that directs the Mapocho River along its course to the center of the city. (Courtesy NPA Group, Edenbridge)

a region and how political representation might better be organized according to watersheds or drainage basins.

City Regions and Agriculture

Copenhagen was included in the collection of maps for the conceptual model that it represents. The post–World War II expansion of Copenhagen fol-lowed the widely acknowledged Five Finger Plan. Urbanization was directed along existing and im-proved rail and highway corridors leaving the land between the fingers available for recreation and agri-culture. When the Five Finger Plan was conceived in the mid-1940s, agricultural production in this part of Denmark was losing importance, but demand for parkland to serve the increasing urban population

Figure 1.19 Tall rain-forest-type street trees in Ho Chi Minh City.

increased. Although the current regional plan for Copenhagen has mutated from a radial pattern into one that is characterized by a combined radial and concentric ring pattern, the original intent of the finger plan can still be seen on satellite images today. Placing the maps of Copenhagen next to Cairo—two cities with very similar land coverage—suggests a radial form with five fingers for the future expansion of Cairo. In Cairo, traces of the five finger pattern already exist. And, as in the Copenhagen region of the 1940s, Cairo needs to continue to preserve agricultural land in the fertile Nile Delta, which is framed by the arid desert. For the foreseeable future foodstuff that is consumed each day is moved into the city from locations nearby.

The transport of food is very much in evidence early every morning. Vehicles of all kinds are pressed into service, piled high with what the people of the city will consume each day in a metropolis where many homes lack refrigeration.

The Randstad remains meaningful as an urban form. It covers a region in Holland as large as the urbanized Tokyo region. The human eye has to do some editing to discover the more intensely urbanized rim that has its origins in medieval settlement patterns. Once the rim is traced on the map and compared to the relative lack of urban settlements in the center, the concept is clear. For a very long time the need for collective water management has forced the cities in the Rhine River Delta to cooperate and to protect the urbanized land and the agricultural land from flooding. But to maintain "the green heart" inside the Randstad required considerable political will. Some Dutch planners appear somewhat apologetic about the preservation of agricultural land at a time when such policy is contrary to European law. The center inside the urbanized rim is no longer essential for dairy farming production and most other forms of agriculture except the highly industrialized production that takes place in vast tracks of greenhouses. However, as a form concept the Randstad continues to have merits because it concentrates regional transportation links in the form of a circular loop to service the cities and towns along the rim of this urban region. Thus public transport has remained accessible, and the development pressure on the green heart remains reduced. That was the Randstad's intent; adherence to the concept will continue to take collective political will. Those who promote the importance of locally grown food have a window of opportunity to convince the planning authorities that the green heart is a unique asset worth saving.

Worldwide new conurbation will form, and if the Randstad model can serve as an example, a strong planning rationale would need to be articulated that ideally has roots in the hydrology of a region combined with a historic settlement pattern. City regions like the Randstad have emerged in other delta locations. They have developed in China's Pearl River Delta. The cities of Guangzhou, Foshan, Nanhai, and Shude accommodate fifteen million inhabitants. Together with cities on both sides of the Pearl River Estuary, Macao, Shenzhen, and Hong Kong, this number included fifty-five million inhabitants in 2003. The characteristics of this urban region are unlike those of a single large city and more closely resemble a string of separate cities. A high-speed train line will reach Foshan in 2008, and a proposed bridge across the estuary near Macao will connect to Hong Kong and close the circular loop that shapes this city region. Similar to the Randstad at the mouth of the branches that the Rhine River forms prior to entering the North Sea, the cities of the Pearl River Delta originated as trading places with access to the river branches that connect to the South China Sea. But that is where the similarity ends. There is no preservation of a green heart yet. Agricultural land is rapidly transforming into industrial zones. Water pollution is a serious issue, and major efforts are under way to improve the health of the rivers and the landscapes alongside them over time.

Seen together and in comparison the maps prompt three general conclusions on the magnitude of change, disparity of resources, and differences in city forms.

Magnitude of Change

The process of change in most cities of this collection has accelerated to such a degree that it is now possible to observe and grasp its effects within a single human lifetime.

The magnitude of change also suggests that what has been added to cities cannot simply be referred to as a logical extension of what was there. The core area might contain urban patterns that seem unchanged. However, outside the core area, change is significant and recent, therefore the shared memory of change must also be recent and can be retrieved. If systematic efforts were made to collect the memory of places from different age groups and different socioeconomic backgrounds, the nature of change would be better understood. A process of reasoning with change would become possible that involves potentially larger segments of the population than currently consulted about matters related to change. Trade-off could be discussed with greater understanding of the possible implications. Such knowledge might not be representative, but it would be suggestive and could give direction for the future. Any observation about the magnitude of change and memory of place would lead to theory developed in the 1960s about people's perception and cognition of urban structures during a time in city history that brought urban renewal and freeway building, notably by Kevin Lynch and others. Local newspapers could invite their readers to mark up regional maps that disclose the reader's mental structure of a region, as was done in the San Diego border region of California.[20] This work would lead to place-specific design principles

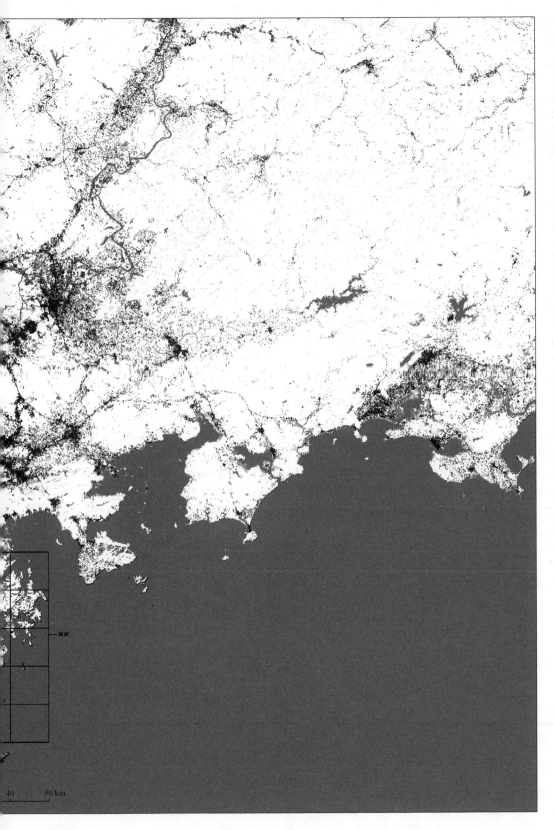

Figure 1.20 A "Randstad" in the Pearl River Delta. The rapidly growing cities of the Pearl River Delta stretch the definition of continuously urbanized area to new dimensions. The map illustrates a large urbanized region that emerged into a nearly continuous urban form. The two main cities of the Pearl River Delta, Foshan and Guangzhou (still better known as Canton), plus Dongguan are now nearly connected with Shenzhen and Hong Kong Hong Kong, inside the fifty by fifty kilometer square, at mid-page, will be connected to Macao by a bridge across the Pearl River Estuary. This bridge will close a loop that connects Macao with Zhulai, Zhongshan, Shunde to Foshan, back to Guangshou, inside the upper fifty by fifty kilometer square—a "conurbation" with fifty million inhabitants. Note: to fit this large image onto two pages of this book we had to reduce the graphic scale compared to the scale of the other city maps in the collection. *Source*: Landsat 7, Path 122/44, 122/45, 121/44, 121/45.

that are based on human values. Such principles could direct the form of city regions.

Disparity of Resources

Any observation about the disparity of resources (space is a resource, just like food, technology, or access to transportation) quickly leads to a discourse about political representation. But the discussion should not end there; nor should the maps hypnotize us about the problems facing the world cities. H. G. Wells's *Anticipations* was mentioned at the outset; in another book, *Fate of Man*, he wrote that salvaging civilization is a race between education and catastrophe. He wrote the book in reaction to emerging fascism in Europe and Asia, but his words equally apply to environmental catastrophe: "There is a worldwide hunger for adequate summarized knowledge on the part of multitudes whom the schools have sent away empty."[21] Laboratories ought to emerge in various parts of the world that monitor the form of conurbations, the magnitude, rate, and nature of change. An important task would be to monitor not only the settlements, the areas rendered in black on the city maps, but also to focus on the patterns of land use that are rendered in white. The productivity of all land categorized as open space is of interest, whether it is set aside to store drinking water, to treat waste, for agriculture, or for forests that improve air quality. These necessary landscapes are the new *commons*, essential for the existence of settlements.

Differences in City Form

The third and final conclusion is that no two city maps are the same. The authenticity of a city is related to its location within a given landform. City form responds to and alters natural systems, but the response happens gradually and rarely obliterates natural systems entirely. The rediscovery of natural systems that existed and that were altered is of growing interest among city design professionals. This interest should make professionals focus on the distinctions between cities, and to find creative solutions where the natural systems inform the design of new cultural landscapes.

At the end of the book, in chapter 7, we will look at the natural systems that inform the design of the shore line around San Francisco Bay.

The comparisons discussed in this chapter reveal distinctions and similarities between cities, a first step in city design. The next step, observation, goes deeper into the meaning of city structures.[22]

CHAPTER TWO

To Observe

Some Observations of Copenhagen's City Form at the Time of Global Change

The process of human perception has fascinated philosophers through the ages. In modern times, human perception has been partially explained by three theories that emerged in the twentieth century.[1] The Gestalt theory laid the groundwork in claiming that the process of perception is holistic: the human mind recognizes the many discrete bits of information that enter through the senses for the contribution they make to a larger organization. The human mind recognizes spatial pattern, chiefly closure of form, similarities, continuity, and proximities.

Not necessarily in contradiction, ecological theory of perception contends that the human mind recognizes sensory information according to what is already known and systemized.[2] Throughout human history human senses have evolved to guarantee survival. One of the important contributions ecological theory has made is to remind us that human perception is not static, but shaped by a developmental process, a process that perceives the world around us in motion, chiefly through a set of eyes, mounted inside the head, which are free to move and to react as part of the human body surrounded by space and time.

Finally, building on Gestalt and partially contradicting ecological theory, a third theory of perception, the so-called probabilistic theory, claims that sensory information is never perfectly correlated with reality.[3]

The observer builds up a repertoire of probabilities that provides likely conclusions by combining trustworthy clues to give an educated guess about the true nature of a situation or place. The probabilistic theory likens the process of perception to an optical lens with the environment on one side and the observer on the other. The observer becomes active in recombining the visual clues, in focusing and testing the validity of what is seen through the lens. The validity of the observed information is strengthened when the observer has access to accuracy tests that verify what is observed through independent means.

Design professionals might take for granted how visual clues influence the design process. Unconsciously or consciously all individuals react to visual clues, interpret their meaning, and act on the information perceived. The probabilistic theory has become important in this context. It gives systematic guidance to the process of observing and verifying visual information. Anyone interested in observation as a method to gain knowledge about a place might practice in an unfamiliar environment such as a foreign culture. There, the observer is likely to ask more astute questions about what is being observed. Honing one's skills in direct and systematic observation will reveal that a surprising amount of clues about a place can be discovered and verified. Allan Jacobs taught systematic observation at Berkeley for many years and his book *Looking at Cities* is important in this context.[4]

In this chapter the inner city of Copenhagen serves as an example. I have been somewhat familiar with the city for several years, but in the year 2000, during a six-month stay, sufficient time was available to take walks through the city and gain insight into the city's spatial structure. Briefly, before we follow a probabilistic approach to dealing with clues, a few words are needed about the ecological theory of perception. The person who is chiefly responsible for articulating the ecological theory of perception, J. J. Gibson, reminded us that perception is a dynamic process that operates under constantly changing conditions and frequently in motion over time. Therefore decisions made based upon direct observation of the real world will differ from those made after viewing visual media that represent conditions frozen in time and in a static state such as plans and other images. For a design professional it might seem contradictory that improvements to professional representation, like the remote sensing from satellites that was used in the first chapter, can lead to an increased remoteness from reality, but technology can produce an alienation from existing urban conditions. Therefore, for a city designer, observation is one of the few methods available to gain primary information firsthand. This is important in a professional culture that has made information abundantly available, but from secondary sources. Are we to trust the information? Rarely do we know how secondary information was gathered, with what focus, at what grain or resolution, for what purpose, and from what sources. This chapter shows how direct experience gained by walking through a city is necessary in making informed decisions about the future of the city.

The narrative is written in a personal style, because what is described here is a process of discovery based upon clues that were perceived, verified—whenever possible—and committed to memory to be recalled as a basis for design decision making.

Copenhagen was chosen because the city center is transforming to conform to the pressures of the changing global economy. Like elsewhere, new employment and cultural centers emerged in formerly underused areas. The scale of these transformations is especially striking in the medium-sized capital cities of the smaller European nations. In a later chapter we briefly visit Milan, Italy, to encounter similar transformations. In Copenhagen, new, large-scale campus-style commercial developments have emerged in marked contrast to the relatively small and finely grained fabric of the historic city center. Through direct observation urban design principles are discovered that can lead to a better integration of new and old: a strategy that can help define a city anew in an age of global change. Such diagnosis can only be made by walking and observing directly because the new buildings or city extensions are no longer seen as objects or distinct projects, which is of course what they are in any method of representation, but when seen enroute the projects are just pieces that will either come together into a larger whole or will need to be repaired to relate to what is already there. What has impressed me most in observing new and old elements of city structure is the principle of connectedness. It might take decades, sometimes centuries, but over time disjointed elements of city structure come together. Not always, and not automatically, but through much design intervention.

My Observations of Copenhagen's City Form at a Time of Global Change[5]

A visitor to the city of Copenhagen is likely to remember the many green towers. For example, the spire of Saint Nikolai's Church towers above the main pedestrian street at Amager Square. Some towers appear in unexpected vistas. It is somewhat

Figure 2.1 The center of Copenhagen seen from the Church of Our Saviour. The towers of Copenhagen from left to right: Christiansborg—the seat of the Danish Parliament; below it to the right: the dragon spire of the Merchant Exchange Building; next: the Church of Our Lady, in brick with a green cap; next and behind it: Saint Peter's Church; below to the right of the canal: Holmen's Church, the new dark copper roof carries a small green belfry; above: Holy Ghost Church also in dark copper; next: Saint Nikolai, a brick tower with an ornate green spire. This church is located near Amanger Square; right behind it: the Roundtower in brick with the small sixteenth-century observatory on top. The Coal Market (Kultorv) is located in a direct line at the foot of the modern building behind the Roundtower. See also the map in figure 2.13 for all locations identified in the view.

of a surprise to get a glimpse of the Parliament tower at Christiansborg Palace, the government seat, while on a walk across the Coal Market, a square at the other end of the historic center.

The human mind recognizes the towers as part of an organization where every element is evaluated for the contribution it makes toward the overall gestalt of the city. Seeing the Christiansborg tower from a distant vantage point reminded me that medieval Copenhagen was not a small city. The towers of Copenhagen dominate street views through their placement, shapes, and color, but more importantly, they helped me understand the structure of Copenhagen's urban form because each tower is associated with an urban district but extends its influence upon the rest of the center.

Understanding a city that had its origin in the early medieval period requires some knowledge of the many fires and acts of war that have erased historic traces in addition to those traces that disappeared through gradual transformation. However, the placement of streets as routes of passage and the placement of churches, not necessarily the church structures or towers themselves, but their location rarely changed. From that conclusion an image of a city structure emerges that describes the early city as an assembly of villages, each clustered around a church and connected by streets that point toward churches in neighboring clusters. This conclusion, however, is not immediately reached; it emerges once many clues are combined over time and becomes apparent when one is standing on a tower with a view like that shown in figure 2.1. When starting observations, it is more likely that the observer reacts first to recent changes and interprets them before an image of the whole city structure emerges.

In the winter of 2000, when I took many walks through the center of Copenhagen, I observed major changes. Military and industrial closures had triggered new developments along the former inner harbor. On the harbor-front, east of the city core, a large financial institution had taken over a former shipyard and had erected a row of administrative buildings. Directly opposite, on the island occupied by the Parliament, a striking black monolith opened to house the new Royal Library. From there to the south, along Christian's Brygge, from where, until recently, ships had sailed to former Danish islands in the North Atlantic, a row of bulky office buildings and a singularly bad hotel tower had been placed with smug and empty confidence. Many of these new structures appeared disjointed compared with the rest of the historic city. The large new bank held the neighboring population at arm's length. Like the former shipyard, the bank now claimed the water's edge, but for the bank's representative purposes. Inside the new library the public was given a magnificent view of the Kalvebod Stream, the waterway to which Copenhagen owes its existence. But the placing of the building directed the movement of people and cars away from the water's edge and once away from it the public was separated from the water by the emerging long row of commercial buildings.

Largely invisible in early 2000, but on the drawing board, a public–private corporation had started construction of Ørestad, a five-kilometer long linear city to connect an area near the Copenhagen airport with the historic center. This large area had been used by the military until abandoned. Finally, the historic naval station, Holmen, had been partially converted to civilian use. New waterfront housing was under construction on leftover land between buildings where ships were once built and serviced. That year, it was announced that a new opera house had been commissioned and approved at the highest level of government outside the customary public approval process for political reasons.

What sent me on my winter walks was the discord between the various projects with the existing spatial patterns of the inner city. It is important to clarify that the architecture of the projects mentioned here is of very high quality, but all buildings are placed like objects to have a space of their own with no relationship to their neighbors. In their separateness the new buildings fragment the spatial structure of the city. Initially my aim was to better understand the essential spatial structure of Copenhagen's center, the geometry of streets and districts that had emerged since medieval times. I wanted to study the edges of districts to better understand how districts of the city had grown together and how the center's orientation to the water had changed. Through the process of walking and observing I hoped to discover principles that might be brought to bear on how current city transformations and expansions could be directed.

The many towers of the inner city provided my first clues; their placement clearly followed a principle: each tower seems to have a domain, and this domain reaches beyond the parish or political boundaries. Regardless of a tower's religious, mer-

cantile, political, or cultural significance, it is an expression of an overlapping spatial structure. Towers are
best seen from a distance when
framed in the cross section of a
street like the tower of Saint Peter's
Church in the center of the Town
Hall Street (Rådhus Strœde) seen
from a far away bridge at the Palace
island Frederiksholm.

Not until I saw the green cupola of
the Roundtower's observatory lining
up with the tower of the Church of
Our Lady in a view from an allée in the
King's Pleasure Garden (Kongens
Have) did I become curious about reg-
ularities between towers and Copenhagen's streets. I could easily imagine
reason and willful design in the layout
of Christianshavn, the fortified harbor
city in relation to Holmen's Church.
The small belfry saddling the main
axis of this beautiful Late Renaissance
church appeared on center in a view
framed by Market Street (Torvegade),
Christianshavn's main street. Both
church and the Christianshavn street plan of the
1620s date from the same period.

Figure 2.2 View of the Roundtower in Copenhagen from the Linden Allée in the King's Pleasure Garden (Kongens Have) with the Church of Our Lady in the Distance.

Consistent with the probabilistic theory of perception, the human mind tries to organize visual
clues into a system that provides likely interpretations and poses questions that need to be verified.
Answering such questions about regularity and co-
incidence between Copenhagen's streets and towers quickly led to the map rooms and picture
galleries of the city. Once I verified that an angular
geometry had dictated the placement of streets and
towers, a new image of the city emerged in my
mind, an image that gave me a general introduction
to the city's transformations and expansions: In
Copenhagen new additions remain anchored
within what existed. Throughout history, when it
came to changing the design of their city center the
people of Copenhagen had a remarkable skill for
not rushing into things but sitting back and watching developments carefully prior to taking action.
When they acted, they did not make too many decisions at one time but left some for later. Although
some bad mistakes slipped through, the most common urban planning disasters, such as large-scale
urban renewal and the building of rows of office or
residential towers in the center to modernize the
city center, have been avoided.

The lessons I learned from my walks through the
city are that really big mistakes in the layout of new
streets are almost impossible to correct, and that the
edges of the urban fabric, where new meets old, require major design consideration for a very long time.

Most importantly, it appeared to me that the
people of Copenhagen were never afraid to change

Figure 2.3 Map of Central Copenhagen. The left arrow, pointing north, indicates the direction of city extensions in the sixteenth century. The arrow pointing to the southeast also refers to a sixteenth century city extension, Christianshavn. The arrow in the center of the map indicates the axis of the Baroque extension, Frederiksstad. Finally, the arrow pointing south indicates the axis of the twenty-first-century extension, Ørestad.

a course of action when it became obvious that a better way of doing things had been discovered. This conclusion made me optimistic about people's ability to reevaluate the complex forces that bring change to the city. If my optimism is justified then even major new developments like Ørestad can be linked to historic Copenhagen in a positive manner, and the city can define itself anew at an age of global change.[6] The political essayist Marshall Berman places the phrase "in a positive manner" into the context of a critique on postmodernity: "The contemporary desire for a city that is openly troubled but intensely alive is a desire to open up old but distinctively modern wounds. It is a desire to live openly with the split and unreconciled character of our lives, and to draw from our inner struggles, wherever they may lead us in the end. If we learned through one modernism to construct haloes around our spaces and ourselves, we can learn from another modernism—one of the oldest but also, we can see now, one of the newest—to lose our haloes and find ourselves anew." His words come to mind when walking through Copenhagen because they describe finding oneself anew by evaluating the merits of what has come to us from the past.

The Old City

During the time I was walking the curving streets in the old city and trying to distinguish old ones from more recent streets, I picked up a simple clue that the difference between straight streets and curved ones might provide the answer to a street's age, with curved streets being old and straight streets newer, and willfully laid out. This proved to be true. In the archives, I found a much-battered map from 1730 depicting the proposed street widening after the great fire of 1728.[7] Fanned initially by strong north-westerly winds, the fire started on Wednesday evening, October 20, burned until Saturday, and destroyed the entire northern half of the city. The map is interesting because it shows Copenhagen's medieval street grid as it existed prior to the fire. To improve circulation and to prevent future fires from

spreading across narrow lanes, a street-widening program was proposed by the authorities. Furthermore, masonry construction was made mandatory instead of the traditional half-timbered building method. The owners of properties were required to start the rebuilding on new stone foundations leaving a uniform street width. The map shows how such requirements defined future property lines after doubling the width of many streets.

Apparently, not all improvements could be carried out. For example, the authors of the map straightened the many curving streets, making them more uniform and orderly in the process. Naturally, a property owner is reluctant to give up land between the existing curve and a new, imaginary line drawn across the front of his property, especially if the neighbor across the street reaps the benefit of that transaction. So the townspeople of Copenhagen kept many of their curving streets. However, I did walk along a number of straight streets that, confirmed by the map, had indeed been willfully laid out after the fire.

Probably the most forward-looking improvement that resulted from the 1728 fire was the introduction of a new continuous east–west axis that made possible Copenhagen's main pedestrian promenade, Strøget. This was done by breaking a new wide street through the rubble in a straight line near the place where the fire had started. Here, between the New Town Square (Nytorv), and the western gate, Saint Clemens, the first church had stood at the edge of Copenhagen's oldest nucleus. Saving the location of the old church must have been secondary to the desire for improved cross-town circulation. Moving goods and people from the city gates through town had become as important as circulation within the center. The second example of a straight street is Fiolstrœde. Parallel to the gentle "S" curve of the Nørregade–Rådhusgade axis, the 1730 map introduced a much-straightened Fiolstrœde as an alternative north–south route and carried it through the entire fire zone in a straight line, almost to the shoreline opposite the island,

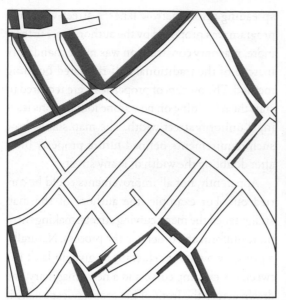
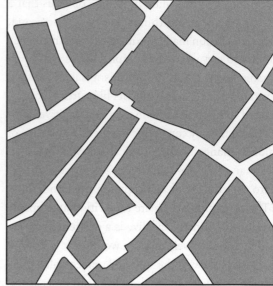

Figure 2.4 Proposed improvements to the street grid of Copenhagen after the 1728 fire. The dark lines in the left frame indicate the street widening proposed in 1730. The map on the right shows the existing conditions. (Redrawn from V. Lorenzen *Haandtegnede Kort over København* plate XXX, Copenhagen, Henrik Koppels Forlag, 1942.)

where the palace stood. In the northern part of the city a new square emerged on the map in nearly present-day shape and placement as that of today's Coal Market (Kultorv). Købmagergade was linked up with the new square and connected directly to the northern city gate.

Streets as routes of passage toward the shoreline like the gently curving Nørregade and Købmagergade have in all likelihood existed since the earliest history of Copenhagen as a settlement. The placement of parish churches in relation to such routes is still apparent from the 1730 map. Early, at the height of medieval expansions, the Nørregade–Rådhusgade axis took on great civic importance. Nørregade became home to the cathedral, Church of Our Lady, on a slight rise of the land, and, running downhill to the old town hall at the Old Town Square, Gammeltorv. Clues that point to the civic significance of the axis consist of two neoclassical porticos, at the cathedral, and at courthouse on Nytorv, the New Town

Square. Both can be seen in one line of sight along Nørregade.

During my walks it was the apparent regularity between church towers and city streets that sent me to the map rooms. Although the church towers we see today—and especially their spires—are of relatively recent design, the placement of these towers is indeed old and they were willfully placed along the historic routes of passage. During my walks I have wondered why the tower of the Holy Ghost Church (Helligaads Kirke) has such little visibility in the image of the city. Although located in the geographic center of the old city, the Holy Ghost Church had its origins not as a parish church, but as a monastery and hospital chapel. I also wondered about the placement of Trinity Church at the Roundtower and Holmen's Church near the old navy yard at Bremerholmen. These last two churches were built after the Reformation when the strict orientation of a congregation toward Jerusalem was no longer as important. The two churches were rotated to follow new geometries. The rotation provided a clue that made me investigate the intent behind the many city extensions of the early seventeenth century. It seems that during the reign of Christian IV (1577–1648) new axes were pointed toward the city extensions of his period. He had Holmen's Church pointed toward Christianshavn and Trinitatis toward the northeast, where he intended to build a new center for his capital, on monastery land acquired by the crown through secularization after the Reformation.[8]

The 1730 map confirmed that the Roundtower seen from where I had seen it, the allée inside the King's Pleasure Garden was visible from that vantage point prior to the 1728 fire; the street Lande Mœrket existed and made a visual connection to the King's Pleasure Garden, then outside the old city walls.

Luckily, a 1649 landscape architecture design plan of the pleasure garden survived, the oldest of its kind in Denmark.[9] That plan showed a linden allée labeled as Ladies Walk; it is indeed in line with the tower of the Church of Our Lady and the Roundtower. In the larger context, the garden design can also be clearly seen on the 1649 Puffersdorf map of Copenhagen.[10]

Apparently, the symbolic quality of the Roundtower (1637–42) was important to the crown. The tower had a dual purpose: it served as a marker for Trinity Church, the new University chapel, but just as important, on its top was the latest technology of Western civilization, an observatory. The professionals working for the King placed the Roundtower on line with the cathedral tower and projected the axis outside of the old city walls, through the pleasure garden toward the northeast. To strengthen the location of the tower they placed two new colleges, Regensen and Borch's near the Roundtower. As a link of the new expansion back to the medieval city, the designers selected the cathedral tower as the most meaningful focal point. Of course when these designs were carried out, the cathedral had a tall, pointed spire that dated from

1514. It was decorated with four much smaller spires in each corner of the church tower, which gave the tower the appearance of a thorny crown. The tower must have been a significant sight, and a person looking at it could make no mistake in recognizing

Figure 2.5 Engraving by G. L. Lahde of a lost painting by Christopher William Eckersberg, *Fire in the Tower of Our Lady's Church*. (Courtesy City Museum of Copenhagen)

the building for what it was—the main church of the city. The spire burned during the 1728 fire, and the architect Lauritz von Thurah (1709–59) designed a new baroque spire, which lasted until 1807, when it became a target during the British bombardment. The painter G. L. Lahde preserved the view of the baroque tower in flames. The artist depicted the scene in a watercolor using the same view axis that started my own inquiry on a walk through Kongens Have.

In the archives I found another postfire map from 1761, prepared by the military engineer Christian Gedde, fashioned after Michel-Étienne Turgot's famous 1731 bird's-eye view over Paris.[11] This map showed most properties rebuilt to a three- or four-story height. All buildings are depicted with strikingly similar building facades, which made me suspect that Gedde used symbols rather than reality as a guide.

Walking through the streets I was looking for the building type depicted on Gedde's map. The unified appearance of new construction apparently must have been a concern. I found few examples

Figure 2.6 Post-1728 fire reconstruction at the Grey Friars' Square. Note the additional flat under the roof illuminated by windows set in gables perpendicular to the roof line. These gables gave Copenhagen's streets a very distinctive appearance.

and only one concentration on the Grey Friar's Square. The Crown's chief architect, Johan Cornelius Krieger, had prepared a building typology, complete with elaborate facade drawings.

Although the postfire buildings I saw were more modestly executed, they generally follow Krieger's design of an additional flat under the roof illuminated by windows set in gables perpendicular to the roof line. These gables gave Copenhagen's streets a very distinctive appearance. As a result of the fire, Copenhagen transformed from a city with low, largely single-story household dwellings, many with stables and of rural character, to a more urban, multistoried city, which allowed Copenhagen to accommodate more people. The trend continued after the second large fire of 1795 and during the rebuilding that followed the British bombardment of 1807.

The City as a Circle

It has been said that the many town-planning schemes of Christian IV lacked coordination. Although the new city geometry that related the spiritual center of the city to science, the pleasure garden, and city expansion had been carefully thought out, when it came to the layout of the town to the northeast of the King's Pleasure Garden, that layout remained apparently unresolved. The reason might be that the king, at the beginning of his reign, imagined for his capital an ideal Renaissance city plan with a clear radial geometry modeled after the latest Italian town planning schemes like Palmanova from 1593.

There is a 1629 map showing such a design.[12] On my walks I could only see fragments of the radial concept. One such trace is in the direction of the King's Pleasure Garden main axis. A set of large marble balls defines a beautiful broad allée that starts at the palace moat, but with no apparent ending. A line drawn on a map does not meet important places; it points to the harbor. Geometry abandoned? Partly, traces have remained and are still visible on today's city map: the row-houses of Nyboder—a garden city concept three centuries before its time. Three wedge-shaped blocks point toward the same common center. Their street defines the pattern of these yellow-ochre row houses built for navy personnel. Secondly, the large star-shaped pattern of the harbor defenses; both are still promi-

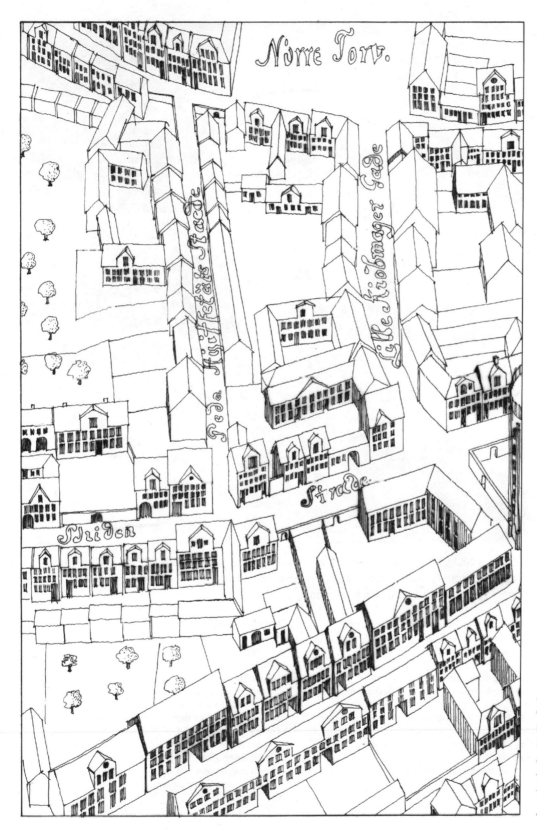

Figure 2.7 Detail of Christian Gedde's 1761 bird's-eye map showing the reconstruction of Copenhagen after the 1728 fire. (Redrawn from the original)

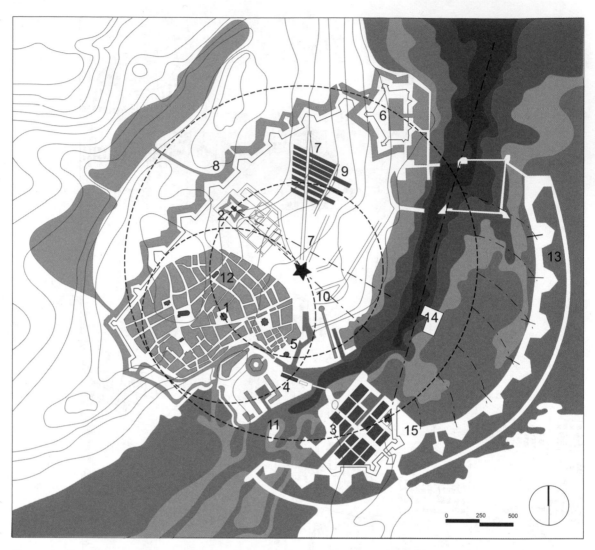

Figure 2.8 The city as a circle. Map showing elements of Copenhagen's urban form that follow a circular city expansion concept, built from 1520 until 1700 and still traceable. The map is drawn on the topography of Copenhagen prior to 1500, after H. V. Ramsing from 1940.

KEY

1) Holy Ghost Church (Helligaads Kirke), chapel, and tower in the center of the old city, 1523.

2) Rosenborg Palace, 1606 and the King's Pleasure Garden, 1649.

3) Christianshavn, fortified harbor city, 1617–19.

4) Mercantile Exchange (Børsen), 1619, with the famous dragon spire, 1640.

5) The Shipyards Church (Holmens Kirke), 1619, expansion of a 1563 anchor forge and conversion into a church.

6) Fortifications at the harbor entrance (St. Annœ Skanse), 1625–29.

7) The "Great Stone Road" (Store Stenbro), new highway to Helsingør, 1630.

8) New eastern city wall, 1630.

9) Nyboder, homes for navy personal, 1631.

10) The "Great and Small Beach Streets" (Store and Lille Strandgade), the old highways out of the old eastern gate along the shoreline.

11) *Leda with the Swan*, a marble column in the harbor, off the palace island (Slotsholmen). The statue is lost.

12) The "Roundtower" (Rundetårn) at Trinity Church that also served as the university observatory, 1642.

13) The navy shipyard and fortifications (Nyholm and Nyvœrk), the star-shaped seaward defense of Copenhagen 1676, 1685–1700.

14) Christiansholmen, 1696.

15) Our Saviour's Church (Vor Frelsers Kirke) 1696, spire 1744.

nent on the map image of the city. It took some time to find the center point of this large star. As I was triangulating lines and circles that resulted in three different center points, all in the vicinity of the King's New Square (Kongens Nytorv) and the Garrison Church (Garnisons Kirke), I was given a beautiful book on the subject of Copenhagen's city expansions between 1500 and 1856 by Nis Nissen.[13] The author tells an interesting story of a Renaissance city extension in the form of a large circle with a star-shaped defense system.

One can easily imagine a group of Renaissance "geometers" practicing with their new magnetic compasses and eyeglasses from Italy or Holland, surveying and triangulating the perfect geometry of a new city and the placement of important buildings. The new plan, hypothetical because an original was never found, is reconstructed in the Nissen book. Drawn around the center at Baron Boltons Gaard is a large circle of 2.4 kilometers. It describes the location of the outer defense lines, both on land and on the Øresund side. The large circle also defined the location of Christianshavn's main square and cuts with stunning precision through the tower of Our Saviour's Church (Vor Frelsers Kirke). I had admired the church before, but now that I knew its place in the geometry of the city, the church took on new importance for me. The church's plan consisted of one large room in the shape of a Geneva cross, a magnificent but simple baroque design. Engraved in the entrance steps I found the construction dates, from 1682 to 1694. A climb to the top reveals a view over the land and water contained by this large, 2.4-kilometer-wide circle. All around can be seen a city expanse that was anticipated in the early 1600s but took until the 1850s to fill to its limits.

The spire of Our Saviour's Church is one of Copenhagen's special features. Lauritz von Thurah designed the tower fifty-seven years after completion of the church in 1749. He modeled his design after Borromini's spiraling staircase of Santo Ivo at the Chiesa Della Sapienza in Rome. Standing up

there in the clear, cold winter air with seemingly boundless visibility, the geometry of Renaissance and Baroque city expansions no longer appeared as arbitrary as it had seemed from a ground-level perspective. There is a clear line of sight from the tower to the harbor entrance and out to sea. Sea captains

Figure 2.9 The spire of Our Saviour's Church, Copenhagen, with the Borromini-inspired design.

were greatly aided by the shining spire in their approach to Copenhagen. A topographic map confirms that the church tower was placed exactly in line with the deep-water channel. Ship pilots would hold their course on the tower until they were in line with the Rosenborg Palace. This was apparent to them when the two smaller Rosenborg towers lined up and shifted in relationship to the main tower. At that point the pilot corrected the ship's course toward starboard and held the new course toward *Leda with the Swan*, a white marble statue on a column placed in the water off Slotsholmen at a location where the new Royal Library extension is located today.

Our Saviour's spire also determined the final geometry of the outer defense line toward the Øresund side, the Holmen Naval Base. Apparently the naval base was too constrained by the geometry of the large circle that had been drawn around Boltons Gaard, and just outside of the circle lay a run of water sufficiently deep for navigation. Thus the circle had to be extended, and this was done in the most ingenious manner. Taking Our Saviour's spire as a centerpoint, radii at the various distances of the anticipated bastions were staked out (in what must have been water) and shifted eastward at equal distances from minded me how important this marker has been for the ecological perception that organizes movement within the city, especially maritime movements. Maritime matters must have guided people's thinking in setting clear priorities: the movement of boats in view of the spire determined the placement of islands and the design of the many specialized buildings. Goods and materials needed inside these

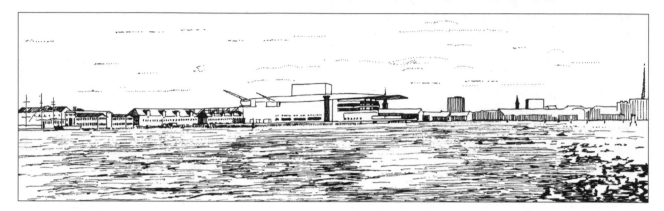

Figure 2.10 Copenhagen's new opera house seen from the harbor entrance with the spire of Our Saviour's Church in the background.

one another. And when the defense work was completed in 1700, Copenhagen had achieved a closure in its form that embraced city, harbor, and defense works on par with any major European city in terms of beauty and elegance.

Within the new semicircular defense line lay a large body of protected water, and on this artificial lagoon a naval city emerged to house the many industries necessary for shipbuilding. Residents from Nyboder came across to Holmen via the "chicken bridge," a movable barrier that closed the harbor at night. Once there, people moved about on boats, and as the number of islands increased drawbridges were constructed wherever needed. I walked out to the very tip of Holmen and looked across the harbor entrance. The Old Customhouse on the other side is only a stone's throw away. From that vantage point, the golden spire of Our Saviour's Church dominates the entire harbor. The spire also re-

buildings came from the water and went back to the water, all under the watchful sight of the tower. For security reasons, a fixed link with the rest of Copenhagen was not desired. The islands grew from north to south; a permanent bridge connecting Holmen with Christianshavn and thus the rest of Copenhagen was not made until the 1880s when the shipyard converted to the production of steel ships, and when the connection was made to enable railroad access, it was routed in view of and alongside Our Saviour's Church.

As I was standing across from the Old Customhouse, where the chicken bridge had once been anchored, I wondered if a future visitor to the city would be able to see and understand the spatial pattern that generated the many islands and the orientation of their buildings. Now that the ships have left the harbor, this large semicircular lagoon looks like an empty room. Among the many silhouettes, the rigging-shears stand out, and other structures are prominent—the dome of Frederik's Church, the spires of Sankt Nikolaj, Christiansborg, and the dragons above the old Mercantile Exchange. But more than all the other structures, the spire of Our Saviour's Church still stands out as a marker for the geometry that created Holmen. Giving meaning to the silhouette of the harbor without taking away from the church spire that created it should be a high priority.

An important by-product of observation is to imagine the future. Any designer knowing about pending projects—like the new opera house that was proposed at the time of these observations— might stand at such a distinct place and not help but imagine the future. Principles came to my mind that permit change without losing the sense of place. The opera house was completed in 2004. In September 2006 I returned to the same spot. The new opera house silhouettes like the bridge of an oversized containership against the skyline. It changed the gestalt of the harbor; not by contributing to the larger organization, but as the first object in a still-missing ensemble made according to different rules.

Subtler, but important to the character, is the building pattern of Holmen. Unlike anywhere in central Copenhagen, where buildings contribute to city blocks and orient themselves to streets, the buildings of Holmen orient toward the water and do not form blocks but stand unattached with shared courtyards to their rear. A design principle consistent with the character of Holmen should be to respect all water edges as places for circulation and primary access to buildings. This strategy keeps the embankments public and allows access to view the towers of the city.

The City as a Grid

The urban form of Frederiksstad, the baroque extension of central Copenhagen, has been imprinted on my mind since I first saw Steen Eiler Rasmussen's axonometric drawing of it in his book on Copenhagen.[14] The main axis extends from the domed Frederik's Church to the harbor right through Amalienborg Palace. The palace is in the form of an open octagon and on axis with the monumental volume of the church, a composition of forms unique in the spatial language of cities. But Frederiksstad is even more memorable on direct encounter. On my walks through Frederiksstad, I saw an area full of design compromises along its northern and southern edges.

In contrast to Holmen, Frederiksstad grew from south to north. Its official history began in 1749, but this northeastern extension was conditioned much earlier with the building of a new city wall in the 1630s between Copenhagen's North Gate and the fortress at the harbor entrance. Thus land be-

Figure 2.11 Store Kongens Gade (King's Great Street), northeastern entrance into the inner city of Copenhagen. The street is centered on the tower of the Parliament at Christiansborg, location number 21 on figure 2.13.

Figure 2.12 *The Flute Players*. A statue placed at the location on Strandgade at the former shoreline in the center of Copenhagen.

new East Gate near the fortress. Between 1647 and 1649, however, in a flurry of design activities, the authorities developed a better circulation system that gave up the diagonal pattern and worked out the beginnings of a new grid geometry. It took 30 years to sort out all the details. The decision to construct a new seawall parallel and closer to the harbor's deep-water channel might have decided matters in favor of an orthogonal street layout for the entire northeastern city expansion. The terminus of the coast highway from the north shifted to the King's Great Street (Store Kongens Gade), and it was laid out in true Copenhagen fashion. A person arriving in town from the northeast through the new East Gate was—and to some extent still is—introduced to the city with a view of the palace tower at Christiansborg.[15]

A map from the late 1640s depicts a new street, Gothersgade, at a right angle to Store Kongens Gade and leaves room for a large square where Kongens Nytorv is now located.[16]

But construction of Kongens Nytorv started in 1672 and took eleven years to complete. A faubourg, a historic suburb outside of the city gates, must have existed here since mediaeval times. Its streets can still be walked today.

One of my winter walks took me to the Garrison Church at Saint Anne's Square in search of the center point of the older radial plan. Naturally, I did not find the center there, the church was built

tween the old and the new walls became available for city expansion. Initially the same radial street design that shaped the naval station's defense line was considered. Consistent with that concept a diagonal "stone road" was built to connect the former East Gate, more or less where the present day King's New Square (Kongens Nytorv) is located, with the

Figure 2.13 Reconciling geometries. The transformation of Copenhagen at the old East Gate (1) is shown here with the medieval walls and moat (2). At the location of the old eastern gate the King's New Square (3) emerged. Property lines still exist (4) that had their origin in the medieval faubourg. The dotted lines show the historic highways that led out of the eastern gate to the shoreline (5) and to the north, for example, the Great Stone Road (6). Property lines and streets were integrated over time into the city extension Frederiksstad (7), *The Flute Players* (8), Amalienborg (9), Frederiks Church (10). The detailed map also shows the location of the Church of Our Lady (11) and the axis from the King's Garden (12), as well as the axis from Rosenborg Palace (13) toward the location of Baron Bolton's court (14) and onward to the New Harbor (15). This was the view axis used by pilots to navigate the approach into the harbor. Also mentioned in the text are the cross-town view from the Coal Square (16) to the Palace Tower at Christiansborg (20). Note the historic location of the Palace Tower; the view from the pedestrian street "Strøget" at Amanger Square (18) toward the Saint Nicolas Church (17) and the view axis from the King's Great Street (21). The location of the Grey Friar's Square is also marked (19).

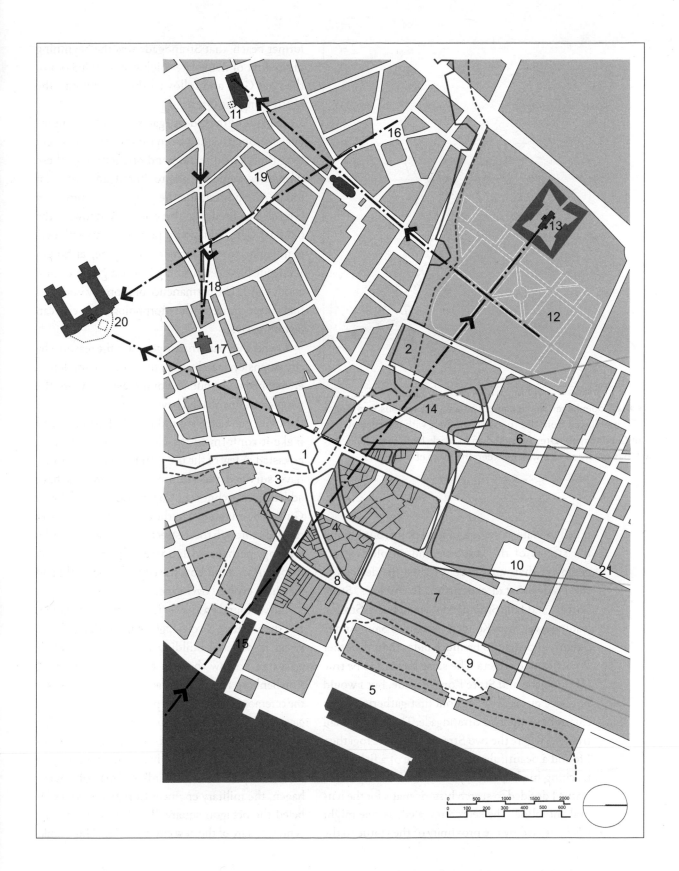

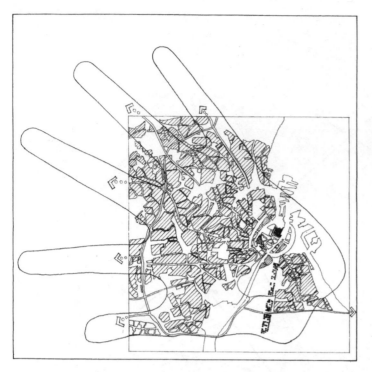

Figure 2.14 Copenhagen in the palm of a hand. The famous Five Finger Plan of Copenhagen from the 1940s shown here with the current form of Copenhagen, Ørestad is shown in black. Note that planned growth has emerged as a web between the roots of its fingers.

---

former beach, that Strandgade was the beginning of the first of many later highways that led out of the East Gate and followed the shoreline to the north along the Øresund.

Outside of the old city gates a significant number of properties had been established for a very long time. The direction and orientation of these properties, perpendicular to Strandgade, still exist today. Along Bredgade the property alignment is even clearer. Bredgade also once curved toward the old East Gate. Today's property lines are still perpendicular to the former street line, although Bredgade has been running in a straight line since about 1660. The permanence of property lines and their importance to the morphology of a city can be impressive.

Ownership patterns are generally the reason why city extensions rarely reach the state of completion envisioned at the outset. For the last 250 years, the people of Copenhagen have tried to straighten out the older geometry around the old East Gate and make it conform to the clear geometry of Frederiksstad. A few of the irregular lots and streets that have survived the slum-clearance process have added to the richness of Copenhagen's urban form. Guided by an interest in the city's history, a person can walk through these streets today and, simply by looking, perhaps with some help from historic maps, understand how the edges between old and new have evolved over time.

I never found an answer to the obvious question, Did the architect Nicolaj Eightved, who designed the street layout and building regulations for Frederiksstad borrow the idea of a central square at Amalienborg from the earlier radial plan, or was it the ceremonial and political pretense of the ruler that gave Copenhagen this flamboyant composition?[17] It is an interesting question because the four Amalienborg palaces were originally not intended for the royal family. On his 1761 bird's-eye map of Copenhagen, the military engineer Christian Geddes labeled the octagon square "Friederichs Stad," the central square of the new city extension. High-rank-

much too late to serve as a focal point, but I found the streets of the faubourg and an older street geometry that must have predated the designs of the Frederiksstad expansion. To my eyes, Store (Great) and Lille Strandgade (Small Beach Street), leading away from Kongens Nytorv to Saint Anne's Square, appeared to be much older than the other Frederiksstad streets. The same seemed to be true for Bredgade and Store Kongensgade. But I would not have guessed so without first gathering some clues about the two Strandgade. There, at a small triangle, where the two Strandgade come together, I found a beautiful green sculpture of a fisherman teaching his boy to play the flute. Looking at the statue I decided to search historic maps for the natural shoreline. The search revealed, as one might have guessed by the proximity of the statue to the

ing court officials commissioned the four palaces: Moltke, Levetzau, Brockdorf, and Schack. The royal family did not move to Frederiksstad until 1794 when the city palace at Christiansborg was damaged by fire. Also, when Geddes prepared his map Frederik's Church did not exist and could not be seen in completed form for another hundred years and more. He drew the proposed volume of the church like a two-dimensional theater backdrop in his otherwise three-dimensional map showing his contemporaries what was proposed, but not there in reality.[18] And it is not the design of Eightved, who died in 1754, but of Nicolas-Henri Jardins that Geddes depicted. None of these designs would be completed, but Ferdinant Meldahl's, who constructed the domed church onto a neo-classical base as late as 1874 and also designed the fashionable flats that surrounded it. The baroque city extension of Frederiksstad with its emphasis on connecting axes gave me some insights on the design of Copenhagen's most recent city extension, Ørestad.

When compared in size, the proposed twenty-first-century Ørestad covers more than eight times the land area of the eighteenth-century Frederiksstad. From the 1630s, the time when the new city walls were built, it took 200 years to connect Copenhagen's northeastern city extension to the rest of the City.

The Linear City

An imaginary future visitor to Copenhagen will in all likelihood make similar observations after a visit to Ørestad. The connections to historic Copenhagen will take a long time to resolve. The emerging form of Ørestad has the appearance of a simple diagram. On first glance Ørestad is a five-hundred-meter-wide and five-kilometer-long city shaped by Copenhagen's first Metro line, which starts at the southern end of Ørestad and runs in a straight line for much of the five kilometers along elevated tracks toward Ørestad's northern end near Islands Brygge. Here the Metro submerges under the historic city.

Spain's early modernist, Arturo Soria y Mata,

and the Soviet planner, N. A. Miliutin, advocated linear city concepts. The intent of a linear city is to concentrate urban development along a transit route and flank it with ribbons of open space. Some examples were built but did not stay linear for long. Allotment gardens separate Ørestad from Amanger to the east. A large marsh defines the new city on the west.

From the outset Ørestad designers have used a combination of linear and radial planning concepts in guiding the design of the new city. Passengers sitting inside the future Metro on elevated tracks will experience the linear planning concept in the best of Copenhagen's planning traditions.

They travel on a straight line toward the Borromini-inspired tower of Our Saviour's Church in Christianshavn. The majority of people, however, will experience Ørestad as a sequence of intersections along concentric-ring roads; most importantly, the intersection of the Metro with the new link to Sweden. Here Denmark's main east–west motorway and Copenhagen's outer ring are joined by the railroad on their way to the airport and the new bridge across the Øresund. The large Fields shopping and entertainment center has been completed at this intersection. A high-rise administrative building for a pharmaceutical company broke ground in early 2000 and is now occupied. Apartment buildings were under construction and are now

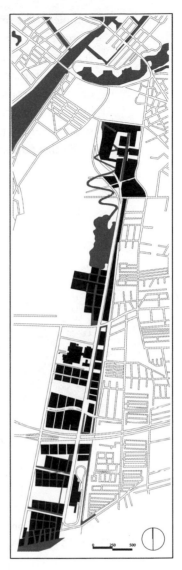

Figure 2.15 The linear city. Plan view of Ørestad, Copenhagen's newest city extension.

- - - - - - - - - - - - - - - - - -

complete. The many people traveling on the submerged rail line and highway through this intersection see very little of Ørestad. The expectation is that motorists will get off the highway and shop or seek entertainment at the Ørestad center. The location was chosen to attract customers from southern Sweden and much of Zealand.

Further north, the next intersection is already es-

Figure 2.16 A view from the front of the elevated Metro, which travels without a driver along Ørestad's main axis.

tablished at the existing Bella Center. North of the Bella Center will be the new City Hospital at Sundby. A future residential community will emerge here. Then Ørestad's urban form is disrupted by a one-kilometer-long gap with an artificial lake and constructed wetlands along the elevated Metro line. (In a typical linear city such features would have no place inside the development along the transit line but would be easily accessible in the flanking open spaces.) Urban form resumes with some concentration at the National Archives, the Broadcasting Center, and finally the Amanger

Campus of Copenhagen University. Here the Metro leaves its straight alignment toward the spire of Our Saviour's Church and aims toward the far less inspiring tower of a Raddison Hotel.

The building of Ørestad was motivated by the need to finance the new Metro. Revenues from properties sold in the new development are intended to pay for the building of the new transit system. Also, an argument has been made for some time that the historic fabric of Copenhagen cannot accommodate new types of buildings required by the rapidly changing demands of office and retail industries. Copenhagen can only remain in the league of "strong European players" if land is made available for such uses. What is argued here is the need for large shopping centers modeled after suburban American examples as well as regional office headquarters of large multinational companies, mainly in the electronics and biochemistry industries. The argument is not new and not only made in Copenhagen but in all major cities of the world. In light of the recent arrival of some of these new headquarter buildings along the southern portion of Copenhagen's harbor, the people of Copenhagen could now relax a little under the apparent weight of a threat that would make their city slip into the backwaters of Europe. One does not need to imagine another row of these buildings in Ørestad to understand that forceful design ingenuity is needed to better accommodate these large structures in any city, new or old.

The new buildings of the global economy are large and frequently ostentatious in their sameness when seen in a row in one place or again on a drive near the airports of Madrid, Milan, or Munich. As building types they resist integration. They are oriented to the automobile and parking lots and not to pedestrians on sidewalks.

At the top of the list for Ørestad was the Field's shopping and entertainment center. Its 110,000 square meters of floor area amounts to only two and a half times the floor area of the Magasin Du Nord department store in downtown Copenhagen, but it measures six and a half times the land area of the same department store. Land for the necessary parking spaces would easily double the surface area needed for such a structure. In the future, pedestrians from nearby residential blocks would be greatly discouraged to walk alongside a 165-meter-long building toward the Metro station.

Ørestad designers need to invent a new buffer-type building; a "liner building" that encapsulates the large structure with neighborhood-oriented stores at ground level. These stores could be part of the shopping center, but most importantly they would open toward the streets that ring the center. The liner buildings would have residential flats on floors above the stores. The buildings would mitigate the large scale of the shopping center with its introverted functions and transition to the smaller residential scale along the neighborhood streets.

The detailed layout of Ørestad's streets and public spaces will be all-important. It isn't the elegant, light-colored Chinese granite curbs that started to arrive on my first walk in April of 2000 that concern me, but the dimensions of the spaces where the curbs will be laid. A granite-covered space of 20,000 square meters is large in scale, if not monumental, when lined with big buildings that have few entrances, and includes a large reflecting pond that covers one quarter of its size. I imagine the square crossed by a pedestrian on a cold and windy winter day—it would seem to take forever. By comparison

Kongens Nytorv measures approximately 24,000 square meters between buildings. But many buses and cars circle around that square. A seemingly large area in the center of 8,200 square meters is dedicated to pedestrian use. The pedestrian area of Copenhagen's Town Hall Square measures half the size of the Ørestad central plaza.

The intent of the Ørestad designers can not

Figure 2.17 Walking alongside Ørestad's new shopping center.

possibly have been to create a public space designed to hold large crowds of people, simply because a large enough crowd will not gather in a place without entrances to buildings, no reason to wait for anyone, and nothing to do. Amangertorv, the most popular square on Copenhagen's main pedestrian street, is about a fifth the size at only 4,200 square meters. The funnel-shaped square lined with many stores holds large crowds extremely well. Here a pedestrian flow of ninety people per minute coming in and out of Købmagergade intermingles in the afternoon with 140 people per minute walking in an east–west

Figure 2.18 Frederiksberg Allée in Copenhagen, a pedestrian-friendly street that can serve as an example for the redesign of Ørestad's streets.

esplanades that people flock to in large numbers. The good ones are well defined by buildings and contain pavilions, or smaller structures detailed to dimensions that make the crossing of pedestrians easier and invite people to congregate along a promenade that is similar in dimension to those comfortable walks on Frederiksberg Allée, a historic boulevard near the center of the city.

What to Take from History

A mirror is held up to our own eyes whenever we examine things of the past. I have focused on the urban form of Copenhagen because I was looking for a trend: how have the people of Copenhagen dealt with large-scale physical changes to their city? I found that city extensions rarely turned out as they were intended. To motivate others in accepting large-scale physical changes to their city, the proponents of city

direction. About four hundred people become stationary and stay in the square to sit in a café, to wait for someone near the fountain, or simply to watch others.[19] Nowhere else in Copenhagen does the movement of people get any better or busier.

Copenhagen is famous around the world for its well-designed public spaces. Extensive research has been carried out over many decades to improve design and use of the city's public realm. It seems that none of the current knowledge of how to design a public space, evident in Copenhagen today, was relevant to those who worked on the initial design of Ørestad. The design of Ørestad Boulevard concerned me as well, when I walked along side the elevated Metro line tracks. The boulevard is five kilometers long and fifty meters wide In addition to the elevated Metro, it accommodates a dual roadway and a canal. Given Ørestad's relatively low density of people and activities, a much narrower roadway would suffice. World cities are full of good examples of linear parkways, urban boulevards, and

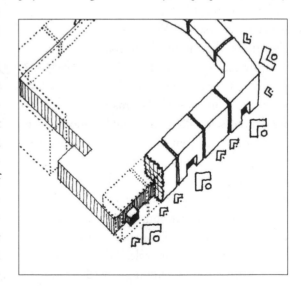

Figure 2.19 A reconfigured Ørestad shopping center where the large-footprint structure is lined with smaller structures that have entrances along the sidewalk.

extensions simplified complex matters into easily understandable abstractions. But the actual building of extensions has proven to be a complex matter. There seem to have been strong voices in Copenhagen advocating change in order to conform to new trends that originated elsewhere. How could it be different in our time? No city can afford to be left outside the global economy. The structures built under this trend have produced sameness. Places that separate people without giving them a sense of place. What is special in the history of Copenhagen are the voices that have calmed the urge to change. Hospitable to people from many cultural backgrounds—English, Dutch, French, German, the nations around the Baltic Sea—and always open to global influences, the city is endowed with a particular talent for receptivity. Thus far in the history of Copenhagen, in an atmosphere of conciliation, outside influences have been loosened and pacified. If history has any currency in predicting the future, than at Ørestad a few important structures will be built according to initial plans, but in all likelihood many other projects will take much longer to complete than anyone wanted to imagine at the outset. Not that those in charge of projects lack a sense of purpose; the initial resolve to proceed will be reconsidered and improved upon. In my view that is good and consistent with the manner in which the people of Copenhagen have dealt with urban expansions throughout the city's history.

A fundamental premise of this chapter is that change can be evaluated through direct observation. Undoubtedly, the reader will have picked up on the author's biases: the center of Copenhagen can be transformed with consideration to the elements already in place, especially those that support public life: change can provide continuity and can be positive. Clearly, any judgment about what constitutes positive change is loaded with controversy unless change is measured over a longer span of time. The center of Copenhagen is a very handsome example of a city that has been developed over time, damaged severely at times, never fully destroyed, worked over, added to, and repaired by many people. In the long range the answer to what constitutes positive change has to do with the ability to integrate new structures into a whole. Each age has left its trace. The city is an endless compression of lives that were lived here with much continuity. It is a cultivated place and a very fortunate one.

URBAN TRANSFORMATION

CHAPTER THREE

To Measure

Vitality, Livability, and Sense of Place

Early in his career, the painter Paul Klee performed as a professional violinist with the Bern Symphony Orchestra; the interpretation of music through visual arts remained important to him throughout his life. His painting *Main Road and Side Roads* makes visible music's temporal and spatial dimensions. The painting originated during Klee's Bauhaus period, and it shows dissecting movements that he referred to as cardinal progressions,[1] successive divisions into halves, quarters, eighths, and sixteenths, or the corresponding additions of intervals.

For me, *Main Roads and Side Roads* has become a metaphor for measurements in general—for measuring those qualities that first need to be placed on a continuum in order to quantify their dimensions, like a tonal scale in Klee's linear structure. That network of interwoven fields of colors symbolizes the relatedness and dependencies between the many dimensions that make up the quality of life in cities. Cities are not a form of art; the visual, auditory, and

kinetic experience of cities very rarely adds up to a *Gesamtkunstwerk*, the German word for artistic expression through multiple art forms. But cities are dynamic spatial networks with interrelated geometries, some messy and unresolved, others clear and intractable. Not only is it possible to measure the physical dimensions of such geometries, it is also possible to measure their implication on social, cultural and political, psychological, economic, and environmental conditions.

Even though the scales for many quality-of-life parameters in cities are missing, it is possible to measure them in relative terms. The *vitality* of urban spaces can be measured by examining three qualities: mixture of activities, density, and public life. Attributes of *livability* include personal safety, well-managed traffic, ease of walking, centrality, and the presence of nature in cities; sense of place and sense of time are dimensions of the *sense of belonging*. These much used but ephemeral concepts, when systematically measured, can be validated or refuted. Without measurement they remain biases.

Livability, Sense of Place, and Vitality

The original meaning of *livability* described conditions in neighborhoods where residents live relatively

Figure 3.1 Paul Klee, *Hauptweg und Nebenwege* (Main Road and Side Roads), 1929. (Courtesy Museum Ludwig, Cologne, © 2008 Artists Rights Society [ARS], New York/VG Bild-Kunst, Bonn)

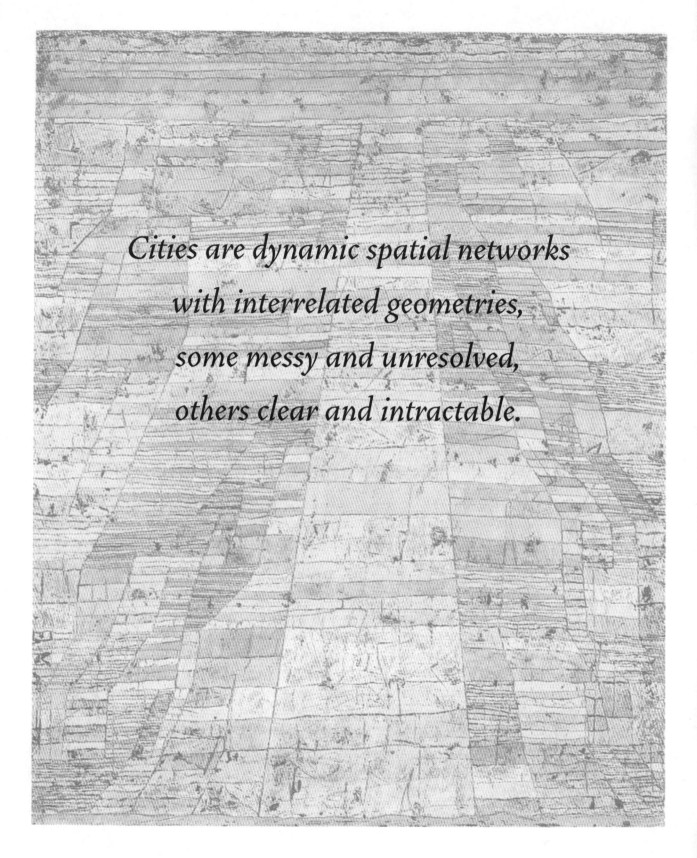

Cities are dynamic spatial networks
with interrelated geometries,
some messy and unresolved,
others clear and intractable.

free from intrusions.[2] The meaning of the term has broadened to include not only the proper management of traffic in neighborhoods but those qualities that are associated with sustainable cities: human life that is well integrated within the social and natural ecology, personal safety, comfort, availability of services, and transit within walking distance to lower the dependency on the automobile.

While covering a large number of elements, livability is focused on the perception of concrete physical elements and is therefore easier to measure than *sense of belonging*. A more abstract concept, a sense of belonging, is defined by the psychological or emotional dimensions of living in a neighborhood, on a street, or in a building, *or when walking through a field without holding any rights to material ownership*.[3] The desire to create places that can be positively identified in a manner that is shared by many is a prominent bias held by urban designers. Designers believe that it is possible to create a design that produces a highly developed sense of place, which in turn gives people a sense of belonging and potentially enriches the personal identity of the occupants. The difficulty with this concept is that designers often consider only the physical design's contribution to a *shared sense of place* when there are many other important variables, chiefly the contribution made by people who also use the space— their memory, expectations, or ambitions, as well as economic conditions and the geographic location. Drawing on selected literature and firsthand experience, the writer Tony Hiss illuminates in a manner understandable for a wide audience many factors in the creation of place that also foster a sense of belonging.[4]

A third concept that has been measured and that will be covered in this chapter is *vitality*. One of the hallmarks of living in cities is the benefit that can be drawn from the presence of other people within close proximity. The underlying assumption designers make is that the design of the built environment can influence both the functionality and the desirability of public places. The concept is applied to the design of plazas, parks, and streets. Designers consider how structures fronting such spaces, through their use and physical form, encourage or discourage public life. Of the three professional biases, vitality is the easiest to measure but is also one that is subject to much cultural relativity.

All three concepts, livability, sense of place, and vitality, suffer from the lack of detailed knowledge that designers could apply with predictable results to many cultural and physical contexts. The three concepts are not mutually exclusive. In fact, they overlap substantially. The distinctions between the three concepts have more to do with the degree of concreteness and ease of measuring. Prerequisites for vitality are the presence of other people and a sense of enjoyment among those who participate in public life; not only those people who have to be there but also those who feel invited to linger and stay for a while, according to the norms of their culture and the choices they have in being elsewhere.

This chapter is divided into three parts; each part demonstrates how to measure one concept: vitality, livability, or sense of place. It should be seen as an invitation to conduct systematic inquiries into professional biases, and as fellow *New Yorker* journalist Brendan Gill said about the importance of Tony Hiss's work, "*to rouse ourselves for the futures' sake as well as our own. The work that lies ahead of us is not one of Sisyphus but one of Hercules*."[5] It examines some of the prominent biases urban designers hold and explains ways to substantiate knowledge through direct measurements. This includes the need to refute some biases that cannot be substantiated.

Since the 1970s, urban design students at Berkeley have been asked to articulate hypotheses about urban form and to carry out evaluations to test their assumptions.[6] Some of the hypotheses were drawn from literature, like Jane Jacobs' norms for "vibrant" neighborhoods. Others might be best called "hunches" that had been articulated in one form or another but had never been tested in any systematic way. At the outset, it should be noted that individual studies suffer from an understandable flaw:

sometimes too many variables are lumped together in an attempt to represent the complex relationships that exist in physical space. But that is part of the reality when students engage in this type of research. They like to study phenomena in a context similar in complexity to the one they observe in reality. Stripping away variables would increase the robustness of their findings, but their studies would also lose relevance for them. Cumulatively, the limitations of the individual studies matter less as results build up over successive studies.

Part One: Vitality

In discussing vitality it is fitting to start with urban critic Jane Jacobs.[7] The vibrant communities she described are places where people can easily interact with one another and benefit from social networks. For Jane Jacobs, human interaction on public streets was an agent of safety; diverse housing stock an agent of social stability and economic vitality, and diversity of business types a preventive measure against economic downturns. She first made these assertions in the early 1960s, at a time when upper and middle-income families were leaving inner city neighborhoods. She was criticized for assuming that residents with sufficient disposable income would adopt the lifestyle of working class communities with ethnic backgrounds. She was ridiculed by no less a luminary than Lewis Mumford in his review of her book in the *New Yorker* entitled: "Mother Jacobs' Home Remedies." But her writings have remained relevant today because of her ability as a journalist to link sociology, economics, and design in a manner that none of the individual disciplines could have done on their own.[8] However, it is fair to say that her theses about vibrant communities, or those of her opponents, were most certainly applied but never tested empirically.

Do density, walkability, and the mix of shops and services on neighborhood streets create a vibrant community independent of socioeconomic conditions? That question was put to an experiment.[9] A research team selected three neighborhood com-

mercial streets in San Francisco. They based their selection on the census to find streets in low-, middle-, and high-income neighborhoods. They made sure that the three streets had the same width and length and the same building typology, with stacked flats above retail stores. They counted mailboxes to check the density; they also counted traffic volumes. They mapped the frequencies of entrances and cataloged the types of stores to establish that each street provided similar services and that the number and size of stores were similar. They also analyzed activities in the public realm and mapped the distribution of public, semipublic, and private spaces. This inventory revealed that the three streets were relatively similar. If there had been significant differences, the team would have had to find substitutes that were a better match.

They then took ten-minute pedestrian counts in the morning, afternoon, and evening on a weekday and on weekends. They mapped the activities they observed and noted them by type. They also walked around the block in each of their three sites during the same times of day and week. During these walks they recorded number, location, age group, and the ethnicity of the people they observed. Knowing that Jane Jacobs had coined the much-used phrase "eyes on the street," the team rated each storefront with regard to its transparency—the ability to look inside as well as out onto the sidewalk. Jacobs focused her "eyes on the street" not as avant-garde flâneur but as an activist concerned about personal safety and the pleasures of chance encounters associated with everyday urbanism.[10]

People walked in and out of stores, walked with purpose, or strolled and stopped to chat on all three mixed-use streets. The middle-income street had the widest range of activities, and residents engaged with each other most frequently. In the middle- and high-income neighborhoods activities only took place on the mixed-use street, and generally not on the surrounding streets. Only in the low-income streets did the team observe additional activities on neighboring streets, such as kids playing and car washing or people hanging out in front of stoops.

The team conducted two surveys; first they interviewed twenty people on each street and then they hand delivered a survey to fifty randomly selected households in the vicinity of each mixed-use street. Residents reported that they used the mixed-use street frequently, most indicated daily. In the wealthy neighborhood, daily use was somewhat less common. Among the residents who responded, most had lived in the neighborhood for ten years or more. The residents in the three income groups gave slightly different reasons for what they found attractive in their neighborhood: the "community" was the most frequent response in the low-income neighborhood, followed by "proximity to family members." In the middle-income neighborhood the residents noted "convenience" of the location, "people," and "culture"; the high-income group also gave "convenience" and "location" as reasons for the attractiveness of their mixed-use street. Interestingly, when asked to select from a list of adjectives that best described the mixed-use neighborhood street, all three groups of residents chose "noisy, crowded, unique, interesting, fun, vibrant, lively, and convenient." Residents in the low-income neighborhood added "unsafe, inexpensive, and dirty." The wealthy residents described their mixed-use street as "homogeneous," which was not a term selected by any of the middle- and low-income groups to describe their neighborhood mixed-use street. When asked to circle on a map the area they considered to be "their neighborhood," almost everybody included the mixed-use street. When asked how likely they were to stop and say hello to someone they would meet on a walk on their neighborhood shopping

Figure 3.2 Three San Francisco commercial streets, vibrant with activities but located in different socio-economic areas. A street (top) in the affluent Pacific Heights district; (middle) a street in the middle income Noe Valley; and (bottom) a street in the low income Mission district.

street, people in the middle-income group felt that such encounters were very likely, the low- and high-income residents indicated that such interactions were less likely.

Social conditions have changed in the half-century that has elapsed since Jane Jacobs wrote about her observations. She never doubted that middle- and higher-income residents would take advantage of mixed-use streets. And, by her standards, the middle-income neighborhood in this study was clearly the most vibrant, but each neighborhood achieved vibrancy in somewhat different ways depending not necessarily on income, but on the design and distribution of the uses that are mixed into the residential neighborhoods. The two more-affluent streets had 1.5 to 3.0 times as many pedestrians on the weekend than the less-affluent street, and the difference was even greater during the week. The middle-income street outshone the other streets on almost every variable, from frequency of visits, to likelihood of seeing someone they knew, to stopping and chatting.

What would have troubled Jane Jacobs in learning about these findings would have been that respondents on the low-income street rarely "meet with friends" along the shopping street: they do so occasionally in front of their homes on side streets but rarely on the shopping street. The contemporary low-income neighborhood commercial street lacks the kind of activities that Jacobs described fifty years ago. Indeed, the range of activities varied by a factor of four for certain days, suggesting that income has an effect on the degree and nature of activities along a local main street. Middle- and high-income groups frequent public places. Higher incomes today are closely correlated with more flexible work schedules, especially for those working in the information technology sector of San Francisco's economy. There is evidence of more leisure in today's society, and those with leisure take advantage of public life, if high-quality public spaces exist. Middle- and high-income people do socialize in public streets. Knowing of and being part of a so-cial network for working-class residents of inner city neighborhoods was of interest to Jane Jacobs. In this example, low-income residents do not seem to have the time and means, or feel discouraged from, taking part in street life to the extent that she described in her book. A possible explanation is found in unrelated research on the effect of youth gang affiliation on various public health outcomes. The research was conducted in the same neighborhood in San Francisco by the City's Public Health Department and found that gang activity can have a significant effect on the nature, frequency, and location of activities, especially of youth.[11] Discouragement from participating in street life could come from gang-related activities. Impressed by the importance of variables unrelated to design, I have recently confirmed that the homicide rate in the low-income area is in evidence and virtually absent in the other two neighborhoods.

Density and Vitality

The study on neighborhoods mentioned in the previous section kept density constant; the main variable was income, or socioeconomic status. In another study researchers[12] used two matched pairs of neighborhood commercial streets to test how residential density affects vitality. The team selected shopping streets located in four neighborhoods with densities of 45, 32, 25, and 15 housing units per acre.

Foot traffic on the shopping street was greater in the two higher-density neighborhoods within each pair, both in terms of the number of pedestrians per hour and proportionally to the square footage of public space available to pedestrians. In the more densely populated areas the majority of pedestrians arrived at the shopping street on foot, and they came from the adjacent neighborhoods. In the lower-density neighborhoods the majority of the pedestrians came from neighborhoods further away and reached the shopping street predominantly by car.

This finding might be obvious, but the team also tested for familiarity with the offerings of a local retail street, resident's affinity as measured

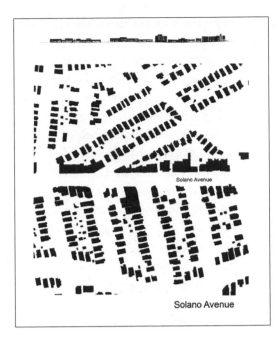

Solano Avenue

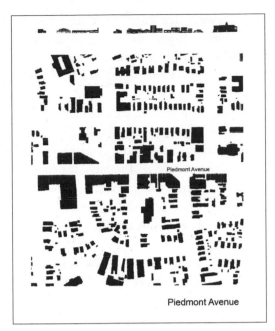

Piedmont Avenue

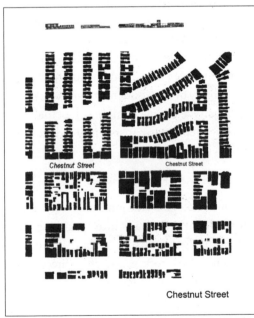

Chestnut Street

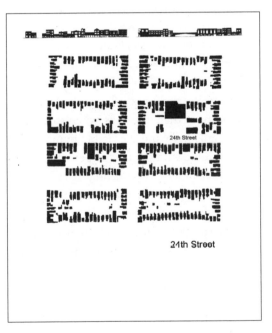

24th Street

Figure 3.3 Four neighborhood shopping streets, with densities ranging from 15 du/acre (upper left), 25 du/acre (upper right), 32 du/acre (lower right), and 45 du/acre (lower left). The building footprint maps show the different densities.

in satisfaction with the local shopping street, friendly encounters with other users, and recall of detailed design features.

The evidence for affinity was ambiguous, with residents in the higher-density neighborhoods slightly more satisfied. Similarly, the evidence of intimacy was weak. The number of chance meetings was slightly higher in the higher-density neighborhoods, while there was no difference in the perceived friendliness from neighborhood to neighborhood.

These results suggest that the internal dynamics of a neighborhood play a significant role in mediating the relationship between density and the listed dependent variables. For example, the rate of turnover in the neighborhood, or tenure of the residents, can overwhelm the positive effects of a larger population associated with higher density.

Importantly, density is a relative measure. Residential streets of identical density, as in housing units or people per acre, can be perceived differently depending upon physical, but also social, variables. Amos Rappoport[13] wrote that the perception of density is influenced by those characteristics that confirm the sense of being in a crowded environment.

A wide variety of studies indicate that facade articulation and the number of visible windows influence people's perception of density more so than other variables. Respondents will judge residential density to be lower than it really is, when architectural detailing is high and the visible number of windows low. One study tested the perception of density on three inner-city residential streets with multifamily row housing and relatively similar densities ranging from 35 to 41 to 47 units per acre. Street frontages with a uniform appearance, many visible windows, and without much detail were judged as denser than street frontages that have individually recessed or protruding entrances and individual roofs facing the street

Respondents, after visiting the three streets in separate groups in random order, ranked the street with the higher articulation as much lower in density compared to streets with relatively similar density but less articulation.[14] The team found that density is perceived differently from the traditional methods customarily used (i.e., people per acre or units per acre), but perceived density is closely associated with actual density when measured as total facade area per linear foot of street. The same team also asked local residents to compare the density of their street to the other two streets by showing photo boards. Residents on the slightly lower density street of thirty-five units per acre ranked their own street highest. These residents, of course, did so with the experience of living on their street. High degree of facade articulation and low window count on their own street were not the clues they used in their judgment. They most clearly related density to available parking and possibly other social conditions such as the number of acquaintances. Residents of the somewhat higher density street of forty-seven units per acre ranked their street lower in comparison to the street with many windows and little facade articulation.

Other studies tested the same research question in lower-density neighborhoods of twenty-four units per acre. At this medium density, it has been demonstrated that design features commonly associated with single-family residences such as individual entrances and landscaped front yards skew the ability by nonresidents to perceive multifamily density as being as high as it actually exists.[15] Here, density is consistently judged to be lower than it actually is.

Creating Vibrant Public Spaces

American sociologist and journalist William H. Whyte made major inroads into specifying standards for urban public spaces.[16] Holly Whyte, as he was known in New York, did so after direct observation, frequently with time-lapsed photography, combined with informal interviews of selected individuals like doormen of office buildings or police

Figure 3.4 Three residential streets with similar density: (top) 47 du/acre, (middle) 41 du/acre, and (bottom) 35 du/acre. The different facade articulation and different fenestration influence people's judgment of density. After a walk-through, subjects ranked the density of the top and bottom streets as low and the density of the street in the middle as high.

GREENWICH STREET
Windows, Entrances and Garage Doors

LEGEND

⊞ WINDOWS

▨ ENTRANCES

▬ GARAGE

Street Building Artculation

LEGEND

▬ Mass Articulation (+45")

▨ Element Articulation (18"-48")

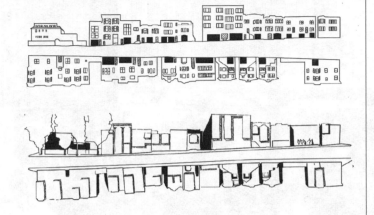

FRANCISCO STREET
Windows, Entrances and Garage Doors

LEGEND

⊞ WINDOWS

▨ ENTRANCES

▬ GARAGE DOORS

Street Building Artculation

LEGEND

▬ MASS ARTICULATION (+48")

▨ ELEMENT ATRICULATION (18" - 48")

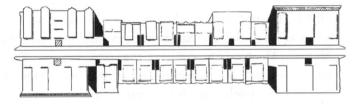

FLORIDA STREET
Windows, Entrances and Garage Doors

LEGEND

⊞⊞ WINDOWS

▨ ENTRANCES

▬ GARAGE DOORS

Street Building Artculation

LEGEND

▬ Mass Articulation (+45")

▨ Element Articulation (18"-48")

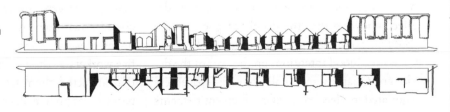

0'   20'   40'

Figure 3.5 Plaza for people watching on San Francisco's Market Street.

design were adopted by the New York Planning Commission as part of the 1982 Midtown Plan together with detailed instruction about the use of trees to provide shade in plazas, the preference for retail frontage facing the plaza, lighting and access, and provisions to sell food. In Manhattan, the redesign of Bryant Park between Fifth and Sixth avenues was the first midtown open-space to benefit from Whyte's research.

San Francisco adopted similar standards in its 1986 Downtown Plan. A research team[18] formed to evaluate the open place standards in 1995, nine years after they had been legislated. While excellent as a research topic, nine years proved to be too short a time to evaluate the new standards because too few plazas had been built to provide a comparable pool of potential users.

The group decided to substitute plazas built prior to design guideline adoption that met all the same requirements. This strategy changed the research question from whether the adoption of San Francisco's plaza design guidelines resulted in higher-quality plazas to whether the guidelines themselves are sound. One of the stronger conclusions was that significantly more people used the plazas that explicitly followed the design standards. This suggests that the mandatory approach toward plaza design has value.

Ten years earlier, in 1985, during a period when many plazas were built, a team[19] studied San Francisco's downtown open spaces suspecting user preferences based upon gender. The team asked office workers at their workplaces about attributes that attracted them to urban plazas and urban parks. Clear preferences emerged that went beyond the convenience of proximity. The team selected two different types of plazas, one a highly *urban*

officers. The importance of his observations was underscored by the fact that public open space in Midtown Manhattan was growing at a staggering rate in the 1960s due to zoning requirements and incentives for public plazas at the ground level of every new office building. By 1972 twenty acres of the world's most expensive plaza space had accumulated, but much of it was useless as an amenity, and as a consequence was not used.[17] Many plazas were cold and windy with no place to sit. Whyte recommended that plazas have places to sit—to be precise, one linear foot of seating for each square foot of plaza area. He included instructions to guarantee the comfort, accessibility, and orientation of the seating. His recommendations were quite detailed, knowing that the details of good design would be overlooked if not specified, as he could not assume good intentions on the part of the developers. Quantity and quality of plaza space were negotiated in a legal context in which entitlements were assigned. There was much at stake for the project sponsors. Whyte's recommendations on plaza

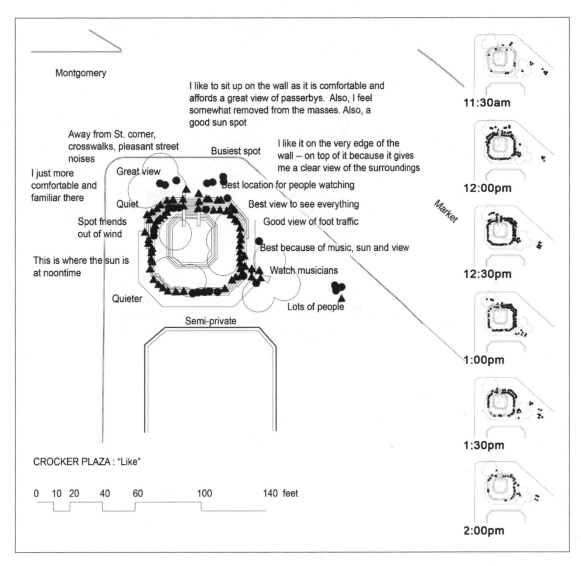

Figure 3.6 The UC Berkeley research team counted people in this San Francisco downtown plaza every half hour and recorded what users had to say about the pros and cons of the plaza.

place at a street intersection, the other more secluded and heavily landscaped. Their results indicated that plazas through their design and location satisfied different values, including some gender-specific differences.

Beginning with a plaza alongside a busy street corner, the team observed a very large number of users, 709 to 779 counted cumulatively every fifteen minutes over three hours; the majority (70 percent) were men. The team observed that women who came here were more likely to arrive in small groups, while men were more likely to come on their own. The plaza clearly attracted those interested in watching other people and being in a public place as passive observers. Holly Whyte made the same observation in Midtown Manhattan. He also wrote that he had never observed a "people watcher" making a "pass" at a woman walking by.

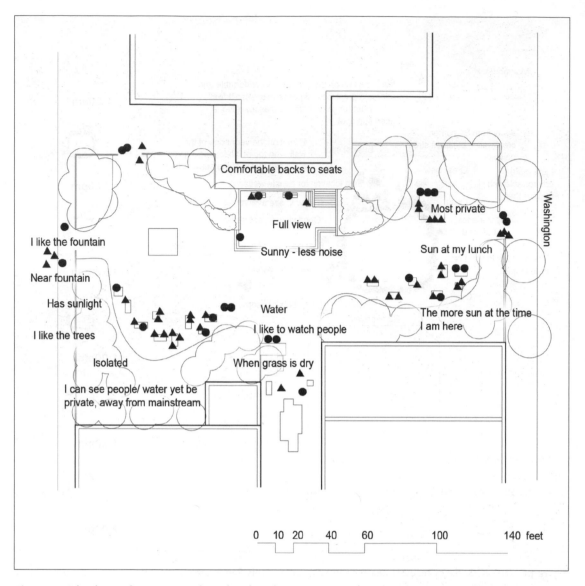

Washington

Comfortable backs to seats

Full view

Sunny - less noise

Most private

Sun at my lunch

I like the fountain

Near fountain

Has sunlight

I like the trees

Water

I like to watch people

The more sun at the time
I am here

Isolated

When grass is dry

I can see people/ water yet be
private, away from mainstream

0   10 20   40   60   100   140 feet

Figure 3.7 A landscaped retreat at Redwood Park in downtown San Francisco. The team recorded what users had to say about the pros and cons of the park.

The team selected a second type of space that users described as closed, intimate, controlled, socially predictable, and green. Counts revealed that men and women appreciate such qualities more equally.

The small park located a few blocks from the plaza was much less used in absolute numbers (approximately 365 people over the same time span,

with half being women), despite being seven times the size of the plaza alongside the busy street corner. Those who spend their lunchtime at the park also came from a larger distance than the users of the street corner plaza. There are multiple possible reasons for this, the most apparent being that the street corner plaza held greater attraction as a people-watching place when it was crowded. The

a

b

c

d

e

Figure 3.8 Bollards in Lucca. On the main square in the Tuscan town of Lucca men gather leaning against bollards (a). Generally one man is joined by another (b), which in turn attracts a third man (c). The little gathering might break up, but once the bollard becomes free, inevitably another man will lean against it (d). Women do not seem to participate in this ritual (e).

design and location of the park, on the other hand, would make people leave, or not even go there, if it was crowded because people did not come to watch others. On the other hand, if nobody was there, people would also be reluctant to sit down. The park had appeal as a place to rest, read a book, or talk to the person one had come with.

The work of Jan Gehl,[20] Lars Gemzoe,[21] and their colleagues at the Public Space Research Center in Copenhagen provides ample evidence that city spaces can be designed or converted to become places full of vitality. After observing public life in the squares of Italian cities, Gehl developed his methods for interpreting human behavior in relation to spatial configuration.

The theoretical underpinnings for Gehl's early work came from the anthropologist Edward T. Hall,[22] the author of the "Proxemic Theory," the study of human use of space within the context of culture. Gehl repeatedly tested a theory that is based on human gathering traits: The presence of people attracts other people. Necessary urban activities like delivery, going from here to there, transit use, or construction activities attract leisure activities such as watching. If there is a chance to sit down, others will join.

Initially Gehl's work was met with much skepticism. True, Italians have been observed to linger in public spaces, but his critics argued, the same was rarely true in cities with a northern climate. Through counts and systematic observations Gehl proved his critics wrong.

For over thirty years, Copenhagen has followed a policy to reduce the impact of car traffic on the city center. As council members over the years could attest, the fact that the city center functions as well as it does with much reduced car access and parking came after much discussion and a great deal of skepticism. But the transformation of streets and squares from the predominant use by cars to the use by pedestrians and bicyclists was done incrementally, and that was the reason for its success. "After successful completion of one stage, it has been possible to find understanding and political support for the next."[23] Early on, the group at the Architecture School of the Royal Danish Academy[24] searched for explanations for what attracted people to spend time in public spaces. Optional activities brought vitality to city streets, and such activities are on a steady increase when high-quality public spaces exist.

Research teams have frequently explored Gehl's interpretation of vibrant public spaces. The comparison of an urban plaza and urban park discussed earlier is one such example, with respondents in both spaces remarking that the presence of other people was the most important draw.

Two public plazas at the edge of the Berkeley campus of the University of California are known for their public quality not only to students but to all those who remember the free-speech movement and the associated political protests. The design of Lower Sproul Plaza, despite being the product of an

Figure 3.9 Social dimensions of space, Lucca. On the same square people who do not seem to know each other sit on steps but keep a predictable distance from each other (above). This is a ritual mainly performed by women, but men can be observed too (below).

international competition, is very much a failure as a public space while Upper Sproul Plaza remains one of the best examples of an urban plaza in North America. Respondents in a study conducted by a research team[25] found few positive qualities with Lower Sproul and generally saw it as a special event space ill-suited to everyday use because better places to linger existed nearby. Conversely, respondents enjoyed Upper Sproul Plaza because of the large number of people walking through. Jan Gehl's basic notion is correct: people attract other people, which in turn invites even more people to stop and linger. This observation was certainly true for the relatively young campus population at Berkeley.

The space at Upper Sproul Plaza is linear and people move through it along a predictable path. The space is not too wide—less than twenty meters. This is important because those sitting on elevated steps on one side and on benches or ledges on the other side can easily observe the whole space and, at this distance, recognize people they know. Respondents also noted the impressive rows of trees that produce comfort for those sitting in the filtered light, and the sequence of spaces, with their central location between highly used destinations and places to eat, to perform, to address groups, to watch, and to protest; all these qualities contributed to the plaza's success.

Part Two: Livability

Of the three concepts vitality, livability, and sense of place, livability is somewhat less concrete than vitality, because it is measured through a process of inquiry that focuses on individual perception and cognition. These terms describe filters that the mind uses to select, store, and act on information from the world around us. Livability research deals with environments where people express preferences for qualities associated with physical settings such as streets with well-managed traffic, comfortable outdoor spaces, places to walk to, and, increasingly, a sound ecology—an integration of human activities with the forces of nature. The overlap

with the other two categories is obvious: such qualities can also contribute to a sense of place, and if sufficient people are involved, even to vitality. For designers, focusing on livability as a central concern can be the prerequisite for a sense of belonging and vitality.

Livable Streets

At a time when in American cities debates take place to demolish urban freeways, it is important to remember that already in the 1960s the intrusion of

Figure 3.10 Amager Square, Copenhagen.

Figure 3.11 Duration of stay. The information was captured from time-lapsed photography; the darker the hatching the longer a person stayed for the maximum duration of an hour, measured in quarter-hour intervals. People obviously had various reasons that influenced their length of stay. Observed repeatedly, the method can be used to locate people's favorite places.

car traffic into people's lives was identified as one of the ubiquitous problems facing residents in cities.[26] The increase in traffic was related to the construction of urban freeways. On and off ramps channeled traffic onto streets that had not been designed to accommodate such a high level of traffic. In these locations, traffic created congestion and unsafe walking conditions, which eventually led to citizen movements against new freeways.

In Manhattan, Jane Jacobs was instrumental in blocking the building of a highway on the west side of the city. Much later, in Toronto, she helped to block the building of an urban freeway that was to go through a neighborhood west of the center of the city. In Copenhagen, the routing of the motorway into the central city from the wealthy enclaves in northern Zealand was blocked by a group of residents who had fixed balloons onto cables along the motorway's proposed alignments through their neighborhoods, through a large park, and alongside a row of lakes. In Paris, the Periferique was constructed and the controversial expressways along the Seine, while a similar proposal was defeated in London.

In the more recent past, at great cost, the Central Artery in Boston was reconstructed below ground. The future of the Alaskan Way in Seattle is still uncertain after a 2007 vote on the question of its demolition. Until recently in San Francisco, traces of the freeway revolt were still visible. Into the early 1990s, unfinished elevated freeway spurs were still pointing toward neighborhoods, where, forty years earlier, citizens had literally taken to the streets and protested the completion of the freeway grid. If a completed freeway system would not benefit San Francisco, a truncated system did not work much better. Freeway spurs had been built up to the Hayes Valley neighborhood as part of the Central Freeway, and instead of freeways connecting from there to the Golden Gate Bridge, a double pair of streets channeled freeway-level traffic through neighborhoods. Traffic on the route through Golden Gate Park and the Panhandle, a handsome linear green that runs from the park toward the center of the City, was taken up by Fell and Oak streets. The second route connected through Pacific Heights and the Marina district via Franklin and Gough streets.

The names of the second pair of streets are well known in the planning literature.[27] They are associated with the "livable streets project." In 1969, just a few years after the final defeat of freeway building in San Francisco, two students in the planning program at Berkeley, Mark Lintel and Sue Gerson, together with their instructor Donald Appleyard, measured the various side effects of traffic on the lives of residents on Franklin Street, which averaged sixteen thousand cars daily; Gough Street, which averaged eight thousand; and Octavia, one block further west, which averaged fewer than two thousand cars. Through measurements they recorded the average speed of traffic, checked traffic volumes, and measured noise. They distributed a questionnaire survey, conducted door-to-door interviews, and solicited responses from residents on selected city blocks, one on each of the three streets. They found that traffic had a detrimental effect on the lives of residents. People on Franklin and Gough streets were fearful of traffic flows. On Octavia, a street with identical width but very little traffic, residents complained about the occasional fast car, but they considered their street safe from traffic hazards. Apparently, families started to move away from the busiest street, Franklin, and leased out their homes there. Traffic formed a barrier to social interaction. Residents on the streets with heavy traffic withdrew from the physical environment of the street and were less involved in whatever took place there than residents on the street with light traffic. Accidents, noise, and fumes were the obvious side effects of through traffic, but traffic also reduced the number of friendships and acquaintances that residents would typically enjoy on a less busy street in the inner parts of the city. On the heavily trafficked Franklin Street residents would rarely consider much of the street space as part of their "home." The opposite was true two blocks away on the neighboring Octavia, the street with little traffic; here the sidewalks and the streets were very much part of people's home territory. Many residents expressed a sense of belonging.

From this initial research, the authors formulated three hypotheses to be tested in further research:

1. Heavy traffic is associated with more apartment renters and fewer owner occupants and families with children.

2. Heavy traffic is associated with much less social interaction and street activity. Conversely, a street with low traffic and many families, promotes a rich social climate and a strong sense of community.

3. Heavy traffic is associated with a with-

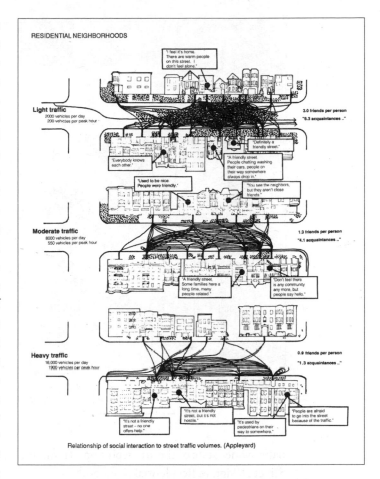

Figure 3.12 The Livable Streets Project of 1969 compared three San Francisco residential streets with different traffic volumes, low, medium, and high, and documented an inverse correlation between traffic volumes and socializing on each street. (Courtesy Appleyard Estate)

drawal from the physical environment. Conversely, residents of a street with low traffic show an acute, critical, appreciative awareness and care for the physical environment.[28]

The study was repeated in other parts of the city as research for a citywide urban design plan that proposed and partially implemented traffic calming for protected neighborhoods in San Francisco.[29] It grew to national importance in 1980 when the Federal Highway Administration funded a

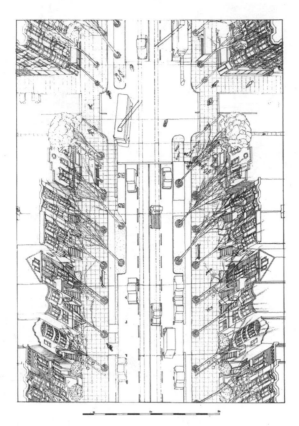
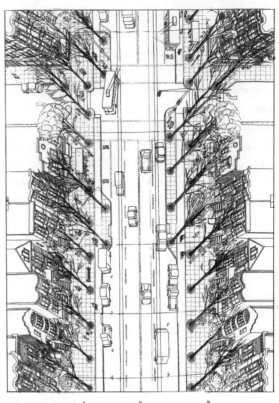

nationwide "state of the art" report on "Traffic and Street Design in Residential Neighborhoods."[30]

Internationally, the results of the study found indirect application in Holland where streets with shared surfaces for cars, pedestrians, and all other street users were introduced. The so-called Woonerven, an area where pedestrians and cyclists have legal priority over motorists, spread to other northern European countries and this type of street was designated with internationally agreed upon signage.

Altogether, the result was a great success for a small-scale research project that had grown out of an advocacy situation. However, rereading the hypothesis so many years after it was written demonstrates how variables are lumped together and how little is known about the way they interact: What else but traffic volumes determines ownership versus rental status? What else influences social interaction? What else could influence

awareness of physical space? Therefore, student research teams were sent out to gather similar measurements over time.

In 1988, almost twenty years after the original research, a team of graduate design students from Berkeley studied the same three San Francisco streets.[31] Traffic volumes on the two busy streets had grown somewhat; however, traffic speed had been reduced due to improved traffic signal timing. This had resulted in fewer accidents and somewhat lower noise levels. Density was not measured in the original study, as it was assumed to be similar along all three streets due to the identical housing stock of three-story row housing. In the new study student researchers compared the density levels of the three streets and reported higher residential density on Franklin Street compared to Gough and Octavia streets. Apparently, in the nineteen years that had elapsed, the remaining family-occupied units on Franklin Street had been converted and subdivided

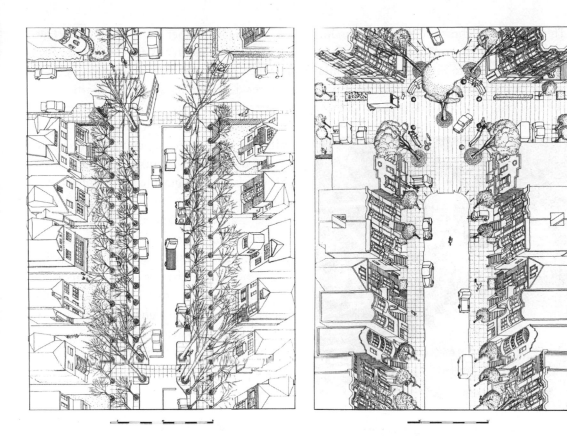

Figure 3.13 Traffic calming suggestions—for one high (far left), two medium (center left and right), and one low traffic volume street (far right). The designs buffer pedestrians from the impacts of traffic.

into smaller rental units. This finding is consistent with the original hypothesis: heavy traffic is associated with more apartment units and fewer owner-occupied units with children. But the higher density on Franklin Street makes the three streets less comparable. No longer can degrees of livability be linked only to traffic volumes.

The next group of student researchers selected two identical streets near the University of California Medical School in San Francisco.[32] The street selection seemed ideal, with two identical residential streets parallel to each other, but with substantially different levels of traffic. The heavy-traffic street, Seventh Avenue, had been designated by the City as the main route over the central ridgeline of the San Francisco Hills into the neighborhoods to the south, while Eighth Avenue remained a quiet

residential street. The results, however, did not substantiate the predicted long-term social effects as a reaction to high levels of traffic. Residents on the heavy-traffic street had lived there longer, the average number of residents per household was smaller, more households had children, and fewer units were occupied by renters than on the neighboring street with low traffic volumes. Similarly, the amount of reported street activity and the perception of home territory were not associated with traffic volumes. However, residents on the heavy-traffic street were more likely to perceive their street as less safe and the traffic as too fast and too heavy. Many had made changes to their living conditions in an attempt to mitigate the negative impacts of the traffic, such as keeping windows closed or using heavy drapes to mute the sound.

This study highlights the difficulties in finding research sites that control for confounding variables. The proximity to the medical school influenced the formation of social networks, since many of the residents on the heavy-traffic street also

Figure 3.14 Traffic calming, a shared narrow street in Copenhagen. Through traffic is discouraged. A sign posted at the beginning of the block mandates a slow speed. At midblock trees are planted to permit only one car to pass at a time. At this "choke point" children at play can be observed.

worked together at the university, thereby minimizing the effect of the traffic on the street's sociability. In addition, San Francisco's tight housing market made occupants protected by rent control stay longer. The same applies to owners, who benefit from fixed homeowner taxes if they remain on their property.

Altogether, over a dozen student research teams have repeated the original livability study in a variety of neighborhoods. Site selection challenges proved difficult to overcome for many groups. Instead of one study providing definitive proof of traffic's effect on social networks, livability, and sense of community, each study contributed some piece of knowledge, often overlapping with other studies. From this layering process, we see trends appear. First, traffic is never benign and residents never seem to get used to it; residents on higher-volume traffic streets consistently cite safety, noise, and pollution more frequently as serious issues than residents on less-trafficked streets. Second, no matter how low a volume of traffic, residents express sensitivity. This sensitivity is augmented substantially if the speed of traffic is perceived as "too fast," suggesting that traffic speed and associated noise, perhaps more than volume, are of great concern.

Third, those studies that included cognitive maps generally find that residents on streets with low traffic draw more extensive and more detailed maps than residents on highly trafficked streets. A fourth finding is related to mitigation: several research teams asked whether dense tree spacing along a heavily trafficked street is perceived to reduce the effects of traffic. The answer is no, although other benefits of densely planted trees were noted by residents, but the presence of trees alone could not mitigate the negative effects of high traffic volumes. A study[33] compared two street segments along an identical street of the same width and with identical and high traffic volumes. One segment had densely planted and majestic trees and the other segment had no trees. Student researchers found that residents on those city blocks with densely planted trees identified a more extensive home territory than residents on city blocks with sparsely planted trees, suggesting that the presence of trees improves residents' ability to identify street segments and possibly improves the overall desirability of the street.

Finally, a study gave detailed insight into the relationship between traffic and how children use and perceive their street environment. A Berkeley team[34] selected two suburban housing tract developments, each with an elementary school. One school was located adjacent to a high-traffic-volume street, with other high-volume streets nearby. The second school was located along a quiet street, and the surrounding neighborhood did not suffer from high volumes of through traffic. Neither neighborhood had extensive sidewalk networks.

As one might expect, children in the low-traffic neighborhood were more likely to walk or bike to school than children in the high-traffic neighborhood. Although the team did not detect differences in travel speeds between the two neighborhoods, parents in the neighborhood with high traffic expressed much greater concern about child safety. Most illuminating, the children seem to fully comprehend the limits that traffic places on their lives. Cognitive maps drawn by children from the low-traffic neighborhood were more complex, contained more information, exhibited greater connectivity between a wider range of destinations, and expressed a greater sense of place around the school, as well as the space between home and school. Conversely, children from the more heavily traveled neighborhood drew maps that showed greater detail immediately around the home, which may reflect the more limited home territory as a result of the proximity to highly trafficked streets. Children from the high-traffic neighborhood also drew more places they did not like, as well as almost seven times more places that they perceived to be dangerous. Interestingly, automobiles were drawn on 80 percent of the maps made by children from the high-traffic neighborhood and only on 20 percent of the maps drawn by the other group. The children, however, reported no difference in the number of homes where friends lived.

One general conclusion to be drawn from the original Livable Streets studies and confirmed by the subsequent studies was to avoid channeling through-traffic along neighborhood streets, but concentrating it along nonresidential streets. Many U.S. cities adopted citywide traffic management plans following this principle, frequently with limited success. In virtually all cities a great number of arterial streets function also as residential streets. Heavy traffic cannot be confined to only nonresidential streets.

Another alternative is to distribute traffic more evenly throughout the street grid. In North America, the Congress for the New Urbanism,[35] an advocacy group for traditional urban development

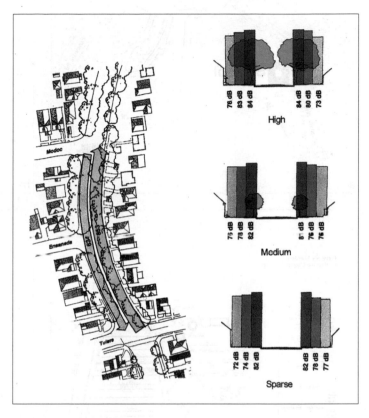

Figure 3.15 Trees, traffic, and noise during afternoon traffic volumes. Trees do not block sound, but a distance of thirty feet from traffic reduces sound by ten decibels. The top street section is lined with mature trees, the middle section has small trees, the bottom section has no trees.

patterns, recommends that cities take advantage of a grid's permeability, distributing traffic over a grid, versus concentrating it. While promising as a theory, perfect citywide permeability is very difficult to achieve because a city's road system is rarely ever robustly connected due to constricted flow conditions or blockages. Instead, in the layout of new subdivisions, arterial streets are increasingly designed as limited access roads.

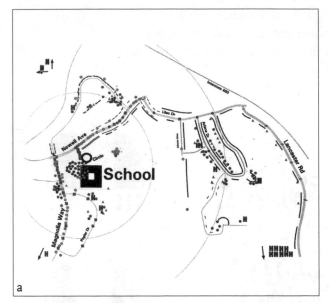

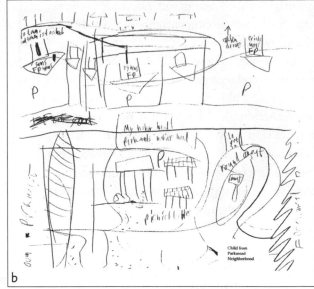

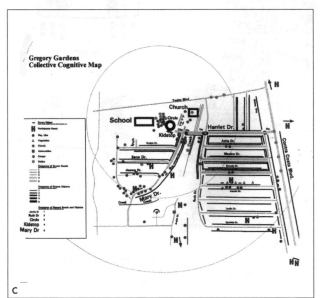

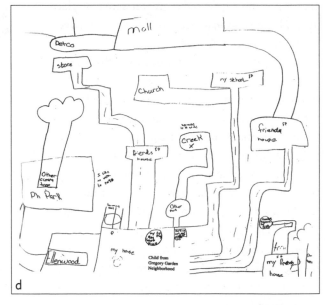

Figure 3.16 Schools and traffic. (a) Composite cognitive map from the Parkmead Neighborhood, a neighborhood with heavy through traffic. (b) A single student's cognitive map. (c) Composite cognitive map from the Gregory Garden neighborhood. (d) A single student's cognitive map.

In subdivisions, residents frequently live alongside, but not with, an address on the arterial streets; only backyards abut the arterial street. Front entrances to homes and driveways are oriented away from the arterials toward local streets in the center of the neighborhood. The arterials run through no-man's-land; they separate neighborhoods and encourage the use of automobiles even for very short trips, like picking up a child from a friend's house in an adjacent neighborhood. The crossing of arterials on foot or on a bicycle is not encouraged, nor, as the previous example showed, are schools or neigh-

Figure 3.17 Reconfiguring the suburb. The existing condition, on the left, shows a road pattern with wide roads. Imagine an additional neighborhood to the left of the one shown. The addition would require a new road along the backyard fences of the existing neighborhood. This arterial street would be designed like a limited-access road connecting the occasional intersections. Instead such a new road should be lined with higher-density multifamily housing and some commerce at the intersection. This would facilitate an intersection with pedestrian crossings and potentially a bus stop. In the image on the right the road width of all interior streets was reduced from thirty-six feet to twenty-five feet without hindering circulation or access by emergency vehicles. The lot sizes and home sizes have remained the same. This change would permit construction of a row of multifamily homes facing the new hypothetical street. (Courtesy John Sugrue)

borhood stores easily integrated into the layout of such neighborhoods.[36]

Great Streets

The repertoire of street types is greatly enriched by a residential boulevard design that carries significant amounts of traffic but is also attractive to live on,[37] such as the Paseo di Gracia in Barcelona (see figure 3.18). The design of the street protects residents from the negative effects of traffic, but also effectively connects neighborhoods with other parts of the city and accommodates all modes of transportation, including walking and bicycling. This street type is not new. After travels to Paris, Thomas Jefferson drew a diagram for a boulevard design for Pennsylvania Avenue in Washington, DC (see figure 3.19).

Through Allan Jacobs' drawings and narrative the residential boulevard has been brought back as a potential remedy for today's traffic problems.[38] In *Great Streets* Jacobs describes, among many other such streets, how two such boulevards designed by

Frederick Law Olmsted and Calvert Vaux function today: Ocean Parkway and Eastern Parkway (see figure 3.20). Both were built in the 1870s as part of what was intended to be an extensive system of parkways weaving through Brooklyn. Their purpose was to structure anticipated suburban development and to serve as linear greenways linking residential areas with parks and the seashore.[39] Ocean Parkway and Eastern Parkway were the only ones built, and they functioned initially as pleasure drives through fields and gardens.[40]

Olmsted separated the center roadways from the local access roads with double rows of trees on side medians that were thirty-five feet wide. In New York these linear strips of green were called malls because they originally accommodated horseback riding trails, but they now function as pedestrian walks.[41] By the early-twentieth century, the parkways became populated with residents who lived in brownstone row houses, and, further from the city, in semiattached single-family homes. Residents began to use the parkway like a linear recreation

Figure 3.18 Paseo di Gracia, Barcelona.

space. They strolled along the malls, used the benches, played games, and gathered after religious services in front of the many churches and synagogues that moved from the inner city. A drive along the parkways today confirms that all these activities are still in evidence and that the homes are well kept and apparently in demand. Yet it is fair to say that streets like Ocean Parkway and Eastern Parkway are unlikely to get built today. Traffic engineers would assume that intersections with separate roadways invite accidents, as cars turning from the local access streets into center lanes might collide with faster moving traffic. But research into accident and automobile safety shows that boulevards are not more prone to accidents than conventionally designed streets.[42]

To determine the livability of the Brooklyn park-ways the author, together with Elizabeth Macdonald and Thomas Kronenmeier, interviewed residents on the Eastern Parkway and the Ocean Parkway, as well as on the Esplanade, a residential boulevard in suburban Chico, California, but not a street designed by Olmsted.[43] All three boulevards follow the same design, center lanes for heavy traffic, and landscaped malls with single or double rows of trees, local access streets, and sidewalks with trees along the curbs. The residential density along the three boulevards differed considerably. The Eastern Parkway block, with two- and three-story brownstone row houses, had a net density of approximately thirty dwelling units per acre. The Ocean Parkway block, with semiattached, two-story, single-family homes, had approximately eleven units per acre. The Esplanade block had the

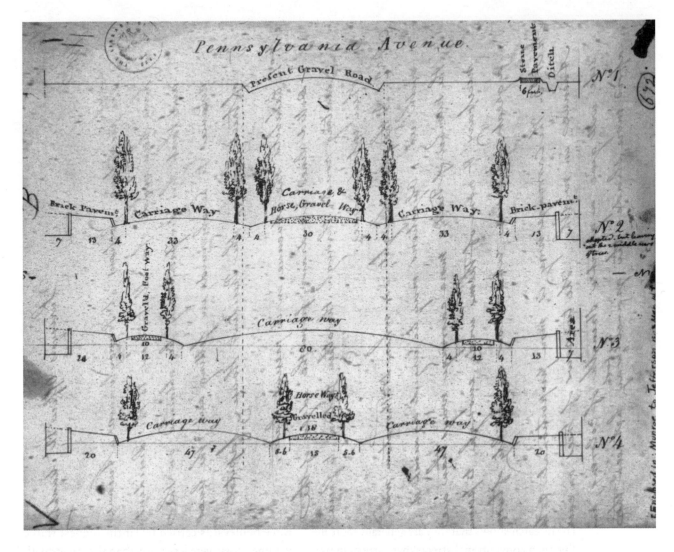

Figure 3.19 Thomas Jefferson, *Alternative Designs for Pennsylvania Avenue, Washington, DC. Source*: CED visual archives, Berkeley.

lowest density, four units per acre. In the immediate vicinity of each boulevard, the team selected two conventionally designed streets with identical density and housing stock, but different traffic volumes, one medium and one low. Through this selection the difference in each of the three settings included a boulevard street, where the placement of homes was significantly removed from the intrusion of traffic by the landscaped malls and the local access streets. On the other two streets in each sample residents lived closer to traffic. Thus they studied a total of nine streets: three boulevards with heavy traffic, three streets with medium traffic, and three streets with light traffic.

The three boulevards are known in their cities for the significant amount of traffic they carry. They are also known as historic streets. But mostly they are known for their strong linear character and their formal design, with evenly spaced trees on the medians. The team asked residents what it is like to live on such a street and to what extent traffic affects livability there. Boulevards are special streets.

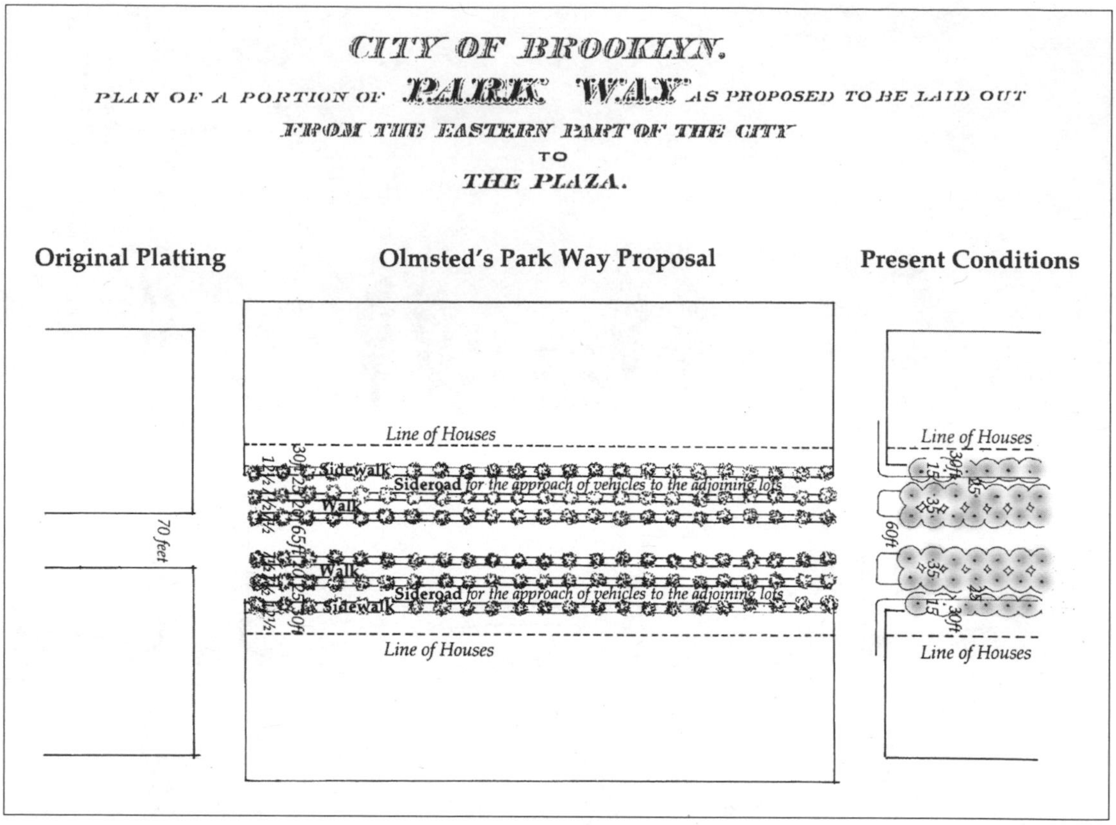

CITY OF BROOKLYN.

PLAN OF A PORTION OF **PARK WAY** *AS PROPOSED TO BE LAID OUT*

FROM THE EASTERN PART OF THE CITY

TO

THE PLAZA.

Original Platting   **Olmsted's Park Way Proposal**   **Present Conditions**

Line of Houses

Sidewalk   *Sideroad for the approach of vehicles to the adjoining lots*   *Walk*

Walk   *Sideroad for the approach of vehicles to the adjoining lots*   *Sidewalk*

Line of Houses

Line of Houses

Line of Houses

Figure 3.20 Frederick Law Olmsted and Calvert Vaux's design for the Eastern Parkway, Brooklyn. (Redrawn from a copy, CED visual archives)

The research shows that they are generally more livable than conventional streets that carry high traffic volumes. Still, boulevards are not a panacea for all the ills of residential arterials. For example, few rights of way in inner cities are wide enough to accommodate a boulevard, which requires at least 120 feet (40 meters), or better yet 150 feet. In places where such width exists, boulevards are possible.

In the field the team measured traffic volumes, speed, and noise. The Esplanade in suburban Chico had the fastest travel speeds of the nine streets. In fact, drivers drove fast on all three Chico streets. The second-highest average travel speed was recorded on Ocean Parkway, followed by East First Street in Chico and the Eastern Parkway.

As the drawings in figure 3.22 show, though the three boulevards carried by far the highest traffic volumes, they were less noisy than the streets with medium traffic. This is an important finding because it helps to interpret the comments residents made in response to door-to-door surveys. The team measured traffic noise at the nearest curb line in front of properties, always at a mid-block location. In the three boulevard examples these curb-lines are at a sizeable distance from the traffic lanes in the center of the roadway, where much of the noise originates.

On the conventionally designed streets with medium and light traffic, the curb-line is in direct proximity to the source of the traffic noise. The noisiest street is East First Street in suburban Chico, where the sixty-five-decibel (dcB) threshold

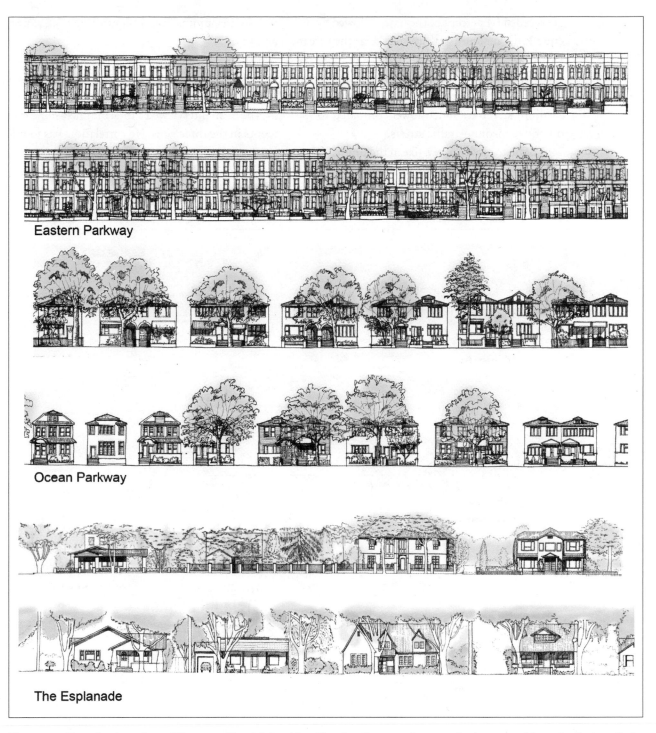

Figure 3.21 Three boulevards at different residential densities. The elevations are drawn at the same graphic scale. Eastern Parkway, Brooklyn (top two rows), Ocean Parkway, Brooklyn (middle rows), Esplanade, Chico, California (bottom rows). (Courtesy Elizabeth Macdonald, top and middle, Thomas Konemeyer, bottom)

is exceeded 65 percent of the time, followed by Avenue P, the medium-traffic street near the Ocean Parkway, followed by the Eastern Parkway, where the sixty-five-decible threshold is exceeded 49 percent of the time, but here the traffic volumes on the medium street are much lower compared to the other two medium-traffic streets.

A door-to-door survey, like in the original "Livable Streets" research, allowed residents to choose an answer from nominally scaled responses.[44] The results are summarized in figures 3.23, 3.24, 3.25 and 3.26.

Four open-ended questions asked residents to describe particular aspects of their street in their own words; one question is summarized in figure 3.25.

The team interviewed a total of ninety-nine residents in the three sites. No correlation was found between traffic volumes and owner or renter occupancy. Seven of the nine streets had an equal number of owners and renters: owners predominated

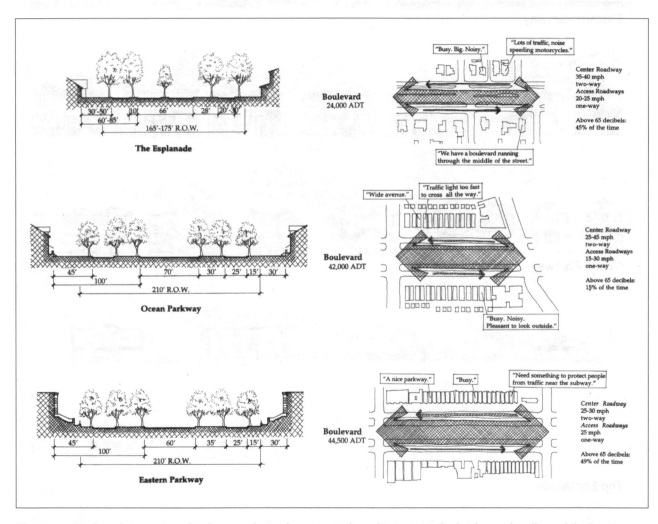

Figure 3.22 Boulevards in section, the diagram shows the main roadway dimensions, the landscaped malls, and the local access streets. The separation of through traffic from local traffic makes higher traffic volumes possible. The diagram also shows speed and noise. Noise levels measured at property lines are lower when compared to noise levels measured in the same location on conventional streets; this is due to the greater distance between traffic and residential homes. (Courtesy Elizabeth Macdonald)

on the two other streets. On all three Chico streets, half the residents surveyed owned their homes and half were renters. The proportion was similar for all three streets in the Eastern Parkway group. The majority of Ocean Parkway residents owned their homes; the same was also true on Avenue P, the street with medium traffic. On East Seventh Street the households were evenly split between owners and renters.

Appleyard and Lintel predicted an inverse correlation between traffic volume and number of households with children. This was true in suburban Chico as well as in the Ocean Parkway group of streets, but not on the Eastern Parkway group. Here the highest number of children lived on the parkway. Friendship patterns on the two Brooklyn boulevards were just as frequent as on the streets with light traffic; residents on the medium-traffic streets had half the number of acquaintances. Judging from the maps where residents drew lines between their home and those of friends and acquaintances, the landscaped malls on the Brooklyn boulevards connected neighbors socially, but neighbors rarely knew residents across the boulevard.

Comparing length of residence with friendship patterns revealed no correlation on most streets. In Chico, Esplanade residents had lived there longer than residents on the other two streets, yet residents on the Esplanade had the fewest neighborhood friends. Eastern Parkway residents had lived there as briefly as two to three years but had the highest number of friends in the entire sample of nine streets, which might be a function of the higher density; yet also higher than the two neighboring streets,

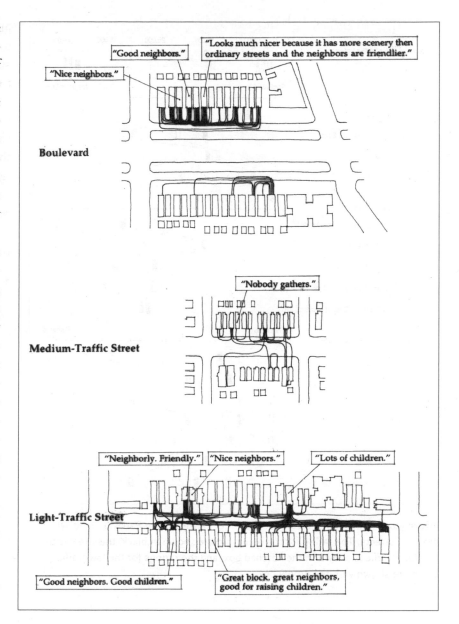

Figure 3.23 Social interaction and activities on the Ocean Parkway, Brooklyn, group of streets. (Courtesy Elizabeth Macdonald)

which are of identical density. The presence of children on the street had a compounding effect on friendship patterns on the Eastern Parkway. However, on the Ocean Parkway, neighbors with fewer children maintained more friendships on their block than on the street with a medium amount of traffic, where a somewhat higher number of children lived.

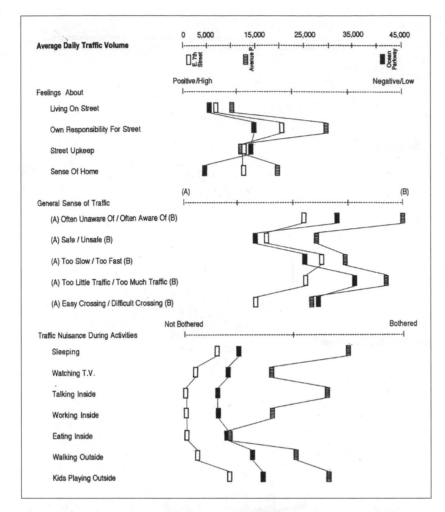

Figure 3.24 Awareness and care for the street for the Ocean Parkway, Brooklyn group of streets. The rating for the boulevard are shown in black, the street with medium traffic is shown in the hatched box, and the ratings for the low-traffic street are shown with the empty box.

gregations that require their members to live within walking distance of their synagogue, so these residents are likely to know each other from social settings other than their street. However, these social issues are conditions that are shared by all residents in each group of the three streets. In all three cases the team had no reason to believe that they affected socializing on the one street more than on another.

Our research led to the following conclusions:

• Overall, residents on heavy-traffic boulevards rated their living conditions as very high. The finding is significant because traffic volumes on the boulevards far exceeded those on the medium streets, where residents rated their living conditions as much lower. Only residents on the streets with light traffic rated their living conditions higher than did residents on boulevards. Therefore, we determined that the distance between the traffic lanes and the property line provided by the landscaped malls and the local access roads on boulevards mitigate the negative impacts of heavy traffic.

This finding is supported largely by the noise measurements. For example, noise levels measured at the property line exceeded the sixty-five-decible thresholds more frequently on the medium-traffic streets than on the boulevards. Exposure to traffic noise is related to the distance between the center lanes, where the noise is generated, and building facades' windows. On the three boulevards this distance was never less than sixty feet, and in most cases eighty-five to one hundred feet, while on the streets with medium and light traffic,

Social issues that might bring neighbors together or keep them apart existed in all three study areas. In Chico, the three selected streets were in a neighborhood where students from the nearby state university lived among long-term residents. The Eastern Parkway streets are located in a section of Brooklyn, which has suffered, in the recent past, from tensions between differing racial, ethnic, and religious groups. Along the Ocean Parkway streets residents frequently belong to orthodox Jewish conit ranged from twenty-five to forty feet. Residents on the three boulevards live more substantially removed from traffic, which is likely to produce the psychological and physiological distance necessary to reduce the impact of traffic on their daily lives. The closely spaced trees do not reduce sound, but they offer a visual screen that reduces people's awareness of traffic. For example, the boulevard residents were generally not bothered by the speed of traffic in the center lanes of their street. The measurements indicated that cars traveled a good deal faster on the boulevards than on the medium-traffic streets, but residents on the medium-traffic streets consistently judged the traffic on their street to be too fast. This also suggests that residents' perceptions of speed are modified by the degree to which desired activities are impacted by fast-moving traffic.

- Boulevard residents are not necessarily renters as Appleyard predicted for a population that lives on heavy-traffic streets, half or more are homeowners who have lived in their homes as long as residents on the other streets.

Again, the findings are significant. The inverse correlation between high traffic volumes and low home ownership or short tenure does not apply to boulevards. In fact, boulevard residents value their street as a special place. They are aware of their street's special configuration, appreciative of its history, and satisfied with the location of their residence despite the high traffic volumes.

Consistently, the three boulevards are used as linear parks by neighbors; people walk, ride their bikes or roller skate, sit on benches, jog, and walk

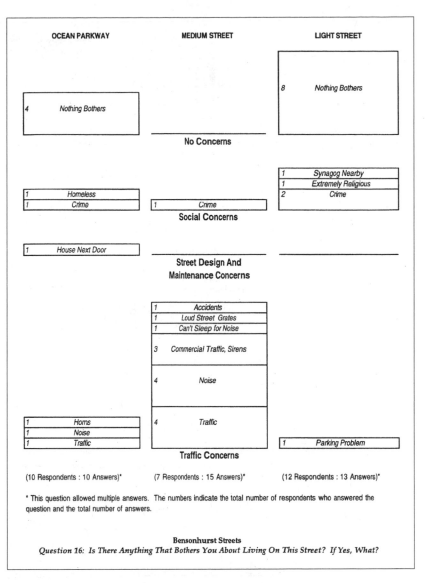

Figure 3.25 Concerns about living on the street, Ocean Parkway, Brooklyn, group of streets.

their dogs, and as they carry out these activities, they interact. Residents on the boulevards observe these activities.

The three boulevards ranked equal or second to the light-traffic streets in terms of residents' awareness and care for their street. The residents were not withdrawn, they suffered less from the negative effects of traffic than residents on

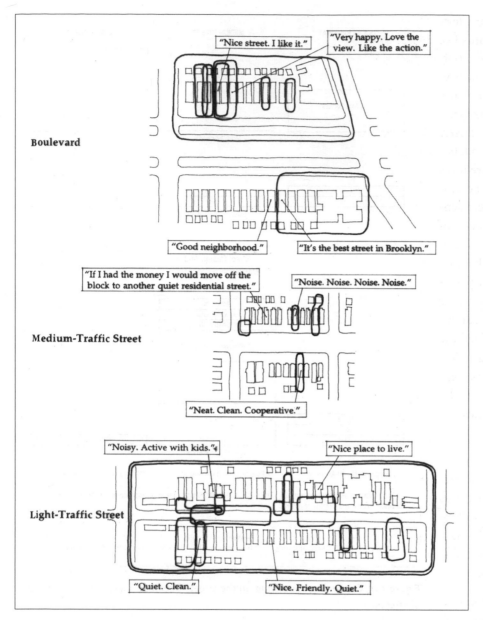

Boulevard

"Nice street. I like it."

"Very happy. Love the view. Like the action."

"Good neighborhood."

"It's the best street in Brooklyn."

"If I had the money I would move off the block to another quiet residential street."

"Noise. Noise. Noise. Noise."

Medium-Traffic Street

"Neat. Clean. Cooperative."

"Noisy. Active with kids."

"Nice place to live."

Light-Traffic Street

"Quiet. Clean."

"Nice. Friendly. Quiet."

Figure 3.26 Sense of home on the Ocean Parkway, Brooklyn, group of streets. (Courtesy Elizabeth Macdonald)

that Appleyard's team had studied over thirty-five years earlier. The removal of the Central Freeway would not have happened if it had not been triggered by the October 17, 1989, Loma Prieta earthquake. It struck at 5:04 in the afternoon, with a magnitude of 6.9 on the Richter scale, and took the lives of 63 people, injuring 3,757 others. Two-thirds of the dead were traveling home on elevated urban freeways during the afternoon rush hour, mainly the Cypress structure in West Oakland. But the quake also damaged the Embarcadero Freeway, the San Francisco–Oakland Bay Bridge, and the Central Freeway in San Francisco.

Of course, it would have been possible to reconstruct the damaged elevated freeways and upgrade the seismic engineering to standards that were revised after the Kobe earthquake in 1996. Instead, in a sequence of public referenda, the decision was made to reroute the freeway structure in Oakland and to replace the two elevated urban freeways in San Francisco with surface roadways.

The 1989 earthquake changed traffic patterns. The Embarcadero Freeway came down first in 1991, and to the great delight of San Franciscans, the downtown waterfront became much more accessible. The Franklin and Gough street ramps of the Central Freeway were demolished in 1992. The Oak

medium-traffic streets, and they were aware of their street's special configuration.

Six years after the research, a boulevard was built to replace an elevated freeway in San Francisco. It opened to traffic in October 2005 to serve the same corridor of Franklin, Gough, Oak, and Fell streets

Street off-ramp and the elevated upper deck of the Central Freeway disappeared in mid-1996; by mid-2003 all traces of the elevated structure had disappeared. Left along the former right of way was a 130-foot-wide "scar" in the urban fabric. In 2005, designed by Allan Jacobs and Elizabeth Macdonald with members of San Francisco's Public Works Department, the first five blocks saw construction of a surface boulevard along Octavia Street. It connected traffic to and from Fell and Oak streets and to the newly reconstructed Central Freeway south of Market Street. The State made plans to sell the surplus land, once covered by the former ramps, and housing will be built that repairs the block structure in the Hayes Valley neighborhood. John Ellis, an urban designer, prepared a three-dimensional drawing of the proposed final condition.

During a three-year time window from 2003, when all freeway structures had finally come down, until 2006, when the new street opened to traffic again, a unique opportunity existed to find answers to a set of questions. Where did the traffic go? Obviously, when the Central Freeway was built traffic was channeled through this part of San Francisco with greater concentration than before. Without the freeway, traffic was dispersed to other routes. While this was advantageous to the Hayes Valley neighborhood, did it create problems elsewhere? Also of interest was the question, How have the residents of Hayes Valley adapted to a "reunited" neighborhood free of the elevated freeway structures?

Two consecutive research efforts in fall 2003[45] and spring 2006[46] answered some of these questions. Both teams followed an identical procedure, measuring traffic volumes, counting pedestrians, and interviewing residents on both sides of the former freeway about their daily movements. They also took a group of nonresidents on walks crisscrossing the former freeway alignment and asked the members of this group to evaluate the walking conditions along the east—west streets that connect the formerly divided neighborhood.

Even without the freeway, the teams concluded

Figure 3.27 The repair of a scar. The diagram shows a condition in the future when the traces of the former freeway will have disappeared. The colored buildings in the upper left of the frame will be constructed on land once occupied by the freeway. (Courtesy John Ellis, Solomon ETC, San Francisco)

that Hayes Valley was still divided, but increasingly residents connected. During the first study, in 2003 when the freeway had already disappeared but the empty "scar" was still left, residents rarely walked along the streets that crossed the scar. Only at Hayes Street did the team observe high pedestrian flows. Those in the eastern half walked to stores and restaurants in their sector. The same was true for those in the western part.

Independent of age, gender, or length of residence,

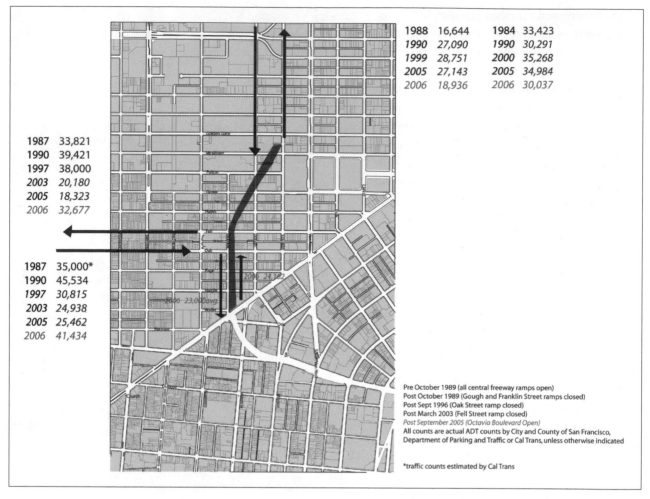

1988 16,644   **1984** 33,423
1990 27,090   **1990** 30,291
1999 28,751   **2000** 35,268
2005 27,143   **2005** 34,984
2006 18,936   *2006* 30,037

1987 33,821
1990 39,421
1997 38,000
2003 20,180
2005 18,323
2006 32,677

1987 35,000*
1990 45,534
1997 30,815
2003 24,938
2005 25,462
2006 41,434

2006 24,182

2006 23,000 avg

Pre October 1989 (all central freeway ramps open)
Post October 1989 (Gough and Franklin Street ramps closed)
Post Sept 1996 (Oak Street ramp closed)
Post March 2003 (Fell Street ramp closed)
Post September 2005 (Octavia Boulevard Open)
All counts are actual ADT counts by City and County of San Francisco,
Department of Parking and Traffic or Cal Trans, unless otherwise indicated

*traffic counts estimated by Cal Trans

Figure 3.28 Where did the freeway traffic go? It returned to the reconfigured surface streets. The numbers columns indicate the traffic volumes measured since the 1989 earthquake by the San Francisco Traffic Department on the four streets that once served as ramps of the Central Freeway. The research team was interested in measuring how traffic contributed to the "barrier" effect between neighborhoods. *Source*: Traffic data, San Francisco DTP.

two-thirds of all reported trips did not cross the scar. Surprisingly, proximity of residence to the scar or roadway had no statistically significant association with a person crossing or not crossing the scar. On maps drawn by the residents, the division of Hayes Valley stood out clearly. Residents provided detail to "their" half of the neighborhood; the other half did not receive equal treatment. The teams' own counts and observations confirmed what the residents indicated in surveys. Few pedestrians walked along the east–west streets with the exception of Hayes Street,

the neighborhood commercial street in Hayes Valley. Here high pedestrian volumes were counted. The outside observers on their guided walk ranked the Hayes Street crossing highest in its potential to bring the two neighborhoods together. Indeed at Hayes Street shops and restaurants on both sides of the empty land held the greatest promise for reconnecting the divided neighborhood for pedestrians.

It seems that residents habitually avoided crossing the empty land just as much as they had avoided walking under the elevated structure. Car drivers also followed habits. After the freeway demolition, car drivers on their way across town were forced to use surface streets, but they do not seem to have shifted routes to other cross-town connectors. Prior to the 1989 earthquake, thirty-three thousand cars would travel northbound on Franklin. Those numbers would drop by only 10 percent during the first few years following the event but went back up to volumes above that level in the late 1990s. Present-day return traffic on Gough has behaved similarly; the thirty-two thousand average daily traffic (ADT) number is also somewhat higher when compared to the preearthquake counts. The westbound Fell Street traffic is also undiminished. Only the eastbound, in-town Oak Street traffic has been reduced. Of all four streets, Oak Street had the highest ADT of forty-five thousand cars. That number has been reduced to twenty-five thousand

since the demolition of the freeway. So, in fact, only some of the freeway traffic dispersed—much of the traffic is still channeling through this corridor, but on surface streets.

The study, when it was repeated 30 months later in 2006, revealed that connections between the neighborhoods on both sides of the former freeway started to improve, but that the "scar" had not yet healed. By now the new Octavia Boulevard had been in operation for six months, and cross-town traffic was directed to use the new boulevard. Tightly planted rows of trees separated the busy center lanes from the local access streets. Granted, the trees were still very small and looked fragile, but the new landscaping and the streetlights delineated clearly a new geometry. Crosswalks had been built on the new boulevard. The number of pedestrians crossing the boulevard had increased; in addition

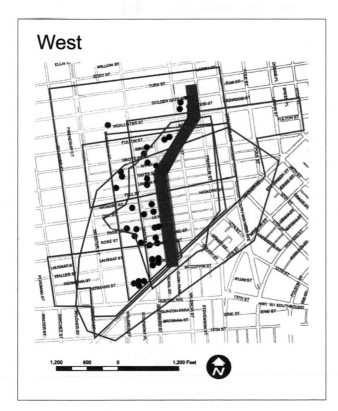

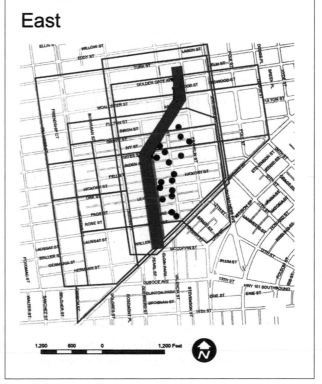

Figure 3.29 Define the boundaries of your neighborhood. In 2006 some overlap starts to emerge. Neighbors living on the west side start to claim parts of the east side. This is less true for neighbors who live on the east side.

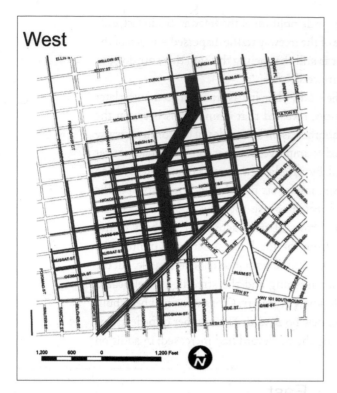
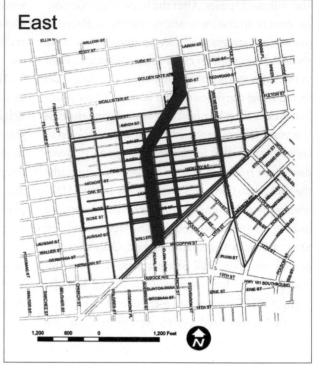

Figure 3.30 Places frequently visited by residents living on the west side and east side of the scar shown here as a red line.

to the Hayes Street intersection, the team counted pedestrians crossing at the Grove Street intersection, and at Oak Street, where very few people had crossed the scar before. The team asked residents on both sides of the former freeway corridor to make maps that delineated the boundaries of their neighborhood. A shift had taken place; there is greater agreement that both sides of the new Octavia Boulevard belong to one neighborhood centered on the intersection of Hayes Street; Octavia no longer functions as a barrier. Only slight differences exist. The residents to the east of Octavia claim slightly less of the western neighborhood portion; those living on the western side claim more of the eastern portion. When comparing the habitual routes that residents take through the neighborhood, the residents on the western half of the neighborhood cross Octavia Boulevard more often and at more locations, while the residents on the

eastern half only cross at Hayes Street. The pedestrian routes appear to be reestablished largely to the benefit of residents on the western side. They use the sidewalks and crossings to reach destinations in the eastern portion, while residents in the east have fewer reasons to cross to the west. This observation is confirmed by comparing the cognitive maps. The residents on the eastern side generally only draw details for their half of the neighborhood, the residents on the western side draw an equal amount of detail on both halves.

As part of the boulevard design, the designers had proposed a small neighborhood park between Fell and Hayes streets in the most northern block of the boulevard, just prior to Octavia Street returning to its original pre-1959 alignment. This small park was built by the time the study was carried out. The park has become a center for the neighbors on both sides of the boulevard.

Residents frequently use it in the evenings and on weekends.

But traffic on Octavia Boulevard is still a major concern. Crossing the entire boulevard in the time span of one green light appeared to be a challenge, not only to elderly people. Pedestrians frequently advanced only to the island between the local access street and the boulevard. There they had to wait until the next green light. With the traffic back on Octavia Boulevard, noise levels in the neighborhood have increased. As in earlier studies, a sixty-five-decibel threshold is used to measure acceptable noise conditions near roadways. During the morning and afternoon peak hours the sixty-five-decibel threshold is exceeded, even at the Hayes Street intersection, one block away from where most of the traffic turns west into Fell Street. There, at Hayes Street, the team measures noise well above sixty-five decibels but below eighty decibels. At Oak Street noise exceeded eighty decibels most of the time.

With much traffic using Octavia Boulevard, sound levels are not likely to improve, but the pedestrian friendliness could improve if a row of buildings were built along its eastern sidewalk. The land alongside the boulevard's eastern sidewalk is still empty. The elevated freeway structure partially took up this five-block strip of land. New building parcels have been reestablished, and new structures on these sites would face Octavia Boulevard. Once built the boulevard will be more pleasant to walk along and to cross. Once that has happened the study should be repeated, because at that time the two halves of the Hayes Valley neighborhood might grow further together. Longitudinal studies are rarely ever done due to their complexity. But when carried out, detailed answers can be given to a complex question, What does it take to reconnect a neighborhood that was severed half a century ago?

Ease of Walking

The role of accessible transit in creating livable neighborhoods remains one of the central themes within urban design. In the pursuit of this topic, various teams studied how the proximity of built form to transit stations defines the degree of integration with the surrounding neighborhood.[47] Born out of the negative reaction to the many commuter stations that are surrounded by parking lots, the team assumed that a true integration can only be achieved if streets and buildings surround the station, as they do in San Francisco where city law does not permit parking lots at station locations. The premise of the team's research is that new stations in suburban locations could perform better if residential and commercial activities were located in the immediate station vicinity and if such uses were better integrated with transit-related activities. The necessary parking for the transit users could be integrated in a less obtrusive manner within structures or below ground.

The group selected three Bay Area Rapid Transit (BART) stations. Based upon their initial observations, they ranked the Twenty-fourth Street BART station in San Francisco as the most integrated. The Orinda station surrounded by parking and a freeway in suburban Alameda County the least, and Glen Park, a second San Francisco station, somewhat in between.

The team chose two physical measurements to gauge integration. They measured what a person would see coming out of the station and counted visible windows and doors that are contained within the view shed. They also defined the various routes available. Their measurements favored Glen Park over Twenty-fourth Street, while Orinda was clearly last. This contradicted their initial ranking, but it sheds light on the terminology used. Integration is a complex concept that is not only explained by visible windows and doors and available routes. The Glen Park Station might be physically well integrated: a person stepping out of the station has the sense of being very close to a concentration of activities, a neighborhood center. The Twenty-fourth Street station, however, generates more social activities due to the density of the surrounding neighborhood. It feels more

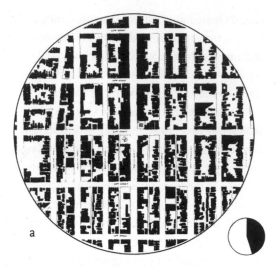

a

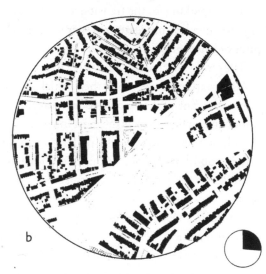

b

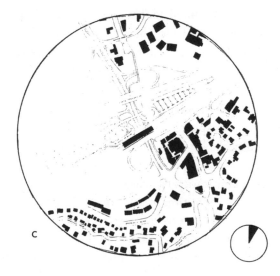

c

integrated, but the measurements did not focus on social activities.

Thus a second team, learning from the results of the first group, hypothesized that pedestrian activity is positively associated with the physical integration of a transit station into the surrounding built environment.[48] Their research demonstrates a more nuanced understanding of the relationship between transit station design and integration into the surrounding area. The team counted people in the vicinity of the station, but, fortunately, raw counts were not the only measure; the group also measured walking times, mapped destinations, and gathering places. The team again included the Twenty-fourth Street station in San Francisco in their study and compared it to a BART station in a former streetcar suburb, Rockridge in the East Bay, and a relatively new suburban station, Pleasant Hill in Alameda County. Focusing on the dependent variables, in this case walking times, destinations, and gathering places, the group counted the greatest number of destinations in close proximity to the Twenty-fourth Street station, followed closely by Rockridge, and then by Pleasant Hill, a distant third. Similarly, Twenty-fourth Street seemed to have the most people lingering around the station. Some, admittedly, engaged in activities that would rouse suspicion by passersby and the police. The team also observed people hanging out around Rockridge, but there is no inviting space available, only an area below a noisy freeway and a narrow sidewalk on the other side of the street. Therefore, lingering at Rockridge means that people only gather because they are delaying the decision to cross the street. In the late 1960s, when these stations were designed, the BART planners made major efforts to prevent people from lingering at stations. The efficient movement of people was a goal. An invitation to linger—then considered loitering—was perceived

Figure 3.31 The integration of three transit stations. (a) Inner-city, (b) streetcar suburb, (c) outer suburbs.

- -

as a discouragement to transit use. Therefore, stations were intentionally designed not as centers for the neighborhoods they served but to function in a peripheral manner. To this day, the design of new BART stations follows this policy. According to Shelly Poticha at Reconnecting America, an advocacy organization promoting transit-related developments, most transit providers have a difficult time actively promoting land-use changes that better connect neighborhoods to transit. New Jersey Transit is the exception;[49] it is their goal to bring existing transit into the community by bringing more housing and more businesses into the station vicinity. Portland, Oregon, provides good examples for new transit stops by integrating the station with the community right from the start.

Walking the Suburbs

In an entirely different type of livability study, student teams have researched the pedestrian permeability in various street grid formations. Teams of students were interested in the relationship between street layout and ease of walking; they assumed that cul-de-sacs and the associated lack of connectivity prevent residents from walking. For the research teams this topic was especially important in the suburban context. In a study[50] that holds density constant, a group examined suburban street form and its relationship to the amount of outdoor activity. To test their hypothesis, the group selected a through street, a cul-de-sac, and a cul-de-sac with pedestrian access at the closed end toward a park. The study generated insights into pedestrian behavior.

Interestingly, despite having no destinations to walk to, a large majority of respondents believed that their neighborhood was well suited for walking and biking. This conflicts with both the observational and survey data that recorded very low levels of walking and no biking. In terms of frequency of walking trips, residents living on the cul-de-sac with the park at the closed end walk more frequently than residents on the other two streets.

The connectivity offered by the park at the end of their cul-de-sac offered destinations like walking to friends' houses and walking for exercise. These were by far the most frequent responses, suggesting for most residents in this setting but without such connectivity that the street layout is devoid of stimulation and opportunity for exploration.

Natural Conditions and Their Influence on Livable Communities

Finally, the concept of livable communities includes the concern for a greater balance between the forces of nature and urban development. "Global warming," or "climate change," refers to recent warming of Earth's near-surface air and implies a human influence. The term was only an abstract concept a decade ago; the International Panel on Climate Change now confirmed that Earth's average surface temperature has increased by 0.74 degrees centigrade (1.33 degrees Fahrenheit) compared to one hundred years ago.[51] There is less agreement on how much warmer the air near Earth's surface will become. For urban designers outdoor comfort is an important criterion in deciding on the form of public spaces. The following work might appear trivial to natural scientists, but when working at the microscale, designers need knowledge about the interplay of climate variables as they are affected by urban form and consequently affect human activities.

Starting in the mid-1980s student teams took climate measurements in downtown streets and on public open spaces. They measured dry bulb temperatures, humidity, the energy radiated from the sun, and wind velocity; they ran the collected data through a mathematical model designed to simulate the human body's thermoregulatory system[52] and printed out maps that showed existing comfort conditions. At the same time they observed human behavior, counted people walking or sitting in the shade versus the sun, and mapped the information. They generally found a correlation between the comfort data and human behavior. Given San Francisco's cool and windy climate, sunlight is essential

Figure 3.32 Measuring thermal comfort. (From top) People prefer to sit in the sun on a cool day; comfort on a warm day (note measuring device in the background); the team and their instruments.

for human comfort on most days of the year. Research teams frequently observed pedestrians sitting or standing in the sun rather than in the shade in places where there was a choice. It is also true, if given a choice, that pedestrians select sidewalks on the sunny side depending on temperatures, but rarely did teams observe pedestrians avoiding adverse wind conditions due to heavy downwinds that high-rise buildings create. Pedestrians can be seen struggling against the wind, but they do not cross the street to avoid it.

The research teams also found noticeable exceptions to behavior in response to comfort. While general findings indicated that respondents' choice of location in a park was directly influenced by available sunlight and sometimes by shelter from wind, the team observed hotel staff members gathering during outdoor breaks in a park on San Francisco's wealthy Nob Hill. The staff consistently gathered along the least comfortable edges of the park.[53] In another study over a six-month period, in one of San Francisco's poorest neighborhoods, benches started to become crowded every afternoon around five o'clock; mostly men selected these seats in the coldest and windiest part of Tenderloin Park. Plenty of comfortable seating was available elsewhere in the park, but the men who lined up on these benches were waiting for the food service to open at Glide Memorial United Methodist Church across the street.[54] Finally, on Union Square, a team consistently counted middle-aged men standing at a corner of the park that was decidedly less comfortable according to the team's measurement. They were clearly waiting and could be seen leaving once rejoined by their spouses, who had "quickly" dropped into Macy's across the street.[55]

On exceptionally warm days a research team compared the comfort conditions on a hard surface plaza with those along a creek on the Berkeley campus. Their intent was to measure the success of the creek as a "cooling agent." Given Berkeley's moderate climate, on only two days out of six warm September days did the team measure climate conditions suitable to test their hypothesis. The climate conditions made the sunny spots on both sites too warm for comfort. On those days the model predicted the shady spots to be comfortable. Accordingly, the team expected most users in both research sites to choose shaded seating. This pattern was weakly apparent on the hard-surfaced plaza, with more users shifting toward the shade. For the creek side area, the distribution of people suggested that users did not choose their location according to predictions made by the mathematical model, since almost all users chose to remain in the sun. Was it the sight of the creek that chilled them sufficiently? Were the instruments sufficiently well calibrated? These and other possibilities make it difficult to control all variables in such a quasi-experiment.[56]

The microclimate studies were carried out at the beginning of a trend to gain better insights into natural processes in cities[57] and how such processes affected human health and human behavior.[58] Since the mid-1980s the interest has continued and has grown: few would have guessed that residents on a street lined with deciduous trees, American sweet gum (*Liquidambar styraciflua*), would indicate that the beginning of fall starts in the month of October, while residents on a street with camphor (*Cinnamomum camphora*) trees, an evergreen, set the beginning of fall—like the calendar—in September, while for residents on a street lined with flowering ornamental pear (*Pyrus calleryama*), autumn did not begin until November. The answers from residents on streets with deciduous trees coincide with the physiological timetable of such trees; the time of year when each species begins to change color based upon the day's length and local climate.[59] When asked what they would miss about their place of residence if they were to move, residents on all three streets agreed that they would miss "the trees" (camphor), "sunlight through the leaves" (sweet gum), and, "the trees during spring, when they are in bloom" (ornamental pear). The residents on the two streets with the deciduous trees ornamental pear and sweet gum most frequently mentioned the

trees, more frequently than anything related to the home itself, neighbors, or the convenience of the location. All three streets were located in the same neighborhood and same proximity to services.

On the increase are studies that test professional biases on biodiversity in city parks. Given the diminishing number of plant species due to environmental causes, parks departments around the world are establishing special areas inside parks that are managed to protect biodiversity. So far San Francisco residents do not perceive or appreciate biodiversity in parks with managed natural areas unless there is signage that educates park visitors. Without signage these managed areas are considered unkempt and unsightly.[60] However, bioswales, storm-water conveyance through vegetation designed to remove impurities, are appreciated and cared for,[61] as one study showed that compared three streets with bioswales in three different socioeconomic areas.

Part Three: Sense of Place

Sense of place has been defined in a number of disciplines, including geography[62] and psychology.[63] In these fields research on sense of place has focused on place attachment, dependency, and identification with place, in natural or constructed settings. To design places that bring about attachment, dependency, and identity clearly goes beyond the setting of dimensions. Tony Hiss[64] describes a bond that exists between a person and a particular setting. This means that an individual has made an emotional investment in a place. Clearly, such a bond is associated with a person's life cycle. Also, place attachment, dependency, and identity depend not only on one particular experience but on an ongoing relationship with a physical setting that in most cases is shared with other people. In this context gender, race, and income are important, as are exposure, familiarity, choice, and cultural norms. That said, the disciplines of psychology and geography have produced little empirical research that suggests what physical characteristics are likely to contribute to sense of place.

When designers think of *place* they might be tempted to think, first of all and quite literally, about the dimensions of a place. Understandable, because designers create spatial geometries; they define proximities and place objects in space. It is only natural for designers to believe that decisions about the correct spatial dimensions influence how people act in space, both functionally as well as emotionally. But what is wide, what is narrow, what is just right to create a certain milieu? Thus many studies by the Berkeley research teams focused on streets and the importance of perceived enclosure. The logical underpinnings for this approach were that a more enclosed space brings people physically closer together. But an emotional connectedness to physical space does not seem to depend on tightly spaced dimensions. Therefore, any hypotheses that tried to discover causal relationships between spatial enclosure and sense of place did so with only with very limited success.

In search of other physical characteristics that influence sense of place, a research team studied two streets on Telegraph Hill in San Francisco and found that a narrow street is associated with a stronger feeling of desirability, uniqueness, coziness, tidiness, and enclosure, while a wide street was associated with stronger feelings of safety, spaciousness, openness, and brightness. That is, both locations had positive feelings associated with them. Both streets in the study are lined with similar architecture and both streets have no street trees. The group, however, acknowledged correctly that most streets on Telegraph Hill are very special due to their location on a steep hill with many memorable views over the City and the Bay. On this hill, places of residence are highly regarded, and the location alone instills a sense of place in many people. Therefore, several years later, when there was renewed interest in the relationship between street dimensions and sense of place, a team[65] formed to study street dimensions in neighborhoods with different socioeconomics. The group found matched pairs of differently scaled streets on Telegraph Hill, in the South of Market district, and in the Mission district. They hypothesized that unique character and an easily distinguishable street form is likely to produce a strong sense of place and a greater sense of community. They found little evidence to support their hypothesis. Only the results from a South of Market neighborhood suggested that the narrow enclosure of alleys was weakly associated with uniqueness, but not necessarily is there a greater sense of place because of the unique street form.

When tests of a favored hypothesis fail, scientists[66] advise that *reclaiming a fruitful path must lie in the empirical record, particularly in scrutinizing basic data for hints of a pattern that might lead to a different hypothesis.* In our case we failed because we focused on narrow streets, a geometry that is too specific. More promising for sense of place is to look at the entire geometry between the street and the private realm. Hoping that a relationship might reveal itself, the study was repeated, but with a difference: a team selected streets with front facades along residential streets that offered the opportunity for a broader range of activities and a better transition designed with attention to detail. A row of buildings, for example, slightly set back by five or seven feet from the sidewalk and with external steps, a low wall protecting a small space suitable for planting, and complemented by regular street trees, provides an environment more suitable for outdoor activities, social or in solitude, than a building placed on the property line, right next to the sidewalk, that is dominated by a blank wall with openings to either a front door or an internal stairway.

Consistently, visitors led around the corner into the street with setbacks would pause and stop to say: "A very nice street, great place to live." While evidence of activities in the transition spaces were frequently observed, research teams still needed to find evidence that such spaces contribute also to a greater sense of place and possibly a greater sense of community. A research group selected this street and compared it to another block without a transition zone. Luckily they found two adjacent blocks along the same street. The reason for this difference was the great fire of 1906. At the beginning of the twentieth century, buildings on both blocks on this street had been recently completed, but the fire destroyed the northern block just up to a marked rise in the land. At the rise the fire had stopped, or it is possible that a trench was laid intentionally to stop the fire at a predetermined line. In any case, the buildings on the next block to the south survived. To encourage rapid rebuilding the city authorities permitted higher land utilization and allowed reconstruction at the property line without setback north of the fire line. Judging from the age of the buildings, reconstruction must have been rapid. There is not much difference in the age of the architecture on both sides of the fire line, only the presence of setbacks differs.

Current demographics indicate similar household income and similar distribution of owners and renters, but more families have moved into the homes on the block with setbacks. On this block 74 percent of the residents spend time on their block outdoors "just because it is a pleasant place to be." On the block without a transition zone only 29 percent did so. Those who do spend time outdoors maintain their front yards, repair things, and supervise children. There is reason to believe that the setbacks in front of the private entrances create a sense of place and that the four or five outside stairs down to the sidewalk, and the associated green space, induce activities that in-

Figure 3.33 Residential street with setbacks (above) and a block further north (below) without setbacks. The geometry of the two streets is virtually identical with the exception of the setback.

crease people's exposure to each other. A resident living at ground level can quickly step outdoors without leaving the privacy of home. On this street,

Figure 3.34 Stepping outside to greet a neighbor and to retreat. The two photos illustrate Appleton's, 1975 "prospect and refuge" theory. The person on the stoop has stepped outside to greet a neighbor. She notices the photographer, says goodbye to the neighbor on the sidewalk (not in the frame), and retreats back inside.

carrier, check on children, or let the dog out. In the case of the person in figure. 3.34, her dog must have made some commotion inside when it noticed a neighbor walking his dog out in front. That made the woman step outside to greet the neighbor while the two dogs became reacquainted.

The team found that on the block with transition zones people knew more neighbors and more by name. And, due to the transition zone, it apparently attracted more families with children. Here, 37 percent of households had children, compared with only 19 percent on the block without a transition zone. More than any other variable, the presence of children explains the finding about knowing neighbors.[67] The presence of the transition zone plays an important role in attracting these families. What is it about such a small area between the front door and the sidewalk that makes young couples decide to move here, and once here to stay here because they feel connected to neighbors and enjoy a sense of place? The observations suggest that the small space is used very well. A resident can relate to other members of the community from the privacy of home, looking down over a few steps and a patch of private space that is also accessible from the public realm of the sidewalk and the street. The availability of this space gives parents the feeling of safety knowing that kids can quickly retreat inside, and can be heard when playing outside. Not only kids, but adults also benefit from both prospect and refuge that the stoop offers. One glance over the street from the front door and one is reassured

where so many people know each other, ample occasion exists to do just that. The research team observed people stepping outside to greet the mail

Lexington, 18th to 19th

Lexington, 20th to 21st

a
b
c
d
e
f

Figure 3.35 Transition zones, (a) without setback and (b) with setback. Details of entrances (c, d, e, f). The setback with the associated stoop plays an important role in the social life of the resident. The details (c) and (d) describe features associated with no-setback design. The details (e) and (f) show design elements associated with setbacks and stoops.

that nothing is out of the ordinary, or if it is, one can see it.[68]

The team concluded that the street with the transition zone produced a greater sense of place, but that does not mean the people on the block without a transition zone had no sense of place, just not as much. When sense of place is meant to include sense of community and is measured in terms of the number of neighbors known, then it appears that transition zones are important. If, on the other hand, sense of community is defined by such qualities as friendliness and neighbors' concern for each other's safety, then the answers are inconclusive because residents answered in the same manner regardless of whether they had a transition space. This suggests that the physical qualities of a space do not necessarily influence perceptions of social behavior, even if they do affect the behavior itself.

Sense of Community

The detailed design of transition zones remained a subject of further research, especially in new communities. In the eyes of neotraditional designers the private garage, especially three in a row as in conventional American suburbs, represents all that is undesirable about suburbia. The correct placement of garages is not the only physical manifestation of neotraditional design. The neotraditional design philosophy importantly calls for mixed land uses, higher residential densities, grid street networks, narrow streets, and vernacular or traditional architecture including porches and other design features that invite interaction. But the placement of garages toward the rear of the property is an important tool in reemphasizing the front of the house and its contribution to the public realm of residential streets. A study[69] compared a conventional suburban street lined with three-car garages with two nearby neotraditional neighborhood streets, with garages to the rear of the properties and entrance porches in the front of the houses. The team observed that the entrance porches were rarely used. The driveway spaces in front of the three-car garage driveways, on the other hand, were used as workspaces and by children. Some garage doors remained partly open for children to retrieve their play equipment and to go inside the house when needed. Children have a strong need for public play spaces, and this need will be met despite the deficiencies in street design. However, there is greater potential for a more diverse range of activities in front of the homes along the neotraditional neighborhood than for the residents on the street with the three-car garages.

The in-person survey results from the same study demonstrate that there was stronger interest in more social interaction along the neotraditional streets than along the typical suburban street, but residents did not necessarily socialize more. Residents on all three streets were asked to indicate on maps who they knew on their block. On the neotraditional streets all neighbors knew each other, but the reason was only indirectly related to physical design features. The residents gathered frequently to draft letters protesting the developer's reluctance to construct the community pool that had been part of the original sales agreement. This effort created a significant degree of neighboring.

Another research team hypothesized on the sense of community in gated neighborhoods. While the team discovered that the residents in the gated community lived there due to a greater concern for security, the sense of community was only marginally higher in the gated community.[70]

Sense of Time

When sense of place is defined as attachment to and dependency on a physical setting together with people in this setting, then it is worth reflecting on how individuals perceive the passage of time in such settings. Perceptions of distance and duration differ according to the amount of information available to the human senses. The more information, and the more to be experienced, results in a perceived slower passage of time. Research teams have tested this hypothesis repeatedly. The first team[71] selected three walks in San Francisco's Marina district. They took respondents on walks in a varied sequence; some started on Union Street, a street with much visual interest, then turned onto Filmore Street, a street with less visual interest, walked for three short blocks, and turned again on Lombard Street, the street with the least amount of visual interest for an equal distance. Others took the walks in reverse order. Respondents were asked about the length of each walk after each segment. Prior to the experiment, the team had measured facade length, frequency of entrances, sidewalk width, signage, and articulation of facades. The Union Street walk made pedestrians encounter more articulation, shorter facades, more entrances, and more signs. Respondents perceived the walk on Union Street as longer, although it took just as long as the other two walks. But after the experiment, the team reported that on their walk along Union Street respondents had encountered more pedestrians compared to the other two streets. The team questioned to what extent their respondents had taken into consideration the encounters with other people along the sidewalk, when asked to estimate the

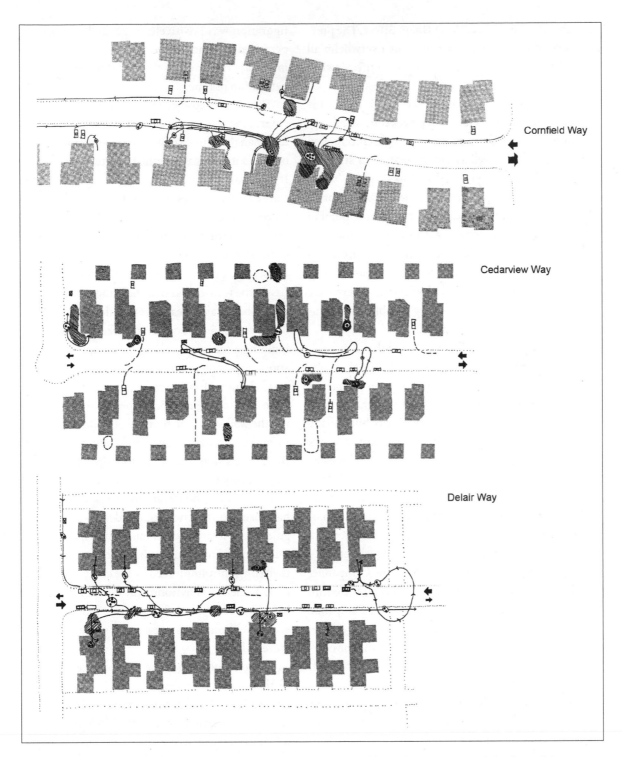

Cornfield Way

Cedarview Way

Delair Way

Figure 3.36 Activities on a street with three car garages (top), compared to activities on two neotraditional streets (middle and bottom). The team observed that the entrance porches were rarely used. The spaces in front of the three-car-garage driveways, on the other hand, were used as work spaces and by children.

time it took to walk along Union Street. The presence of other people might easily overwhelm all other visual information related to the physical world. They were correct.

Therefore, a year later, a second group of students tested the relationship between the perception of time and the number of people encountered along walks as well as the articulation of street facades by selecting two urban walks and two walks on campus of equal distance. The four walks varied in street width, architectural articulation, number of people, and automobile density. Again, the team took groups of participants, in varied order, on each walk.[72] The inclusion of people density as an independent variable proved problematic. There were simply too many confounding variables that influenced the perception of time.

Finally, a third team understood that a successful research design would need to reduce the number of variables. They took groups of people on walks of identical length but through environments of different spatial complexity but equally busy with people. The team[73] selected two walks through the parklike setting of the Berkeley campus. The first walk could be attributed to its designer, John Galen Howard, who laid out the central portion of the campus in the tradition of the Ecole de Beaux Arts, a straight walk through a sequence of formally designed spaces, slightly uphill, directed toward a monument, the Campanile. The bell tower remained in view during the entire walk. The second walk also ended at the Campanile but took a more circuitous route across a bridge, through a gate, and along a narrow path. The campanile would frequently appear in the view ahead. Both walks followed a slightly uphill route, measured the same in length, and took the same amount of time. The team hypothesized that the straight walk with the view of the bell tower constantly in sight would be perceived as shorter compared to the more circuitous route. The respondents confirmed the hypothesis. Groups of people took both walks in different order: complexity of route con-

figuration was positively associated with longer perceived time, and route directness was the most important reason given that influenced the shorter perception of time.

The team discovered three other useful relationships. First, the perceived time for both routes was less than the actual time. This observation is curious, and it was made in the two previous studies. If the actual time is not checked using a watch, the elapsed time it takes to travel relatively short distances is consistently overestimated, and by a large margin. Second, respondents ranked the more complex route as more interesting, enjoyable, and satisfying, despite its perceived greater length. Lastly, the team found that the things respondents remembered along each walk differed. Along the direct route, respondents remarked primarily on buildings; conversely, along the complex route respondents remembered details, trees, an ornate gate, along with observed human activities. The team counted the number of people they met during the walks and the number of buildings visible from the two walks and found them to be equal. Both walks were taken at lunchtime when both were equally busy.

For John Galen Howard these responses would have been consistent with the design theory that guided the creation of monumental space, which intended the individual to be, if not overwhelmed, then constantly impressed by the composition and scale of the built environment. What he might not have noticed is that moving inside monumentally scaled environments appears to make time pass more quickly.

Respondents judged the elapsed time according to the spatial complexity of their experience.[74] Smaller spatial dimensions, more variation, more changes in direction, and shorter block dimensions influenced people to estimate longer duration, close to 50 percent longer than the actual time it took to walk the distance. The experiment confirms what William James[75] wrote in 1892: "A time filled with varied and interesting experiences seems short in

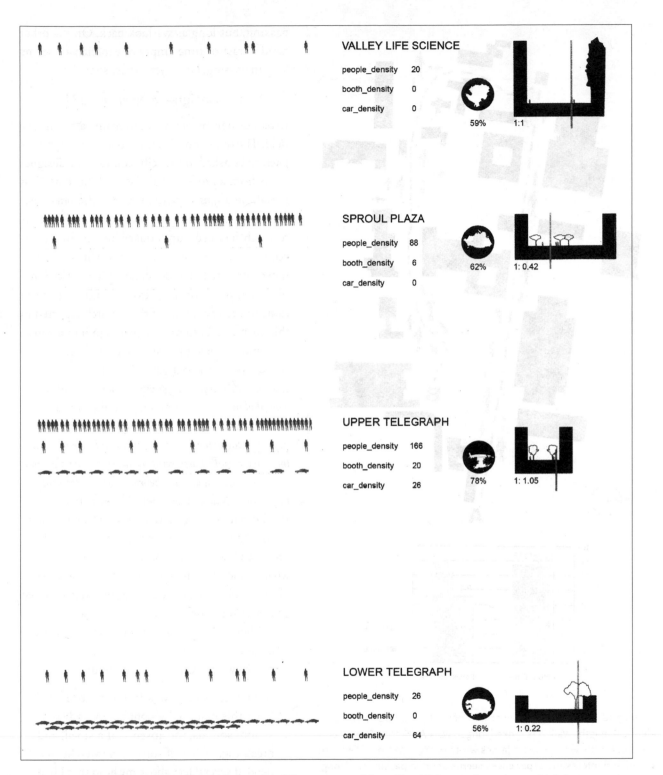

VALLEY LIFE SCIENCE

people_density	20
booth_density	0
car_density	0

59% 1:1

SPROUL PLAZA

people_density	88
booth_density	6
car_density	0

62% 1: 0.42

UPPER TELEGRAPH

people_density	166
booth_density	20
car_density	26

78% 1: 1.05

LOWER TELEGRAPH

people_density	26
booth_density	0
car_density	64

56% 1: 0.22

Figure 3.37 Four walks of identical length but with a different sense of time. The third street from the top had the greatest visual interest, and walks along it seem to last longer.

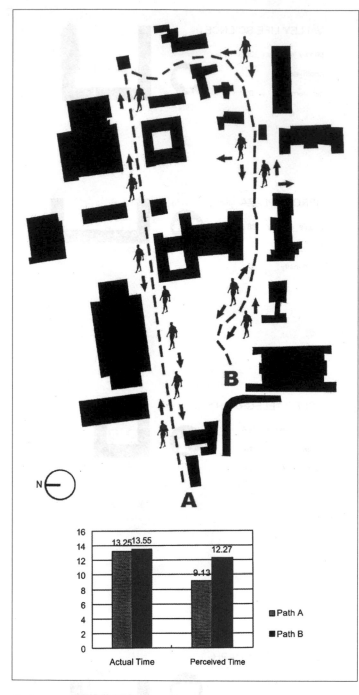

Figure 3.38 Comparing the sense of time on two campus walks of identical length. Walk B is ranked longer, walk A shorter. The experiment confirms what William James wrote in 1892: "A time filled with varied and interesting experiences seems short in passing, but long as we look back. On the other hand a tract of time empty of experiences seems long in passing, but in retrospect short."

passing, but long as we look back. On the other hand a tract of time empty of experiences seems long in passing, but in retrospect short."

Urban Design—a Normative Field

Urban design by definition remains a normative field. The question, What is good urban form? is likely to be asked in a specific context. The designer starts from a professional bias, and this bias *"is as partial in its way as the prevalent functional theories so unconsciously are in their own peculiar ways."*[76] Ample research has been undertaken to explain socioeconomic aspects of settlements. Theories guide those interested in understanding how cities function; many descriptions exist on how city form came to be. The intent of the research reported in this chapter was to move city design into a somewhat more robust professional discipline. This includes systematic fact gathering with greater rigor than customary. *"Objectivity cannot be equated with mental blankness,"* Stephen Jay Gould[77] used to tell his incoming science students, *"rather objectivity resides in recognizing your preferences and then subjecting them to especially harsh scrutiny and also in a willingness to revise or abandon your theories when the tests fail (as they frequently do)."* Designers, like scientists, can be stubborn in holding on to their beliefs. They might assume that it was a flaw in the test that caused failure. Even if we have not been able to prove robustly what physical features contribute to a sense of place, place exists and designers have created places that give people a sense of place, even a sense of belonging without holding material ownership. Tony Hiss' description of a walk through Grand Central Station in New York City comes to mind:

In another step, I was in the concourse. I knew this first not by sight but by body sensation, sounds, the absence of a smell, and breathing. I felt as if some small weight suspended several feet above my head that I had not till then even been aware of, had just shot fifteen stories into the air. I straightened up, my breathing slowed down, and I noticed that the scentless air around me was warm. I was walking at the same fast clip, and on the same kind of marble floor, but now, and for the rest of the minute it took me to walk the length of the concourse, I could no longer distinguish the sounds of my own footsteps. All the sounds that reached me seemed to have fused into a single sound. Vast and quiet, it seemed to be evenly distributed throughout the great room. This sound, pleasant in all its parts, regular in all its rhythms, and humorous and good-natured, seemed also to have buttoned me into some small, silent bubble of space.

This sound was produced by five hundred or more people talking and walking on marble through the bottom part of eleven million cubic feet of air. Within two or three feet of where I stood, I could hear separate voices: "Take Care, now" and "Yep, see you tomorrow" and "All 'board." And from quite far away, I could hear laughing. The rest of what I heard was just the single comingled sound. I could see, quite clearly, two things: an unmoving framework made up of marble floor, tall piers, arched windows, high barrel vault, daylight, and faint electric stars; and the swirling, living motion of five hundred people walking, two and three abreast, from and toward the fourteen entrances and exits of the concourse.

I thought, as I have many times in the concourse, that if I were a stranger to this overwhelming city, it would be helpful to me to know that something in me and in everybody around me already knew how to fit in with all the people circulating through the city and going about their business. After emerging onto Vanderbilt Avenue, I found that when I crossed over and walked along the south side of Forty-third Street, I could for a while keep with me this awareness of the cooperation that makes a city possible."[78]

The range of topics discussed is broad, but the chapter focuses only on a subset of topics that city designers need to address. Therefore, as stated in the beginning, this chapter is intended as an invitation to form city design research centers in different cultural contexts that introduce fact-finding evaluations into the qualitative, sometimes intuitive, design traditions. The goal is not to come up with prototypes, or to be overly proscriptive, but rather to make the normative approach less partial, to question normative theories and verify them when possible.

CHAPTER FOUR

To Transform

Rebuilding the Structure of the Inner City

Urban morphology is a field of knowledge that describes the form of cities and changes to city form over time. A related discipline, typology, describes the variation that can be observed in specific elements of city structure such as buildings or streets. Both fields of knowledge, morphology and typology, are part of a tradition that relates the socioeconomic processes in cities to the form of public spaces and buildings. The interest in urban form is less concerned with architectural style, and more with the contribution that built and unbuilt spaces make to the fabric of the city. A fabric in which buildings are solids and streets are voids, together with yards, gardens, squares, parks, empty lots, and much else not covered by a building. The study of urban morphology leads to an understanding of the elements that make up the form of a city. The geometry of these elements is defined by the units of land they occupy. Such parcels are generally under the control of owners who have well-defined rights and obligations that govern their utilization and manipulation of the land.

The approach is rooted in the work of M. R. G. Conzen from the early 1900s in Berlin, at a time when he and other geographers tested a morpho-logical approach to the study of urban settlements.[1] Architects and urban designers, chiefly in Italy, have been influenced by a typomorphologi-cal approach to city design[2] because of their early interest in classifying the elements of the urban structure in the context of district preservation.[3] In the English-speaking world, through the writings of Aldo Rossi,[4] interest in typology began to increase. He and others have argued that the study of buildings as types can be as valid as the under-standing of cities gained through the social sciences: the city is understood as a product of history because traces of the past are inescapably ingrained in the dynamics of urban form. Direct observations and measurement combined with archival information can lead to the discovery of a city's essential structures. Such structures include elements of city form that have mutated through time but have constantly adapted to change, thus remained viable in their contribution to the fab-ric of a city.

This chapter explores how information from archival sources and historical maps can be retraced and combined with tentative designs to discover how new elements can contribute to the essential spatial structure of a city.[5]

Figure 4.1 Edward Hopper, *Sunday Morning*, 1953. (Courtesy the Phillips Collection, Washington, DC)

Transforming the Structure of the Inner City

The resurgence of the inner city on the West Coast of America, as in Vancouver, Seattle, Portland, and San Francisco, distracts from the fact that many smaller and medium-sized cities continue to struggle in maintaining the centrality of their downtown areas. The ability to attract a permanent residential population, lured by good regional transit, has be-

come a prerequisite for attracting new commercial uses back to the inner city.

For example, downtown Oakland in Northern California has experienced significant loss of population and retail commerce in a process that started in the 1950s and has lasted over the course of the past fifty years.

In January of 1998, Jerry Brown, a former State of California governor and one-time aspirant of the U.S. presidency, took office as the mayor of Oakland. In his inaugural speech, he promised to bring ten thousand new residents to the downtown area of his city. The announcement received nationwide attention. For city officials in the San Francisco Bay Area the announcement echoed what other cities hoped to do as well. San Jose, for example, has made major efforts to bring a residential population back into the urban core as its role in the regional high tech economy has become increasingly more central. San Francisco's chronic housing shortage has resulted in a number of new, inner-city neighborhoods, even in former industrial areas. But San Francisco never lost as many downtown residents as other American cities. Its inner-city neighborhoods have remained attractive to many, to the extent that residents in inner-city neighborhoods like Chinatown, the Mission District, and the Tenderloin experienced economic pressures to move. Traditionally, these inner-city districts accommodated a population of the less mobile, the elderly, and immigrant families who could not easily find homes anywhere else.

The Oakland mayoral election promise was not simply a proposal to bring back a population that left long ago, or to bring back physical compactness where the urban fabric had been fragmented for a long time. The new housing had to make inner-city living an attractive choice compared to suburban living. Repairing the inner city to the social and physical conditions similar to what existed in the first half of the twentieth century is not possible or even desirable. People left the inner city for many good reasons: to exchange crowded flats for ownership of a freestanding single-family home with tax benefits, increased mobility, access to open space, schools, and living among people of one's own social background. In this context, a visit to an art gallery might be useful; the faces that an Edward Hopper painted or a Karl Stieglitz photographed frequently show expressions of alienation, phobia, even despair, and only sometimes personal triumph over, mastery of, and curiosity about city life.

Attracting people to live in the inner city requires new models that draw creatively on present-day conditions. Although past redevelopment models have recognized the need for reinvention, they have often resulted in housing that was too uniform and too institutional in character. The federally supported urban renewal projects of the 1950s and '60s lacked true diversity and, in the long run, were rejected by those with mobility as a viable alternative to the suburban choice. Although urban renewal produced some high-quality inner-city housing, in Oakland and elsewhere urban renewal is chiefly associated with the wholesale clearance of neighborhoods, closure of streets, creation of superblocks, and relocation of residents. Only some former residents found their home inside the new structures within their old neighborhood. Those who did moved into modern apartment blocks that soon would show signs of neglect. The majority of the housing became inflicted with social problems.

A lesson learned from urban renewal was to avoid the clearance of neighborhoods but to encourage the filling of vacant land within the existing parcel structure of city blocks.

The process starts with identifying the remnants of existing vitality in inner-city neighborhoods and carefully adding new development to strengthen the qualities that have survived. Such a model of urban transformation is rooted in an understanding of a city's morphology, the geometry of its streets and blocks, and a division of land that is relatively small but used by many overlapping activities, all in need of access to public streets and entrances along sidewalks. With the insertion of new development the opportunity exists to improve and reform elements of the public realm, such as streets, squares, or a waterfront. Such a model requires a strategy; it cannot be accomplished by making individual development decisions in an ad hoc fashion.

On first reading, the new model does not sound too different from the mandate that has guided redevelopment for the last half century. The important difference is that one instrument of urban renewal is used with the greatest restraint or ideally

developable parcels available. Instead, development takes place within the existing parcel structure in a manner that best avoids any further fragmentation of existing social and physical conditions. Such a model is now used in inner-city neighborhoods, where just the mentioning of urban renewal would cause a storm of protest. In downtown Oakland the population to mount such a protest was largely absent, not organized, and silent.

The mayor's proposal to build housing for ten thousand new residents equaled a volume of approximately eight to ten million square feet of floor space. The anticipation of such a considerable amount of building activity created a momentum that could have further eroded what was left of downtown Oakland's existing social and physical conditions, especially if the remnants of downtown neighborhoods had been perceived as particularly marginal by those taking responsibility for the proposed redevelopment efforts. Judgments about marginal conditions are easily made, but they are also very consequential. Is the one-room apartment of a waiter in a Chinatown rooming house marginal? The current state law would support such an assessment if the rooming house were to be located on a city block that has an "irregular property configuration." The assessment of marginality would become the first step in a process that results in condemnation of structures and displacement of residents.

It might come as a surprise that the methods of

Figure 4.2 Aerial view of downtown Oakland in 2000. (Courtesy City of Oakland, Redevelopment Agency)

not at all, and that is the consolidation of land through "eminent domain," a process in which government disowns present landowners and consolidates adjacent parcels of land to make large

urban renewal are still in place and that a legal instrument like eminent domain is still seen as a necessary tool to trigger a process in which market forces can freely operate. In *Cities Without Cities* Thomas Sieverts reminds us that those individuals attracted to the planning profession generally belong to a left-leaning bunch on the political spectrum and that the tradition of balancing competition and cooperation has been one of the fundamental functions of planning; that is, if planning is understood as an extension of city government.[6] Since the beginning of the profession in the early 1900s, city planners and urban designers have seen it as their professional challenge to tame and cultivate what we now call market forces in a constant effort to protect the weaker components of the city: culture, people, and nature. These three components will remain weak because market forces will only selectively address their concerns.

City Culture

City culture is the manifestation of a collective history. Therefore an understanding of the current spatial pattern requires knowledge of how these patterns have come about. A city designer might start interpreting city culture by planting seeds of an educational nature. Among the members of the planning staff and among politicians little was known about the history of Oakland's urban form. Given that Oakland's history is limited to 156 years, its morphology is quickly explained. Not everybody will draw the same conclusions from historical analysis; however, when subsequent actions are indeed taken, they will be made with knowledge of the city's past.

A History of Oakland's Morphology

The Swiss engineer Julius G. Kellersberger laid out Oakland's street pattern in 1852. Kellersberger was born on February 9, 1821, near Baden in Switzerland. He came to New York in 1847 where he worked as a surveyor on Central Park. We hear of him in the context of Frederick Law Olmsted's de-

sign of Central Park, which was excessively over budget in 1859. A state senate committee brought in Kellersberger to evaluate the work on Central Park in detail. He attested to its high quality and excellence in overall organization. "'Much better than any other public work in the United States,' Herr Kellersberger reported."[7] News of California gold brought Kellersberger and his wife to San Francisco. In California he made a name for himself as surveyor responsible for the Humboldt Meridian, a survey of the northern portion of the new state toward the Oregon border, and the Mount Diablo Meridian, a survey from the Central Valley to the coast. Prior to taking on these federal commissions, three New York investors—E. Adams, H. W. Carpentier, and A. J. Moon—hired him in 1852 to lay out the new city of Oakland at the mouth of the San Antonio Creek and Contra Costa Bayou.[8]

Kellersberger selected a rise of the land for the center of the new town. From the vantage point on this hill only forty feet above sea level, the site must have evoked the feeling of an island surrounded by water and tidal marshes.

In 1852, three years after the discovery of gold in California, the new city was intended to function as a supply base to support the gold miners in the foothills of the Sierra Nevada. An existing Spanish highway, now San Pablo Avenue, had become well used by those who traveled toward the gold fields. The road reached the hill in what was to become the center of Oakland from the north across a narrow land bridge between two low-lying wetlands. The old road continued across the mouth of the tidal estuary, now Lake Merritt, toward the San Jose Mission. Across the estuary, hills rose steeply. The site was well chosen for a new town; it offered trees as building material growing in the valleys, fresh water, plenty of fish in the bayou, and grazing land on the hills. The estuary provided a natural harbor directly opposite San Francisco, where goods and people passed through in both directions. Aesthetically, the place must have been of exceptional beauty and comfort. There are very few

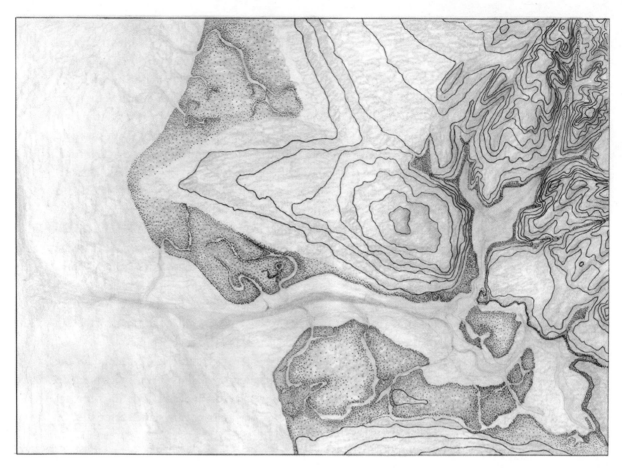

Figure 4.3 The place that became Oakland was located near a tidal marsh at the mouth of the San Antonio Creek and Contra Costa Bayou.

cities in the world, especially at sea level, with as temperate a climate as Oakland.

Right there, at the center point of that rise, Kellersberger laid out a street one hundred feet wide at an angle of twenty degrees east of north, and ran it down the slope toward the bayou to a landing place. The street became Broadway, and to both sides Kellersberger staked out eight parallel streets, giving them names like Webster, Castro, Clay, and Harrison. Starting at the water's edge, he ran fourteen numbered streets perpendicular to Broadway, creating a grid of 224 city blocks measuring three hundred by two hundred feet each. He designated seven blocks as public open spaces and arranged them symmetrically across the grid. Two of them

together, centered on Broadway between Fourth and Fifth streets, were intended to become the town center. Apparently the double square served that purpose for a short while until it became the site of the county administrative buildings. Kellersberger designated four additional squares and distributed them evenly to serve each of the four city quadrants as neighborhood squares. The seventh he named after his wife Caroline and placed it by itself near the eastern edge of town.

Each block was divided into twenty-eight lots, sixteen on the narrow side of each block and twelve on the long side. The buildable land totaled 325.5 acres, and if individual families had settled every single one of the 3,276 lots the density of the city

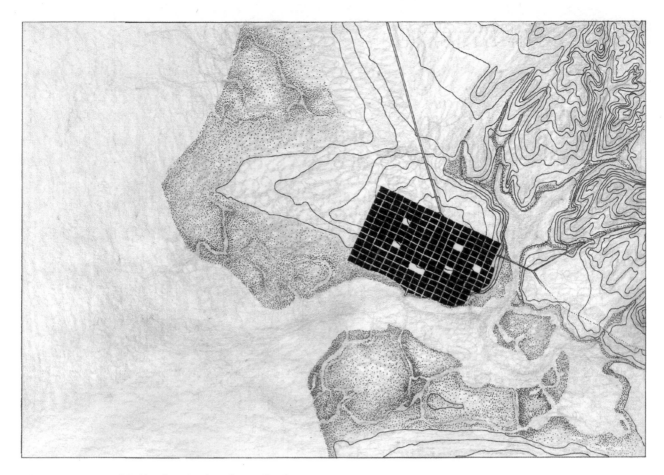

Figure 4.4 Layout of Oakland in 1852 by Julius Kellersberger.

would have been approximately ten units per acre and would have accommodated between ten and fifteen thousand people. But a population, stable in numbers, could not be expected for some time.

The city blocks were settled from the waterfront upward; most blocks along the estuary required extensive pilings to lift structures above the high tide or flood level. We do not know the approximate population he was trying to accommodate. We do know that the city grew rapidly as a result of population influx due to the gold rush. Kellersberger was soon appointed city engineer, and in 1854 he was officially elected to that position. In 1857, just before he left the Bay Area to return east, he revised his Oakland design and introduced a new diagonal street, Market Street, to connect the Embarcadero at Bush Street directly to the San Pablo Highway. Such a new street and the erasure of one whole row of city blocks were only possible because the western flank of the city had not been settled. Market Street became necessary as a route for freight traffic that could now avoid the climb up the hill to Fourteenth Street but could still reach the highway directly from the wharf and on level ground. Market Street also defined Oakland's westerly expansion centered on Seventh and Eighth streets. For Kellersberger, the western expansion of Oakland apparently held greater promise than the northern expansion. In his mind Market Street, like its counterpart in San Francisco, would become the city's main divider, and people of Oakland would refer to the city's two parts as West Oakland and

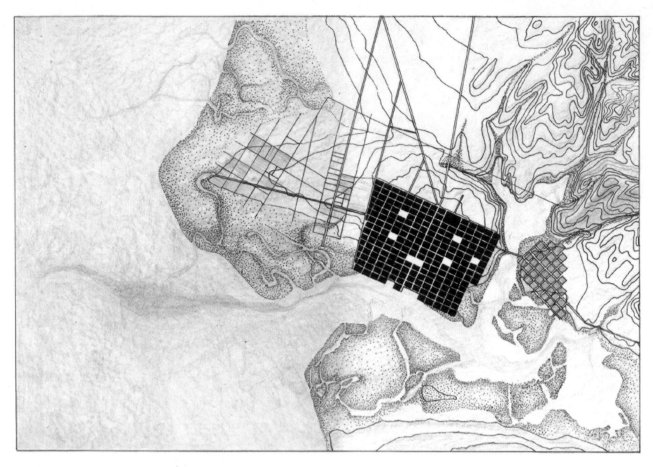

Figure 4.5 Kellersberger revised the plan for Oakland in 1857 to better connect the harbor to the highway. He did so by introducing a new diagonal street, which also became the baseline for future city extensions.

East Oakland. That division still exists today, but not necessarily along Market Street. The revised map also introduced Telegraph Avenue as a continuation of Broadway. Near the foot of Telegraph and Fourteenth Street Kellersberger combined four of the regular blocks and designated them for the use of the California College. That institution would move up Telegraph Avenue to Berkeley as the University of California in the late 1860s. Across the narrow mouth of the estuary another extension to Oakland appeared on Kellersberger's revised map, called Brooklyn. The two settlements were linked by a bridge at Twelfth Street.

In 1857, Kellersberger surveyed land in Mexico for the Tehuantepec Railroad, the first to cross the continent from the Gulf to the Pacific. With the outbreak of the Civil War in 1861, he enlisted in the Confederate Army for a career as a military engineer. He died in 1900, back in Switzerland, after forty-nine years in America.[9]

The street pattern of Oakland is not unusual for the design of a new town in the Western United States.[10] It follows a colonial pattern of regular blocks and lots that efficiently accommodates a growing population. As a pattern such a design had longevity because it is almost infinitely expandable upon demand. The creativity of the surveyor came to the foreground not in the specific design of the physical street pattern, but in the selection of a precise location and the imposition of a regular street

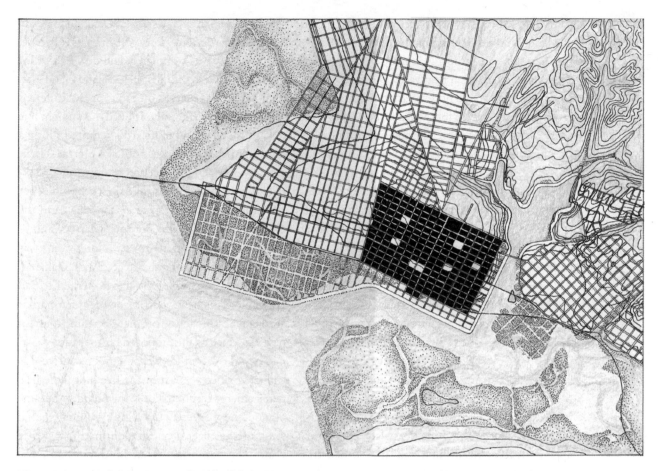

Figure 4.6 W. Bordman's survey of Oakland from 1884 introduces a continuous waterfront street.

pattern onto an existing topography. Therefore, Kellersberger did what most surveyors would have done with very much the same tools in the long town-planning tradition for colonial towns that date back to pre-Roman times. However, this tradition is not without its limitations.

The 1850s and '60s were the formative years for the San Francisco Bay Area. A large portion of the population that had rushed out to search for gold did not have the means or desire to return to their place of origin; many stayed and made the territory their permanent home. As Oakland grew, the limitations of Kellersberger's tradition must have become increasingly apparent, for the formal pattern of blocks and lots that allowed for fast and efficient development also invariably allowed for overcrowd-

ing and the rise of conflicting uses at a time when the use of land was not regulated through zoning. Most importantly, the people of Oakland had to clarify the three edges of their city along the San Antonio Creek and Estuary, as Kellersberger had simply run blocks and streets against the water without defining the city's edge. Without design intervention, the city would turn its back toward the water. The shallow tidal basin would fill with debris.

Soon Frederick Law Olmsted would change the tradition of town planning in the United States by following a strikingly different design ethic; one not based on the explicit aesthetic rules determined by design traditions that draw solely from the past. Rather, Olmsted developed a concept in response to firsthand observations of the landscape. His art combined functional organization, city planning, and landscape design in response to the natural setting. He came to California in 1863 to manage the Mariposa Gold Mine at Bear Valley. During the two-year stay he continued his profession as a landscape architect in the design for the California College on a site at the foot of the Oakland Hills. Eventually the site was not chosen for the college, but instead the college that later became the University of California was established on its present site in Berkeley. But near the earlier site Olmsted designed and supervised the construction of the Mountain View Cemetery. He also urged the City of San Francisco to consider a large central park.

Olmsted did not work on the design of Oakland, but his presence in California must have inspired others. One can imagine that an Olmsted-inspired design of Oakland would have created a greater unity of city blocks and streets with a constructed waterfront, ensuring an accessible and permanent place for Oakland in this otherwise fragile estuary landscape. The opportunity to create a continuous urban promenade along the city's water edges was apparently recognized, but to Oakland's great detriment never fully implemented.

By 1880 the city of Oakland housed a population of 34,550 inhabitants. A map, partly a survey partly a plan, prepared by W. Bordman from 1883, shows a promenade street that, if built, would have been spectacular. This new street started as Lake Shore Boulevard along Lake Merritt's eastern shore and circled the entire lake as it does today, but Bordman introduced a complete new row of blocks east of Fallon Street, turned at a ninety-degree angle, and proposed to complete the edge that Water Street occasionally forms along the inner harbor. At Castro Street the new promenade street would have turned again to follow the shoreline of what must have been part of a tidal marsh but is now the container terminal. There, the new street connected north to the foot of the Wharf at Seventh Street. This new street would have given Oakland a clearly delineated edge to build along.

The Bordman survey showed Oakland in nearly completed form. Barely forty years into its existence, the inner city was completely laid out. Except for the subdivision in the hills, all level land—and even tidal land—was platted into four or five different grid patterns. Broadway continued in a straight line toward the Oakland Hills. This required filling a portion of the marsh west of Lake Merritt. (Incidentally, it was in this section of downtown Oakland where most structural damage would occur after the 1989 Loma Prieta earthquake.) On the more pragmatic side, the Bordman plan accommodated two competing railroads. A long wharf was built at the end of Seventh Street in West Oakland; ferries took passengers and cargo from there to San Francisco. This new wharf made the inner harbor at the foot of Broadway obsolete, opening it up for new uses such as the proposed promenade.

The motivation for writing this narrative was triggered when the last of the five morphological maps emerged from the drawing board. It became obvious how severely Oakland's original spatial structure has been truncated during the last fifty years. The new streets that Bordman had envisioned and that would have formed an edge along the water were never built. More severely, the city was truncated in several places. First, in 1955, the city was separated from its waterfront by the elevated Nimitz Freeway (I-880). Second, and as recently as the early 1980s, the wide trench of the submerged Interstate 980 severed the connection between Central and West Oakland. Third, and still ongoing, the process of urban renewal has encouraged the consolidation of city blocks and abandoned major sections of the historic street grid. Within the original Kellersberger grid the city intentionally lost ten thousand linear feet of street frontage due to block consolidation and the associated vacating of streets as public rights-of-way. In producing these maps one cannot help wondering whether knowledge of the city's history would have changed the routing of freeways and the course of urban renewal during the 1950s and

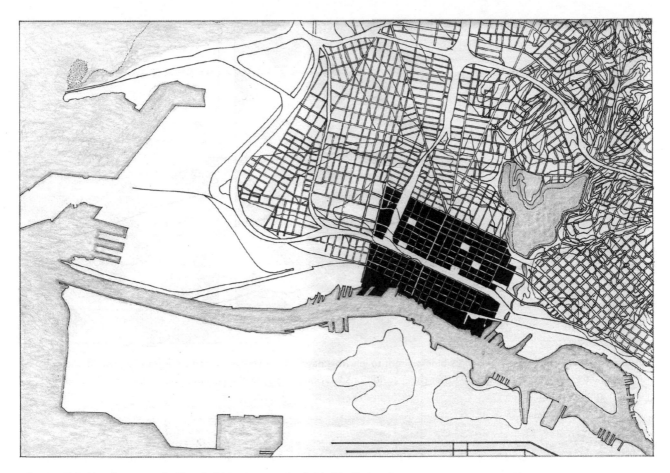

Figure 4.7 Oakland in 2005. Oakland's historic center is divided by freeways.

'60s. In all likelihood it would not have. Oakland like many other American cities had lost its inner-city population. With much abandoned property city blocks started to become vacant because those among the inner-city population with economic means started to move to suburbs that had become accessible, first by streetcars and later by private automobiles. For the planners of the time Kellersberger's grid must have represented an empty slate that could be filled with new structures.

A Strategy for an Urban Transformation

The maps in figure 4.8 trace the physical form of a select group of blocks through history. The first frame shows the lines that Kellersberger drew to define the parcels of each block. Each block contained the same twenty-eight properties. Once parceled in this manner sales agents—not necessarily located in Oakland—started to sell the land as a commodity. A buyer could purchase more that one lot, but a single lot was the smallest amount of land available. After deciding on a given block, the buyer did have one choice, the desired lot could be located on the short side of the block and be seventy-five feet deep, or on the long side of the block and be one hundred feet deep—a subtle difference, but important in its intention. The short block was intended to face a commercial street because the lot configuration encouraged a continuous retail frontage. The long side of the block was intended as a residential street, with setbacks in front to make room for a small yard.

Figure 4.8 The morphology of Oakland's blocks. Right to left (this page), Kellersberger's platting from 1852; conditions in 1912, from a cadastre map; conditions in 1951; (far page) conditions in 2000; proposed changes in 2000; alternative development plan, not implemented.

The next frame shows the same set of blocks in 1912, drawn from the earliest cadastre map that I could find. Fifty years into its history the city blocks have filled up. We can already see that the location of the two lot types on each block did not necessarily influence the use of the property. Commercial buildings without front setbacks and residential with front setbacks became mixed. Prior to the advent of zoning, a residential home could easily end up next to a wholesale meat market, or a row of homes could be built next to an industrial shop

The third frame is from 1951. Oakland is now nearly a century old and the fabric has started to disintegrate. The process started a decade earlier and would last for fifty years. By fire or through other forms of demolition buildings disappeared because the occupants had left or were in the process of leaving. Some properties were simply abandoned.

The fourth frame records the conditions in 1999. Remnants of the old fabric are still visible;

they are scattered over several blocks. Earlier in the same decade, the process of development had started to reverse its course. A new residential structure, a trendsetter, had been built and appeared on the uppermost block in the frame. Its single structure covered all of Kellersberger's twenty-eight original lots on this block. Where in 1912 a total of twenty-three properties existed with individual entrances, this number was reduced to one property. Relatively intact is the block just below. In Oakland this block is known as the Ratto Block. As long as anyone can remember, at the eastern corner stood Ratto's Hotel. The building still exists and houses a deli of the same name located on the ground level of the former hotel. In clockwise direction, next to Ratto's we find another small restaurant, followed by a rooming house at the corner. Around the corner is a former industrial shop that the present owner of Ratto's converted into a residential loft for himself. An empty dou-

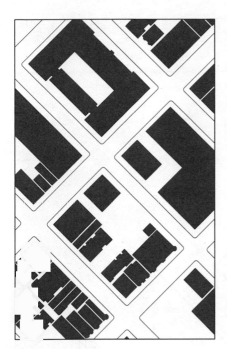
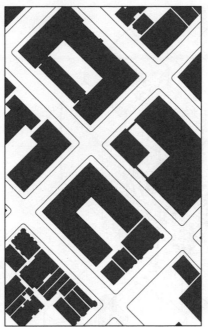
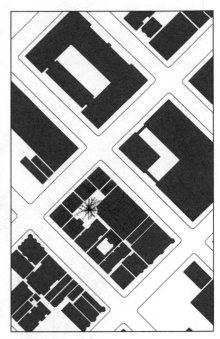

ble lot separates the loft structure from another rooming house. This one has a Chinese lunch counter on the ground floor. The Salvation Army occupied the next corner within a one-story structure, and there is a single empty lot between them and a wholesale meat market on the northern corner. The circle closes with one empty double lot and vacant triple lot that the Ratto customers use for parking. In 1999 the block held eleven separate properties and thirteen different uses.

The fifth frame shows the result of decisions made that year, but the building that would have resulted from such decisions was never constructed. The City proposed to consolidate all land on the Ratto block, except for the three properties on the south side of the block, and permit the construction of one four-story residential structure above a one-story parking garage. The design would be similar to the "trendsetter" on the block above. A similar structure was also proposed on the neighboring block to the west, where properties had already been consolidated and where a developer was also proposing to construct a single building on the entire block.

The sixth and last frame shows a condition that is informed by the morphology of Oakland's block and parcel structure. The development process would proceed incrementally. It starts with building a six-story city garage on the parking lot behind Ratto's. The new parking would be supported not only by Ratto's Deli and several other nearby owners of commercial properties, including the owners of Swan's Market across the street. In 1999 these owners had completed the renovation of an old housewife's market inside a historic structure that also included a children's museum and a cohousing community with twenty condominium units. In this location, the garage property could accommodate a retail store on the ground level, or—like a similar structure in San Francisco's North Beach—a neighborhood police station. Next to the garage, a forty-four-unit housing development could be placed on the northern portion of the block. The new housing would not need to be built on top of a parking garage. Instead, the ground floor could accommodate a row of shops, and the residents could use the parking structure next door.

To propose a housing development in a California

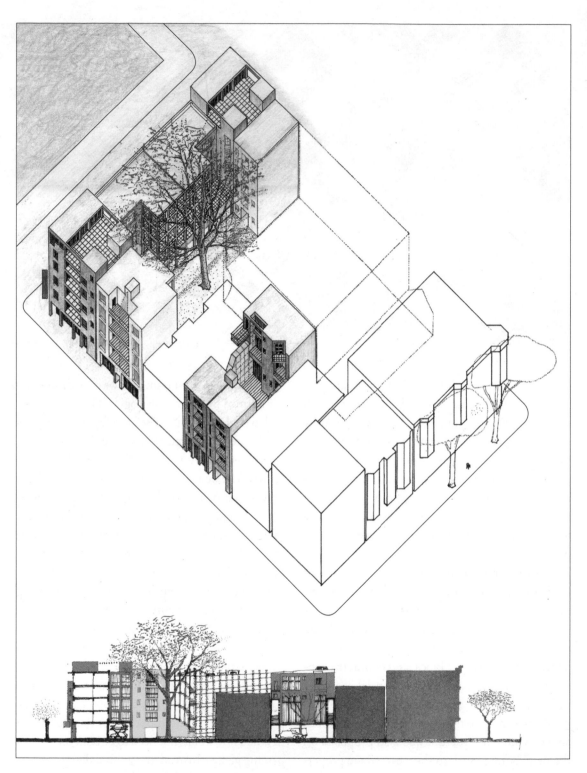

Figure 4.9. Isometric drawing of the Ratto block showing the alternative development plan. The proposal introduces a range of building types with a pedestrian-friendly frontage.

city without parking sounded utopian in 1999, but developers have since become accustomed to sell or rent downtown housing units separately from parking spaces. Also, city governments no longer insist on having developers build parking inside inner-city residential structures. Of course, the future owners or tenants of the new housing might directly benefit from such an arrangement, if the developer would pass on the cost saved from not building a parking podium. The indirect benefit is that the land in the rear yard of the housing can instead be landscaped in a manner that goes significantly beyond what can otherwise be planted on the roof of a parking garage. A single majestic tree is drawn in the illustration. Future residents looking out of their rear windows would have the sense of living inside a large tree.

Most importantly, the alternative proposal for the Ratto block would not eliminate any of the existing housing, including the Chinese lunch counter and the rooming house above. On the empty double lot next to it, the proposal would create an apartment building with eight units in the front and four residential lofts in a rear structure. The alternative proposal for the Ratto block would create high-quality living quarters with a range of densities. Instead of empty facades with parking behind, the proposal creates active sidewalks with many entrances into buildings around the entire perimeter of the block. The count of entrances to properties on the Ratto block would increase to seventeen, serving eight properties. Counting entrances into structures is important when making comparisons, because a greater frequency of entrances holds greater interest for pedestrians and makes urban districts more walkable. Importantly, the proposal does not displace any existing residents; it does not contribute to further fragmentation of the existing building fabric. Rather, it attempts to transform the fabric with new buildings of only slightly larger scale but greater utility because of the commercial use at ground level.

The vacant lots on blocks around the Ratto block

contained one of five such clusters with potential for development in downtown Oakland. Together, each of the five clusters offers much empty land that could be transformed under the mayor's initiative. Figure 4.10 shows each of the five clusters and indicates in yellow the land available.

First priority should be given to the main streets of the city that converge at the center of Oakland—Broadway, San Pablo Avenue, and Telegraph Avenue—which evolved into the city's principal commercial streets early in its history. One of two former vaudeville theaters had been restored in the 1970s, but a second theater, several department stores, and smaller retail outlets had been largely abandoned. Sears moved into one department store that Macy's had closed in the mid-1970s. Until recently the city has pursued other large-scale retailers to locate behind the ornate, but empty, facades. There is little hope that department stores will return; smaller retailers might locate here, but they will only follow a new and substantial increase in residential population, which is starting to happen. The many vacant sites along the three main streets provide opportunities for in-fill housing in direct proximity to transit. In 2008, near one of the regional transit stations, new housing is nearing completion on formerly empty parcels. The development will make street improvements possible and improve the chances for street-level retail to provide services to residents and downtown office workers.

Recognizing the future importance of the ornate old commercial structures like the second former vaudeville theater, the City supported an effort that made the structure seismically stable. It can now be partially used. Unfortunately, the new housing development near there is configured like a gated community with few, but controlled, entrances of the kind described earlier. The development closes itself off from the streets and sidewalks by placing large parking podiums on the ground level with housing above. As a result, empty walls, hostile toward pedestrians, line the sidewalks.

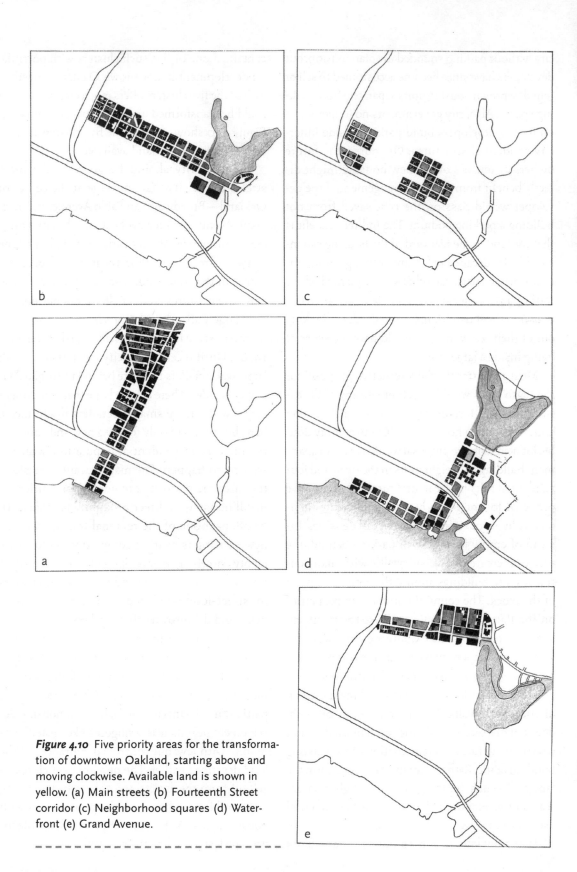

Figure 4.10 Five priority areas for the transformation of downtown Oakland, starting above and moving clockwise. Available land is shown in yellow. (a) Main streets (b) Fourteenth Street corridor (c) Neighborhood squares (d) Waterfront (e) Grand Avenue.

A second opportunity existed on empty land along the Fourteenth Street corridor that connects downtown to Lake Merritt, shown clockwise in figure 4.10b. One would hope earlier mistakes could be avoided here and that new buildings could be built along tree-lined sidewalks that would make this street a civic promenade. The street design invites downtown office workers to stroll to the lake and employees of the county courthouse near the lake to walk to the transit station at the Civic Center. Fourteenth Street also functions as the main street for the Gold Coast neighborhood, an inner city district that has kept its appeal because of its location near the lake.

The third priority is the transformation of the residential squares. The symmetrical distribution of the squares is an element of Oakland's historic town pattern; they are shown in figure 4.10c. One of them, Lafayette Square, was redesigned by the landscape architect Walter Hood, and the success of his design serves as evidence that the transformation of the other residential squares is possible. The playground on Lafayette Square is in use again, and elderly people sit near an old oak tree that—judging from its age—must have been planted here not too long after Kellersberger laid out the square. The empty parcels and their future configurations surrounding the square are shown in figure 4.13.

Lincoln Square, on the other side of Broadway, has been used as a schoolyard for many years, but it is open to the public and could be designed in much the same civic manner as Lafayette Square. Madison Park in the eastern portion of downtown is one block away from the former Caroline Square, which now accommodates a subterranean Bay Area Rapid Transit Station. Once upgraded and surrounded by

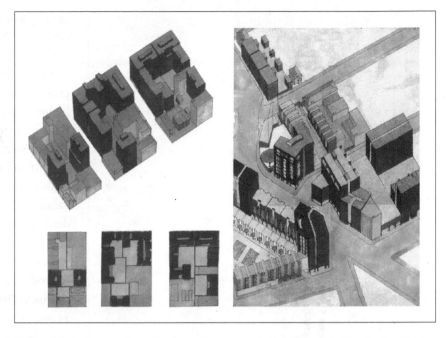

Figure 4.11 A cluster of possible new development centered on Oakland's San Pablo Avenue that would follow an incremental development pattern. Each cluster contains a mix of building types. Small townhouses for single families are combined with stacked flats with dual orientation to light and double-loaded corridor buildings with single orientation to light.

new homes Madison Park would become a center of the eastern portion of downtown Oakland. Finally, Washington Square, now called Chinese Garden, and Jefferson Square have been neglected because of their proximity to the elevated freeway. It would take a major commitment of funds to improve these two squares. This could be done by building narrow structures alongside the freeway to shelter the squares from the noise of the adjacent freeway. Alternatively, but it would be very costly, the freeway could be routed underground and covered as it is in Boston. The advantages to reconnect the city above a subterranean freeway would outweigh the great expense in the long run.

Fourth, figure 4.10d shows the design potential of Oakland's waterfront along the inner harbor and the Lake Merritt channel, first demonstrated by the Bordman survey of 1884. A comprehensive design approach is still feasible. The city planners would

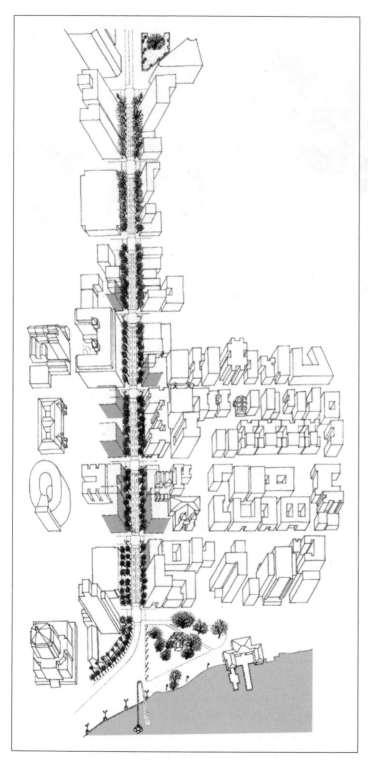

Figure 4.12 The improved Fourteenth Street promenade connecting Lake Merritt with Oakland's city hall.

need to coordinate all future housing projects in the vicinity of the water's edge to design an urban waterfront promenade.

Finally, shown in figure 4.10e, along Grand Avenue, a linear greenway could repair the currently fragmented neighborhood conditions north of the Kaiser Center. Such a greenway would continue Grand Avenue's handsome design north of Lake Merritt and carry it through to San Pablo Avenue across Broadway and Telegraph Avenue. Enough vacant land is available to build high-density residential development including high-rise towers in selected locations near the existing towers of the Kaiser Center. There is also enough room for a new inner-city school and a large open space adjacent to the linear greenway; this school could be organized as one of the new charter schools the City has established downtown. Good schools would be essential to attract young families to live in downtown Oakland.

The explanation of such "design principles" helped much to take advantage of the potential opportunities that lie within the physical form of the city. In 2006 Mayor Brown completed his second term; his goal of bringing ten thousand new residents to downtown Oakland was reached, with some delay, in 2008.

People

The residents that are expected to move back into the inner city are, in all likelihood, empty nesters and young professionals, who can be classified as children of the suburbs. That is the place where most anchor their references. That is where many have grown up, and, if they are still young, that is where they might return to raise their own families. If they are in the middle of their lives or older, they will make comparisons and carefully weigh the advantages of suburban living with those of living in the inner city. At the turn of the previous century, when people migrated in large numbers from the countryside to live in cities, there was little opportunity to return to their places of origin. Today there is. However, sociology takes two divergent views on urban migration:[11] some people at one or more stages in their lives will find life in the inner city culturally and intellectually stimulating and will appreciate the walkable access to amenities. Others will not easily tolerate the confinement of limited space, diverse crowds, and the lack of consumer choice that is alternatively available in suburban shopping environments.

Technological advances in information linkages and personal entertainment have allowed people to remotely access the centers of news and thrills. Still, some prefer the "freedom" of a drivable suburb. Family vans and sport utility vehicles are an excellent example of a trend that has fulfilled people's expectations for comfort when it comes to personal mobility and access. But, not even focusing on the environmental impacts, which are obviously caused by a dispersed population, this freedom, for many, coming from many remote locations, has created the traffic congestion that often makes locations like the inner city seem more attractive.

Life in the inner city can be attractive to the young and some of the old. The young have been the pioneers; early on in Oakland they took over industrial lofts and converted them to live–work spaces, causing small, informal residential pockets to emerge. The former mayor himself made his home in one of the converted structures. Developers have noticed the trend (lured by incentives) and have created a greater number of new loft structures, including those on several city blocks in the former warehouse area near the inner harbor. The building code treats apartment lofts more like commercial workspace than like typical residential space. For example: the code does not insist on private open space, such as

Figure 4.13 The transformation of Lafayette Square, Oakland. (Top to bottom) Existing condition in 2000; possible building footprints drawn in the Gianbatista Nolli tradition, graphic method to distinguish ground floors of public buildings that are accessible from the sidewalks; and allowable building heights.

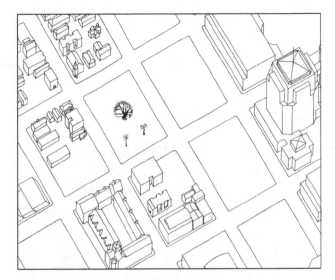

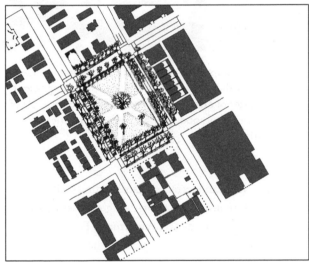

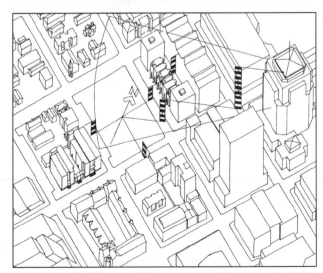

Figure 4.14 A new high-density neighborhood along Grand Avenue near Lake Merritt in Oakland. (Above) The proposed building heights transition from a cluster of existing high-rise buildings to the scale of the adjacent Valdez neighborhood; (at right) an axonometric view. (Courtesy S. Pellegrini)

balconies and terraces. Also, building codes contain strict requirements for daylight access to living spaces of residential structures. For commercial spaces, and lofts are regulated under the commercial building codes, such daylight requirements are much relaxed. As a result, loft apartments, although used as residential units, do not have the same general utility as regular residential units.

A strategy has to be developed before middle-aged couples, most elderly, and certainly families would consider moving downtown. These social groups need an opportunity to make a "home," not just a temporary place to dwell. Even in the form of "stacked homes" housing has to offer private realms to a much greater extent than is available in the residual inner-city fabric that has survived urban renewal and freeway building.

But success in the creation of a home for a small group of people like a family, or a middle-income and middle-aged couple, depends on many qualities that start with the dwelling and extend to virtually everything within some proximity of the home. Personal safety will be a prime concern. Those responsible for children will only let children venture outdoors into inner-city streets if accompanied by an adult. Most families will also be extremely concerned about access to local and regional services, including good schools, proximity to nature, and good regional transportation, ideally by private car.

Within a discussion on the needs and values of prospective downtown residents, it is necessary to include some thoughts about the cost of housing and its affordability. It was, of course, the high cost of housing in the larger San Francisco Bay Area that opened a window of opportunity to bring ten thousand new residents to downtown Oakland. In 1999, when the mayor made his announcement, the cost of a single-family home in a modest neighborhood bordering downtown Oakland approached $400,000; in 2007, prior to the setback in the real estate market due to the subprime mortgage crisis, the average home price rose to $575,000. Starting around 1999, the Bay Area's regional housing shortage made it necessary to look at opportunities for housing in areas where few people with medium to higher income would have searched in the past.

The high cost of housing elsewhere favored downtown Oakland, and throughout the year 2000 there was sufficient interest: 1,000 housing units were under construction priced to sell at $255/square foot, or $2.50/square foot for rental units. A year earlier, the City had invited proposals for five City-owned parcels and spontaneously received offers from several developers; two projects totaling 180 units were approved very quickly. Indeed the City was expecting an additional 3,600 units; if they had been built the mayor would have indeed reached his goal during his first term. In early 2001, however, the economy of the region slowed significantly. Substantial layoffs and failures, first in the Internet and multimedia industries and then among the computer hardware producers, made developers and lenders more cautious.

Since 2003, development proceeded at a much slower pace; however, there was time to do more outreach and better define the kind of housing that should be built and how it should be phased. Housing, transportation advocates, environmental groups interested in using land more efficiently, and downtown business owners have continued their support of the effort.

Figure 4.15 "Market Doorway, Oakland: Tenth Street Market" in 1942, photographed by Dorothea Lange. (Courtesy Oakland Museum)

Urbanity

Urbanity has meant a polished courtesy, politeness, or sophistication and elegance of manners. Although today urban areas are less likely to be associated with courtesy, urbane people are still considered to be sophisticated, worldly, and welcoming of diversity. It is easy to understand why tourists seek urbanity, but the consideration needed for others with diverse ethnic and cultural backgrounds and tolerance for people of all ages might go beyond the civil virtues that can be expected from members of our individualistic society. The creation of new urban neighborhoods thus does not guarantee urbanity; the everyday tools of modern society, such as private automobiles, will continue to give many the opportunity to live removed from social diversity.

Urbanity is a concept that fascinates designers. They claim to know what it takes to create it, but can they be certain that prospective residents will like their idea of urbanity? Designers rarely use the term to describe the characteristics of a population, but rather of a place. For them a city with urbanity is compact and dense and has many services and activities in close proximity to one another.

Presently, Oakland is not without urbanity: one of the city's unique experiences is for one to sit in a busy restaurant where world-class jazz is performed late in the evenings. Periodically and seemingly without warning, the restaurant's big windows are filled with the view and sounds of a large passenger or freight train traveling through the middle of the street. A few blocks further south, in the early morning hours, a person on a stroll might stumble upon the hustle and bustle of a wholesale fruit and vegetable market. This activity takes up several city blocks. Restaurant owners and retailers come to pick up boxes of produce, an activity once common to the center of most cities but made invisible by the move of these markets, long ago, to the outskirts of cities.

These activities, once commonplace, are in many ways "leftovers" of a nineteenth-century urbanity. Today they take place in the immediate vicinity of new upscale loft housing. The train operation and the wholesale market may not be robust enough to remain in their locations much longer, but these are nonetheless experiences that a designer would associate with the specific urbanity of Oakland.

This unique character manifests itself in a variety of ways in this city. The streets of the Gold Coast have a more stable urbanity, in both the cultural and the physical sense of the word. A multicultural community has held out here for some time in appreciation of the Lake Merritt setting. Chinatown in Oakland is smaller than in San Francisco, but walking on its sidewalks is a step into a different world. On weekends customers from the entire region come to shop. Chinatown provides the main retail services for downtown residents.

Admittedly these "cells" of urbanity are modest when compared to what designers think about when they refer to the handful of "truly urban places" of this world. But a designer can work with these places and add to them; there is clearly something there upon which to build.

Centrality

Centrality in downtown Oakland is synonymous with regional transportation. The regional and local transit providers serve downtown very well. One can commute from here to schools or places of employment in virtually all parts of the Bay Area. From a regional transportation perspective the centrality of Oakland's location is not sufficiently exploited. But the center of Oakland as a transportation hub is only a geographic centrality; related yet different is the importance of its location in the region. Oakland never had much centrality and lost what it had to shopping malls and office parks in once rural and now suburban Walnut Creek, Concord, and Bishop Ranch. It is doubtful that Oakland could have its own city-region ever again in the sense that Jane Jacobs defines it in *Cities and the Wealth of Nations*.[12] The city is part of an extensive supply region in support of San Francisco and the South Bay. The new federal and state office buildings in downtown Oakland were indeed built with the intent of giving the city more centrality; lawyers and brokers have subsequently opened branch offices, but not at the expense of downtown San Francisco. Local politicians might still aspire to a downtown with centrality. For them to imagine downtown Oakland as a set of inner city neighborhoods might require a lowering of expectations.

Density

Density, when related to livability, is not sufficiently understood even by city designers. Homes per acre or people per acre do not correlate directly or indirectly with the quantity and quality of human interaction and social contacts. There is likely to be a range of density with good social conditions and this range of density has to satisfy many other concerns, such as the need for privacy, light and greenery, access, open space, and parking. In addition to physical density designers know about visual, or perceived, density. The term implies that physical density can be willfully manipulated to appear lower than actual.[13] Research shows that Bay Area residents have a higher tolerance for multifamily densities if such living arrangements are combined with related services, such as transportation, neighborhood open space, and neighborhood retail. Not much research is done on people's preference for density, but the majority in a sample of 160 individuals from eight Bay Area communities, when interviewed about their preferences, clearly understood and accepted densities higher than twenty-four units per acre because these densities support more services than do lower densities.[14]

In Oakland the number of new residents nec-essary to revitalize downtown was arbitrarily chosen. When the mayor announced he would bring in ten thousand new residents, the number was not in any way related to the amount of available land but had political significance. To determine the anticipated range of density, a recently completed development of one hundred units on a typical Kellersberger block of 1.5 acres provided the prototype. Four floors of flats combined with a row of townhouses, built over a partially submerged parking podium with some retail on one of the four block frontages, yielded a density of sixty-eight units per acre. When this density was applied to all the available vacant sites in downtown Oakland, only half the units necessary for ten thousand new residents could be accommodated. Clearly some sites had to be built to higher densities. The best

Figure 4.16 The Oakland planning staff views a room-sized model demonstrating the distribution of residential density to accommodate ten thousand new downtown residents. The planning staff is preparing for a meeting with Mayor Brown in 1999.

way to explain the implications of the mayor's proposal was to lay out a large room-sized model of downtown Oakland and cover empty lots with building types, color coded by density. The distribution of new buildings on this map revealed clusters of new housing, and when seen in this way, city planning staff, politicians, and members of the community could weigh the opportunities and difficulties associated with each location.

Housing Types

For those potential downtown residents who have lived in the suburbs, the housing market for the inner city seems to provide only limited choices. The predominant type is the double-loaded corridor building with apartments on both sides of a central corridor, two separate sets of communal stairs to reach floors above the second level, and a shared elevator for buildings with four or more floors. This type is cost-efficient because it can be constructed on a parking podium of similar dimensions. As a building type, however, it presents significant shortcomings: windows open to only one side of the building; thus natural light and cross ventilation are limited. It would be reasonable to require that housing units with more than one bedroom have an orientation to natural light from two directions, a requirement in European and in most Asian countries, but not in North America. Such flats with dual orientation are referred to as single-loaded flats. Generally, two or more flats are accessible from a shared landing. In the hypothetical development scenario in the Ratto block near the Lafayette Square development cluster and shown in figure 4.9, the single-loaded building type with four residential floors over retail reached a density of eighty units per acre. Each unit has windows to two sides and a sizeable terrace or loggia opened to sun, air, and views.

Row houses combine some of the advantages of single-family living with the assets of inner-city locations. They do not necessarily result in low densities: small, single-family row houses with a setback from the street and a private rear yard can reach twenty units per acre, while three story townhouses in rows can be built at densities of up to fifty units per acre. Only 60 percent of a given lot area is covered by structures, allowing sufficient land area on each lot to remain available for backyards and private gardens. Row housing has an additional advantage: the density is low enough to accommodate car parking in the footprint of each row house structure. Row housing, with its frequent entrances, fine-grain texture, and clearly identifiable typology is in many ways best associated with urban living in American cities. Using a row house typology to line a significant public space was shown at Lafayette Square in figure 4.13. If built, the idea of an urban quarter might easily return to the consciousness of downtown residents. Many doors and windows open to the square, ensuring a sufficient population will have a stake in keeping Lafayette Square maintained and safe. The new housing thus contributes to a positive transformation of the public realm.

Rather than building apartment buildings of one consistent density, mixing density yields a more varied urban fabric. In order to reach a density sufficiently high for a downtown district, the combination of densities from as low as fifty units per acre to 150 units per acre would produce a variety of types, including row housing, stacked flats with light coming from the front and the rear, and tower configurations. Recent examples in Portland, Oregon, and Vancouver, Canada, have demonstrated that it is possible to arrange the different building types inside the same city block, right next to each other, and reach a density of 80 to 150 units per acre. Proposals for high-rise towers in the past have sparked confrontation and controversy due primarily to the drastic contrast of their immediate surroundings. High-rise towers must also accommodate higher numbers of parking spaces and thus are prone to large building footprints with potentially continuous and uninteresting facades at the pedestrian level. Con-

Figure 4.17 Diagrammatic model of downtown Oakland with color-coded blocks explaining the distribution of building types—townhouses, midrise apartment buildings, and high-rise towers.

centrations of high-rise buildings near existing large uses, such as the office towers at the Kaiser Center near Lake Merritt, however, can take advantage of a concentrated employment center while providing new residents with visual access to the lake. Their large footprints can become useful in locating larger-scaled retail uses, such as supermarkets, at accessible corner locations; these uses will invariably become necessary with an influx of new residents.

A mixture of activities is desired in downtown locations but should give special consideration to the diversity of small-scale commercial activities. The challenge is to sustain those activities that make the area vibrant and inviting, and will be an asset to the future population.

Nature

It is important to think of cities as areas that continue to be subject to the forces of nature. The 1989 earthquake brought to people's awareness the fragility of structures built on former tidal wetlands. The continuous struggle to keep the water quality of Lake Merritt healthy serves as another example. The lake, left to its own devices, would turn back into a wetland. On a different note, Oakland residents can observe directly that the lake continues to play an important role on the Pacific flyway for migrating birds. Firestorms, and erosion after heavy rain are all examples of natural forces that people in Oakland have experienced. Early city maps, like Kellersberger's design of Oakland, show the contrast between nature and the city with great clarity. The city blocks demarked the difference, outside the blocks, nature, inside the blocks, city. As settlements have encroached further upon natural areas, however, cities have become increasingly a component of a constructed nature with no wilderness left.

This concept of "city as nature" is not without its contradictions and thus not easily embraced by everyone; moreover, there is no denying that this concept is not without imposing design challenges. Consider, for example, the current demand for office buildings that are naturally ventilated and lit, a major departure from past practice. People in cities with a hot climate have grown to understand the need to arrange allowable building heights in a manner that does not block prevailing cool air breezes, for example, from water to land. Or, in cities with strong winds, planning officials have realized the importance of enacting laws that direct tall building configurations to behave in the face of a strong wind much in the same way that a gradually rising terrain might direct a wind upward without violent disturbance.[15] Whether it is in the planting of trees to increase air quality, or in the management of rainwater that gets channeled into swales by removing concrete and asphalt wherever possible, these design responses do not occur unless they are designed and directed on a citywide basis. The design community has embraced standards (such as the United States Green

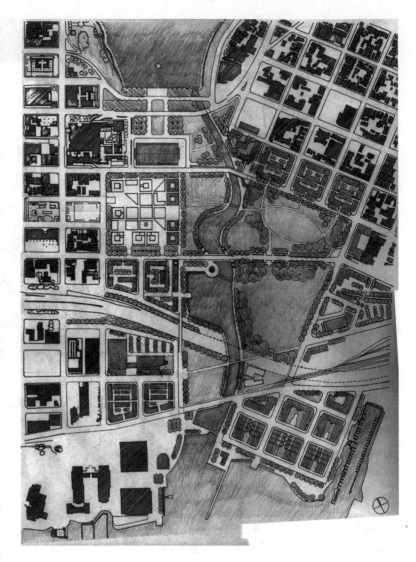

Figure 4.18 Urban design study of the Oakland estuary. (Above, courtesy J. C. S. Huang; above right, courtesy D. Davis)

Building Council [USGBC] Leadership in Energy and Environment Design [LEED][16] standards), largely self-imposed, referred to as the green building movement. These measures deal positively with the forces of nature while satisfying the needs of existing and future populations.

In Oakland, the proposal to build a new inner-city ballpark for the As in the former estuary—literally on top of the former estuary that connects Lake Merritt and the Inner Harbor—brought up the age-old ques-

the channel would need to function as a constructed tidal marsh. The channel could potentially act as a cleaning filter for the runoff waters of the Oakland Hills as well as the polluted seawaters of the Inner Harbor, all made visible in the modest, and yet constant, rhythm of the tide. A new design that deals with nature in the city *and* heightens the experience of natural processes will require the invention of an aesthetic that is different from the picturesque water's edge and sculptured lawns that slope down toward it. Instead there would be a geometry of reeds, gravel, and potentially some mud. None of this geometry would be entirely predictable—not at the beginning at least—but a constructed geometry of shapes and textures nevertheless.

Urban Transformation Instead of Urban Renewal

In conclusion, we need to return to the central argument that distinguishes urban transformation based upon urban morphology from the more functional urban renewal.

We were surprised to learn how much credibility the old urban renewal model still had in Oakland. To make potential development on vacant parcels more efficient, the Redevelopment Agency staff is

tion of how Oakland should relate to water bodies to which it owes its existence. Enough remains of the estuary to deal with it constructively as a body of water connected both to the creeks draining water from the hills as well as to the tidal action of the Bay; admittedly, this is a challenge. An extensive redesign of the estuary could never restore the original, natural conditions. However, a constructed water landscape of high quality can easily be imagined: such an innovative design would repair the ecological conditions of Lake Merritt, which is maintained artificially as a lake only with a constant removal of plant material below the waterline. Instead, parts of the lake and

ready to condemn marginal homes or businesses on adjacent properties. Ideally, the agency would like to develop at a scale of not less than one full city block. The staff is ready to go further and close existing streets that are not necessary for vehicular circulation, thus increasing the size of developable land over several blocks. Granted, this model is efficient because it gives control over decision making to few entities. It serves the developer and the lender. There is ample evidence in Oakland and elsewhere that this model created large structures with an institutional character, city districts that are not walkable, are unsafe, and without a mix of uses (i.e., single-use structures). Should the financing of a new project not be secured, or if the project becomes unfeasible for a variety of reasons, entire city blocks remain empty, and many blocks have been empty for a long time.

Figure 4.19 Urban design study of the Oakland estuary. (Above, courtesy S. Pellegrini; above right, courtesy R. Vargas-Hidalgo)

A new model of urban transformation would protect existing properties from condemnation and consolidation. It does so by protecting the existing parcel structure. After decades of land assembly and consolidation associated with urban renewal, few blocks with an intact parcel structure remain in the inner city. On city blocks where multiple parcels exist, new development would proceed in an incremental fashion. As parcels become available, the smaller-scale development can provide the downtown area with a neces-

sary fine grain that will inevitably create greater value over time because it will reduce the institutional quality of development. Smaller parcels are associated with frequent entrances, architectural diversity, and variety in the otherwise coarser grain of the urban fabric. Importantly, smaller parcels can offer a richer and more diverse pedestrian experience along sidewalks. There is nothing as important to the pedestrians of the inner city as attractive and well-functioning sidewalks.

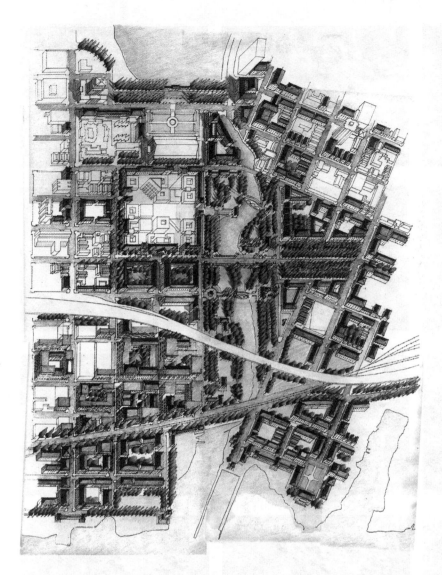

than to foster a tradition of living together in central locations. The individual, regardless of income or social status, has thus become isolated from urban places, losing membership in city society. This is a global phenomenon. Thomas Sieverts refers to the French sociologist Alain Touraine, for whom the question is of a high political priority; shall we accept the fragmentation of the city and society, or shall we try to invent a new kind of wholeness in our communities?[17]

A word of caution is in order: for design and planning professionals it is important to understand that the responsibility for creating inner-city communities does not solely rest with them. It takes more than physical structures to invent a new wholeness. But designers and planners have a special skill to communicate abstract concepts so others can imagine what life in the contemporary city could be like.

The call to move back into the inner city comes at a time when city culture is reemerging only in selected locations. Collectively as a society, planning has done more to dismantle the civic nature of cities

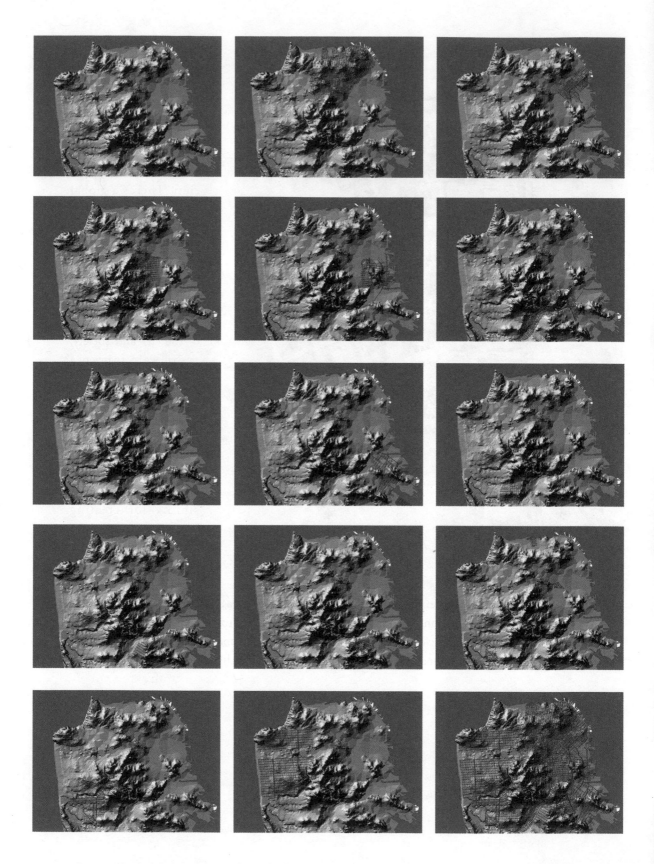

CHAPTER FIVE

To Define

Urban Design Principles for City Streets

This chapter is about design principles. Defining a principle in city design is similar to the activity suggested by the dictionary: to invent an abstract rule that can be applied by choice in a great number of situations and with consistency. The manner or style in which a design principle is executed matters less; more important is that the principle expresses a certain truth or generally applicable rationality that can be fulfilled in a number of ways. To be associated with "truth" lifts the interpretation of city structures to a moral level where structures do not seem to belong in common terminology. But urban structures should fulfill, in addition to the basic needs of human habitation, values and aspirations. To achieve this, the structure has to be conceived with ingenuity. Only then can a structure be uplifting, repair damage, and address neglect. Structures remain things; I am not interested in associating the "animus" of ancient et-ymology with structure, only with the creators of structures whose designs support life.[1]

City Design Principles That Define Street Design

Streets as routes of passage have permanence. It is therefore important to understand their origins. In cities with significant topography, the routing of streets influences the connectivity of the street grids. In San Francisco the regular grids of blocks and streets were stretched over hills and valleys in a fashion that seems to defy the natural topography. Upon closer examination, however, it becomes clear that topography played a major role in how various street grids were laid out, or platted. I counted twenty-seven distinct grids, many identified by name as neighborhoods, or districts. When each grid is drawn separately, but in the context of the topography, the directions of its streets in relation to important features in the city's landform and to shorelines becomes obvious.[2]

To find the oldest routes of passage one has to imagine first how settlers, and then road builders, established connections between places. In cities with strong topography, ridgelines offer the greatest challenge for the road builder. A saddle along a

Figure 5.1 Streets and topography. San Francisco has twenty-seven distinct street grids. The maps were made from an abstraction of two geographic information system layers, topography and streets. There is reason to believe that the early surveyors used topography to orient the street grids toward prominent topographic features.

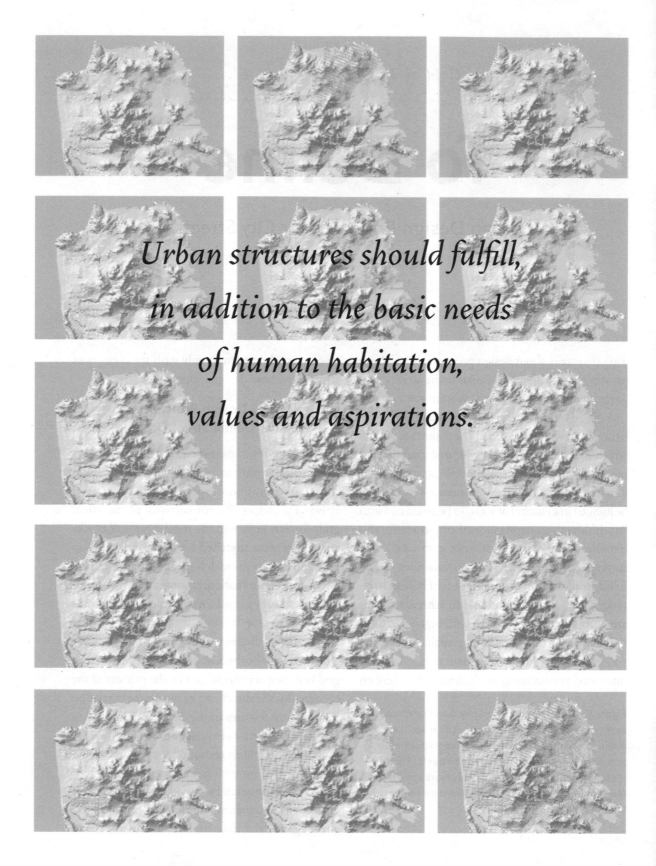

Urban structures should fulfill,

in addition to the basic needs

of human habitation,

values and aspirations.

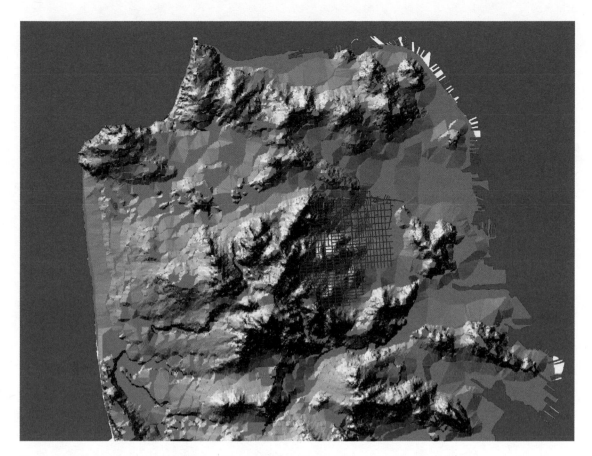

Figure 5.2 The street grid of the Mission District lies nestled inside topography.

ridgeline comes as a relief. It will inevitably become a place of passage.

A saddle in the landform of a city is a very interesting feature. Prior to reaching a saddle the traveler is directed toward the unknown; the anticipation of a new experience lies ahead. Like going around a turn, but stronger, the traveler prepares to move into a new place. Looking back, it is clear where the traveler came from, but approaching the saddle produces anticipation. Once at the saddle, the traveler is able to see what lies ahead and has a clear sense of arrival.[3]

San Francisco has sixteen major saddles (see figure 5.6); each is a distinct location. Their passage leaves a lasting impression upon the traveler. Generally a view opens up of the next district, frequently of the bay or ocean; sometimes the view opens to re-

veal a sense of the region beyond the city. Committed to memory, saddles will be recalled because they remain of strategic importance in finding one's way. For example, San Franciscans traveling between the Castro and the Haight districts use the saddle at the end of Seventeenth Street. Coming from Pacific Heights and traveling to Chinatown they use the saddle at Pacific and Jones. The experience is strong and does not wear off upon repeated encounter. In fact, the ascent and decent across saddles is a quintessential experience of moving through the city. First-time visitors might only find these saddles by chance. But once found, the experience is uplifting and memorable to visitors and locals alike.

To find reasons for the direction or orientation of grids, one needs to imagine the surveyor and the equipment that was used. If a prominent feature

Figure 5.3 The street grid of the Hunters Point Shipyard neighborhood in San Francisco near the former shipyards.

existed in the landform, nineteenth-century survey-ors selected station points and directed a baseline toward such a feature to plat parallel and perpendicular lines on the land.

Evidence for grids platted in relation to major features in the landform exist in thirteen instances in San Francisco. The most noticeable hill in the city, Twin Peaks, dominates Market Street and streets parallel to it. The Mission District is nested in a ring of hills with South Van Ness directed to the peak at Bernal Heights. The surveyor directed Dolores Street toward the saddle between Mission Heights and Bernal Heights, and Twenty-fourth Street is located between the peaks of Diamond Heights and Potrero Hill. The result is a regular grid with streets slightly askew to the cardinal directions.

The shipyards at Hunters Point are long gone, but the streets will always point toward piers and dry docks and toward the slips where once ships were launched. War effort priorities dictated the street geometry in this part of San Francisco.

On the south slope of Bernal Heights we find a very fine grid of narrow streets and small lots originally platted for weekend cottages. The location of these streets, on a slope that is oriented toward the sun and sheltered from the northwest wind, made these properties very valuable to families residing in the inner city; they could escape frequent summer fogs and strong winds.

Next to the experience of traversing a ridgeline, the crossing of a valley from one ridge to the next evokes a strong experience. The traveler has some-

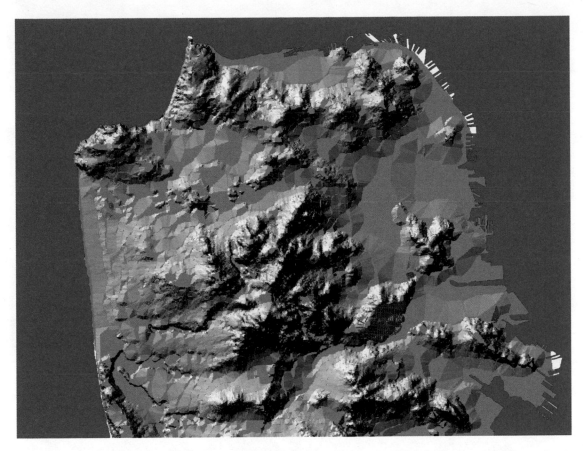

Figure 5.4 Bernal Heights, a San Francisco neighborhood that started as a weekend cottage subdivision, oriented toward the sun and protected from the northwest wind.

what of a roller-coaster experience. Upon descent there is a sense of joy because the opposite slope is revealed very clearly. Upon ascent toward the opposite ridge there is a sense of accomplishment in having crossed a major geographic feature. Ten such major valley crossings are firmly established (see figure 5.7). They are of citywide importance. Locals will know about others.

Memorable streets also run along ridges, never for any great length, because natural ridgelines soon separate from the straight line of streets, but long enough for the traveler to feel a sense of mastery. Each intersection on a ridge provides sweeping views downhill in both directions. Memorable ridgeline streets are found on Pacific Heights, Mission Heights, and Potrero Hill (see figure 5.8).

From these observations, one can conclude the following principle:

The relation of streets to the topography of a city holds special meaning. Streets with topographic distinction give residents a sense of orientation; help them understand the spatial structure of a city; and aid in way finding. In cities with strong topography, like San Francisco, special design attention has to be taken so that the experiences of saddles, ridges, valleys, and peaks are not diminished.

In addition to the twenty-seven grids there are two accumulations of smaller street grids. One is the historic remnant of small separate communities that existed along the Old Spanish Highway

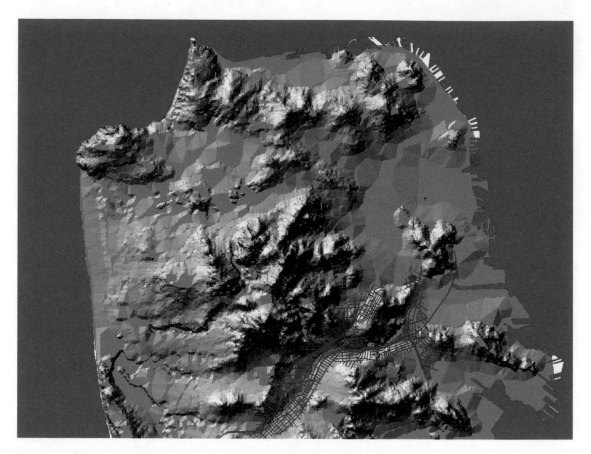

Figure 5.5 Early street grids alongside the historic highway into the city of San Francisco. We have to assume that the geometry of the street grids is old. Each subdivision of land might have started as an agricultural field along a small river that runs on the floor of the valley. The river is known as Islais Creek, named after wild cherries that grew along its banks. The flow line of the creek provided a convenient grade for the "Camino Real," the highway that was laid out by the Spanish colonial government and ran north to connect the California missions. In San Francisco, this road transformed into Mission Street. In the late-nineteenth century the railroad used the same flow line to create a grade for its tracks. Running parallel to Mission Street, the railroad grade became San Jose Avenue. Over time the fields were transformed into small neighborhoods with a village character that is still in evidence. During the decades following World War II, freeway builders and the Bay Area Rapid Transit planners placed modern infrastructure into the same creek bed. It is fair to say that the geometries we see today have all been influenced by Islais Creek. The creek is gone, few traces are left. The water that drains inside culverts along the flow line carries domestic sewage.

that led into the city from the south starting in the late eighteenth century. The other was a planned addition done in direct response to contour lines. There are also six special smaller grids that make transitions between the larger grids. They form adjustments between different street directions. Altogether, we are looking at a rather complex geometry that evolved over a nearly two-hundred-year period, changed here and there by human intervention, but now in a relatively stable state. All available land is used and no further extensions are possible.

For San Franciscans, the relation between the street grid and topography is not as esoteric as it might sound to someone who has never visited the

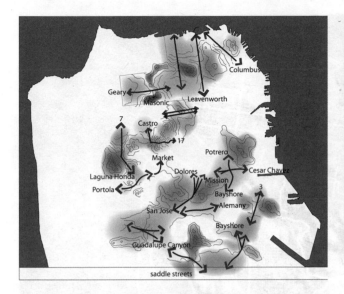

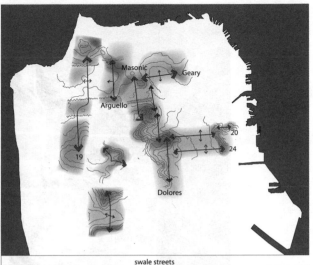

Figure 5.6 Saddles as places of passage. Crossing a saddle in the form of the land means to traverse from one neighborhood to the next. San Francisco has sixteen major saddles; each is a distinct location. Their passage leaves a lasting impression upon the traveler.

Figure 5.7 Streets that cross valleys or swales. The crossing of a valley from one ridge to the next evokes a strong experience in San Francisco. The traveler has somewhat of a roller-coaster experience.

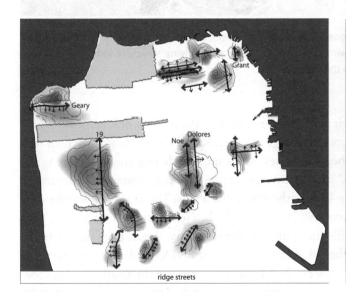

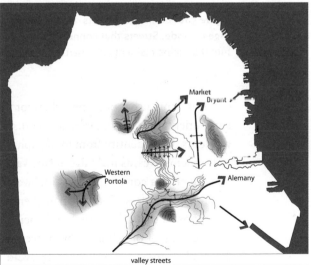

Figure 5.8 Streets along ridges. Memorable streets also run along ridges, never for any great length, because natural ridgelines soon separate from the straight line of streets, but long enough for the traveler to feel a sense of mastery when stopping at an intersection, where views down slopes in both directions become available.

Figure 5.9 Streets inside valleys. These are streets that follow the flow lines of former creeks.

Figure 5.10 Connector streets. Not all streets connect across hills between neighborhoods, only some allow passage citywide. Streets that connect are well known. They play a special role in giving structure to the city, a structure that helps residents link parts of the city to the whole.

city. Residents use topographic clues for their personal orientation. Topography defines districts and residents draw identity from topography. They do so for themselves, as in: "I live in Noe Valley," or as a member of a constituency, as in, "we, the Telegraph Hill Dwellers." The group frequently objects to proposals that take away from "their" hill—in any meaning of the phrase—by protecting the hill under the landmark ordinance to avoid further quarrying its steep northern face, as in the past, or by fighting any high-rise construction that takes away from the shape of the hill—and their views.

Streets That Connect

In San Francisco topography also influences the hierarchy of streets. Not all streets connect across hills between neighborhoods, only some allow passage citywide. Streets that connect are well known. They play a special role in giving structure to the city, a structure that helps residents link parts of the city to the whole. The most well known connector might be Geary Street, a street that runs through the entire city, almost from the bay to the ocean. The Geneva–Ocean Avenue connector is less known, it connects the southern neighborhoods. Nineteenth Avenue is dominated by through traffic; it carries the Coast Highway from the south and continues as the Presidio Parkway. It leaves the city at the Golden Gate. Mission Street is the longest street in San Francisco. As part of the Old Spanish Highway it enters at the city's southern border and ends at the northeast waterfront.

Figure 5.11 Consistent use of trees. Along an existing connector street (above) the trees unify the appearance; along a steep commercial street (below) the trees are concentrated in close proximity and placed to alternate with lights. The design emphasizes the stair stepping of this street as it runs down a hill toward the water.

Figure 5.12 Map shows the potential for promenade streets. Many miles of pedestrian promenades can be gained from lining the city parks with pedestrian walkways.

Connectors like Junipero Sierra, Portola Drive, and Market Street form a sequence of streets, the most important north–south link across the central ridge of the city. Seventh Avenue is less recognized but also makes such a connection.

A total of twelve major and fifteen minor connector streets exist in San Francisco. These streets connect the parts of the city and they should be redesigned according to their noteworthiness. These streets stand out and should be made distinct through consistent tree planting, signage design, lights, and special designs at intersections.

Streets as Promenades alongside Parks

The land for the large parks of San Francisco was claimed early in the history of the city. Their exact boundaries were defined in the successive platting of the land, but prior to significant development that later sprouted up around them. For that reason they are clearly demarked by streets along their edges, and these streets are lined with homes that face the park. Nature and city exist in clear juxtaposition. The abrupt juxtaposition was apparently

Figure 5.13 A potential pedestrian promenade alongside Golden Gate Park in San Francisco.

intended as a contrast; frequently there are no side-walks on the park side of the street. A person approaching the park after crossing the street emerges straight into the constructed wilderness. This design has advantages: city-dwellers can quickly transplant themselves into "nature" and be surrounded by green, but it also has disadvantages: the crossing from city to nature has always been associated with a certain sense of fear, especially at dark.

Along the edges of the major parks, pedestrian and bicycle promenades should be built that allow residents to move alongside parks and draw all the benefits from walking or bicycling through a green landscape, ideally on permeable surfaces, but a short distance to homes and urban activities. Citywide, the gain in walking and bicycle routes would be substantial.

Boulevard Designs That Protect Residents from Heavy Traffic

As early as the 1920s, well prior to the construction of urban freeways, high-capacity roadways were built, or existing streets improved, to accommodate the increased commuter traffic from suburban communities into the city. San Francisco has a number of such parkways or boulevards, including the Great Highway, Sunset Boulevard, Presidio Parkway, and

Figure 5.14 Map shows the potential for multilane boulevards citywide. Frequently configured as precursors to urban freeways, high-capacity roadways were laid out prior to World War II in San Francisco to accommodate growing commuter traffic. With the subsequent freeway building these roads are designed for access capacity. They can now be redesigned to improve the quality of life for residents that live alongside such roads. This is best done by including local access roads for residents, bike lanes, and wider sidewalks that are lined with trees.

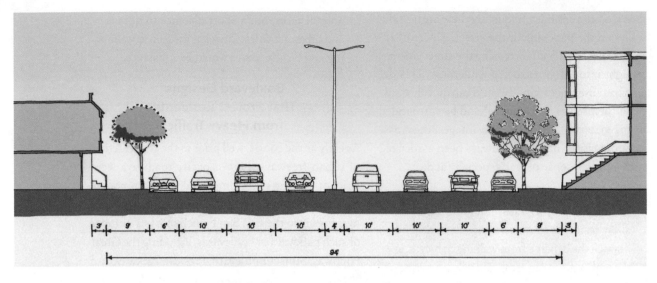

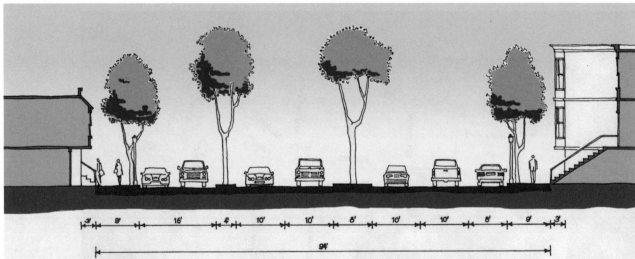

Figure 5.15 Redesigning the street to increase the distance between moving traffic and residents. (At top) The existing condition; (at bottom) increased usage of the same area for pedestrians, bicyclists, and parking.

Junipero Sierra Boulevard. These roadways are well designed and only need minor design attention. Third Street, once a historic highway into the city and the main supply route to former port activities, has recently been redesigned to reflect its changed role as a major transit connector between the city's eastern neighborhoods and downtown. Problematic are Nineteenth Avenue, San Jose Avenue, Alemany Boulevard, and Bay Shore Highway; their

designs should be reconsidered. Also, a section of Potrero Avenue, as it borders the Mission District, needs design attention. Potrero Avenue once functioned as the southern highway entrance prior to the construction of US 101 as a freeway.

The street design of major arteries that are wide, with extra moving lanes and a design that encourages fast traffic, should be reconsidered, especially in those areas where these streets are lined with residential homes and where they run parallel to freeways. Here, the roadway design should be changed wherever possible to increase the distance between homes and through traffic. Already a twenty-foot increase in the separation of homes and traffic reduces sound levels. In such a buffer zone, which includes the sidewalks and can include parking lanes, trees should be planted as closely spaced as possible to visually separate the residents from the moving traffic.

Streets as Conduits for Nature

In addition to the many functions that streets have, they also play an important role in the natural ecology of the city. Street design influences microcli-

mate, their design contributes to the health of the city's vegetation, and, because streets traverse watersheds, their design can be important for groundwater recharge. Of course it is primarily their linear form and the fact that streets cover long distances that make them so important for the natural ecology of a city.

Streets as Green Connectors

Selected streets could take on an important ecological function as connectors between major urban parks. Not only does the Presidio Parkway connect major traffic to and from the Golden Gate Bridge, it also connects two major urban forests, Golden Gate Park and the Presidio. Ecologists stress the importance of such connectors as migration corridors with high biological value. Plant

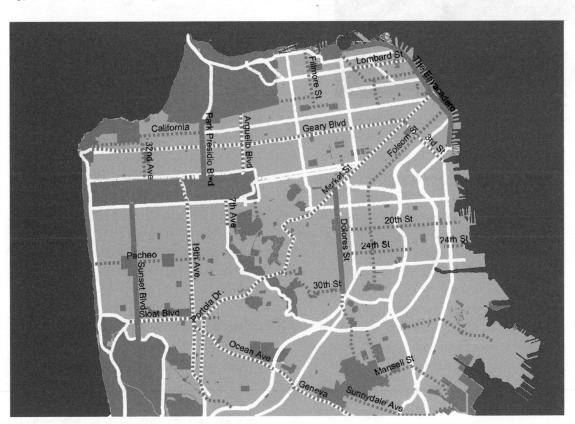

Figure 5.16 Map shows the potential for ecological connector streets citywide. Designated streets in San Francisco can be redesigned to connect the major parks of the city.

 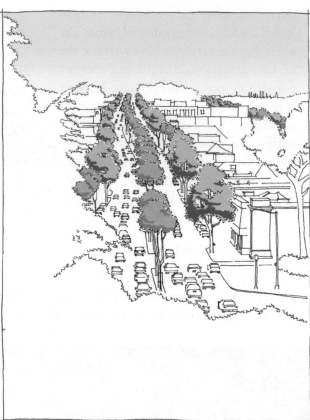

Figure 5.17 Streets as ecological connectors: options for change. Nineteenth Avenue in San Francisco seen (at left) from Golden Gate Park and (at right) with proposed addition of continuous trees.

species and small animals, including birds, migrate along such routes and thereby increase the health of vegetation; this in turn makes plants more resistant to diseases. Healthy trees contribute to improved air quality and a more comfortable microclimate. It is possible to lay a green weblike structure over the entire city that connects all major parks. Like most other design principles, the creation of a green web of streets is possible in many cities.[4]

Selected streets can be designed to become green connectors with high ecological value. For example McLaren Park needs to be connected via Persia and Naples Street to the San Bruno Mountains, to Candlestick Park via Mansell Street, and to Golden Gate Park via Bosworth Street and Seventh Avenue. A green corridor along California Street would connect the Presidio Parkway with Lincoln Park. Construction of these connectors would form the beginnings of a new green network that connects all parks and stretches across the entire city from the bay to the ocean.

One additional link would be beneficial along the western flank of the city. This link would connect Golden Gate Park and Stern Grove to the Zoo and onward to Fort Funston. In the extreme west, Sunset Boulevard partly makes this connection, but Nineteenth Avenue plus its two neighboring streets, Eighteenth and Twentieth, would together

Figure 5.18 Streets as ecological connectors: options for change. Neighboring Eighteenth Avenue (above left) and with a proposed center mall (above right). Below, and aerial view, transformed (at right) in an aerial drawing of the completed ecological corridor.

provide a more meaningful connection because they can also be connected to Mount Davidson and Mount Sutro, thus to Twin Peaks and Glen Park. The two streets flanking Nineteenth Avenue could be designed with an eighteen-foot-wide median that reaches from Golden Gate Park to Stern Grove and St. Francis Wood. A green mall to allow pedestrians and bicyclists to reach the parks with greater comfort, or for diagonal parking, could be created using a permeable-surfaced median with a continuous tree cover.

Heavy fog during the summer makes San Francisco residents in the western parts of the city regard sunlight as a precious resource. In the past, there has been much opposition to inten-sive tree planting in the neighborhoods near the ocean. However, the planting of trees in the center of the street, versus along sidewalks, should alleviate such concerns. Unlike trees along sidewalks, trees along the center mall of the roadway cast less of a shadow onto windows and yards, especially during the summer months when the sun angles are high.

An organization that actively promotes tree planting in North American communities is the Home Depot Foundation. In addition to ecological reasoning and advocating improved roadway character, this organization has also gathered data on the economic benefits of additional tree growth in cities.[5]

Streets and Watersheds

The city of San Francisco has seven watersheds. They are named after the creeks or small rivers that once ran along their slopes. Mission Creek and Islais Creek are the best-known examples. The two small rivers, together with all other brooks and creeks, have long been covered over by streets and buildings. Rainwater is directed into sewer lines. The natural water system has all but disappeared. However, after rains, water still drains along the old flow lines down slopes into the valleys and out to the bay or ocean. The pattern of these flow lines can be seen on aerial photos, especially after the winter rains. Lines of healthy trees can be seen that wind through backyards and travel down slopes to gather at the bottom of valleys.

Using modern mapping techniques, flow lines can be traced in the contour lines of the city's topography. Wherever such flow lines cross streets the opportunity exists to design retention areas that have permeable surfaces. The flow lines will direct rainwater into such recharge areas and replenish the groundwater table. Depending on the available space these groundwater recharge areas can be extensive or small. They can be placed at the edge of the pavement or in the middle of the street. To be effective, they will have permeable surfaces with trees or other vegetation. Their distribution will delineate the natural topography of the city as these groundwater recharge sites stair-step up slopes from block to block. It will be important to coordinate

Figure 5.19 San Francisco's watersheds and former wetlands.

Figure 5.20 The flow lines made visible by the health of backyard trees. This photo was taken after the winter rains in the early spring. The diagonal lines of trees that cross backyards and streets diagonally grow where ground water is available in a linear fashion along the natural drainage lines of the terrain.

the design of these groundwater recharge sites with neighborhood groups.

Streets and Climate

Good city design can influence outdoor comfort for pedestrians at street level. Pedestrian promenades, but also gathering places elsewhere and sidewalks along streets, can be designed to take advantage of ambient airflow to provide comfort on hot days, protect from adverse wind conditions, and offer direct sunlight for much of the year. Such conditions can be provided even at relatively high urban densities.

To improve the microclimate in cities special attention should be given to the natural airflow between cool and hot surfaces. In most climates this ambient wind is beneficial to human comfort; it cools the air, especially on warm or hot days. For example, along waterfronts a natural heat exchange takes place between the cool air above the water surface and the warmer air above hard surfaces on land. As air rises above surfaces that have been heated by the sun, it is replaced by cooler air. This airflow is continuous; its strength depends upon differences in temperature and decreases with distance. The airflow occurs wherever such a heat exchange takes place. In new settlements streets can be aligned parallel to the wind flow that is predominant during the hottest time of year. In existing

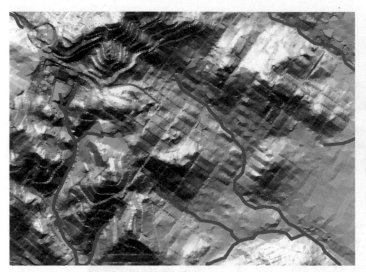

Figure 5.21 Designing streets that retain water. Aerial views (top left and right) tracing the flow lines; (mid-page) cross-section through a flow line; and (bottom) street designs with storm water retention. (Courtesy Noah Friedman)

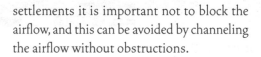

settlements it is important not to block the airflow, and this can be avoided by channeling the airflow without obstructions.

Streets That Channel Wind

Streets that run through urban districts where high buildings are permitted should be subject to special wind protection measures that shelter pedestrians from the mechanical forces of the wind. High buildings reach to altitudes where the wind's velocity increases and can direct the stronger wind downward to ground level, causing strong gusts that impede the movement of pedestrians. Wind velocities of up to eleven miles per hour are acceptable along sidewalks and seven miles per hour in areas where people sit.

High buildings can generally be designed to reduce the mechanical force of the wind, but high-rise structures in groups need to be tested as part of the permitting process to demonstrate compliance with wind standards.

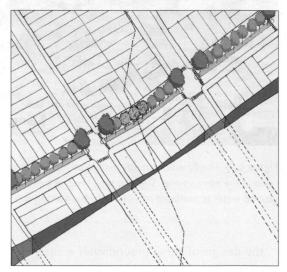

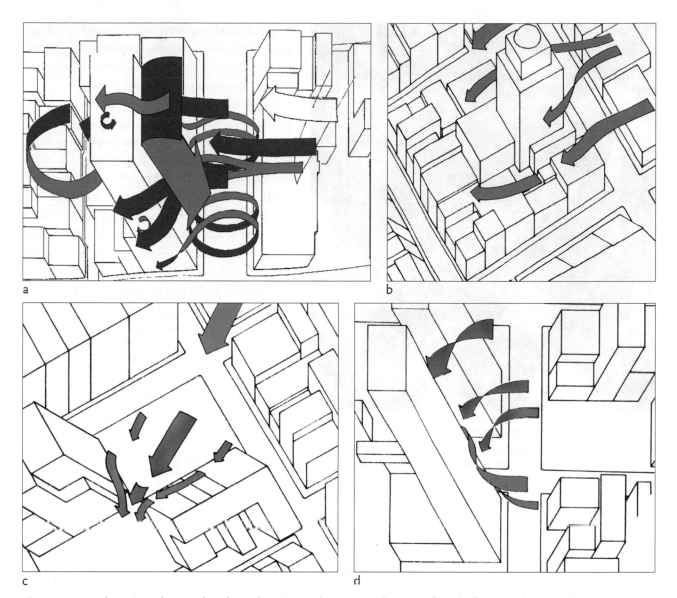

Figure 5.22 Avoiding street designs that channel strong winds. (a) A combination of wind effects, predominantly the *downward vortex* and the *corner* effects, (b) the *hill* effect that directs wind above buildings, (c) the *venturi* effect, and (d) the *gap* effect.

Streets That Should Stay Sunny

Given San Francisco's cool climate, direct sunlight is important for thermal comfort outdoors. On sunny days there should be a choice to walk in the sun or in the shade. In those districts of the city where building height is limited to four or even six floors such a choice exists.

In areas where greater heights are permitted, allowable building heights along heavily traveled sidewalks should be set to avoid intensive shading during the middle of the day for as many months as possible. Figure 5.23 explains how limits to building heights can be set without reducing densities in a district of high-rise buildings.

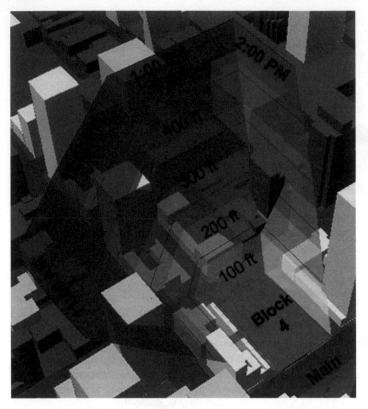

Figure 5.23 Streets and plazas that stay sunny for the physical comfort of park users. Sun access planes for midday sun exposure determine allowable building heights in the vicinity of a small new park in a residential high-rise zone.

Streets and Traffic

Streets have permanence because they give access to properties. But for the same reason they are places of conflicts between various users. Once defined in space, property owners will strongly resist any change to a street's routing. Streets are frequently made wider to accommodate more traffic and parking but are almost never made smaller. Seemingly small elements along streets like the placement of curbs, crosswalks, lane width, parking spaces, trees, and lights receive much attention because improvement to such elements are expected to settle deeper conflicts between those parties that lay claim over streets: between those who live locally and those who customarily pass through; between institutions and neighbors, commerce and

neighbors, and frequently between neighbors themselves. This was the argument made by Donald Appleyard who described the conflicts and suggested solutions to some of these problems.[6]

The deepest conflicts exist on streets that are residential but that also carry a significant volume of through traffic. Here residents are exposed to noise, fumes emissions, and the dangers of traffic, especially at crosswalks. A 1970 map shows streets in San Francisco that carry ten thousand cars or more each day and that are predominantly residential. Thirty years later, conditions have not improved. To the contrary, the number of streets that carry heavy traffic has increased and so have traffic volumes. The conflict between traffic and residential livability might never be solved completely, but it can be alleviated if nonautomobile travel is made more attractive.

Clearly, streets need to be designed to accommodate car traffic, emergency services, and logistics (i.e., the movement of trucks). But the emphasis is on *accommodate* in a manner compatible with other street activities. Comparing the 1970 statistics with the 2000 map should make us conclude that a city like San Francisco, with a rather stable population, should not and cannot accommodate more traffic without a loss of livability.

Streets as Centers to Be Reached on Foot

In San Francisco, 31 percent of the working population takes transit to work, 13 percent primarily walk or use nonmotorized transport, and half the population commutes by car—40 percent drive alone and 10 percent use carpools. These statistics from the year 2000 show a lower automobile use compared to many other West Coast cities, but conditions could improve. This can be best accomplished by strengthening the neighborhood centers as places for public life.

Half the population of San Francisco lives in a convenient five-minute walking distance to

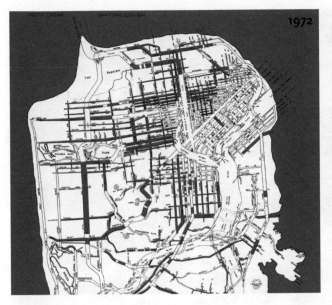
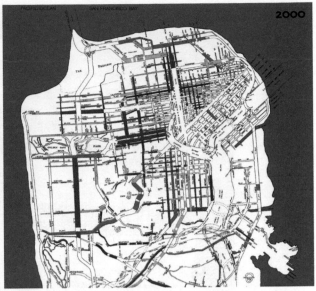

Figure 5.24 High traffic volumes on residential streets in San Francisco. The width of the bars shows average daily traffic volumes (ADTs). The color indicates streets that are lined with predominantly residential land uses on streets with traffic volumes in excess of ten thousand cars. At left above, the colored streets are associated with low livability, high interference of traffic into daily routines, low social interaction among neighbors, and low residential tenure or with residents of low mobility (City of San Francisco, City Planning Department, "Citywide Urban Design Plan, 1972"). At right, the four colors show in light yellow those streets that experienced no increase in traffic volumes in 2000 (some experienced a reduction, and that would be shown in the width of the bar associated with each street). As the color intensity increases, traffic volumes increase by up to 25 percent, 26 to 75 percent, and 76 to 350 percent. Thus the traffic conditions on a significant number of city streets have further reduced the livability for residents. (Traffic counts by San Francisco Department of Transportation and Planning)

- -

neighborhood centers and to transit stops located there. The rest of the population lives ten minutes away from such centers. It is imperative that streets and sidewalks are designed for good pedestrian connectivity; that barriers of any kind are removed, and that the most direct pedestrian routes are made available. By providing a convenient and interesting walking experience an important step is made to lower the dependency on the automobile and to further increase the number of trips made by transit.

San Francisco has a total of sixty-six neighborhood centers, all served by public transit. These are the main streets of the city; they are the places where public life takes place. Thirty-six of these centers

have a length that is rather substantial, three to four city blocks long, thirty are smaller, the length of one or two city blocks. The significance of the five-minute walk to centers for half the population, and ten-minute walks for the rest, cannot be stressed enough. Physical improvements to pedestrian connectivity need to go hand-in-hand with improvements to public transit and ease of transfer between transit carriers. Physical improvements also need to be coordinated with policies that protect the economic vitality of the centers.

City design protects the distribution of the existing neighborhood centers and strengthens their conditions through design that is attractive to pedestrians.

The urban design principles in this chapter are

Figure 5.25 Half the city's population lives within a five-minute walk of a neighborhood center (in red) with transit stops.

intended to improve conditions for the nonmotorized users of streets, chiefly pedestrians. Design principles that improve conditions for bicyclists are also included, but San Francisco's strong topography places some serious limitations on bicycling as a commuter choice. In other cities this will vary. However, the topography of the city is a welcome challenge for recreational bicyclists.

It will take a major appeal to balance easy access by car with more consideration for pedestrians, including transit. These appeals have been made periodically with some success. The last time, in the 1970s, such appeals led to traffic calming and protected neighborhoods. The current concern for public health, especially for the health of children and others without sufficient physical exercise, gives strength to an argument that improves conditions for pedestrians.

We start with the social conditions: If half the population enjoys a five-minute walk to and from some sixty concentrations of shops and transit, 350,000 people live within easy contact of each other in communities of roughly 6,000 people. If the sidewalks that lead to neighborhood centers, schools, libraries, and parks are pleasant to walk on and the streets are easy to cross and otherwise safe, an important step is made to increase walking as well as the face-to-face contact between residents. Detailed design principles describe the continuity of the pedestrian experience within each center.

Figure 5.26 A neighborhood center. San Francisco has a total of sixty-six neighborhood commercial centers serving an average of six thousand residents each.

Neighborhood shopping streets should have a continuous frontage of stores, especially around street corners. In addition to on-street parking, additional parking can be organized in the rear of properties, below ground, or above stores, but never on vacant properties facing the sidewalks. Curb-cuts for vehicular access should be limited to ten feet. Sidewalk widths should measure a minimum of fifteen feet. This allows for some retail-related activities to extend onto the sidewalks in front of shops. This width also allows for street trees in a planting strip near the curb. Shopping streets work best when they are not too wide. At sixty feet across the

other side of the street is easily seen. The human eye recognizes details, smaller signs, and the identity of individuals.

In addition to the sixty neighborhood centers, San Francisco's financial district and adjacent commercial and tourist centers have regional, sometimes national, or even international importance. Here, a concentration of streets serves 130,000 office workers daily. San Francisco's "transit-first" policy and the lack of parking inside or near office towers forces the majority of workers to travel by public transit. To a lesser extent, people drive private cars to parking garages. But regardless of their mode of transit, upon arrival in the downtown districts every person becomes a pedestrian.

Figure 5.27 Successful neighborhood centers have (a) continuous frontage of stores, (b) convenient sidewalks, (c) tree canopy made of deciduous trees, (d) and transit.

City design should give priority to pedestrians in the center of the city, and this is done by setting design standards for wide sidewalks and safe crossings. To give centers distinction, street furniture, such as lights fixtures, signage, and pavement, is unified, or willfully coordinated by color, material, and design. Downtown plazas and squares are designed for the comfort of office workers who spend an average of thirty minutes outdoors during lunch breaks prior to returning to their air-conditioned work spaces.

Some Final Observation about Public Life in Streets

Even the multicultural background of San Francisco residents does not make it socially permissible to be stationary in public places without any apparent activity. Public opinion has it that parks should serve those with leisure. Outside the downtown area, with its plazas and squares for office workers and tourists, it is rare to watch people simply sitting or standing along sidewalks with nothing to do for any extended period of time. Small setbacks in front of banks are better used by vending stalls or a flower shop than left empty with benches or ledges.

This observation about public life reflects on how public space is used in many North American cities. But there is evidence that cultures do change and the reason for such changes is related to the nature of leisure activities.[7] With more people working a more freely scheduled day on activities that are not tied to a common downtown workplace, neighborhood centers will potentially accommodate more activities, and they will contribute to more public street life. So far this increase in activities has been directed into coffeehouses, and they have grown in numbers.

That people like to gather where other people are, or at least near them to observe the activities that predictably take place out of necessity, is almost universally seen.

For example, the comings and goings near a transit stop are attractive for many; in turn, people will attract other people, and not necessarily only transit users. Therefore, good city design should consider modestly scaled public places for outdoor leisure activities near transit stops as a city design principle. It is important to use the term "modestly dimensioned," because outdoor public places that are too large will not be used. Selected transit locations should be improved to increase the distribution of public places in the city.

To implement this principle in San Francisco, the four neighborhood rapid transit stations would make a good beginning. Here the plazas should provide direct access to the neighboring stores, and the stores or cafes should be permitted to sell to customers on such public transit squares. In San Francisco this principle calls for reconsideration of current policy established long ago by the regional transit provider. Direct access from transit property to commercial establishments was not permitted, nor does the transit provider tolerate customers consuming on their public squares leading to transit. This policy is slowly changing because of the need to use the station locations more intensely as transit-related developments in order to increase transit ridership.[8]

To connect public spaces to commercial activities, it is prudent to introduce improvements to the public spaces incrementally. Eventually new space will need to be found by using leftover street space or obsolete turning lanes, or by consolidating traffic islands and median spaces.

Demand for more pedestrian-dedicated public street space does not appear overnight, but happens gradually. Residents in large Australian cities have taken to the streets, despite their slim history for gathering on sidewalks or in squares. This happened after incremental changes were made and more well-designed public spaces became available. As a result the city's capacity to accommodate people outdoors increased. The Australian cities mentioned here have their share of social problems, drug-related activities, and petty crimes, but city designers have managed to design inviting spaces that are used by a good cross-section of the population. With more pedestrians outdoors using streets, a stronger argument can be made for a better balance between spaces dedicated to cars and to people on foot.

Summed up briefly and in the spirit of Holly Whyte and Jan Gehl: start by improving a small place, and, if the space is successfully used, make it a little bigger, then add other spaces incrementally. It is likely that they will be used. This use in turn will attract new people, who have previously not been in the habit of using public space outdoors. Thus the population of outdoor users will increase exponentially.

Figure 6.1 Modeling human vision. The photo collage shows the Ryoanji Temple in Kyoto photographed by David Hockney in 1984. (Courtesy David Hockney Trust Fund)

Sitting in the Zen Garden at the Ryoanji Temple Kyoto Feb. 1983

To Model

Authenticity, Modeling, and Entitlement

With his photo collage of the Ryoani Temple in Kyoto the artist David Hockney explains a notion that is not obvious to most. To capture a view with a camera, it makes more sense to use the camera as a scanning device with a fixed focal length than opening the focal length by turning the zoom ring to a wider lens setting. The collage of images that results represents the view more closely to the way a set of eyes moves over the scene. With each slight movement of the head the eyes create a new perspective. When viewing the collage the reader needs to hold the page closer to the eyes than customary, but if the reader does so, the scene will be perceived as it was in reality and the reader will be drawn into the scene, in this case, the Zen garden.

Through modeling, urban designers gain knowledge about how a new structure may perform, and how compatibly it may fit with existing physical, social, and economic conditions.

In common with abstract modeling, three-dimensional modeling is chiefly done to enable a process of reasoning; modeling takes an abstract idea and transforms it toward the realm of the concrete. Not yet reality, urban form and the associated conditions become more understandable, thus

more real. Because it allows for greater clarity, models are useful for explaining urban conditions to those who may not otherwise understand the implications of decision making, such as politicians, community representatives, and the news media—thus the public at large. Modeling alone cannot claim to deliver judgment about good performance, fit, or compatibility—the evaluators will make such judgments—but modeling provides accessible evidence and makes possible an open, public discussion among evaluators about the nature of change, its perceived degree of faithfulness to a recognized tradition—authenticity—or a conscious break with tradition—a new beginning.

Authenticity, Modeling, and Entitlement[1]

In the creative fields like dance and music, but also in architecture and city design, the direct meaning of "authenticity" describes a condition, or an artifact, that is true to the intent of its creation or authorship. Authenticity can be applied, first of all, to the original form of the land that a city was built upon; the creation, without evoking religion, through natural processes.

The rock formation below Manhattan holds authenticity as it slopes alongside the Hudson River

Modeling takes an abstract idea and transforms it toward the realm of the concrete.

Sitting in the Zen Garden at the Ryoanji Temple Kyoto Feb. 1983

Figure 6.2 Landform and settlement, Paris, Ile de France.

toward the Atlantic Ocean. The Seine, meandering through the Ile de France gives Paris authenticity.

The satellite images in the first chapter show the forms that give these urban regions such authenticity. The form-giving elements of the natural topography (more evident in some cities than others) distinguish one region from the other.

Authenticity of place, however, is an ephemeral notion, open to much interpretation. While few would argue against the fact that a city's original landform has authenticity, many would question whether structures that have been placed upon the land can be considered to hold authenticity—clearly, not in all cases. Only a historic perspective can be useful to arrive at some consensus. Any decisions about authentic or inauthentic contributions to city form would need to be based upon principles arrived at through open, public debate.

As a result of such a debate principles can be established that can guide city design. Chapter 5 illustrated a number of principles that followed a generalizable rationale. In those cities where such discussions have taken place proposed change can be evaluated to conform to such principles.

Yet authenticity is a dynamic concept. Debates about the appropriateness of change continuously take place in cities. One only need think about the Eiffel Tower in Paris, one of the first, if not the first, profane structure that violated the city's height limits, or the Transamerica Pyramid in San Francisco that violated the law preventing street closure. Interpretations of authenticity are not only made at the time when structures are first proposed, but also change with time. Parisians reportedly hated the Eiffel Tower as an eyesore, but when asked where they would go on their last walk, if exiled from Paris, the majority would take the lift up to the Eiffel Tower, "the only place from where this thing can not be seen."[2]

In San Francisco, the pyramid-shaped building was certainly not perceived as authentic when it first appeared on the skyline under much protest in the early 1970s. The shape was controversial, but discussions about symbolic shapes frequently obscure other important concerns. In the case of the Transamerica Pyramid, the building size violated a number of publicly agreed upon rules, including the one stating not to close a street in order to incorporate its public land area into the proposed private project. The violation set a precedent. More recently, the same provision of the law was again violated when city government gave permission to revitalize a block in the retail district with a refurbished department store. In both cases, only the signifi-cant public contribution of street space made the large new structures possible.

Thirty years later, the pyramid-shaped building has become an icon of the city. The same claim is already made regarding the 180-meter-high "Gherkin" in the city of London (see figure 6.3). In 2000, Swiss Re's curved office building was approved on the site of the historic Baltic Exchange structure near St. Paul's Cathedral under similarly intense protest.

In 2006 the residents of St. Petersburg were confronted with the proposal of a 400-meter-high tower sponsored by Gazprom, the Russian energy monopoly. This twisting glass tower, if built, will dwarf St. Petersburg's highest building, the 123-meter Peter and Paul Cathedral.

An elected official in St. Petersburg voiced ap-

Figure 6.3 London's new skyline, 2006. (Courtesy Brendan Nam)

preciation "for the city's horizontal cityscape, which has remained largely unaltered for two centuries and is embedded in city law." A different interpretation of authenticity came from the architect, who claims—somewhat self-servingly—"the tower was designed with an eye towards St. Petersburg's cityscape, with its baroque architecture and punctuating spires."[3]

While the pressure to build high-rise office towers has slowed considerably in North American cities due to high vacancy rates, the security concerns after the attack on the World Trade Center in New York, and the preferred campus-style office model more frequently built on more affordable suburban sites, in European and Asian cities, proposals to build high-rise structures in inner-city locations constitute a major force for change. The models of these projects cause a considerable stir with the general public.

The array of curious building shapes that emerged during the first decade of the millennium in Shanghai might have inspired architects to propose twisted shapes in other largely horizontal cityscapes like St. Petersburg, London, Milan, Copenhagen, Paris, Berlin, or Vienna. Contemporary modeling tools available to architects certainly make it possible to conceive fluid shapes with great ease. The shapes are selected for their novelty as symbols; they become the focus of attention.

Symbols have their own associated risks. In order to enter the collective consciousness, symbols are in need of interpretation as a reference to an idea or concept. As the Swiss linguist Ferdinand de Saussure (1857–1913) pointed out, "the connection between the signifier and the signified is arbitrary." For symbols to be understood they need to be grounded because the shape of a symbol neither resembles nor is causally connected to its reference. Meaning depends upon agreement, upon a shared convention. However, the large volume and height of tall structures have far greater consequences on urban conditions than the structure as a symbol. Once entitled and built the buildings become a commodity. Swiss Re sold the Gherkin to a German real estate management company after five years of ownership in early 2007. The approval of high-rise structures as a symbol in one location raises expectations among neighboring property owners for higher development intensity on their parcels. Unless the land utilization is bridled by rules—or at least channeled into special districts, like La Defence in Paris—land speculation frequently leads to population displacement because it is coupled with a decrease of those activities that cannot survive near highly valued properties.

Next to the authenticity of location and the more questionable authenticity of symbols, there is a third authenticity involved, though many do not acknowledge it, and that is the authenticity of legal process. What is questioned here is the legitimacy by which public representatives grant entitlements to private individuals, including corporations. Buildings of the kind we are discussing did not conform to current law and were approved outside the democratic processes, but at a higher level of government. As if a natural disaster would strike, the applications to construct such buildings are treated like an emergency, where normal rules are suspended.

In the case of London, the Swiss Re application was discussed at a time when the British government was fearful that Europe's main banking activities would move to Frankfurt. Symbols are important in the context of such a threat; the deputy prime minister approved the application and decided that no further consideration was needed. Thus a form of authenticity—the most fragile of them all, the authenticity of a legal tradition—was challenged. In this case, it is the British tradition of a formal public inquiry designed to address important issues with some objectivity.

The process of public inquiry is not used in Shanghai, and in St. Petersburg local democracy is still very tentative. Here the application by Gazprom is discussed in strategic terms. The central government will use the authenticity of St.

Petersburg to attract foreign financial institutions. This move is expected to turn the city into a global economic center. Without the resources of such a center, the government claims, the city's unique architectural heritage cannot be preserved. It is precisely the authenticity of the city that has become a marketable asset.

Similar reports come from Tivoli Gardens in Copenhagen, where the new owners[4] proposed a high-rise residential tower and hotel to improve the revenue stream for Tivoli by marketing the famous amusement park's assets. If not granted entitlement, the owners claim that Tivoli's future is seriously threatened. By demanding that city government grant an entitlement to build a volume not permitted under current laws, the owners step beyond property rights and into the domain of the public. In early 2007 the Copenhagen city council was undecided but leaning toward approval. Only modeling the tower and significant community opposition made the civic leaders change their minds.

Buildings like the Gherkin or the Gazprom City project appear unique. Throughout history, presidents, prime ministers, and their equivalents have approved signature projects outside the normal process. Numerous public buildings, like the French National Library, promoted and approved by President Mitterrand, stand as examples. But the approval of building applications that were initiated by private corporations and approved outside the legal tradition at the highest level of government are a relatively new phenomenon that has become increasingly common, and not just in London. Here the Swiss Re tower will be joined by three additional towers, including the "Shard of Glass" or London Bridge Tower. At 310 meters, approved by the deputy prime minister in 2003, the tower was meant to be Europe's tallest building—until Gazprom came along. No longer is there validity to height limits set by law and the rationale that supported such laws. Nor does the financing available necessarily dictate the height of buildings at the time when such entitlements are sought. Mascu-

line ambition to outdo each other provides the rationale to set the heights of proposed projects.

In 2007 the authorities in Rotterdam were discussing the fate of a proposal to bring a row of towers to the Lijnbaan, the city's well-known pedestrian street. Opponents to the proposal gave ammunition to their protest by arguing correctly that the comfort of pedestrians walking along the Lijnbaan would be compromised. The four proposed towers would cast a solid shadow onto pedestrians at midday, every sunny day of the year. The Lijnbaan would also become much windier. Such rationale should be sufficiently strong to limit building heights on adjacent properties.

Public opposition toward the projects mentioned is fierce and strong, but rarely effective. In the case of London the opposition has lobbied the United Nations Educational, Scientific and Cultural Organization (UNESCO) to add the nine hundred-year-old Tower of London to the list of endangered world heritage sites unless the threat from encroaching skyscrapers is resolved. The Tower of London's visual integrity will be threatened by the 2010 expected completion of the 310-meter-high Shard of Glass project, according to the World Heritage Center.[5]

A resigned mind might perceive a shift in society's values toward decision making that follows market forces and attribute this change to abstract notions of postmodernity or globalization. Excusing a lack of accountability by elected officials and attributing it to conditions of a postmodern society is an argument with potentially disastrous consequences. What might unfortunately be the case is that abuse of political power has become more common, but it is undesirable and should not be accepted as a condition of our time.

Modeling

One partial remedy toward a better balance of power in city design controversies is to invest more resources in monitoring change prior to implementation. For a long time, modeling techniques have offered tools to aid meaningful discussions about change. This type of modeling is generally referred to as simulation, because the models of proposed changes should evoke a sense of reality in the mind of the viewer and produce a reaction that is similar to an experience of the real world. Indeed, without simulation, even a politically involved citizenry could not understand the effects of cumulative change, driven as they often are by speculative forces.

Seemingly despite, but really because of, the high publicity value of the type of project discussed here, specific information about such projects is not revealed to the public. The proponents of such projects manipulate the information with great care. The opponents do the same. Both sides try to influence the decision-making process; the proponents will persuade decision makers of a proposal's merit; the opponents will do the opposite. Only narratives and imagery are made public that portray a proposal at its very best, or worst. Therefore, any strategy that improves the balance of power for the benefit of a more open debate calls for a special commitment among those who produce the work. The simulations should be representative of the change that a new project will impose on the conditions that exist and on possible future conditions— ideally, they should consider cumulative change—without exaggerating or diminishing the impact of change. And the modeling should be open to accuracy tests.

Realistically, such work could not be expected from proponents or from opponents, but could be performed by individuals outside the controversy, for example, at research universities. Simulation laboratories exist in Tokyo at Waseda University.[6] Another laboratory has existed at the New School in New York City; a new one is emerging in Milan. The first laboratory of this kind existed at Lund University in Sweden,[7] followed by others in Holland, Finland, and Germany.[8] The early laboratories used physical models to test proposed buildings. In the late 1980s, when computer-modeling applications became available, a technology transfer took place.

Most three-dimensional urban modeling is now done with geographic information systems (GIS) applications, but scale models are still used for detailed discussions and presentations to the public. The laboratory in Milan[9] uses computer modeling techniques but also employs physical modeling. As a first project, an area in Milan was modeled that is located near the Porta Garibaldi train station. Several very large structures are proposed for the area. The architect I. M. Pei was commissioned to design a new tower for the regional government. Near there, a set of high towers was proposed in 2007; initially intended for the fashion industry and called Città de Mode, but renamed Porta Nova.

Modeling the experience of what it will be like to see a large set of structures inside a cityscape that has been without such structures, like Milan, is not a trivial task. The viewer is not accustomed to seeing them, and depending on distance will not be able to see them because a backward movement of the head will be needed to see the new towers above the roofs of the existing buildings. For example, figure 6.5 illustrates what a person in Milan sees from the roof of the Duomo looking toward the Alps. People from Milan do not regularly climb up to that platform, but it is a favorite spot for school classes and tourists. The lower image of figure 6.5 shows what the future will bring as seen from the same vantage point. That view came as a surprise when projected publicly in a room at the university in town. Once the first surprise wears off, viewers understand the visual logic of the simulated view. They relate the gargoyles in the foreground to the Duomo, the main cathedral; the glass dome on the left to the famous Milan Galleria; and everything else to the Alps in the distance. The information makes sense to a local, even if few people in Milan have seen the Alps from this location on a regular basis. The same is not true for the images in figure 6.4. Here the viewer is looking at the Porta Nova project from the neighborhood to the north of the Garibaldi Station, across a new park that does not yet exist. The viewer stands 150 meters away, as a

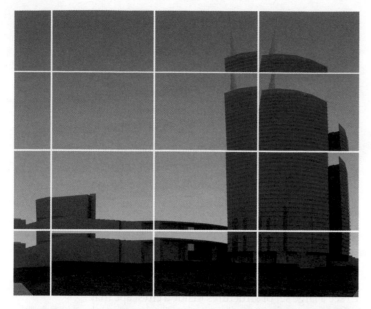

Figure 6.4 Simulating human vision. Above, the Gerald Hines proposed Porta Nova project at Milan's Garibaldi Republica is large and cannot be seen in one single perspective. A grid is superimposed to remind the viewer that the human mind needs to construct twelve perspectives in order to understand the true size of the project. Below, the image below has the horizon line superimposed to indicate the scale of the proposed project.

ways, very much like David Hockney did in creating figure 6.1. The frame lines in upper figure 6.4 show how many discrete perspectives the human mind will have to create in order to take in all information that gives reliable clues about the true size of the proposed structures. In this case twelve perspectives are required. Of course human eyes do not operate like a camera. The eyes scan the view continuously, but between each vertical frame the head must be tilted by fifteen degrees. To see the top of the structure a person would need to stand there with the head turned back all the way. That is, until it hurts a little in the rear of the neck.

To view the model of such a large structure projected as a single image on a flat computer monitor or screen can be misleading. A red horizon line and a few correctly scaled people have been introduced on the lower figure 6.4 image. Without these visual helpers a viewer cannot imagine how tall this structure will end up rising. The project is big, very big for any city, but especially in a city with a dense building fabric and a horizontal cityscape. The model that was employed for these simulations used a computer application called "sketch up." It allows for free rotations of the three-dimensional model. Sketch up is used in combination with a GIS application that allows one to georeference locations in Milan. Thus the modeler can freely match a view of the three-dimensional model to any desired location from which photographs can be taken. Until the industry invents multiple station point projection devices that imitate David Hockney's method, the modeler has to live with the shortcomings of a single station point perspective. The point is that single station point perspectives are very misleading when it comes to showing large structures in one view. They seriously understate the true size of buildings.

The Gerald Hines Interests proposed the Porta Nova project at Milan's Garibaldi Republica and kept much of their proposal hidden from the public.

The Texas-based developer hired the architect Cesar Pelli to design the two large towering half

person would upon entering the new park in the future. In order to see the entire structure visitors would need to move their head backward and side-

Figure 6.5 The Porta Nova project when seen from the roof of the Duomo against the background of the Alps in Milan before, *top,* and after, *below.*

round slabs, one of them decorated with an antenna in the form of a very much enlarged version of Francesco Boromini's lantern for Sant' Ivo alla Sapienca in Rome.[10] In June 2007 the project was entitled but the building design was still in a conceptual state. The simulated views also give an indication of the hard work ahead. The designers have to turn the diagrams into a building, and this does not always happen automatically, especially if the designer has not fully grasped the true size of the project.

At the University of California at Berkeley a modeling laboratory has continuously operated since the early 1970s.[11] Here changes to San

Francisco's urban form have been modeled. The lab's work has focused on the downtown area and the compliance of proposed development with policies imbedded in the General Plan, for example, the city's well-known "Downtown Hill Policy." This policy arranged the allowable heights of future buildings in a manner that created a constructed hill compatible with the city's natural topography.

Modeling and Entitlement

Computer-based modeling is not only available at selected university locations. With only minor capital investments, it has become quite accessible. A form of consultancy has emerged that furnishes developers and their architects with their own simulation studies. In San Francisco, as in most major cities, a sizeable industry of lawyers, designers, and technical support staff has grown around this activity. Their prime occupation is in assisting developers in their successful navigation through the approval process. Equipped with their own digital models developers now routinely try to persuade decision makers to increase entitlements. Not that developers and their technical support staff would openly lie; they simply distort the truth by presenting information selectively, showing the proposed building from only the most opportune angle, or leaving out important aspects of its context. Also, a developer has no interest in showing the effects of cumulative change. That is, to show what would happen if neighboring properties receive similar increases in entitlement. Such images and narratives could be a major distraction from a single developer's proposal and might easily lead to a negative decision for the developer. But cumulative change is important, and the Berkeley laboratory has developed methods which show all factors that are representative of the existing and proposed conditions, including other potential projects in the vicinity. The staff also provides openness to accuracy tests. Anyone doubting the accuracy of a particular simulation has access to its underlying data files. As part of a public university, information produced at the laboratory is in the public domain and disclosed upon request.

Interestingly enough, proponents of development have rarely challenged the accuracy and representative nature of the laboratory's simulation work. Instead, developers have attempted to influence city government by preventing the laboratory from getting involved in the first place. Their efforts have sometimes been successful, especially when backdoor political channels are used. For example, contracts for simulation work between the city and the university have been quietly canceled by the mayor's office without informing the planning staff that commissioned the work.

The reader should not assume that any undue level of conspiracy has operated in these matters. Viewed from a financial standpoint, the proponents operate in a most predictable manner. They attempt to benefit from sizeable increases to entitlements through the political influence at their disposal. The stakes are high, and if increased entitlements are granted the potential financial gain for property owners, investors, and developers may be substantial.

Modeling a New Downtown Residential Neighborhood

Between the late 1980s and the late 1990s, high-rise office space was in oversupply in American downtown locations. Existing buildings had high vacancies and there was little demand for additional downtown office buildings. The San Francisco Bay Area was no exception; new office space, especially in the new technology fields and biochemistry, was accommodated in suburban office

Figure 6.6 Transbay terminal site in San Francisco (above) in 1962, soon after the completion of the Embarcadero Freeway (source: CED visual archives) and (below) in 2005, 15 years after freeway was demolished. The state-owned land where freeway ramps once ran is readied for development. (Courtesy of B. Rokeach)

parks that styled themselves after university campus settings.

In the beginning of the new millennium, instead of high-rise office development, demand emerged, first slowly, then more forcefully, for high-density residential developments in downtown locations. San Francisco invited such demand for high-rise residential towers when the State of California resolved to modernize the city's main commuter bus terminal with an ambitious design that included high-speed train service linking San Francisco and Los Angeles. Such service might be in the distant future, but as an early step toward increasing the future ridership and to finance the new terminal, the State took steps toward developing ten acres of land adjacent to the terminal on parcels that had been previously occupied by the elevated Embarcadero Freeway. These parcels had been vacant for almost ten years after the structure, damaged in the 1989 Loma Prieta earthquake, was demolished. The State proposed building a high-rise residential neighborhood for ten thousand residents on ten acres of vacant land, expecting to offset the costs of the new terminal. One can only wonder about the origins of such numbers. When they were first announced, certainly nobody at the state level and in the city understood their implications.

Therefore, modeling such new vertical neighborhoods is essential. The list of topics that needed to be modeled was long, all focusing on the livability for residents in such a downtown neighborhood. In a city with an average of thirty-five units per acre density, a projected density of three hundred units per acre for a ten-acre site was unprecedented. Such a high density is more common in Asian cities, but on the West Coast of the United States there are no precedents. Even Vancouver, where vertical neighborhoods have emerged, one hundred to two hundred units per acre are high densities. Throughout the city the highest existing density on an equivalent ten-acre site was built in the 1960s following urban renewal, and even here residential densities only reached 150 units per acre.[12] Designers did not admit to it publicly, but to produce a livable downtown neighborhood at this density would be a significant design challenge. Many residents who will live in this vertical neighborhood will, of course, enjoy spectacular views, but once they descend to street level they behave not so differently from residents in a horizontal neighborhood. As pedestrians they will cross over to the sunny side of the street, if there is one. They will curse the wind at street corners, unless designers have dealt with this issue. The main attraction of the location, apart from the views from their windows, is the fact that they can walk to work or to high-frequency regional transit and save time for more enjoyable things than driving on congested freeways. The sidewalks need to be well designed to offer direct routes along commercial frontages to restaurants, parks, or the water's edge as destinations. The streets need to be light and airy, with trees that mediate the scale of large buildings. All those qualities can be designed, and living there can be quintessentially urban—or dreadful to imagine: long empty podium walls with cars parked behind them.

High-rise towers follow their own logic, guided primarily by structural engineering, fire codes, and the desire to provide light, not only to the upper floors but also to their base and to the land below, including the streets that surround the property. These reasons dictate the form of the high-rise structure, its spacing next to other structures, and how the towers meet the ground. A designer would wish towers to be slender and to have them meet the ground in a graceful manner. The first, a slender tower for a speculative development, remains wishful thinking. Engineering conventions in an area susceptible to earthquakes, conventions about elevators and the number of people they should serve efficiently, and local fire codes make slender towers a very expensive building type. These concerns dictate that the dimensions of the typical floor measure not less than one hundred feet, ideally square or nearly square. The second, a good transition of the tower structure to the ground, can only be achieved if the tower, prior to meeting the

Figure 6.7 High-rise towers with a pedestrian-friendly facade. The drawing in the middle shows a combination of building types on one city block: a high-rise tower, a row of townhouses with loft apartments above, stacked flats with a dual orientation to light on the left side, and an eight-story, double-loaded corridor building for small apartments. The design can yield a density of three hundred units per acre. The enlarged drawing on the right shows the two-story townhouses with the loft apartments above. Important is the direct access to the townhouses from the sidewalk. Access to the lofts above is provided via a corridor that connects to the high-rise tower and to the building with the stacked flats, plus one additional access point in the middle of the row. The drawing on the left shows the corner condition with a street-level market, a café on the second floor, and four floors of stacked flats, where all flats, not only those at the corner of the building, have a dual orientation to light.

ground, first transitions to the roof of a lower structure. Naturally, for structural reasons, the structural forces need to travel straight down to the ground, but for *quality of life* reasons, the design of this lower structure should be scaled to the dimensions of pedestrians that are expected to walk alongside it.

In addition to the tower entrances, the lower building should have entrances and activities that create street life. There should be a good interaction between the activities inside the building and the public sidewalk. Without the lower building serving as an intermediate, the scale of the towers would deaden the street frontages and make walk-

ing alongside them an unpleasant experience. The sidewalks would also be much windier.

Even at the high residential densities projected, not all street frontage could accommodate stores and restaurants. There would be room for commercial activities, but even ten thousand new residents would not provide enough buying power to support commercial frontages around all blocks, facing all streets. Stores and restaurants would be concentrated on selected blocks, ideally along one very active street that makes a good connection to the waterfront and channels many pedestrians along a convenient route toward transit stations.

Figure 6.8 Tower spacing existing in 2003 (above), and a simulation (below), both seen from the tower of the St.Regis Hotel in San Francisco's South of Market district. *Source:* SOM, San Francisco/Urban Explorer.

The concentration of commercial frontages along one street implies that the remaining block frontages would need to accommodate residential units. But placing residential units at street level is another major design challenge. The need for privacy of the inhabitants at street level requires an effective separation, or transition zone, between the building facade and the public sidewalk. And this transition zone needs to be arranged in a relatively small space. Instead of having ground-floor windows level with the sidewalk, the first floor should be raised for privacy; in addition this floor needs to be set back by a

few feet. Six to eight feet will suffice, and in this space, four feet above the sidewalk, there can be a small private space that is accessible from inside the flat. This private outdoor space should be somewhat enclosed to provide a sense of security and privacy as shown in figure 6.7. From the same space, it is possible and desirable to give the units close to the ground their own entrances. Thus the units could be designed as townhouses, and to make them function as townhouses their entrances would not necessarily be accessible from the lobby inside the large structure but directly from the sidewalk.

The spacing of the towers needs to be considered. Office towers in North American cities are permitted on adjacent properties, right next to each other, with a minimum separation dictated only by fire safety rules. Residential towers, for reasons of privacy, views, and light, need more separation. There is no set rule; precedent informs design.

In San Francisco, a 110-foot minimum separation was observed in the 1960 example mentioned earlier. (In Vancouver this dimension shall not be less than 80 feet, but in most cases the distance between towers is greater.) The 110-foot dimension was judged to be too narrow, and a 150-foot separation was applied to all the residential housing towers. In addition, a different criterion for adequate separation needs to be considered that places the towers well into the overall skyline of the city. Cumulatively, new towers associated with one project should not form a wall that blocks the views of the city for people who approach downtown, nor should the towers solidly block the views from the rest of the city into the regional landscape. These two criteria for good spacing are quickly articulated; however, they need to be modeled before detailed decisions can be made because their implications are far-reaching. Of great consequence as a result of modeling was the fact that not every parcel, but only selected parcels, can be entitled to accommodate a high-rise residential structure.

Again there is no set rule, the rules that exist are from the early years of zoning, but good planning practice suggests that a project of this density and acreage needed one, ideally two, public squares. Such public gathering spaces should be located at street level, not on the roof of an underground garage. The direct connection to the ground would permit large trees to grow, trees that would not be dwarfed by the scale of the surrounding buildings. When they reach maturity, these trees should be

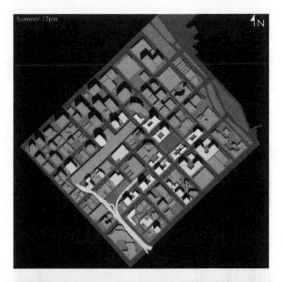

Figure 6.9 Sunlight to parks at mid-day (top to bottom) summer, fall/spring, and winter.

taller than the five-story structures at the base of the towers. To receive direct sunlight, high-rise towers were placed in such a manner that sunlight would reach the entire square from eleven o'clock in the morning until two o'clock in the afternoon for six months of the year, at a minimum. The laboratory's GIS model of downtown San Francisco was employed to test this rule and alternative rules.

To test the correct tower separation in the model a drive across the San Francisco–Oakland Bay Bridge was recorded. This entry into San Francisco must surely rank among the most memorable urban experiences in America. Only an animated simulation shown in motion can demonstrate the importance of adequate tower separation. The proper separation will avoid creating a wall and blocking views of the skyline and the hills beyond.

Without creating the model the designers could not have effectively explained the proposed plan to the public.

Modeling a Plan versus Modeling Speculative Development

One important side effect of the State's plan was that nearby property owners began to hire developers to perform feasibility studies for high-rise structures on their own neighboring parcels. This process started soon after the State had announced its intentions to develop the ten-acre site. Responding to pressure from developers, in January 1999, the mayor's office asked the City's zoning administrator to send out letters informing property owners in the vicinity that a raising of existing height limits to a new four hundred–foot level was under consideration for all properties in the area adjacent to the State's former freeway properties. According

Figure 6.10 Traveling across the Oakland–San Francisco Bay Bridge in 2005. Read images from bottom to top, scanning them upwards with your eyes as a progression in space. *Source:* Bosselmann/Vasileva/ Urban Explorer.

to San Francisco's constitution, the final decision to raise height limits rests with the city's legislative body, the Board of Supervisors. The board had not sanctioned the letter, nor had the mayor's office consulted with the planning staff.

The message to the property owners clearly broke with a thirty-year tradition, a provision in the planning law to concentrate all high-rise building into a well-defined area and to gradually increase the allowable heights from the edge of the district to the center. Thus high buildings contribute to the shape of a constructed "hill" that is compatible with the hills in the natural topography. The peak or ridgeline of this hill is found along Market Street. The State's former freeway parcels are located on the southeastern slope of the downtown hill. The proposed plan would now fill in this slope, or extend it gradually toward the hill's toe line. But, according to the hill policy, the adjacent properties further to the south and east would continue to be located in an area where a transition would have to be made to the building heights that prevail in the surrounding neighborhoods. This downtown hill policy is based on the authentic geography of San Francisco because it is tied to the original form of the land that the city was built upon. In the 1970s the hill policy had become official as a component of the City's General Plan, and since then allowable building heights have been set accordingly.

Whoever advised the mayor on the development choices for the neighboring properties made the argument that downtown San Francisco would eventually become more of a neighborhood. More people would soon want to live downtown, in addition to the 130,000 commuters employed there.

Figure 6.11 The drive continues, showing potential buildings that would be possible under the Transbay Plan; the last frame shows buildings possible under the Rincon Hill Plan. Read images from bottom to top, scanning them upwards with your eyes as a progression in space. *Source:* Bosselmann/Vasileva/ Urban Explorer.

Granted, they will live on land originally intended for commercial development, but with no demand for additional downtown office space, housing is now the highest and best use of the land. The downtown location is in many ways ideal for housing. Residents can live near their work; or if they do not work downtown, they can walk to a range of transit providers that will take them to employment centers anywhere in the region. Museums and other places of culture can be reached on foot or by streetcar.

A total of ten thousand units could be accommodated on the State-owned properties, and an equal number on adjacent privately owned properties on the slopes of neighboring Rincon Hill. Many of the new units would have sweeping regional views over the city, the bay, and toward the Berkeley Hills. One can be sure that the mayor's advisers also cited Vancouver as a precedent, where a high-rise community had emerged over the last twenty years on former industrial land.

Anticipating the inevitable counterargument, the mayor would have been concerned about equality. He would have asked who could afford to live downtown? Naturally, the advisers would have pointed out that the tower units would be expensive, the equivalent of a traditional single-family home in a very good location, or more, depending on views. But the advisers would have assured the mayor that for every tower unit there would have to be a unit in the podium of the project. Those would be more difficult to sell or lease at the same cost per square foot as the tower units because they lacked views and light. The lower units could easily be set aside to fulfill the inclusionary zoning requirements that stipulate the availability of a quarter of all units for people with a fixed household income. (In this San Francisco loca-

Figure 6.12 The same drive in 2007. Read the images from bottom to top, scanning them upwards with your eyes as a progression in space. (Courtesy S. Bosselmann)

tion the combined income of two schoolteachers is used as a benchmark and in 2005 was approximately $100,000.) These units would need to be subsidized by the sale of units on the upper floors.

In the American ethos, equality does not mean equal access, certainly not equal distribution. As Martin Lipset so aptly pointed out, all it means is "fair opportunity."[13] The fair housing policies of the City will guarantee that units be made available at, or somewhat below, market rates, with physical access to the lower prized units though lobbies separate from those for the upper units.

Tishman-Speyer, a developer acting for the property owners of two city blocks across the street from the State properties hired an architect and other consultants to seek entitlement for four towers under the four hundred–foot height limit that had been sanctioned by the mayor but—at the time—not approved by the city's legislative body.

Tishman-Speyer and their architects placed the four towers of nearly equal height on two half-city blocks. Given the available dimensions, the towers had to be placed in a checkerboard configuration, only separated by sixty-five feet on the diagonal (the towers are given a yellow tint in figure 6.13c). The tightness of the block dimensions did not allow for five-story structures along sidewalks. The demand to maximize the use of the site left no choice: the towers had to rise directly out of the street wall, from a podium of eight to nine floors in height. The units in the podium received light only from one side, from the street, or from an interior courtyard, inside one of the blocks. On the second block, the

Figure 6.13 San Francisco abandons its downtown hill policy. (a) Conditions in 2005, (b) the simulated view of buildings possible under the Transbay Area Plan, (c) in yellow, approved buildings on a site next to the Transbay Planning Area, (d) buildings possible under the Rincon Hill Plan, (e) a rendered version of the previously shown volumes. *Source:* Bosselmann/Urban Explorer. The last frame, (f) shows existing conditions in 2007. (Courtesy S. Bosselmann)

Figure 6.14 The view from the city (a) was taken in 2005 from the roof of the police officers union; (b) shows the buildings possible under the Transbay Area Plan, plus the approved project across the street from the Transbay Planning Area; (c) shows buildings possible under the Rincon Hill Plan; (d) shows a rendered version of all previously shown buildings; and (e) was taken in 2007 showing the existing conditions seen from the hill in the upper Market Street neighborhood. *Source:* Bosselmann/ Urban Explorer.

units wrapped around a multistory parking structure. And in these lower units, inside the podium, the developer would accommodate lower-income tenants required by inclusionary zoning.

The Tishman-Speyer proposal on the adjacent development site was far from becoming reality in 2004. At that time the developer's goal was to gain entitlement, which was granted. Once entitled the developer would be free to develop the property, or to sell the rights. By 2006, the developer had committed to half the project, and by 2007 had completed one of four towers, but with a different team of architects. Across the street, once the State has completed the work related to the highway and bus terminal, individual developers will opt to purchase the associated development rights for each parcel. This process had not started in 2008. Nor will the State release the properties until all roadwork and work on the terminal are completed.

Quite separately from all the attention, and in a nearby, but separate, location, one tower was completed in 2008 and sits on top of Rincon Hill measuring six hundred feet in height. It stands alone on the choicest spot, just above the anchorage of the San Francisco–Oakland Bay Bridge. The bridge is the gracefully designed double suspension structure from the 1930s; it has four towers that measure four hundred feet in height. From the new residential tower residents have breathtaking views of the bridge (see figure 6.14). Looking out over the city, the residents on the San Francisco hills wonder how such a structure ever got approved (figure 6.14e). It violates the policies of the General Plan.

Public Trust

The public should be given an opportunity to understand the implications of decision making and have input into the process—not an unreasonable proposition in a democracy. Public assets are at stake. Topography and sunlight are assets protected by City charter. A well-designed public space is an asset; so are views of the natural setting, shorelines, and hills.

In this regard, modeling makes an important

Figure 6.15 Modeling laboratory at Waseda University, Tokyo. (Courtesy Shigeru Satoh)

contribution to the political discourse in cities. Therefore, it is important that those who do the work adopt a neutral stance toward those who assign the work. Not neutral in values, which would be undesirable, but neutral in regard to affiliations with those who have a stake in the outcome. For that reason, the work is best done at facilities affiliated with a university. Work of this nature has been done by advocacy groups like those in New York City. The Municipal Art Society commissioned work on Times Square, so did the Parks Council on developments associated with the Upper West Side. But better yet, the modelers should be somewhat removed from the pressures of political influence and insulated by the circumstances of their employment from the temptation to tailor their findings to the needs of high-paying clients.

Admittedly, it might sound idealistic to advocate public involvement through modeling as a solution in the current era of planning deregulation, but there are success stories. In Tokyo, a large developer constructed a physical model of the Ginza district to explain a future scenario, when some of the historic department stores would need to consider changing their stores to high-rise hotel and residential towers. In order to implement such a plan, the city government would need to consolidate the blocks and give up the many narrow side streets.

There was a fair amount of reality to the threat for the department stores, because of the aging customer base and drops in sales. But the Ginza district is not only made up of expensive department stores lining the main streets at a uniform height. In the same area, but on the narrow side streets, a highly varied building typology exists that accommodates small, high-quality stores. Through modeling done by a team at Waseda University, landowners and local merchants realized the interdependence of the two Ginza environments and concluded that the protection of the more varied side street environment was key to sustaining the whole Ginza district. The local merchants conducted gaming sessions around a model. The process resulted in a request to the government to establish "Special District Zoning," a provision under the Japanese planning law that is designed to supersede the general planning provisions, which are general and tailored to fit all Japanese cities, with rules for entitlements that can be shaped by a community or district. The request was granted. Merchants and property owners began to understand that a community needs to respond to development proposals made by a developer who is interested in benefiting from a higher utilization of land through

Figure 6.16 Model of Tokyo's Ginza district. (Courtesy Academy Hills modeling laboratory)

Figure 6.17 Transit tower in San Francisco, proposed as a result of a competition but not approved as of 2008. (Courtesy Bosselmann/Yon Te Kim)

speculation, and that the community can become an active participant in modeling the future of their district based upon a consensus they have reached.

The crux of the matter is the timing of the modeling. Ideally, modeling needs to be done early in the process, prior to a time of raised expectations about entitlements. When done early—and early ideally means done in a proactive mode by the city planners—there is an opportunity to compare a proposal to the design traditions that are consistent with the collective will of a community. If only a hint is made that creates the expectation of a change to the zoning rules, the simulations have mainly shock value for those who have not been involved in the decision making. Once a policy has been breached it is virtually impossible to reestablish it.

In San Francisco the hill policy is dead. In the fall of 2007, the State held an invited competition

for the terminal site itself. Hines Interests with Cesar Pelli as architect won with a 1,200-foot tower proposal. If approved the result will change the skyline as shown in figure 6.17.

On April 30, 2008, a public meeting was held to present the official reaction to the State's 1,200-foot high Transit tower proposal. No conclusion was presented, but an indication was given that the city-planning department will recommend approval of the structure, although at a somewhat reduced height of 1,000 feet. If approved, San Francisco will have a new landmark. But not for long. The potential approval of the somewhat reduced tower has already triggered the expectations among property owners of three adjacent parcels that their property can also be utilized with buildings twice to three times the height of what was permitted at the time of their initial construction.[14]

CHAPTER SEVEN

To Interpret

A Canvas for an Emerging Commons

The visual arts can serve as a method to interpret urban transformations. I am thinking primarily about the mutual reinforcement between detailed observation and the knowledge of causes that influence art as a form of seeing, expressing, and interpreting. The subject of interpretation is the metropolitan landscape and specifically the San Francisco Bay as a body of water surrounded by an urbanized region of seven million people.

The Metropolitan Landscape

The majority of the world's population now lives in urbanized areas. Not everywhere does the term "urbanized area" mean cities in the traditional sense of the word, but an urbanized landscape with multiple centers, connected by corridors of movement, represented by multiple political institutions and economic activities. Rarely is this landscape shaped by the collective will of the community that is contained within its geographic boundaries; it is shaped by growth, decline, waste, and only sometimes collective aspirations.

In North America, Australia and to a lesser extend in Europe, people who live in urbanized regions frequently travel large distances on a daily basis, but they are transporting themselves through a relatively small segment of an urban agglomeration. The individual traveler is likely to know certain routes, but much of the metropolis is unknown territory. Seen through the windshield of a car the landscape appears accidental, not planned nor willfully designed. Only a view from space will explain a certain order, clarify the components of such a landscape and how the elements relate to each other. Such images reveal the original landform, the presence of water—or where water once was, the routing of highways, the distribution of centers and subcenters. In such a view, nature appears as an important component of this landscape, but it is largely a constructed nature. Continuously subject to natural processes, the metropolis has mutated climate, landform, water, and vegetation. The study of satellite images implies that it should still be possible to achieve a more thoughtful integration of city regions into the cycle of nature because all the important natural elements appear to remain, or they can be traced. The same satellite view does not reveal the social segregation associated with the metropolitan structure. The view through the windshield explains better the uneven distribution of wealth in this landscape of capital.[1]

The topic is complex; no quick answers can be

expected. A new urban culture that seeks to refine the conditions of this landscape has not emerged at present time. At the edge of metropolitan areas in North America, the large dispersion of single-family homes over the formerly agricultural urban perimeter has continued despite the collective understanding of the environmental problems.

Building a regional culture will take time, and many critics question whether the foundation for such a culture exists. Regrettable as it might seem, culture will not be based on the egalitarian principles of a "Great Society"[2] that inspired government programs like "operation breakthrough," which gave access to housing and distributed schools and parks throughout regions in the past (namely, during the Johnson administration 1963–1969). The hopeful signs come from an increased awareness of the environmental conditions. Real economic impetus for change to the low density, commute intensive land-use patterns comes from the rise in the cost for energy.

"Managing the Sense of a Region"[3] was an early foray by Kevin Lynch into the discipline that explored metropolitan form. Now the collection of books on the meaning of metropolitan form is growing. (In 2007, as a result of a conference on the Metropolitan Landscape the journal *Places* summarized some of the recent literature.) The contributions mainly came from Europe, where there is agreement that a shrinking population will not need much land for housing or parks. Not the kind of parks that we generally see in front of our eyes when the word is mentioned.[4]

A broad philosophical basis is needed by planners and designers that acknowledges the metropolitan landscape as a system shaped by socio-economic and cultural forces as much as by geography and ecology. When the metropolitan landscape in the developed world is seen in the

Figure 7.1 An emerging commons, San Francisco Bay Area, the setting for seven million people. (Courtesy K. Stanke)

context of large-scale economic restructuring, demographic shrinkage, dispersion of population, and major threats to ecological systems, nothing short of enlightenment is needed for its reformation. For some authors, like Thomas Sieverts,[5] it is doubtful that such a reformation can be imposed upon a region from above—and be democratic at the same time. Instead, he would advocate that society look at the metropolitan landscape like a large *commons* for the whole region, or many connected commons, where local responsibility can develop. How else can a community understand the interrelatedness of health and survival for all life forms, if not applied to a commons?

In "The Tragedy of the Commons," by Garrett Hardin,[6] a much-cited piece in political sciences, the author evokes Aristotle, who said, "that which is common to the greatest number has the least care bestowed upon it." The negative experiences with commonly used land motivated activists in the 1960s to establish a regulatory agency to manage the San Francisco Bay as a resource for the metropolitan region. The activists understood the conflict over recourses between individual interests and the common good. Such conflict occurs when there is a tendency toward free access and unrestricted demand for a finite resource. With that in mind let us pursue the idea of a commons and consider art as a method to interpret a well-managed regional space.

An Example of a Commons

A visitor looking at a map of the San Francisco Bay Area will immediately recognize the bay as the major form-giving element for this metropolitan region of seven million inhabitants. A glance at a map of the bay might also promise the discovery of a great range of conditions for the enjoyment of life at the water's edge. But the opportunities to interact with the water's edge as part of one's daily routines are not as plentiful as one might expect. There are only limited opportunities to stroll along a waterfront promenade crowded with people and enjoy an, admittedly rare, balmy evening in a Mediter-

ranean climate, with choices of entertainment and activities, with lights and music, all set against the sound of moving water only a few feet away. The waterfronts of places like Circular Quay in Sydney, Kungstradgarden in Stockholm, Allegheny Riverfront Park in Pittsburgh, and the Rhine River Promenade in Düsseldorf all boast such opportunities for activities, thereby allowing residents and visitors to experience their unique location in the world. However, those experiences are very rare along the waterfronts of Bay Area cities, and, when proposed in new developments, they are somewhat frowned upon. The residents of the Bay Area like their waterfronts to be "natural" and there is good reason for that. Very little natural shoreline can be found; the entire shoreline was constructed on land gained from the bay. Indeed, the loss of water surface is stunning. In 1850, when California was admitted as to the Union as a state, the bay measured 680 square miles; one hundred years later it measured only 430 square miles.

Landscape architects and urban designers cannot resist playing with contradictions like "nature," constructed nature, natural wilderness, or natural habitats versus constructed wetlands and constructed habitats. These terms describe interesting phenomena in the contemporary landscape that call for interpretation. Nature in its natural state is an extremely rare occurrence along the shoreline, where once Ohlone Indians trapped fish and gathered mussels and abalone. But if we are talking about natural processes that act on constructed landscapes, many examples come to mind. Abandonment of industry and military airfields during recent decades made natural processes evident within the sites of ruins from the industrial past. Early in the history of the Bay Area extensive portions of the shore were reclaimed for commercial salt production. This activity is much reduced; the levees have been breached intentionally to introduce tidal action. The reemergence of constructed tidal marshes provides breeding ground for brine shrimp, a food source for many water birds that visit the bay in their migration along the Pacific Flyway.

The reintroduction of "nature" as a shoreline improvement excites Bay Area residents. In growing numbers, urbanites put on windbreakers and binoculars to drive to one of the access points in order to walk or bicycle along portions of the new Bay Trail. The aesthetics of the new shoreline landscape has emotional meaning for the Bay Area population, and these emotions can only be understood as a reaction to the lack of access to the bay that existed throughout the 150-year history as an urbanized landscape.

Not only the local Ohlone natives but any sensitive human being must view the history of the bay as a tragedy. When seen from a Eurocentric perspective, the San Francisco Bay is a relatively recent discovery. On November 4, 1769, the Spanish sea captain Gaspar de Portola was the first European to set eyes on the bay together with sixty-three men of his crew who had climbed up to a 1,200-foot-high ridge south of San Francisco to look down at what they believed to be an impressive inland sea. The entrance to the bay would not be found until six years later, when Juan de Ayala sailed into the bay and claimed the large natural harbor for the Spanish crown. Urbanization of Bay Area communities was very slow until the discovery of gold in 1849, but boomed thereafter.

Already at the time of the great earthquake in April of 1906, it would have been difficult for anyone to set foot on a piece of urban waterfront unless he or she had business to be there. The military claimed the choicest spots to guard the entrance at the Golden Gate and at Mare Island, where the Napa River joins the Sacramento River at the Carquinez Strait. Later, in anticipation of air traffic, the military reserved large salt marshes at Hamilton Field, Alameda, and Moffat Landing and turned the marshes into airfields. By the early 1880s, rail lines were routed along the shoreline. The railroad companies filled former estuaries to provide straight alignments for their tracks and offered the remaining new land to industry. The 1960s saw the construction of freeways paralleling the rail-

roads. Barrier upon barrier emerged that kept the towns away from the water's edge. Unless an urban waterfront had been built early in the process, as in Sausalito, it had little opportunity to emerge. Even in the city of San Francisco, the entire shoreline along the bay was a working waterfront, claimed by industry, rail transportation, and ocean shipping. Large sections were fenced off, with access controlled by customs officials.

In the post–World War II decades an industrial landscape had closed a solid loop around the bay. By 1960, forty garbage disposal sites existed along the shoreline; water quality was poor and the demand for new, flat land appeared insatiable. Entire mountainsides were slated for removal to serve as fill to create new islands and city extensions. The Army Corps of Engineers continuously researched locations for additional fill. The Corps published a report in 1959 on the potential for future landfill areas to 2020. Not until a local paper published the engineers' map of proposed land reclamation in December 1959 did the public realize what was planned.

Where the bay had been, the map, redrawn in figure 7.2, showed a large flat valley with two shipping channels. The 1959 publication of the map triggered two reactions, the first locally well known. Three women residents formed an organization, Save the Bay, to begin encouraging community action and to engage state politicians. Their advocacy eventually brought into being a regulatory commission to oversee planning and building along the bay shore. Theirs is a story of a grass roots initiative that changed the course of history in the region and saved the bay.

The second reaction—less well known—was the 1963 publication of a report by Mel Scott, a historian on the faculty at UC Berkeley, "The Future of the San Francisco Bay." For the preparation of this report Mel Scott commissioned a professional photographer to record from the air images of the shoreline. One hundred and eighty images are on file in the archives. They were recorded on slow speed Kodachrome film and have survived in beautiful color for over forty years. For the illustrations of this chapter an aerial photographer[7] repeated the 1962 flight pass in April 2005.

The comparisons invite reflections about the changing cultural landscape. Shown in figures 7.3 to 7.7 are five locations and the changes between the 1962 and 2005 conditions. Access to the shoreline improved. But large developments continue to restrict access to the bay and only provide it at designated points. Movement of people along the shoreline on the Bay Trail is now possible to a much greater extent. Eventually the five-hundred-mile-long trail will circle much of the San Francisco Bay, but privatization of land adjacent to the shoreline is still dominant. The ecology of the edge has improved along many stretches of the shoreline, but sedimentation at the mouth of former streams is more noticeable due to creek canalization. Finally, reclamation of land has not stopped entirely. Some major projects slipped through the net of rules adopted in 1964 with the establishment of the San

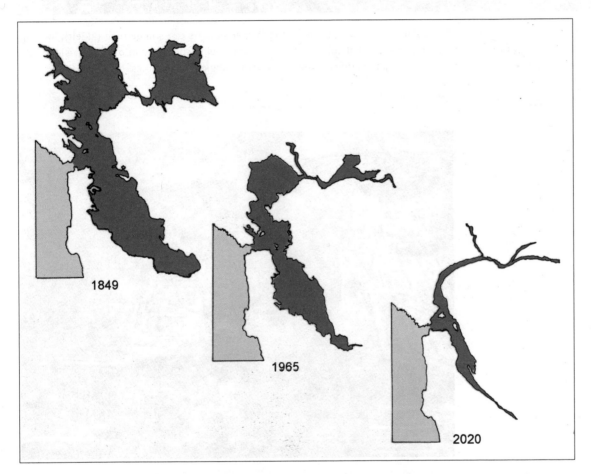

1849

1965

2020

Figure 7.2 Save San Francisco Bay. A famous graphic produced in 1965 that led to the establishment of the San Francisco Bay Conservation and Development Commission and protection of the shoreline, and prevented further landfill. From 787 square miles in 1849 the surface of the bay was reduced to 548 square miles in 1965. If filling were to continue, the bay would be reduced to three riverbeds by 2020: the Napa River in the north, the Sacramento and San Joachim rivers in the east, and the two Guadalupe rivers in the south. The 2020 map is based upon information provided by the Army Corps of Engineers that was published in the early 1960s and showed all land that could be gained by filling the bay.

Figure 7.3 Foster City in San Mateo County, California. In 1962, traces of the former sloughs can still be seen (at left), looking from the shoreline across a former salt marsh that was filled and is in the process of being converted into a subdivision with artificial lagoons. *Source:* CED visual archives. In 2005, the artificial lagoon lined with single-family homes. (Courtesy Barry Rokeach)

Figure 7.4 Crissy Fields, San Francisco, 1962 (left) and 2005 (right). From the air the straight line of the former airfield stands out. The line continues and is a trace of the long-abandoned rail line that served the Presidio military base until closure when the base was converted into a park as part of the Golden Gate National Recreation Area. *Source:* CED visual archives. In 2005, George Hargreaves' design of the constructed estuary promenade and beach is one of the most popular sections along the San Francisco Bay shoreline. (Courtesy Barry Rokeach)

Figure 7.5 Redwood Point: A geometry of large ponds (at left) used to produce salt to the south of San Francisco. *Source:* CED visual archives. The ponds are turned into constructed wetlands on the 2005 picture (right). Major high voltage utility lines crossed the marsh in the past and more have been added. Note the extensive sedimentation in the sloughs and along the shoreline. (Courtesy Barry Rokeach)

Francisco Bay Conservation and Development Commission. A comparison of the five comparisons is quickly explained. We start at Foster City, figure 7.3, a community in the northern portion of Silicon Valley, South of San Francisco. Here in the 1960s extensive portions of the bay marshland were filled to build homes for suburban commuters. Traces of former sloughs that meandered through the marsh can still be seen on the 1962 image, but the fresh traces of artificial lagoons are more pronounced. The 2005 image shows the "Islands" community forty-five years later, still a highly desired location where residents can keep a boat in their backyard. Around the bay a number of communities exist that have privatized edges of the commons.

The second comparison takes us to the entrance of the bay. The Presidio was claimed by the military early in settlement history. Prior to World War I a cove was filled to build an airfield, Crissy Field, the first landing strip in the Bay Area. Together with Fort Mason, the Presidio remained a staging area for military conflicts in the Pacific basin. It closed in 1990 and a slow transformation began. The military post became a national park, and a shoreline promenade was built on the former airfield. Of all

public places along the bay shore, Crissy Field fits best into the concept of an urban commons. Thousands of people visit this destination. Since its inception, the promenade from the Marina Green to Fort Point has become a modern day "paseo" for old and young, who walk the two kilometers with the wind in their faces and views of container ships entering the bay underneath the Golden Gate Bridge. This promenade contributes to the shared identity of living in the Bay Area.

The third comparison shows Alameda Island opposite San Francisco on the Oakland side of the bay. The view includes Bay Harbor Isle, a golf course community constructed on landfill. The landfill operation was still in progress when the 1962 picture was taken. A levee had been built to enclose a large wetland in the south for further fill. That operation was long completed in 2005. Noticeable are the deposits along the canals. The deposits have increased and a new marsh has emerged on the bay side of the landfill.

In its natural, pre-mid-nineteenth-century condition, the creeks and small rivers that brought water from the surrounding hills into the bay continued as sloughs inside the bay marsh. Subject to

Figure 7.6 San Leandro, 1962: Gated subdivisions replace salt marshes (left). *Source:* CED visual archives. Industry located on reclaimed land (right). The former San Lorenzo creek runs inside a channel on the San Leandro Bay Shore, California (Courtesy Barry Rokeach)

Figure 7.7 Bay Harbor Isles, Alameda. The former San Antonio (left) creek flows into the Bay between Alameda Island and a new island that was still under construction in 1962. *Source:* CED visual archives. The 2005 image (right) shows a green park on top of the former Alameda garbage refuse site and the emerging new shoreline in front of the levee that protects Alameda Island. (Courtesy Barry Rokeach)

the tide, these sloughs took on a strongly meandering form. The marshes with their sloughs were surrounded by levees and filled. It appears that in the 2005 image a new marsh is emerging in front of the levee. The new marsh is a creation of predictable natural processes, made from deposits that are transported down the canalized creek beds and distributed by tidal action. Thus, as the bay shore ex-

tends, a new edge of the commons is emerging. It is not an edge anyone can step on, but it is an edge nevertheless that will result in a new shoreline over time that people will see from a distance.

The fourth comparison looks north toward San Francisco on the west side of the bay. The marshland is extensive and has changed very little. The salt production on former mudflats has stopped. The levees have been breached in places and the land is now subject to flooding by the tide. Several large sloughs connect where Redwood Creek enters the bay at Redwood Point. Rafts of redwood trees were floated down this river and tugged to San Francisco as building material. The river has remained navigable, even for oceangoing vessels. Although not currently used as a ferry route, the possibility exists for a future water connection between Silicon Valley and the two international airports on the east and west sides of the bay. Here ferry riders will see the new commons from the water.

In the fifth comparison, the camera points south along the East Bay shoreline toward the San Mateo Bridge at San Leandro. In the distance are the salt marshes that were commercially used until the 1990s. With the levees now breached the tide is free to move in and out. In addition to the geometric shapes of levees, new shapes will appear that are part of the natural processes associated with tidal flow. Birds will transport seeds and successive vegetation will grow. Largely inaccessible by car, a water landscape will grow. Similar experiments in The Netherlands[8] show that it will take less than thirty years for such a landscape to emerge. Residents will be able to walk out to it on plank-ways and will look out over the commons.

Five conditions and five aspects of a commons include a place for a water landscape largely inaccessible to humans by car, water-based transportation, a new artificial tidal marsh to explore by kayak, a highly popular waterfront promenade, and a waterside residential area.

These are five scenarios for the commons. It also includes a former rail yard (see figure 7.18) that is turning into a neighborhood at Mission Bay, a medical research complex, an active shipyard (see figure 7.19) where dry-docks can be seen in operation, a sizeable mountain (see figure 7.20) that has beautiful views, airports (see figure 7.21), and much more. It is a strange assortment of landscapes that shows the wear and tear of a half-century with many contradictions. Only the promenade at Crissy Field follows an aesthetic that people associate with a designed landscape. The other parts of the commons will look accidental, uncared for, and not willfully designed. The contradictions will remain so for some time because the area is very large. The designer's task will be to establish large-scale elements in this horizontal landscape that emphasize the importance of the horizon and the silhouette of power lines against the background of hills in the distance. As future designers conceive rows or lines in the landscape they will address the basic functions of this new landscape.

As a commons the bay shore's chief function will be to transform itself into a productive landscape, a range of vegetation in proximity to water, sometimes below the shallow water table that is subject to the tides. Once established, this vegetation will create oxygen and improve the local climate. The biological process of decay and growth will create nutrients for more advanced vegetation. If this landscape is well designed, it will clean water, support animal life, and create food—a commons as a necessary landscape for human-centric reasons, enjoyment as well as survival

Defining the activities is necessary so that it can be managed as a commons to prevent them from the tragedy that political scientists like Garrett Hardin[9] talk about, and that the Bay Area experienced when its resources were exploited to a point where there was a danger that the bay would almost disappear.

When seen from the air, the bay shore looks like a canvas of shapes, patterns, and colors. Five geometries were noteworthy because they relate directly to management of the commons for human experience and ecological gain. They are interpreted here through visual art. Katie Standke produced the ten plates in oil and with mixed media after studying the net change on the photo image pairs. In producing the art she brought out preexisting geometries—commonalities—and then labeled them. Thus art has been employed as a method to learn about landscape.

Figure 7.8 *Edges 1.* Early in the history of the Bay Area extensive portions of the shore were reclaimed for commercial salt production. This activity is much reduced; the levees have been breached intentionally to introduce tidal action. A new landscape will emerge over time. (Courtesy K. Standke)

Edges

The first pair of paintings she called *Edges.* Edges are zones of transition. Much accumulates along edges: constructed patterns, debris, traces of shapes created by nature: figure 7.8 illustrates the geometry of sloughs in shallow water. These passages are inaccessible to humans unless by a shallow boat. For a person on foot, the horizon toward the water's edge appears infinite and can never be reached; it opens up anew at each bend. In figure 7.9 a built edge confronts the water. Paths that lead toward the edge offer a clear sense of first recognition followed by a sense of arrival.

When design evokes a shared meaning among many people, its value has a high public significance.[10] Well-designed edges can be such places because they are recognized for their symbolic quality as places of transition or borderlines. Edges can take on multiple forms.

Figure 7.9 *Edges 2.* Many shapes are found along the edge: formal patterns, incidental shapes like this one, both subject to wind and water. (Courtesy K. Standke)

Figure 7.10 *Connections 1.* The shape of sloughs in shallow water. These passages are inaccessible to humans unless by a shallow boat. The horizon towards the water appears infinite and can never be reached; it opens up anew at each bend. (Courtesy K. Standke)

Connecting Land and Water

Constructed elements that willfully connect land and water are designed for human exposure to the tide, wind, smells, and the special light that exists wherever water meets land. The design elements that provide such connections offer unique experiences and therefore can be memorable. Throughout the bay shore, designed tidal steps, piers, plank-ways, view towers, and beaches should give residents a sense of proximity to the water's edge. Streets that lead to the water should provide clear vistas. Elements at the waters edge should remain visible from afar.

Figure 7.11 *Connections 2.* Lines continue into the water that are anchored inside the city. (Courtesy K. Standke)

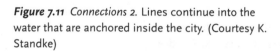

Figure 7.12 *Place 1.* Places in their natural condition are an extremely rare occurrence along the shoreline. But if we are talking about natural processes that act on constructed landscapes, many examples come to mind. Abandonment of heavy industry during recent decades made natural processes evident within the ruins from the industrial past. New places can emerge here. (Courtesy K. Standke)

Place

People identify with a location as a distinct place when it offers unique experiences. For example, places will be memorable if people are invited to move upward, to look out over, and to have mastery of a landscape, a vista. Locations with a sense of place invite visitors to move alongside water, to be next to things and other people. Selected places should be designed to have centrality, which is achieved when a place attracts the largest possible number of people for the activities it provides. By definition, places with centrality strive to be multicultural. Places along the shoreline are public and should be inclusive of individuals and population groups.

Figure 7.13 *Place 2.* This image reminds us that connections need to be designed in areas where we are close to water, but separated from it by strong barriers. (Courtesy K. Standke)

Figure 7.14 *Heterogeneity 1.* Ideal is an access pattern toward the shoreline that increases the number of access ways. (Courtesy K. Standke)

Multifaceted Landscape

If the bay is to be understood as the centerpiece of a commons and the land between the cities and the water is its frame, the landscape near the water's edge should be of a fine grain. This is achieved by introducing frequent access routes and paths. Frequent paths will increase connectivity between cities and water. Their alignment as public rights of way will also structure development and break down potentially large parcels into smaller properties. Not only will smaller buildings and structures create less of a barrier along the water's edge, they will also produce a greater variety of activities and create a multifaceted landscape with a greater chance for incremental development.

Figure 7.15 *Heterogeneity 2.* Currently the shoreline is met by developments with long frontages of a single use. Industry, office parks, or residential subdivisions dominate the experience. The shoreline was more frequently designed for the experience of moving toward it. Wherever possible, the land uses at the shoreline should offer a greater variety to those moving along it. (Courtesy K. Standke)

Figure 7.16 *Ecological Gain 1.* A new marsh is a creation of predictable natural processes, made from deposits that are transported down the canalized creek beds and shaped by tidal action. Thus, as the Bay Shore extends, a new edge of the commons is emerging. It is not an edge anyone can step on, but it is an edge nevertheless that will result in a new shoreline over time that people will see from a distance. (Courtesy K. Standke)

Ecological Gain

Visits to the shoreline make evident that ecological systems can be integrated with city design. The exit of a drainage channel that was once a creek can be designed for enjoyment and a sound ecology instead of only engineered for safety. Nature cannot be re-created back to its natural form, but into a new form. Instead metropolitan form needs to be made compatible with the cycles of nature. The water's edge in an urban area is largely a constructed feature that reveals the dynamics of water: tides, sediments, potential floods, and wind. A good design of the edge acknowledges this complex system, and in doing so design helps to produce an ecological gain. For example, breaching the levees to reintroduce the tide into former salt ponds will create a not

Figure 7.17 *Ecological Gain 2.* A special quality of light exists on the waterfront. The high reflectivity of the water surface and the sky above tint the light to strengthen the blues and greens in the color spectrum during the mid-day. In the afternoon the warmer tones of the color spectrum become stronger. On days with much moisture in the air the mist changes the visibility of objects. Shapes become silhouettes. (Courtesy K. Standke)

Figure 7.18 Elements of an emerging commons; a rail yard turning into a neighborhood at San Francisco's Mission Bay. (Courtesy CED Archives/B. Rokeach)

Figure 7.19 A shipyard that is holding on. The Central Waterfront of San Francisco, 1962–2005. (Courtesy CED Archives/B. Rokeach)

entirely predictable pattern of new drainage channels. Alongside these shallow waterways vegetation will emerge from seeds brought there by birds. The plant life will evolve over time, but the constructed regular grid of the ponds will remain; so will the high-voltage transmission lines and the plank-ways that serve their maintenance crews. With the tides a small type of shrimp will colonize the marsh, more birds will come, more seeds, more vegetation. A designer will find much inspiration from the constructed geometry to distinguish willful design elements from the geometries of natural processes.

The challenge is to find commons in metropolitan areas. They are generally found in relation to a water system. Seen from a satellite view the large drainage basin that defines the form of the Los Angeles metropolitan area is impressive. The challenge is to transform the Los Angeles River so that the water system from the mountains to the Pacific Ocean can be experienced as a commons, a necessary landscape for all residents—that would be truly impressive.[11] The challenge has not only been recognized, the Santa Monica Mountain Conservancy[12] is working on the acquisition of land in

Figure 7.20 Parts of the San Bruno mountains that were slated for removal, 1962–2005. (Courtesy CED Archives/B. Rokeach)

Figure 7.21 The Oakland airport built on a former tidal march. In the future some passengers will arrive there by ferry, 1962–2005. (Courtesy CED Archives/B. Rokeach)

neighborhoods near the river. This not-for-profit organization has thus far established eleven miles of riverfront where reeds, willows, mulefat, and native riparian plants have returned. At their Los Angeles River Center, near the confluence of the Arroyo Secco with the Los Angeles River the organization describes the history of the Los Angeles River, its current status, and a vision for the river's future.

Another example is found in Japan. The Sumida River is a large river running through Tokyo. It is not the only large river; Tokyo has numerous sizable rivers, many invisible or hidden below express-ways. Tokyo, a fiercely modern city, grew out of the ruins of the 1923 Kanto earthquake and then again out of the ruins left after aerial bombings at the end of World War II. As a result few historic traces are left. The Japanese population is on the decline. The priorities of a mature society differ in comparison to those that were set by the two previous generations. The challenge has been recognized to transform Tokyo in ways consistent with the qualities of a river landscape, the essence of its location.[13]

The notion of a commons matters greatly in China, in one of the world's fastest-growing metropolitan areas, the Pearl River Delta with Hong Kong and Guangzhou as its two main cities. The city Guangzhou suffered from one hundred days of unacceptable air pollution in 2007. In an article published by the Swedish Academy of Sciences, the water quality of the Pearl River contained 204 million cubic meters of degraded water resources in 2002. While such a number will not mean much to a layperson, the Swedish authors estimated that quality would further deteriorate to 252 million cubic meters by 2010 and toward 537 million cubic meters by 2020.[14] Instead, the conditions have improved somewhat because the political leadership has recognized the importance of a commons. In this region the commons are largely a maze of interconnected rivers. In their highly polluted condition they impose a threat to the populations health, but improved as a shared river landscape they become an invaluable public asset. As a small first step, in March 2007 the World Bank made 96 million dollars available to the region to improve the water quality of the Pearl River Delta.

City design is a subfield in the disciplines of planning and landscape architecture that tries to direct design decisions over an extended period of time. The work described here falls into this category. Visual art was chosen as a medium to represent principles, rules that define a generalizable rationale. Each principle can be executed in many ways. It was the artist's intent that representations give inspiration to designers, who will carry out the work over time. Designers will interpret images and words with their own concerns in mind, and these concerns are based upon individual experiences, knowledge of science, and values. Art tries to capture their essence.

Interpretation, the subject of this chapter, can be understood as the foundation for comparing, transforming, measuring, defining, and modeling. It is the last chapter, but as an activity, interpretation should very well be listed first. How we interpret what is before us sets the parameters for everything that follows. The very act of interpretation brings bias, opinions, and judgments as well as insights, evaluations, and explanations. The interpretation of the metropolitan landscape as a commonality requires listening, remembering, and understanding the whole before we can understand parts and their connections. Understanding an existing order, "hearing what has never fallen silent" was the poet W. S. Merwin's[15] way of describing the morphology of a system.

Conclusion

Principles of Precedent

This book has examined the process of reasoning about place by employing a logic that is referred to as the principles of precedent.[1] This ancient line of thinking is based upon experience of the environment and the observation that all things are interrelated: when events reliably follow each other, we can understand and describe simple processes. These processes become precedents based upon the evidence created by their successful performance—successful because a precedent reinforces a truth that relates to our life. When precedent is added to precedent and articulated we can make rational assumptions about how to use the existing force of a place toward future transformations.

But if a designer's process of reasoning with place is limited only to subjecting change to the rational order of settled, pre-existing rules, the designer is not an agent of change, but an agent for the status quo—stability and continuity with the past—good or bad.

This is where politics come into play. If designers act and think of themselves as agents of change they become responsive to interests and pressures that seek to abandon some precedents and establish new ones. What good is change, if it is not for greater livability, vitality in cities, and a better sense of place for most?

In this book I have argued that it is possible to be both an agent for change and committed to place. It is possible to design cities that are dense—in many cases denser than customary—but also connected to land, water, the essential city structure, and character of a place. When I consider the question of how places, over time, grow toward greater livability and vitality, it is through transformations according to principles that have a basis in the existing city structure and in natural processes.

Notes

ACKNOWLEDGMENTS

1. Melvin Webber, in his "Explorations into Spatial Structures," took issue with the importance of material space relative to its socioeconomic dimensions. He found local place constricting in a society that increasingly had—we would say today—global ties. In Webber's society people had become independent of local community and were in fact placeless. Helped by media and new modes of communication people had overcome their dependencies on local community for support and services through increased mobility.

INTRODUCTION

1. Stephen J. Gould, an evolutional theorist, 1941–2002. The reference is taken from: *Rocks of Ages: Science and Religion in the Fullness of Life* (New York: Ballantine Books, 1999).
2. Peter Hall and U. Pfeiffer, *Urban Futures 21* (London: E&FN Spon, 2000).
3. Thomas Sieverts, *Cities without Cities* (London: E&FN Spon, 2003).
4. Bernardo Secchi, *La città del ventesimo secolo* (Rome: Laterza, 2005).
5. Anne Vernez Moudon, "Catholic approach to what urban designers should know," *Journal of Planning Literature* 6, no. 4 (1992): 331–49.

CHAPTER ONE

1. The phenomenon of the dispersed city has been discussed in literature since H. G. Wells, *Anticipations* (London: Chapman and Hall, 1901).
2. Arien van Susteren, *Metropolitan World Atlas* (Rotterdam: 010 Publishers, 2005).
3. Institute of Sustainability, Technology and Policy, Peter Newman, Director, Curtin University, Perth, Australia. Peter Newman, "The Environmental Impact of Cities," *Environment and Urbanization* 18, no. 2 (2006): 275–95.
4. *Foshan Daily* http://www.fsonline.com.cn/life/car/csxw/200712270150.htm.

5. *World Urbanization Prospects Report, 2005*, United Nations.
6. Emrys Jones, *Towns and Cities* (London: Oxford University Press, 1966).
7. Wolfgang Ribbe and Jurgen Schmadeke, *Kleine Berlin Geschichte* (Berlin: Stapp Verlag, 1988).
8. United States Agency for International Development (USAID)-sponsored meeting of Planning Commissioners and Heads of Planning Departments, Calcutta, September 1998.
9. The phrase is taken from Daniel Solomon, *Global City Blues* (Washington, DC: Island Press, 2003), 173.
10. Steen Eiler Rasmussen, *Byer og Bygninger* (Copenhagen, 1949).
11. Richard Saul Wurman, *Cities: Comparisons of Form and Scale* (Cambridge, MA: MIT Press, 1976).
12. Peter Bosselmann, *Representation of Places: Reality and Realism in Urban Design* (Berkeley: University of California Press, 1998).
13. Raymond Isaacs , "The Subjective Duration of Time in the Experience of Urban Places," *Journal of Urban Design* 6, no. 2 (2001).
14. William James, *Psychology: The Briefer Course* (New York: 1892).
15. Paul Goldberger, "Shanghai Surprise, The radical quaintness of the Xintiandi district," *The New Yorker* New York, December 28, 2005.
16. Emrys Jones, *Towns and Cities* (London: Oxford University Press, 1966).
17. Patrick Geddes, *Cities in Evolution* (London: Ernest Benn, 1949).
18. Hidenobu Jinnai, *Tokyo: A Spatial Anthropology* (Berkeley: University of California Press, 1995).
19. Alistair Horne, *Seven Ages of Paris* (New York: Alfred A. Knopf/Random House, 2002).
20. The project referred to took place in 1975 and was funded by the Marston family, the publisher of the "San Diegan." Kevin Lunch and Donald Appleyard, *"Temporary Paradise"* (Cambridge, MA: MIT, Department of Urban Studies and Planning, 1975).
21. H. G. Wells, *The Fate of Man* (London: Chapman and Hall, 1939).

22. Discrepancies exist in the listing of population numbers. In addition to the UN statistics, we have frequently also listed numbers found in the latest edition of the *Oxford Essential Geographic Dictionary* and the population estimates by World Gazetteer, www.world-gazetteer.com and by Thomas Brinkhoff, "City Populations" at www.citypopulation.de.

CHAPTER TWO

1. For a brief review of the theories of perception see C. Holahan, *Environmental Psychology* (New York: Random House, 1982).
2. J. J. Gibson, *An Ecological Approach to Visual Perception* (Boston: Houghton Mifflin, 1979).
3. E. Brunswik, *Perception and the Representative Design of Psychological Experiments* (Berkeley: University of California Press, 1956).
4. A. Jacobs, *Looking at Cities* (Cambridge, MA: Harvard University Press, 1985). Allan Jacobs taught a class on observation at UC Berkeley in the 1980s and '90s. Much of what I am practicing here I learned from him.
5. Part of this narrative on Copenhagen has been published by the author in *Urban Design Journal*, Nottingham, UK, Vol. 7, no. 1 2002.
6. M. Berman, *All That Is Solid Melts Into Air* (New York: Penguin Books, 1988).
7. The map is reproduced in Vilh. Lorenzen, *Haandtegnede Kort over Kobenhavn*, Vol. 2, 1660–1753 (Copenhagen: Henrick Koppels Forlag, 1942).
8. A portion of the structure had housed an anchor forge for the naval shipyard.
9. A. Lund, *Guide til Dansk Havekunst, 1000-1996* (Copenhagen: Danish Architectural Press, 1999).
10. V. Lorenzen, *Haandtegnede Kort over København*, Vol. 2, 1660–1753 (Copenhagen: Henrick Koppels Forlag, 1942).
11. The three-dimensional map of Copenhagen by Christian Gedde was commissioned by the Crown in 1757 and completed in 1761. The horizontal scale is 1:2500. The vertical scale is somewhat randomly chosen. The map measures 2.5 meters square. A copy is kept on display at the archives of the Copenhagen City Museum. Gedde also prepared twelve district maps at the scale of 1:1600.
12. Vilh. Lorenzen, *Haandtegnede Kort over København*, Vol. 2, 1660–1753.
13. Nis Nissen, *Kobenhavns Bybygning 1500–1856, Visioner Planer Forfald* (Copenhagen: Danish Architectural Press, 1989).
14. Steen Eiler Rasmussen, *København* (Copenhagen: G.E.C. Gads Forlag, 1969).
15. This effect was even stronger in the past. The historic tower of old Christiansborg Palace was placed further out in the square that is in front of the palace, thus in a perfect line with Store Kongens Gade.
16. Vilh. Lorenzen, Vol. 1, ibid., plate VII dated 1647–1649.

17. Eightved, Niels or Nicolai, court architect 1701–1754.
18. The three-dimensional map of Copenhagen by Chr. Geddes was commissioned by the Crown in 1757 and completed in 1761. The horizontal scale is 1:2500, the vertical scale is somewhat randomly chosen. The entire map measures 2.5 meters square. A copy is kept on display at the archives of the Copenhagen City Museum.
19. Jan Gehl and Lars Gemzø, *Public Spaces—Public Life* (Copenhagen: Danish Architectural Press, 1996).

CHAPTER THREE

1. Hajo Düchting, *Paul Klee: Malerei und Musik* Munich: Prestel Verlag, 2005).
2. D. Appleyard, *Livable Streets* (Berkeley: University of California Press, 1982).
3. The phrase is taken from Christopher Alexander, *Empirical Findings from the Nature of Order* (Berkeley: Center for Environmental Structures, 2006).
4. T. Hiss, *The Experience of Place* (New York: Alfred A. Knopf, 1990).
5. The quote is borrowed from Brandan Gill, who wrote for the book jacket of Tony Hiss' "The Experience of Place."
6. The course, Environmental Design Research Methods, was initiated by Donald Appleyard when he joined the Berkeley faculty in 1968 and was taught by him until his death in 1983. From 1984, the author has taught the course; from 1985 to 1995 together with Allan Jacobs.
7. Jane Jacobs, *Death and Life of Great American Cities* (New York: Random House and Vintage Books, 1961).
8. The phrase originated with Jason Hayter, PhD candidate at Berkeley, 2006
9. J. Katoh, M. Spencer, and S. Tencer, "Vibrant neighborhoods: The role of mixed-used design," *Ontario Planning Journal* 18, no.1 (2003).
10. John Chase, ed, *Everyday Urbanism* (New York: Monacelli Press, 1999).
11. C. Auerswald, K. Greene, A. Minnis, I. Doherty, J. Ellen, N. Padian. "Qualitative assessment of venues for purposive sampling of hard-to-reach youth: An illustration in a Latino community," *Sexually Transmitted Diseases* 31 no. 2 (2004): 133–38.
12. K. Aaron, D. Davis, N. Hrushowy, K. Irani, A. Patel, S. Pellegrini, and S. Shum, Density in Urban Neighborhoods. Unpublished student research report, UC Berkeley, Department of City and Regional Planning, 2004.
13. A. Rappoport, "Towards a redefinition of density," *Environment and Behavior* 7 no. 2 (1975): 133–58.
14. J. Bergdoll, R. Williams, "Density perception on residential streets," *Berkeley Planning Journal* 5 (1990): 15–38.
15. M. Foster, D. Parolek, B. Suchy, Density and the Perceived Edge. Unpublished research report, UC Berkeley, Department of City and Regional Planning, 1998.

16. William H. Whyte, *City: Rediscovering the Center* (New York: Doubleday, 1988).

17. J. Kaydon, *Privately Owned Public Space: The New York Experience* (New York: Wiley, 2000).

18. A. Danielson, T. Goto, W. Ryan, and C. Wilson, A Study of the Success of Urban Plazas in San Francisco. Unpublished student research report, UC Berkeley, Department of City and Regional Planning, 1995.

19. Louise Mozingo and Robin Anderson, Urban Plazas and Parks Unpublished student research report, UC Berkeley, Department of City and Regional Planning, 1985. Mozingo published the research in "Women and downtown open spaces," *Places* 6 no. (1990): 118–47.

20. Jan Gehl, *Life between Buildings* (New York: Van Nostrand Reinhold, 1987). Translated into several languages and republished in English in 1996, 2001, 2003, 2006 by the Danish Architectural Press, Copenhagen. The most recent English edition, 2008 was published by Island Press, Washington, DC.

21. Jan Gehl and Lars Gemzø, *Public Spaces: Public Life* Copenhagen: Danish Architectural Press, 1998). J. Gehl and L. Gemzø, *New City Spaces* Copenhagen: Danish Architectural Press, 2001); J. Gehl and L. Gemzø, *New City Life* Copenhagen: Danish Architectural Press, 2006).

22. Edward Hall, *The Hidden Dimension* (New York: Doubleday, 1966).

23. Quote taken from Bente Frost, mayor for traffic and planning, City of Copenhagen, 1996, from her introduction to Gehl, Gemzø, 1998, ibid.

24. Jan Gehl and Lars Gemzø started their work in the early 1970s as part of an urban design study program in landscape architecture under Professor Sven Ingvar Andersson, chair in landscape architecture. The group enjoyed much support, but in successive reorganizations the group ended up under various administrative units until it formed its own research center with a major grant from Realdania in 2000. During this time a number of publications emerged that were cited earlier. Since 2007 the group operates outside of the Royal Academy.

25. E. Osth, A. Tennant, Pei Zhu, Upper and Lower Sproul Plaza Comparative Study. Unpublished student research report, UC Berkeley, Department of City and Regional Planning, 1999.

26. Colin Buchanan, *Traffic in Towns* (London: Minister of Transport, Her Majesty's Stationary Office, 1963). See also Peter Bosselmann, Terrance O'Hare, "Traffic in urban American neighborhoods: The influence of Colin Buchanan," *Built Environment* 9 no. 2 (1983): 127–39.

27. Donald Appleyard and Mark Lintell, "The environmental qualities of city streets: the residents' viewpoint," *Journal of the American Institute of Planners* 38 (1972, March): 84–101.

28. D. Appleyard and M. Lintell (1972): 97.

29. City of San Francisco, *City-Wide Urban Design Plan*, 1972.

30. D. Appleyard and D. Smith, *State of the Art Report* Report FHWA/RD- 80/09. (Washington, DC: Federal Highway Administration, 1980).

31. L. Patterson, D. Gunter, and P. McGovern, Livable Streets. Unpublished research report, UC Berkeley, Department of City and Regional Planning, 1988.

32. A. Lopez, M. Goodavish, and J. Woo, Livable Streets. Unpublished research report, UC Berkeley, Department of City and Regional Planning, 1991.

33. M. Carroll, S. Chan, J. Mason, and S. Thuilot, Trees, Traffic and Livable Streets. Unpublished student research report, UC Berkeley, Department of City and Regional Planning, 1998.

34. B. Appleyard, B. Dietrich, M. Jayachandran, Effects of Automobile Traffic on Children's Sense of Place. Unpublished research report, UC Berkeley, Department of City and Regional Planning, 1995.

35. Congress for the New Urbanism (CNU), 13th, Pasadena, 2005.

36. M. Southworth and E. Ben-Joseph, *Streets and the Shaping of Towns and Cities* (Second Edition, Washington, DC: Island Press, 2003).

37. The residential boulevard as a street type was illustrated by the author for the American Institute of Transportation Engineers handbook, *Residential Street Design and Traffic Control* (Washington, DC: Institute of Transportation Engineers, 1984).

38. A. B. Jacobs, *Great Streets* (Cambridge, MA: MIT Press, 1993).

39. I. D. Fisher, *Frederick Law Olmsted and the City Planning Movement in the United States* (Ann Arbor, MI: UMI Research Press, 1986).

40. Elizabeth Macdonald, *Pleasure Drives and Promenades: A History of Olmsted and Vaux's Brooklyn Parkways* (Washington, DC: Center for American Places, 2008).

41. M. B. Dietrich, *A Historic Summary of Grand Army Plaza and Eastern Parkway* (New York: Department of Transportation, Bureau of Highways, 1982).

42. A. B. Jacobs, Y. Rofè, Y., and E. Macdonald, *The Boulevard Book: History, Evolution, Design of Multiway Boulevards* (Cambridge, MA: MIT Press, 2002).

43. The research was published in P. Bosselmann, E. Macdonald, with Thomas Kronemeyer, "Livable streets revisited," *Journal of the American Planning Association* Vol. 65, No.2, (1999): 168–181.

44. Appleyard and Lintell (1972), ibid.

45. C. Hilger, K. Mauney-Brodek and R. Orduña, "A highway run through it." Unpublished student research report, UC Berkeley, Department of City and Regional Planning, 2003.

46. Noelle Cole, Sadie Graham and Aaron Odland, "Octavia Boulevard: healing an urban scar." Unpublished student research report, UC Berkeley, Department of City and Regional Planning, 2006.

47. J. Ferrucci, C. Hamilton, and E. Miramontes. "The Integration of BART Stations in their Surrounding Neighborhoods." Unpublished student research report, UC Berkeley, Department of City and Regional Planning, 1996.

48. J. Bahng, A. Buss, K. Dwarka, and R. Walking, "BART Station Integration and Pedestrian Activity". Unpublished student research report, UC Berkeley, Department of City and Regional Planning, 1999.

49. In 2002, New Jersey Transit Authority created a transit friendly land use program, also referred to as "Transit Village Initiative."

50. S. Suzuki, M. Larkin, and A. Keller, Street Configuration and Outdoor Activities in a Residential Area. Unpublished student paper, UC Berkeley, Department of City and Regional Planning, 1997.

51. United Nations, IPCC Web site: http://www1.IPCC.ch/.

52. The outdoor comfort model referred here was documented in: A. Pharo Gagge, A.P. Fobelets, and L. Berglund, "A standard predictive index of human response to the thermal environment," *ASHRAE transactions* 92 (1986), and E. Arens, L. Berglund, R. Gonzales, "Thermal comfort under an extended range of environmental conditions," *ASHRAE Transactions* 92 (1986).

53. T. Babich, C. Gimmler, and E. Leon-Guerrero, Huntington Park: Comfort and Microclimatic Study. Unpublished student paper, UC Berkeley, Department of City and Regional Planning, 1987.

54. Christopher Castorena and Lewis Kraus, Bodecker Park Comfort Study. Unpublished student paper, UC Berkeley, Department of City and Regional Planning, 1985.

55. Shih Cheug Chung, H. Schless, D. Shaw, and S. Ziegler, Plaza Comfort Study. Unpublished student paper, UC Berkeley, Department of City and Regional Planning, 1984.

56. Chao-ti Chen, Eli Ilano, Chia-ning Yang, Creek-Side Chilling. Unpublished student paper, UC Berkeley, Department of City and Regional Planning, 2000.

57. Michael Hough, *City Form and Natural Processes: Towards a New Urban Vernacular* (Beckenham, Kent: Croom Helm, 1984).

58. Roger S. Ulrich, "The View through a Window May Influence Recovery from Surgery," *Science* 224 (1984): 420–21. Edward O. Wilson and Stephen R. Kellert, eds., *The Biophilia Hypothesis* (Washington, DC: Island Press, 1993).

59. J. Dinh, H. Kiers, N. Luzier, Street Trees and Seasonal Change. Unpublished student paper, Department of City and Regional Planning, UC Berkeley, 2000.

60. Mara Baum, Shay Boutillier, Duane DeWitt, Rosey Jencks, Doug Kot, and Leslie Webster. Perceptions of Accessibility and Biodiversity. Unpublished student research report, UC Berkeley, Department of City and Regional Planning, 2004.

61. Andrea Gaffney, Trudy Garber, and Kirsten Johnson. Water Where? Permeable landscape sidewalk projects and their affect on environmental awareness and social interactions on urban residential streets. Unpublished student research report, UC Berkeley, Department of City and Regional Planning, 2007.

62. Yi-Fu Tuan, *Space and Place: The Perspective of Experience* (Minneapolis: University of Minnesota Press, 1977).

63. Jonathan D. Sime, "Creating places or designing spaces?" *Journal of Environmental Psychology* 6, no. 1 (1986): 49–63.

64. Tony Hiss, 1990, ibid.

65. F. Araneta, T. Ariga, M. Schelly, and J. Rutherford, Enclosure and Sense of Place. Unpublished student paper, UC Berkeley, Department of City and Regional Planning, 1993.

66. Stephen Jay Gould, *I Have Landed: The End of a Beginning in Natural History* (New York: Three Rivers Press, 2003), 42.

67. C. Goldade, J. Isbill, J. McCray, and L. Newman, The Transition Zone. Unpublished student paper, UC Berkeley, Department of City and Regional Planning, 1987.

68. J. Appleton, *The Experience of Landscape* (New York: Wiley & Sons, 1975).

69. T. Kirk, B. Lasko, and A. Torney, Neighboring in Neo-traditional Neighborhoods. Unpublished student paper, UC Berkeley, Department of City and Regional Planning, 1994.

70. B. Brack, L. Glass, and M. Lamboy, Subdivisions Surrounded by Walls. Unpublished student paper, UC Berkeley, Department of City and Regional Planning, 1989.

71. M. Andrews, Fei Li, Hiroyuki Sasaki, Ying Ling Sun, Kronos in the Marina District: A Study of the Effects of Scale on the Perception of Time. Unpublished student paper, UC Berkeley, Department of City and Regional Planning, 1999.

72. A. Bukojemsky, J. Longhenry, C. Mezzino, and M. Shirgaokar, Unpublished student paper, UC Berkeley, Department of City and Regional Planning, 2000.

73. Emelie Cheng and Yu Cao, Time on Campus: A Study of Visual Elements and the Perception of Time. Unpublished student paper, UC Berkeley, Department of City and Regional Planning, 2004.

74. Raymond Isaacs, "The Subjective Duration of Time in the Experience of Urban Places," *Journal of Urban Design*. 6, no. 2, (2001): 109–27.

75. William James, *Psychology: The Briefer Course* (New York: 1892).

76. Kevin Lynch, *A Theory of Good Urban Form* (Cambridge, MA: MIT Press, 1981). The quote is taken from the prologue, A Naïve Question.

77. Stephen Jay Gould taught the introduction to natural sciences at Harvard University. He was a zoologist by training, a prominent evolutional biologist as well as a splendid essayist. He died in 2002. The quote is taken from his obituary prepared by Harvard University.

78. T. Hiss, ibid., 6–7.

CHAPTER FOUR

1. M. R. G. Conzen, *Altwick, Northumberland: A Study in Town-Plan Analysis*. Publication No. 17 (London: Institute of British Geographers, 1960).

2. G. Caniggia, G. L. Maffei, "Compositione architectonica e tipologia edilizia." *Lettura Dell'edilizia dibase* (Venezia: Marsilio, 1979).

3. Prominent and internationally known are works by Carlo Aymonino (et al. 1966), Aldo Rossi (Rossi 1964, 1982), and the Krier brothers (Vidler 1976). All were early advocates of a typomorphological approach to city design.

4. A. Rossi, *The Architecture of the City* (Cambridge, MA: MIT Press, 1982).

5. See also A. Vernez Moudon, *Built for Change* (Cambridge, MA: MIT Press, 1986).

6. Thomas Sieverts, *Cities Without Cities* (London: Routledge, 2003).

7. Witold Rybczynski, *A Clearing in the Distance: Frederick Law Olmsted and America in the 19th Century* Touchstone ed. (New York: Simon & Schuster, 1999), 184.

8. Jack J. Struder *A Swiss as Surveyor and City Planner in California, 1851–1857.* (Sacramento: California Historical Society, 1968).

9. Julius G. Kellersberger, *Erlebnisse Eines Schweizerischen Ingenieurs in Kalifornien, Mexico und Texas zur Zeit des Americanischen Bürgerkrieges* (Zürich: Juchli and Beck, 1897).

10. John W. Reps, *The Making of Urban America: A History of City Planning in the United States* (Princeton, NJ: Princeton University Press, 1965).

11. R. Fishman, *Bourgeois Utopia: The Rise and Fall of Suburbia* (New York: Basic Books, 1987).

12. Jane Jacobs, *Cities and the Wealth of Nations: Principles of Economic Life* (New York: Vintage Books, 1985).

13. Amos Rappoport, "Towards a Redefinition of Density," *Environment and Behavior* vol. 7, no. 2, (June 1975): 133–58. Also, William Michelson, *Environmental Choice, Human Behavior, and Residential Satisfaction* (New York: Oxford University Press, 1977).

14. Peter Bosselmann, *Representation of Places* (Berkeley: University of California Press, 1998), ch. 8. The chapter reports on research done by Robert Cervero and Peter Bosselmann, "An Evaluation of the Market Potential for Transit-Oriented Development Using Visual Simulation Techniques," Monograph no. 47. (Berkeley: Institute of Urban and Regional Development, University of California, 1994).

15. P. Bosselmann, R. Wright, K. Dunker, and E. Arens. "Urban form and climate," *Journal of the American Planning Association* 20 (1995): 226–39.

16. See www.usgbc.org.

17. Alain Touraine, *Die Stadt: Ein überholter Entwurf* (The City: An Outdated Design). (Bonn: Monatzeitschrift für Kommunalpolitik, March 1996).

CHAPTER FIVE

1. Animus, Latin for the Greek ανεμος, meaning wind. In Greek mythology, "anemos" also refers to things that are personified, are conscious, and have spirit or soul—a view of the world that was opposed by Thales, the Greek philosopher (625–547 BC), who is referred to as the father of science.

2. See also F. Lipsky, *San Francisco, La grille sur les collines* (Marseille: Editions Parenthèses, 1999).

3. Inspiration for relating buildform to landform came from many sources. Wilhelm Landzettel, *Das Bild der Dörfer*, (Hannover: Ministry for Agriculture, State of Lower Saxony, 1989).

4. C. Girling and R. Kellett, *Skinny Streets and Green Neighborhoods: Design for Environment and Community* (Washington, DC: Island Press, 2005).

5. Home Depot Foundation, http://www.homedepotfoundation .org/support__trees.html.

6. Donald Appleyard in the foreword to Anne Vernez Moudon, ed., *Public Streets for Public Use* (New York: Van Nostrand Reinhold, 1987).

7. Jan Gehl and Lars Gemzoe, *City Spaces* (Copenhagen: Danish Architectural Press, 2006, 2003).

8. R. Cervero and P. Bosselmann, "An Evaluation of the Market Potential for Transit-Oriented Development Using Visual Simulation Techniques," MG-047 (UC Berkeley: Institute of Urban and Regional Development, 1998), www.iurd.ced.berkeley.edu/monograph__titles.htm.

CHAPTER SIX

1. A small portion of the material contained in this chapter was first published in *Urbanistica*, Milan, Italy. P. Bosselmann, "Autenticità, simulazione e diritto a costruire," *Urbanistica*, 126.

2. Stanley Milgram reported on his experiment with "Psychological maps of Paris, " pp. 104–24, in S. Milgram *Environmental Psychology: The Individual in a Social World, Essays and Experiments* (New York: Holt, Rinehart and Winston, 1977).

3. The quotes were taken from an article by Steven Myer, who wrote a cover story on the Gazprom tower proposal for the December 2/3, 2006, issues of the *International Herald Tribune*.

4. The controlling shareholder of the publicly traded corporation that operates the amusement park in the center of Copenhagen is no longer the Carlsberg Brewers but Scandinavian Tobacco.

5. UNESCO, World Heritage Center, Paris, Jan. 8, 2007.

6. Shigeru Satoh, "Creating community through Machidukuri with the help of visual simulation," *Territorio*, no. 43 (2007), Rome, Italy.

7. C. A. Acking, R. Küller. Presentation and judgment of planned environments. In *Environmental Design Research*, ed. W. F. E. Preiser, vol. 1, 72–83 (Stroudsburg, Pa.: Dowden, Hutchinson & Ross, 1973).

8. A. Markelin, B. Fahle, *Umweltsimulation, sensorische Simulation im Städtebau* (Stuttgart: Karl Krämer Verlag, 1979).

9. Fausto Curti, et al. "Il Laboratorio di Simulazione Urbana e Valutazione dei Progetti; uno strumento di sperimentazione didactica e di ricerca applicata. [The Simulation Laboratory at the Politecnico di Milano]," *Territorio* no. 43 (2007), Rome, Italy.

10. Peter Bosselmann, "Nature of change," *Territorio*, no. 43, (2007), Rome, Italy.
11. Peter Bosselmann, *Representation of Places, Reality and Realism in City Design* (Berkeley: University of California Press, 1998).
12. The Golden Gateway Center, 480 Davis Court, San Francisco.
13. Seymor Martin Lipset, a political sociologist, 1922–2006. The reference is from *The First New Nation* (New York: W.W. Norton, 1963).
14. Visit, http://www.sfgov.org/City__Design__Group/CDG __transit__center.htm, accessed June 18, 2008.

CHAPTER SEVEN

1. P. Bosselmann and D. Ruggeri, eds., "The Future Metropolitan Landscape." Special issue, *Places* (19 March 2007).
2. Richard Goodwin coined the phrase for a speech by President Johnson on May 22, 1964, at the University of Michigan, Ann Arbor. It is generally the label given to legislation enacted during the following years that addressed civil rights, urban issues, transportation, and education. Goodwin had borrowed the phrase from the social theorist Graham Wallace.
3. K. Lynch, *Managing the Sense of a Region* (Cambridge, MA: MIT Press, 1976).
4. References to the literature summarized here can be found in a special issue of *Places* (19 March 2007). P. Bosselmann and Deni Ruggeri edited the issue: "The Future of the Metropolitan Landscape," held at the University of California, Berkeley, in March 2005. Contributors from Europe, Japan, Canada, and the United States included Francois Ascher, Bernardo Secchi, Thomas Sieverts, Michael Hough, Hideneou Jinnai, Randolf Hester, Robert Fishman, and others.
5. T. Sieverts, ibid.
6. G. Hardin, "The tragedy of the commons," *Science* 162, no. 3859 (Dec. 13, 1968), 1243–8.
7. Barrie Rokeach repeated the 1962 flight-pass in April of 2005. He matched thirty images with those from Mel Scott's original survey. The production of the comparisons was made possible with funds from the Geraldine Knight Scott Landscape Architecture History Fund, established by Geraldine Knight Scott in memory of her husband Mel Scott, who commissioned the original 1962 photo survey of the San Francisco Bay Area.
8. The best-known example is Oostvaardersplassen National Nature Preserve in The Netherlands, an area located near the city of Almere of 3,600 hectares that was originally part of the Ijsselmeer but became part of a new polder (reclaimed land from the sea bounded by a levee) in Flevoland and has become a densely vegetated refuge after the incomplete and only partially drained polder was abandoned in the 1970s.
9. G. Hardin, ibid.
10. Wilhelm Landzettel, "Das Bild der Doerfer," Minister for Agriculture, State of Lower Saxony, Germany (1989).
11. R. Hester, "Reciprocal and recombinant geometries of ecological democracy," *Places* 19, no. 1 (Spring 2007): 68.
12. Berkeley faculty in Landscape Architecture and Environmental Planning, Marcia McNelly and Randy Hester have worked with the organization on the Los Angeles River project. See R. Hester, *Design for Ecological Democracy* (Cambridge, MA: MIT Press, 2006).
13. H. Jinnai, ibid.
14. Zhu Zhaoyo, et al., "Water pollution and degradation in the Pearl River Delta, South China," *Ambio* 31, no. 3 (May 2002), Stockholm.
15. The quote is taken from "Learning a Dead Language" (1956) by the poet W. S. Merwin, *New and Selected Poems* (Port Townsend, WA: Copper Canyon Press, 2005), 41.

CONCLUSION

1. Robin West, *Re-imagining Justice* (Aldershot: Ashgate Publishing, LTD, 2003).

Bibliography

Acking, C. A., and R. Küller. "Presentation and judgment of planned environments." In *Environmental Design Research*, ed. W. F. E. Preiser, vol. 1, 72–83. Stroudsburg, PA: Dowden, Hutchinson and Ross, 1973.

Alexander, Christopher. *Empirical Findings from the Nature of Order*. Berkeley, CA: Center for Environmental Structures, 2006.

Appleton, J. *The Experience of Landscape*. New York: Wiley and Sons, 1975.

Appleyard, Donald, and Mark Lintell. "The environmental qualities of city streets: the residents' viewpoint." *Journal of the American Institute of Planners* 38 (March 1972): 84–101.

Appleyard, Donald. "Foreword"*Public Streets for Public Use* Anne Vernez Moudon, ed. New York: Van Nostrand Reinhold, 1987.

Arens, Edward, and Peter Bosselmann. "Wind, Sun and Temperature: predicting the thermal comfort of people in outdoor spaces" *Building and Environment* 24, no. 4 (1989): 315–20.

Auerswald, C., K. Greene, A. Minnis, I. Doherty, J. Ellen, and N. Padian. "Qualitative assessment of venues for purposive sampling of hard-to-reach youth: An illustration in a Latino community." *Sexually Transmitted Diseases* 31, no. 2: 133–8.

Aymonino, Carlo, M. Brusatin, G. Fabbri, M. Lena, P. Loverro, S. Lucianetti, and A. Rossi. *La Città di Padova: saggio di analisi urbana* Rome: Officina Edizoni, 1966.

Bechtel, Robert, R. Marans, and W. Michelson, eds.*Methods in Environmental and Behavioral Research.* New York: Van Nostrand Reinhold, 1987.

Berman, M.*All That Is Solid Melts Into Air.* New York: Penguin Books, 1988.

Bosselmann, Peter. "Redesigning American Residential Streets" *Built Environment* 12, no. 1-2 (1986): 98–106.

———. "The Documentary Quality of Computer Simulations" *Spazio e Società* 28, no.75 (1996): 74–83.

———. "The Transformation of a Landscape" *Places* 10, no. 3 (1996): 26–35.

———. *Representation of Places: Reality and Realism in Urban Design* Berkeley: University of California Press, 1998.

———. "Københavnske Anatomier" *Arkitekten* 104, no. 15 (2002): 2–7.

———. "Transformations and City extensions: Some observations of Copenhagen's city form at a time of global change" *Urban Design Journal* 7, no. 1 (2002): 75–95.

———. "Autenticità, simulazione e diritto a costruire." *Urbanistica* 126, (2005): 103–112.

———. "Nature of change." *Territorio* 43 (2007): 9–16.

Bosselmann, Peter, and Terrance O'Hare. "Traffic in urban American neighborhoods: The influence of Colin Buchanan." *Built Environment* 9, no. 2 (1983): 127–39.

Bosselmann, Peter, and D. Ruggeri, eds. "The future metropolitan landscape." *Places* 19, no. 1(2007): 4–77.

Bosselmann, Peter, E. Macdonald, with T. Kronemeyer. "Livable streets revisited." *Journal of the American Planning Association* 65, no. 2 (1999): 168–81.

Bosselmann, Peter, et al. "Urban form and climate." *Journal of the American Planning Association* 20 (1995): 226–39.

Branch, C. Melville.*An Atlas of Rare City Maps: Comparative Urban Design, 1830–1842* Princeton, NJ: Princeton Architectural Press, 1997.

Broadbent, Geoffrey. *Emerging Concepts in Urban Space Design.* New York: Van Nostrand Reinhold, 1990.

Brunswik, Egon. *Perception and the Representative Design of Psychological Experiments.* Berkeley, University of California Press, 1956.

Buchanan, Colin. *Traffic in Towns.* London: Minister of Transport, Her Majesty Stationery Office, 1963.

Conzen, M. R. G. *A Study in Town-Plan Analysis.* Publication No. 17. London: Institute of British Geographers, Altwick, Northumberland, 1960.

Craik, Kenneth. "The psychology of the large scale environment." In N. R. Feimer and E. S. Geller, eds. *Environmental Psychology, Directions and Perspectives.* New York: Praeger, 1983.

Curti, Fausto, et al. "Il Laboratorio di Simulazione Urbana e Valutazione dei Progetti; uno strumento di sperimentazione didactica e di ricerca applicata. (The Simulation Laboratory at the Politecnico di Milano). *Teritorio* 43 (2007): 17–23.

Düchting, Hajo. *Paul Klee: Malerei und Musik.* Munich: Prestel Verlag, 2005.

European Space Agency *Mega Cities.* Salzburg, Austria: Geospace, 2001.

Fisher, I. D. *Frederick Law Olmsted and the City Planning Movement in the United States.* Ann Arbor, MI: UMI Research Press, 1986.

Fishman, R. *Bourgeois Utopia: The Rise and Fall of Suburbia.* New York: Basic Books, 1987.

Gagge, A., A. Pharo, P. Fobelets, and L. Berglund. *A Standard Predictive Index of Human Response to the Thermal Environment.* ASHRAE Transactions 92, pt.2, 1986.

Geddes, Patrick. *Cities in Evolution.* London: Ernest Benn, 1949.

Gehl, Jan. *Life between Buildings.* New York: Van Nostrand Reinhold, 1987.

Gehl, Jan and Lars Gemzø. *Public Spaces: Public Life.* Copenhagen: Danish Architectural Press, 1996.

———. *New City Spaces.* Copenhagen: Danish Architectural Press, 2001.

———. *New City Life.* Copenhagen: Danish Architectural Press, 2006.

Gibson, J. J. *An Ecological Approach to Visual Perception.* Boston: Houghton Mifflin, 1979.

Girling, C., and S. R. Kellert. *Skinny Streets and Green Neighborhoods: Design for Environment and Community.* Washington, DC: Island Press, 2005.

Gould, Stephen Jay. *Rocks of Ages, Science and Religion in the Fullness of Life.* New York: Ballantine Books, 1999.

———. *I Have Landed, the End of a Beginning in Natural History.* New York: Three Rivers Press, 2003.

Hall, Edward. *The Hidden Dimension.* New York: Doubleday, 1966.

Hall, Peter. "The changing European urban system." In *Politicas Urbana: Tendencias, Estrategias e Oportunitades.* Lisbon: Foundacao Calouste Gulbenkian, 2003.

Hall, Peter, and U. Pfeiffer. *Urban Futures 21.* London: E&FN Spon, 2000.

Hardin, G. "The Tragedy of the Commons." *Science* 162, no. 3859 (Dec. 13, 1968): 1243–48.

Hester, Randolf. *Design for Ecological Democracy.* Cambridge, MA: MIT Press, 2006.

———. "Reciprocal and recombinant geometries of ecological democracy." *Places* 19, no. 1 (2007): 68–75.

Hiss, Tony. *The Experience of Place.* New York: Alfred A. Knopf, 1990.

Holahan, C. *Environmental Psychology.* New York: Random House, 1982.

Horne, Alistair. *Seven Ages of Paris.* New York: Alfred A. Knopf/Random House, 2002.

Hough, Michael. *City Form and Natural Processes: Towards a New Urban Vernacular.* Beckenham, Kent: Croom Helm, 1984.

Isaacs, Raymond. "The subjective duration of time in the experience of urban places." *Journal of Urban Design* 6, no. 2 (2001): 109–27.

Jacobs, A. B. *Looking at Cities.* Cambridge, MA: Harvard University Press, 1985.

———. *Great Streets.* Cambridge, MA: MIT Press, 1993.

Jacobs, A. B., Y. Rofè, and E. Macdonald. *The Boulevard Book: History, Evolution Design of Multiway Boulevards.* Cambridge, MA: MIT Press, 2002.

Jacobs, Jane. *Death and Life of Great American Cities*, New York: Random House and Vintage Books, 1961.

———. *Cities and the Wealth of Nations: Principles of Economic Life.* New York: Vintage Books, 1985.

James, William. *Psychology: The Briefer Course.* Ed. Gordon Allport. New York: Harper and Row, 1961.

Jinnai, Hidenobu. *Tokyo: A Spatial Anthropology.* Berkeley: University of California Press, 1995.

Jones, Emrys. *Towns and Cities.* London: Oxford University Press, 1966.

Katoh, J., M. Spencer, and S. Tencer. "Vibrant Neighborhoods: The Role of Mixed-Used Design." *Ontario Planning Journal* 18, no.1 (2003).

Kaydon, J. *Privately Owned Public Space: The New York Experience.* New York: Wiley, 2000.

Kellersberger, Julius G. *Erlebnisse eines Schweizerischen*

Ingenieurs in Kalifornien, Mexico und Texas zur Zeit des Americanischen Bürgerkrieges. Zürich: Juchli and Beck, 1897.

Kostof, Spiro. *The City Shaped-Urban Patterns and Meanings through History*. London: Bulfinch Press, 1991.

———. *The City Assembeled: The Elements of Urban Form through History*. London: Thames and Hudson, 1992.

Lange, Bente. *The Colors of Copenhagen*. Copenhagen: Danish Architectural Press, 1998.

Lipset, Seymor Martin. *The First New Nation*. New York: W. W. Norton, 1963.

Lipsky, F. *San Francisco: La grille sur les collines*. Marseille, France: Editions Parenthéses, 1999.

Lorenzen, Vilh. *Haandtegnede Kort Over København*. Vols. 1, 2. 1600–1753. Henrik: Koppels Forlag, 1930.

Lund, A. *Guide til Dansk Havekunst, 1000–1996*. Copenhagen: Danish Architectural Press, 1999.

Lynch, Kevin. *What Time Is This Place*. Cambridge, MA: MIT Press, 1972.

———. *Managing the Sense of a Region*. Cambridge, MA: MIT Press, 1976.

———. *A Theory of Good Urban Form*. Cambridge, MA: MIT Press, 1981.

Macdonald, Elizabeth. *Pleasure Drives and Promenades: A History of Olmsted and Vaux's Brooklyn Parkways*. Washington, DC: Center for American Places, 2008.

Marans, Robert, and D. Stokols, eds. *Environmental Simulation, Research and Policy Issues*. New York: Plenum Press, 1993.

Markelin, A., B. Fahle. *Umweltsimulation, Sensorische Simulation im Städtebau*. Stuttgart: Karl Krämer Verlag, 1979.

Merwin, W. S. *New and Selected Poems*. Port Townsend, WA: Copper Canyon Press, 2005.

Michelson, William. *Environmental Choice, Human Behavior, and Residential Satisfaction*. New York: Oxford University Press, 1977.

Milgram, Stanley. *Environmental Psychology: The Individual in a Social World, Essays and Experiments*. New York: Holt, Rinehart and Winston, 1977.

Moudon, A. Vernez. *Built for Change*. Cambridge, MA: MIT Press, 1986.

———, ed. *Public Streets for Public Use*. New York: Van Nostrand Reinhold, 1987.

———. "Catholic approach to what urban designers should know." *Journal of Planning Literature* 6, no. 4 (1992): 331–49.

Mozingo, L. "Women and downtown open spaces." *Places* 6, no. 1 (1990): 118–47.

Newman, Peter. "The environmental impact of cities." *Environment and Urbanization*. 18, no. 2 (2006): 275–95.

———. *Cities as Sustainable Ecosystems*. Washington, DC: Island Press, 2008.

Nissen, Nis. "København's Bybygning 1500 - 1856,Visioner, Planer, Forfald," Danish Architectural Press, Copenhagen, 1989.

Oxford Atlas of the World. New York: Oxford University Press, 2003.

Oxford Essential Geographical Dictionary. New York: Oxford University Press, 1999.

Rappoport, Amos. "Towards a Redefinition of Density." *Environment and Behavior*. 7, no. 2 (1975): 133–58.

Rasmussen, Steen Eiler. *Byer og Bygninger*. Copenhagen, 1949.

———. *København*. Copenhagen: G. E. C. Gads Forlag, 1969.

Reps, John W. *The Making of Urban America: A History of City Planning in the United States*. Princeton, NJ: Princeton University Press, 1965.

Ribbe, Wolfgang, and Jurgen Schmadeke. *Kleine Berlin Geschichte*. Berlin: Stapp Verlag, 1988.

Rossi, Aldo. *The Architecture of the City*. Cambridge, MA: MIT Press, 1982.

Rybczynski, Witold. *A Clearing in the Distance, Frederick Law Olmsted and America in the 19th Century*. Touchstone Edition. New York: Simon and Schuster, 1999.

Satoh, Shigeru. "Creating community through Machidukuri with the help of visual simulation." *Territorio* 43 (2007): 24–6.

Secchi, Bernardo. *La città del ventesimo secolo*. Rome: Laterza, 2005.

Sieverts, Thomas. *Cities without Cities*. London: E&FN Spon, 2003.

Sime, Jonathan D. "Creating places or designing spaces?" *Journal of Environmental Psychology* 6, no. 1 (1986): 49–63.

Simmonds, Roger, G. Hack, eds. *Global City Regions: Their Emerging Forms*. London and New York: SPON Press, Taylor and Francis, 2000.

Solomon, Daniel. *Global City Blues*. Washington, DC: Island Press, 2003.

Southworth, M., and E. Ben-Joseph. *Streets and the Shaping of Towns and Cities*. New York: McGraw-Hill, 1997.

Touraine, Alain. *Die Stadt: Ein überholter Entwurf (The City: An Outdated Design)*. Bonn: Monatzeitschrift für Kommunalpolitik, 1996.

Tuan, Yi-Fu. *Space and Place: The Perspective of Experience*. Minneapolis: University of Minnesota Press, 1977.

Ulrich, Roger S. "The view through a window may influence recovery from surgery." *Science* 224 (1993): 420–21.

United Nations. *World Urbanization Prospects Report*, 2005.

Van Susteren, Ariel. *Metropolitan World Atlas*. Rotterdam: 010 Publisher, 2005.

Vidler, Anthony. "The Third Typology." *Rational Architecture* ed. Robert L. Delevoy. Brussels: Archives d'Architecture Moderne, 1978.

Webber, Melvin W., ed. *Explorations into Spatial Structures*. Philadelphia: PA, University Press, 1964.

Webster Online Dictionary, www.Merriam-Webster.com.

Wells, H. G. *Anticipations*. London: Chapman and Hall, 1901.

———. *The Fate of Man*. London: Chapman and Hall, 1939.

Weschler, Lawrence. *True to Life—Cameraworks—David Hockney* New York: Alfred A. Knopf, 1984.

West, Robin. *Re-imagining Justice*. Aldershot, UK: Ashgate Publishing LTD, 2003.

Whyte, William H. *City, Rediscovering the Center*. New York: Doubleday, 1988.

Williams, Rick, J. Bergdoll. *Perception of Density*. Berkeley Planning Journal, Vol. 5. Berkeley: UC Berkeley, 1990.

Wilson, Edward O., and Stephen R. Kellert, eds. *The Biophilia Hypothesis*. Washington, DC: Island Press, 1984.

Wurman, Richard Saul. *Cities: Comparisons of Form and Scale*. Cambridge, MA: MIT Press, 1976.

Index

Note: Italicized page numbers indicate figures and their captions

Moon, A. J., 197
Moscow, Russian Federation, *62–63*
Mount Diablo Meridian survey, 197
multifaceted landscapes, 283
multispectral analysis in map making, 11
Mumbai, India, *64–65*
Mumford, Lewis, 144
Municipal Art Society, New York City, 269

Nanhai, China, 113
natural areas, managed, 181
natural light requirements, 216
natural systems
    and city form, xix, 1, 4, 116, *198*, 217–19
    constructed landscapes and, 235, 273–74
    and livable communities, 179–81
    mapping of, 12–13
    satellite views of, 271
    trees and drainage lines, *239*
    and urban form typology, 107–11
neighborhoods
    boundaries of, *175*
    effects of freeway scars on, *173*, 173–77
    income and vitality of, 144–48
    of Oakland, 209, *212*
    of San Francisco, 180, 182, 226–27, *226–27*, 242–43,
        244–46, 247
    traffic and street design in, 158
neotraditional streets, 185–86, *187*
Netherlands, The, 279
New Jersey Transit Authority, 179, 294 n.49
New Territories, China, *41*
New York City, USA, *66–67*, *97*, *104*
New York Planning Commission, 150
Nimitz Freeway, Oakland, 202
Nineteenth Avenue, San Francisco, 230, *236*
Nissen, Nis, 129
Nob Hill park, San Francisco, 180
Noe Valley, San Francisco, *145*
Noise, traffic and, *161*, 166–68, *168*, 177
Nørregade–Rådhusgade axis, 124
Nyboder, Denmark, 126

Oakland, USA
    city blocks of, 203–7, *204–5*
    density in, 214–16
    downtown, aerial view, *196*
    downtown residents, needs of, 212–13
    estuary study, 218–9, *218–19*, *220–21*
    Fourteenth Street promenade, *210*
    historic center and freeways, *203*
    housing in, 207–8, 211–12, 216–17

    layout of, 197–99, *199*, 200–202, *201*
    model of, *215*, *217*
    natural location of, *198*
    Ratto block area development plan, 204–7, *204–7*
    structural transformation of, 194–95
    transformation strategies, *209*, 211–12
    urbanity in, 213–14
    urban renewal projects in, 202
    urban transformation vs. urban renewal in, 219–21
    waterfront opportunities, 209–10
    See also specific streets and places
Oakland airport, *286*
Oakland Redevelopment Agency, 219–20
Oak Street, San Francisco, 175
observation
    and art, xix
    direct, and urban design principles, 118
    imagining the future as by-product of, 131
    as method, xxi
    spatial complexity and, 188
    of urban public spaces, 148–50
Ocean Parkway, Brooklyn, 163–64, 166–67, *167*, 168,
    169–70, *170*, *171–72*
Octavia Boulevard, San Francisco, 175–77
Octavia Street, San Francisco, 156–59
Oglethorpe, James, 99
Ohlone Indians, 273–74
Olmsted, Frederick Law, 163, *166*, 201–2
open-space systems, as context of urban agglomerations, 12
Opera house, Copenhagen, 131
Ørestad, Copenhagen, 120, *122*, *135*, 135–38, *137–38*
Øresund strait, *35*
Orinda transit station, San Francisco, 177–79
Our Lady's Church, Copenhagen, *119*, 121, *121*, 124–25, *125*
Our Saviour's Church, Copenhagen, *119*, *129*, 129–31, *130*
outdoor comfort model, 294 n.52
outdoor public spaces, scale of, 247
Oxford Atlas of the World, 11

Pacific Heights, San Francisco, *145*
parcel dimensions and structure, 98–99, 195–96, 203,
    205, 220
Paris, France, *68–69*, 99, 109, *252*
parking, in California housing developments, 205–7
parks, 181, 246–47
Parks Council, New York City, 269
parkways, 163–65, *166–67*, 166–68, *169–70*, 170, 235–37
    See also boulevards, residential
Paseo di Gracia, Barcelona, 163, *164*
Pearl River, China, 287
Pearl River Delta, China, 113, *114–15*, 286–87
Pearl River Estuary, China, *115*